Unpublished Writings
from the Period of *Unfashionable Observations*

Volume Eleven

Based on the edition by
Giorgio Colli & Mazzino Montinari
as adapted by Ernst Behler

The Complete Works of Friedrich Nietzsche

EDITED BY BERND MAGNUS

University of California, Riverside

Friedrich Nietzsche

Unpublished Writings
from the Period of *Unfashionable Observations*

Translated, with an Afterword,
by Richard T. Gray

STANFORD UNIVERSITY PRESS
STANFORD, CALIFORNIA

Assistance for the translation was provided by Inter Nationes, Bonn.

Translated from Friedrich Nietzsche, *Sämtliche Werke, Kritische Studienausgabe*, ed. Giorgio Colli and Mazzino Montinari, in 15 vols. This book corresponds to Vol. 7, pp. 417–837; Vol. 14, 529–54.

Stanford University Press, Stanford, California
Printed in the United States of America

CIP data appear at the end of the book

Contents

Unpublished Writings
from the Period of *Unfashionable Observations*

Contents

Reference Matter

A Note
on This Edition

This is the first English translation of all of Nietzsche's writings, including his unpublished fragments, with annotation, afterwords concerning the individual texts, and indexes, in twenty volumes. The aim of this collaborative work is to produce a critical edition for scholarly use. Volume 1 also includes an introduction to the entire edition. While the goal is to establish a readable text in contemporary English, the translation follows the original as closely as possible. All texts have been translated anew by a group of scholars, and particular attention has been given to maintaining a consistent terminology throughout the volumes. The translation is based on *Friedrich Nietzsche: Sämtliche Werke. Kritische Studienausgabe in 15 Bänden* (1980), edited by Giorgio Colli and Mazzino Montinari. The still-progressing *Kritische Gesamtausgabe der Werke*, which Colli and Montinari began in 1963, has also been consulted. The Colli-Montinari edition is of particular importance for the unpublished writings, comprising more than half of Nietzsche's writings and published there for the first time in their entirety. Besides listing textual variants, the annotation to this English edition provides succinct information on the text and identifies events, names, titles, quotes, and biographical facts of Nietzsche's own life. The notes do not have numbers in the text but are keyed by line and phrase. The Afterword presents the main facts about the origin of the text, the stages of its composition, and the main events of its reception.

ERNST BEHLER

Abbreviations
and Conventions

The following symbols are used throughout the text and the notes:

[ ]	Deletion by Nietzsche
| |	Addition by Nietzsche
[?]	Uncertain reading
{ }	Addition by the translator
⟨ ⟩	Addition by the editors (Colli and Montinari)
— — —	Unfinished or incomplete sentence or thought
[+]	Gap in text
Italics	Underlined once by Nietzsche
Bold	Underlined twice or more by Nietzsche

Variants are referred to with the following abbreviations:

Pd	Preliminary draft
Sd	Second draft

The four *Unfashionable Observations* are referred to as:

"Strauss"	"David Strauss the Confessor and the Writer"
"History"	"On the Utility and Liability of History for Life"
"Schopenhauer"	"Schopenhauer as Educator."
"Wagner"	"Richard Wagner in Bayreuth"

Page and line citations to these essays refer to page and line numbers of the *Unfashionable Observations*, Volume 2 of this edition.

Unpublished Writings
from the Period of *Unfashionable Observations*

[19 = P I 20b. Summer 1872–Early 1873]

19 [1]

At the proper height everything comes together and harmonizes—the philosopher's thoughts, the artist's works, and good deeds.

The object is to show how the entire life of a people reflects in a flawed and confused manner the image presented by its supreme geniuses: they are not the product of the masses, but the masses exhibit their aftereffect.

Or what is the relationship?

There is an invisible bridge connecting one genius with another—that is the truly real "history" of a people, everything else amounts to shadowy, infinite variations made of inferior material, copies formed by unskilled hands.

The ethical strengths of a nation, as well, are exhibited in its geniuses.

19 [2]

Characterization of post-Socratic ethics—all are eudaemonistic and individual.

19 [3]

To mark off the world in which the philosopher and the artist are at home.

19 [4]

Preface dedicated to Schopenhauer—entrance to the under-world—I have sacrificed many a black sheep to you—which has caused the other sheep to complain.

19 [5]

How they philosophized in the splendid world of art! Does philosophizing cease when life attains perfection? No: that is only the beginning of true philosophizing. Its judgment *on existence says more* because it has before it this relative perfection, as well as all the veils of art and all illusion.

19 [6]

The ancients were much more virtuous than we are because they had so much less fashion.

The virtuous energy of their artists!

19 [7]

Antithesis of the press—it the *opinionator of the public*—we the *informers of the public*.

We concern ourselves with the *imperishable cares of the people*—we must be free of the momentary, transitory ones.

Depiction of the task facing the new generation of philosophers.

The demand that one overcome oneself, that is, overcome the *saecular*, the spirit of the age.

19 [8]

Characterization of Schopenhauer: isolation in the highest society.

19 [9]

Those Greek philosophers *overcame the spirit of the age* in order to be able to gain a sense for the spirit of the Hellenic: they express the need for solutions to eternal questions.

19 [10]

In the world of art and of philosophy, human beings contribute to an "imperishability of the intellect."

The will alone is imperishable—how wretched that imperishability of the intellect achieved through education, which
5   presupposes human minds, looks in comparison:

we see the lineage in which this belongs for nature.

—But how can at the same time the genius be the supreme aim of nature!

Establishing a legacy by means of history and establishing a legacy
10   by means of *procreation*.

This is where Plato's procreating in the realm of the beautiful belongs—thus, the overcoming of history is necessary for the birth of genius, history must be immersed in beauty and made eternal.

15   Against *iconic historiography*! It contains a barbarizing element.

It should speak only of what is great and unique, of the exemplary model.

With this we have grasped the task facing the new generation of philosophers.

20   All the great Greeks of the age of tragedy have nothing of the historian about them: ———

19 [11]

The *indiscriminate* drive for knowledge is on the same footing as the indiscriminate sex drive—signs *of vulgarity*.

19 [12]

The task of the philosopher, to consciously combat all the
25   temporalizing elements—and therefore to support the unconscious task of art.

In each of these a people achieves the unity of all its characteristics and their supreme beauty.

The present task over against the sciences.

19 [13]

The Philosopher of the Tragic Age.

The philosopher does not stand so completely apart from the people, as an exception: the will also wants something of him. Its intention is the same as in the case of art—its own
5   transfiguration and redemption. The will *strives for purity and ennoblement*: from one stage to the other.

The form of existence as cultivation and culture—the will on the heads of human beings.

19 [14]

The Limited Drive for Knowledge.

10   The seven wise men—the epic-Apollinian stage of philosophy.

19 [15]

The drives that distinguish the Greeks from other people are expressed in their philosophy.

But these are precisely their *classical* drives.

15   Their way of dealing with history is important.

The gradual degeneration of the concept of the historian in antiquity—its dissolution into mere curiosity and the thirst to know it all.

19 [16]

Task: to discern the *teleology* of the philosophical genius. Is he
20   really nothing but a wanderer who appears by chance? In any case, if he is a true genius, he has nothing to do with the chance political situation of a people; on the contrary, in comparison with his nation he is *timeless*. But that does not mean he is connected to this nation by chance—what is specific in this people
25   comes to light here as an individual: the drive of the people becomes a universal drive, applied to solving the riddle of the universe. By *separating* them, nature succeeds this once in viewing its drives in their pure forms. The philosopher is a means for coming to rest in the rushing current, for becoming con-
30   scious of the enduring types by disdaining infinite multiplicity.

19 [17]

The philosopher is a self-revelation of nature's workshop—philosopher and artist tell nature's trade secrets.

The sphere of the philosopher and the artist exists above the tumult of contemporary history, beyond need.

5   The philosopher as the *brake shoe on the wheel of time*.

Philosophers appear during those times of great danger—when the wheel keeps turning faster—they and art take the place of disappearing myth. But they are thrown far ahead of their time, because they only gain the attention of their con-
10 temporaries very slowly.

A people that becomes conscious of its dangers produces genius.

19 [18]

Freedom from myth. Thales. **One** *element as Proteus*!
The tragic nature of existence. Anaximander.
15 The artistic play of the cosmos. Heraclitus.
Eternal logic. Parmenides. Logomachy.
Compassion with all living things. Empedocles. The slave.
Measure and number. Pythagoras. Democritus.
(The competition. Heraclitus.)
20 (Love and education. Socrates.)
The *νοῦς* most basic assumption. Anaxagoras.

19 [19]

We will not put up with just anyone's philosophizing, for example, not with David Strauss's, who cannot be rescued once he steps out of his specifically historical-critical atmosphere.

19 [20]

25 After Socrates it is no longer possible to preserve the commonweal, hence the individualizing ethics that seeks to preserve *individuals*.

19 [21]

The immoderate, indiscriminate drive for knowledge, along with its historical background, is a sign that life has grown old: there is a serious danger that individuals are becoming *inferior*, which is why their interests are so passionately attached
5 to objects of knowledge, regardless of which ones. The universal drives have become so feeble that they no longer keep the individual in check.

By means of the sciences, the Teuton transfigured all of his limitations simply by transferring them: fidelity, modesty, self-
10 restraint, diligence, cleanliness, love of order; these are hereditary virtues: but also formlessness, that entire lack of vitality in life, that pettiness—his limitless drive for knowledge is the consequence of an impoverished life: without it he would become—and often is, in spite of them—petty and malicious.
15 Today a higher form of life has been bestowed upon us, an ambience of art—and now the immediate consequence is a selective drive for knowledge, that is, *philosophy*.

Terrible danger: a fusion of the American kind of political hubbub with the groundless culture of the scholar.

19 [22]

20 With the selective drive for knowledge, *beauty* once again emerges as a power.

Most remarkable that Schopenhauer *writes beautifully*! His life also has more style than that of the university professor—but backward surroundings!

25 Today no one knows what a good book looks like; they must be given a model: they do not understand composition. Moreover, more and more the press is ruining their feeling for it.

To be able to hold onto what is sublime!

19 [23]
Opposition to iconic historiography and to the natural sciences requires vast *artistic* powers.

What should the philosopher do? Amid this antlike swarming, he must emphasize the problem of existence, the eternal
5 problems in general.

The philosopher should *discover what is needed* and the artist should *create* it. The philosopher should have the utmost empathy with universal suffering: just as each of the ancient Greek philosophers expresses a need; this is where he places his sys-
10 tem, in the void. He constructs his world within this void.

We must gather together all the means that make it possible to rescue the human being for repose: while religions die out!

The difference between the effect of philosophy and that of science must be made clear: and likewise their different genesis.

19 [24]
15   It is not a matter of destroying science, but rather of *controlling* it. In all its aims and methods it is wholly reliant on philosophical views, *though it easily forgets this. But the philosophy that is in control of science must also consider the extent to which science should be allowed to develop: it must determine its* **value**!

19 [25]
20   Proof of the *barbarizing* effects of the sciences. They easily get bogged down in the service of "practical interests."

19 [26]
Schopenhauer's value, because he calls to mind *naive, universal* truths: he dares to express so-called 'trivialities' in a beautiful way.

25   We have no noble popular philosophy because we have no noble concept of the *peuple publicum*. Our popular philosophy is for the *peuple*, not for the public.

19 [27]

If we are ever to attain a culture, we will need unheard-of artistic powers so as to break the limitless drive for knowledge, so as to produce a unity once more. *The supreme dignity of the philosopher is revealed when he gives focus to the limitless drive for knowledge,*
5 *controls it by giving it unity.*

This is how the earlier Greek philosophers are to be understood, they control the drive for knowledge. How did it come about that after Socrates it gradually slipped from their grasp? To begin with, we see that *Socrates and his school* displayed the
10 same tendency: it is supposed to be controlled out of *individual* concern for *living happily.* This is a final, inferior phase. Previously it had not been a matter of *individuals,* but of the *Hellenes.*

19 [28]

The great ancient philosophers are a part of *general Hellenic life: after Socrates, sects* are formed. Gradually philosophy loses its
15 hold on the reins of science.

In the Middle Ages, theology takes hold of the reins of science: then a dangerous period of emancipation begins.

The general welfare once again requires its *control,* and with this simultaneously its elevation and concentration.
20 The *laissez aller of our sciences,* just as with certain *dogmas of political economy*: the faith in their unconditionally salutary consequences.

In a certain sense, *Kant's* influence was also detrimental: for the belief in metaphysics has been lost. No one will be able to
25 rely on his "thing in itself" as if it were a controlling principle.

With this we comprehend what is so remarkable about *Schopenhauer*: he gathers together all those elements that are still useful for controlling science. He arrives at the most profound primordial problems of ethics and of art, he raises the question
30 of the value of existence.

The marvelous unity of Wagner and Schopenhauer! They issue from the same drive. The most profound qualities of the

Germanic spirit arm themselves for battle here: just as in the
case of the Greeks. Return of *circumspection*.

19 [29]

Portrayal of the immense danger of secularization in the
sixth and fifth centuries {B.C.}: the extravagance of the colo-
5 nies, the wealth, the concupiscence.

19 [30]

The problem: *to find the culture appropriate to our music*!

19 [31]

The aim is to designate the method by which the philosophical human being must *live*.

19 [32]

Toward a characterization of the superficiality of our culture:
10 David Strauss, our theaters, our poets, our critics, our schools.

19 [33]

My task: *to comprehend the inner coherence and the necessity of every
true culture*. The protective and healing capacities of a culture,
its relationship to the genius of the people. The consequence
of every great artistic world is a culture; but due to hostile
15 countercurrents, the work of art often never achieves its full
resonance.

Philosophy should hold onto the *intellectual mountain chain* that
extends throughout the centuries: and thereby onto the eternal
fruitfulness of everything that is great.

20 Science makes no distinction between great and small—but
philosophy does! The value of science is measured in terms of
this statement.

Holding onto what is sublime!

What an extraordinary *deficiency* today of books that breathe
25 a heroic strength! Even Plutarch is no longer read!

19 [34]

Kant says (in the second preface to the *Critique*: "*I must, there-fore, abolish knowledge to make room for faith*; and the dogmatism of metaphysics, that is, the presumption that it is possible to advance in metaphysics without a critique of pure reason, is
5 the true source of all that unbelief—which is always very dog-matic—that opposes morality." Very important! He was driven by a cultural need.

Curious opposition, "*knowledge and faith*"! What would the Greeks have thought of this? Kant *knew of no other opposition*! *But*
10 **we** *do*!

A cultural need drives Kant: he wants to *rescue* one domain from *knowledge*: this is where—Schopenhauer—sets down the roots of all the highest and most profound things, art and ethics.

15 On the other hand, he assembles everything that is *worthy of being known for all time*—the ethical wisdom of nations and individuals (standpoint of the seven wise men, of the Greek popular philosophers).

He breaks up the elements of that faith and shows just how
20 insufficient the Christian faith is in answering our most pro-found need: the question concerning the value of existence!

The struggle of knowledge with knowledge!

Schopenhauer even calls attention to that mode of thought and knowledge of which we are *unconscious*.

25 *Controlling the drive for knowledge—whether for the benefit of a reli-gion? Or of an artistic culture?* That is about to become evident; I favor the second alternative.

I add to this the question concerning the **value** of *historical, iconic* knowledge, of *nature* as well.

30 In the case of the Greeks it is control for the benefit of an artistic culture (*and* religion?), control that seeks to *prevent* a complete unleashing: we seek to *control* once more what already has been completely unleashed.

19 [35]

The philosopher of tragic knowledge. He controls the unleashed drive for knowledge, not by means of a new metaphysics. He does not establish a new faith. He senses it to be *tragic that the ground of metaphysics has been cut away* and can never be satisfied
5 by the colorful kaleidoscope of the sciences. He works toward the construction of a new *life*; he returns to art its rights.

The philosopher of *desperate knowledge* will be consumed with blind science: knowledge at any price.

For the tragic philosopher the *image of existence* is made com-
10 plete by the insight that the metaphysical only appears in an-thropomorphic form. He is not a *skeptic.*

Here it is necessary to *create* a concept: for skepticism is not the aim. Once it reaches its limitations, the drive for knowl-edge turns against itself in order to proceed to the *critique of*
15 *knowledge.* Knowledge in the service of the best life.

One must even *desire illusion*—that is what makes it tragic.

19 [36]

The last philosopher—it can be entire generations. He sim-ply must help them attain *life.* "The last," of course, in a relative sense. For our world. He demonstrates the necessity of illu-
20 sion, of art, and of the kind of art that dominates life. It is not possible for us to produce once again a series of philosophers like that in Greece during the age of tragedy. Their task is now accomplished by *art alone.* Only as *art* is such a system still pos-sible. Viewed from the standpoint of the present, that entire
25 period of Greek philosophy also belongs within the domain of their art.

The *control of science* can *only* take place today by means of *art.* It is a matter of *value* judgments about knowledge and exces-sive knowledge.

30 *Enormous task and dignity of art in performing this task!* It must create everything anew and *all on its own give birth anew to life! The Greeks* show *us what art is capable of*: if we did not have them, our faith would be chimerical.

Whether a religion can establish itself here, in this vacuum, depends on its strength. *We* have turned to *culture*: what is "German" as a *redeeming* force!

At any rate, any religion able to do this would have to have
5 an enormous *power of love*: on which all knowledge is dashed, as it is dashed on the language of art.

But might art perhaps be capable of creating its own religion, of giving birth to myth? This was the case among the Greeks.

19 [37]

10   The philosophies and theologies that have now been *destroyed* still continue to exert their influence in the sciences: even if their roots have died off, here in the branches there is still some life for a while. *History* has been widely developed in particular as a counterforce to theological myth, but also to philosophy:
15 here, as well as in the mathematical sciences, *absolute knowledge* celebrates its saturnalia; in these realms, the most trivial matter that actually can be *decided* counts for more than all the ideas of metaphysics taken together. Here it is the degree of *certainty* that determines value, not the degree of *indispensability* for
20 human beings. It is the old struggle between *faith* and *knowledge*.

These are barbaric biases.

The only thing philosophy can do now is emphasize the *relativity* and *anthropomorphic character* of all knowledge, as well as the universally dominant power of *illusion*. That is why it no longer
25 can restrain the unleashed drive for knowledge, which increasingly *judges* according to the degree of certainty and seeks ever smaller objects. Whereas every human being is happy when a day has passed, the historian grubs, digs, and combines so as to reconstruct this day, in order to save it from oblivion: what
30 is *small* shall also be eternal, *because it can be the object of knowledge*.

The only criterion valid for us is the aesthetic criterion: what is *great* has a right to its history; however, not to an iconic history, but instead to a *productive, stimulating historical portraiture*.

We leave the *graves undisturbed*: but we take possession of what
is eternally alive.

Favorite topic of the present age: the *great effects of the smallest
thing*. For example, historical grubbing, when taken as a whole,
has something grandiose about it: it is like the feeble vegetation
that gradually erodes away the alps. We see a great drive that
makes use of small instruments, but a *grandiose number* of them.

One could oppose to this: *the small effects of what is great!* —
at least when it is represented by individuals. It is difficult to
understand, the tradition often dies out, but the hatred toward
it is universal, its value is based on quality, which always finds
only few admirers.

Only what is great has an effect on what is great: just as the torch
signals in Agamemnon leap only from crest to crest. It is the
task of *culture* to ensure that what is great in a people does not
appear among them as a recluse or an outlaw.

That is why we seek to express what we feel: it is not our way
to wait until the dull reflection of what to me appears bright
has descended into the valleys. Namely, that ultimately, the
great effects of the smallest things are simply the aftereffects
of *great things*; they have set an avalanche in motion. Now it is
difficult for us to stop it.

19 [38]

History and the natural sciences were necessary to combat
the Middle Ages: knowledge versus faith. We now oppose *art*
to knowledge: return to life! Controlling the drive for knowledge! Fortifying the moral and aesthetic instincts!

This appears to us as the *redemption of the German spirit so that
it might again be a redeemer*!

The essence of this spirit first became apparent to us in our
music. We now understand how the *Greeks* made their culture
dependent on music.

19 [39]

In order to create a religion one would have to *awaken belief* in a mythical edifice that one has constructed in a vacuum, which means that he would be satisfying an extraordinary need.

Since the *Critique of Pure Reason* it is *unlikely* that this will ever
5 happen again.

On the other hand, I can imagine a wholly new sort of *philosopher-artist* who fills the void with a *work of art*, with one that has aesthetic value.

Fortunately, goodness and pity are independent of the de-
10 cline or flourishing of any religion; by contrast, good *actions* are largely determined by religious imperatives. By far the greatest proportion of good, dutiful actions have no ethical value, but instead have been performed under *compulsion*.

Practical morality will suffer greatly with every collapse of a
15 religion. A metaphysics that punishes and rewards appears to be indispensable.

If we can only create *mores*, powerful *mores*! Then we would also have morality.

But *mores* are formed following *the example set by powerful indi-*
20 *vidual personalities*.

I do not reckon with the awakening of *goodness* in the bulk of the propertied class, but one could probably bring them to accept *mores*, a sense of duty toward tradition.

If humanity were to spend for education and schools what
25 it has already spent for the building of churches, if it were to devote to education the intellect it now devotes to theology.

19 [40]

The *free poetic* manner in which the Greeks dealt with their gods!

We are too accustomed to the opposition between histori-
30 cal truth and untruth. It is funny that the Christian myths are supposed to be absolutely *historical*.

19 [41]

The problem of a *culture* rarely grasped correctly. The aim of culture is not the greatest possible *happiness* of a people, nor the unhindered development of *all* its talents: rather, it manifests itself in the proper *proportion* of these developments. Its aim
5 points beyond worldly happiness; its aim is the production of great works.

All the drives of the Greeks evince a *controlling unity*: let us call it the Hellenic *will*. Each of these drives attempts to exist on its own into infinity. The ancient philosophers attempt to
10 construct a world out of them.

The *culture* of a people reveals itself in the *unifying control of this people's drives*: philosophy controls the drive for knowledge, art controls ecstasy and the drive to give form, ἀγάπη controls ἔρως, etc.

15 Knowledge *isolates*: the earlier philosophers represent in isolation what in Greek art is able to appear together.

The content of art and of ancient philosophy is identical, but in philosophy we see the *isolated* elements of art being used to *control the drive for knowledge*. We ought to be able to demon-
20 strate this in the case of the Italians, as well: individualism in life and in art.

19 [42]

The Greeks as discoverers and voyagers and colonizers. They know how to *learn*: enormous power of appropriation. Our age should not believe that it stands so much higher with
25 regard to its drive for knowledge: except that for the Greeks everything became *life*! For us it merely remains knowledge!

19 [43]

When it is a question, on the one hand, of the *value* of knowledge, whereas, on the other hand, a beautiful illusion, as long as one believes in it, has the same value as an item
30 of knowledge, then one realizes that life requires illusions, that is, untruths that are held to be truths. It requires faith in

the truth, but illusion is ultimately sufficient; that means that truths establish themselves not by means of logical proofs, but by means of their effects, proofs of strength. The true and the effective are held to be identical; here, too, one submits to force. How is one then to explain that logical proof of truth ever even occurred? In the *struggle between "truth" and "truth"* both seek an alliance with reflection. *All true striving for truth came into the world through the struggle for a sacred conviction*, through the πάθος of struggle: otherwise human beings have no interest in its logical origin.

19 [44]

Purpose, to determine the teleology of the philosopher amid culture.

We ask the Greeks, in that period in which their culture displayed unity.

Important: even the richest culture has its philosophy. For what purpose?

We ask the great philosophers. Alas, they have perished! How reckless nature is!

19 [45]

How does the philosophical genius relate to art? Little can be learned from his immediate conduct. We have to ask: Is there anything in his philosophy that is art? Work of art? What *remains* when his system, as science, has been destroyed? But it must be precisely this remaining element that *controls* the drive for knowledge, that is hence the artistic element. Why is such control necessary? For, when considered scientifically, his system is an illusion, an untruth that deceives the drive for knowledge and affords only temporary satisfaction. In this control, the value of philosophy does not lie in the sphere of knowledge, but in the sphere of life: the *will to existence uses philosophy* for the purpose of a higher form of existence.

It is impossible for philosophy and art to be turned *against* the will: but morality is likewise in its service. Omnipotence of the *will*. Relative nirvana one of the most fragile forms of existence.

19 [46]

Everything must be said as precisely as possible, and every technical term, including "will," must be set aside.

19 [47]

The beauty and magnificence of a construction of the world (alias philosophy) now passes judgment on its value—that means that it is judged as *art*. Its form will probably change! The rigid mathematical formula (as in the case of Spinoza)—which had such a soothing effect on Goethe—is now only justified as an aesthetic means of expression.

19 [48]

The proposition must be established—we live only by means of illusions—our consciousness only scratches the surface. Much is hidden from our gaze. Moreover, we never will have to fear that the human being ever will understand himself *completely*, that he will fathom in every moment all the laws of leverage and mechanics, all the formulas of architecture and chemistry that are necessary for life. However, it is quite possible that everything will be understood on the basis of a schema. This will change next to nothing where our lives are concerned. Besides, these are nothing but formulas for absolutely unknowable forces.

19 [49]

Due to the superficiality of our intellect, we do indeed live in one ongoing illusion: that means that in every moment we need art in order to live. Our eyes do not permit us to get beyond the *forms*. But if we ourselves are the ones who have gradually trained our eyes to do this, then we realize that an *artistic power* holds sway within us. Thus, we see in nature itself mechanisms that protect against absolute *knowledge*: the *philosopher* **recognizes** *the language of nature* and *says*: "we need art" and "we need only a limited amount of knowledge."

19 [50]

5   Every type of *culture* begins with a host of things being *veiled*. Human progress depends upon this act of veiling—life in a pure and noble sphere and detached from the more common allurements. The struggle of virtue against "sensuality" is fundamentally aesthetic in nature. When we employ *great* indi-
10 viduals as our lodestars, we veil much about them; indeed, we hide all the circumstances and contingencies that made their emergence possible, we *isolate* them from ourselves in order to venerate them. Every religion contains such an element: human beings under divine protection as something infinitely
15 important. Indeed, all ethics begins when the single individual is considered to be something *infinitely important*—in contrast to nature, which acts in a cruel and playful way. When we are better and more noble, it is the isolating illusions that have made us this way!
20 Natural science opposes to this the absolute truth of nature: to be sure, advanced physiology will comprehend the artistic powers already present in our development; and not only in human development, but in that of animals as well: it will claim that what is *artistic has its inception* in the *organic*.

19 [51]

25 The consequences of Kantian doctrine. End of metaphysics as scientific discipline.
     The barbarizing influence of knowledge.
     Control of knowledge as the drive of art.
     We *live* only by means of these artistic illusions.
30 Every higher culture has become such by means of this control.

The philosophical systems of the early Greeks.

The world they reveal is the same one that was created by
tragedy.

In this we grasp the unity of philosophy and art for the purpose of culture.

The aesthetic concept of the great and the sublime: the task
is to educate people in accordance with it. Culture dependent upon the way in which one defines what is "great."

19 [52]

Absolute knowledge leads to *pessimism*: art is the remedy
for this.

Philosophy is indispensable for *education* because it *draws
knowledge into* an artistic conception of the world, and thereby
ennobles it.

19 [53]

The concern that the eternal work not be withheld from
humanity and not perish had an absolutely formative influence
on **Schopenhauer**: he was well acquainted with Heraclitus's
fate, and his first edition was pulped! He displayed the precau-
tion typical of a father: all the unpleasant traits of his being, his
friendships with litterateurs like Frauenstädt, can be explained
by this. In this context, his passion for fame is a precaution-
ary instinct for the benefit of humanity: he was well acquainted
with the course of the world.

It is certainly possible to conceive of a greater superiority
over humankind: but in that case he never would have written
anything! He longed for procreation in the realm of the beautiful!

19 [54]

Perhaps chemical transformations in inorganic nature also
can be called artistic processes, mimetic roles that are acted out
by a force: but there are *several*! that it can play.

19 [55]

I have not made it easy for those who only want to derive a *scholarly* satisfaction from it, since ultimately I did not consider them at all. Quotations are lacking.

19 [56]

The age of the seven wise men was not very meticulous when it came to the attribution of wise sayings, but considered it very important when someone dared to adopt a saying.

19 [57]

The Chronology of the Greek Philosophers.
Metrics.
Choephori.

19 [58]

The philologists of the present age have proven themselves unworthy of being permitted to include me and my book in their number: it hardly needs to be asserted that, in this instance as well, it is entirely up to them whether or not they want to learn something; but I am not in the least inclined to compromise with them.

May what today calls itself "philology" (and which I have intentionally designated in this neutral manner) ignore my book once again: for it is masculine by nature and is not suited for castrati. They are better suited for sitting at the loom of textual reconstruction.

19 [59]

On the Διαδοχαί and their origin (in the history of the earlier {Greek} philosophers).

Apollodorus struggles against it: who first postulated it?

19 [60]

The emergence of philosophical sects in Greek antiquity.

Out of the most profound transformation of the Hellenic spirit.

Begins with the Pythagoreans; *Plato* learns it from them.

5   The academy establishes the *model.* They are subversive institutions opposed to Hellenic life.

The earlier philosophers manifest in isolation the individual drives of the Hellenic being.

We experience the transition from the spirit of philosophi-
10 cal sectarianism to cultural awareness, *transition from philosophy to culture*. In the former, the *segregation* of philosophy and culture.

The superficiality of all post-Socratic ethics! The profound, earlier Hellenic ethics could not be expressed in words and concepts.

19 [61]

15 Heraclitus in his hatred of the Dionysian element, also of Pythagoras, also of excessive knowledge. He is an Apollinian product and speaks in oracles whose meaning one must interpret for oneself and for him. He has no sense for suffering, but he does for stupidity.

19 [62]

20 Great quandary: whether philosophy is an art or a science.

In its aims and in its results it is an art. But its means, conceptual representation, it shares with science. It is a form of poetic artistry. —It cannot be categorized: consequently we must invent and characterize a species for it.

25 *The physiography of the philosopher.* He arrives at knowledge by poeticizing and poeticizes by arriving at knowledge.

He does not grow; I mean, philosophy does not follow the same course as the other sciences: even if some of the domains of philosophy gradually fall into the hands of science. Hera-
30 clitus never can be obsolete. It is poetry beyond the limits of experience, continuation of the *mythic impulse*; also essentially

in images. Mathematical portrayal is not part of the philosopher's nature.

Overcoming knowledge by means of *the power to create myths*. Kant remarkable — knowledge and faith! Inherent kinship between *philosophers* and *founders of religions*!

19 [63]

Curious problem: the self-consumption of philosophical systems! Unheard of both in science and in art! The situation is *similar* in the case of religions: that is remarkable and significant.

19 [64]

Illusion necessary for sentient beings to be able to live.
Illusion necessary for progress in culture.
What is the purpose of the insatiable drive for knowledge?
— It is, at any rate, hostile to culture.
Philosophy seeks to control it; is an instrument of culture.
The earlier {Greek} philosophers.

19 [65]

Write in a completely impersonal and cold manner. No "I" and "we."

19 [66]

Our reason is a surface force, is *superficial*. This is also called "subjective." It arrives at knowledge by means of *concepts*: which means that our thought consists in categorization, name-calling. Hence something that comes down to an arbitrary human convention and does not capture the thing itself. Only when *calculating* and only in the dimensions of space does the human being achieve absolute knowledge, which means that *quantities* are the ultimate limits of everything knowable; he does not *comprehend* a single quality, but only quantity.

What can be the purpose of such a surface force?

In the first place, the concept corresponds with an image,

images are primal thought, that is, the surfaces of things focused in the mirror of the eye.

Image is one thing, *mathematical calculation* quite another.

Images in human eyes! This governs the entire nature of the
5 human being: from the *eye*! Subject! The *ear* hears sound! An entirely different, marvelous conception of the same world.

Art is based on the *imprecision* of *sight*. In the case of the ear, as well, imprecision in rhythm, temperament, etc., which once again is the basis for *art*.

19 [67]

10 There exists within us a power that allows us to perceive the *major* features of a mirror image with greater intensity, and another power that stresses similarity in rhythm despite actual imprecision. This must be an *artistic* power. For it *creates*. Its primary operations are *omitting*, *overlooking*, and *failing to hear*.
15 Therefore antiscientific: for it does not have equal interest in everything that is perceived.

The word only contains an image, from this {comes} the concept. Thought thus calculates by means of artistic magnitudes.

20 All categorization is an attempt to arrive at the image.

We relate superficially to every true *being*, we speak the language of symbol, of image: we then artistically add something by emphasizing the primary features and forgetting the secondary ones.

19 [68]

Apologia for Art.

25 Thales long gone—but a sculptor, standing at a waterfall, will still admit that he was right.

19 [69]

Our public, civic, and social life comes down to an equilibrium of egoistic interests: answer to the question concerning how, lacking any power of love, one can achieve a bearable existence based solely on the wiles of the egoistic interests involved.

Our age hates art, as it does religion. It will be put off neither by the promise of an afterlife nor by the promise of the transfiguration of the world of art. It takes this to be useless "poetry," amusement, etc. Our "poets" *conform*. But art as terribly serious! The new metaphysics as terribly serious! We want to alter the world so drastically by means of images that it will make you shudder. And that is within our power! Plug up your ears, your eyes will see our myths. Our curses will rain down upon you!

Science must now demonstrate its utility! It has become a source of nourishment for egoism: state and society have made it their servant so as to exploit it for *their own* purposes.

The normal condition is the state of *war*: we make *peace* only for limited periods of time.

19 [70]

I have to know how the Greeks philosophized during their age of art. The *Socratic* schools sat amid a sea of beauty—What can one discern of this in their work? Immense expenditures are made for art. The Socratics have either a hostile or a theoretical attitude toward it.

By contrast, the earlier philosophers are governed in part by an impulse similar to the one that created tragedy.

19 [71]

The concept of the philosopher and the different types {of philosophers}.—What do they all have in common?

Either he issues from his culture or is hostile toward it.

He is contemplative like the visual artist, empathetic like the religious person, thinks in terms of causality like the man of science: he tries to let all the tones of the world resonate within him and to project the totality of this sound outside himself by means of concepts. *Swelling up to encompass the macrocosm* and simultaneously *circumspect observation*—like the actor or the dramatic poet who transforms himself, but still retains circumspection so that he can project himself outward.

Dialectical thought as a cold shower for this type of thinking.

5   Plato remarkable: enthusiast for dialectics, that is, for that circumspection.

19 [72]
The Philosophers. Physiography of the Philosopher.

The philosopher compared to the scientific person and the artist.

10   Controlling the drive for knowledge by means of art,

              the religious drive for unity by means of the concept.

The juxtaposition of conception and abstraction rather curious.

15   Significance for culture.

Metaphysics as vacuum.

19 [73]

The philosopher of the future? He must become the supreme tribunal of an artistic culture, the police force, as it were, that guards against all transgressions.

19 [74]

20   We certainly will not call all categorization, all general concepts "philosophical." Nor everything unconscious and intuitive: even in the case of philological reconstruction, there is a creative moment that cannot be completely reduced to conscious thought.

19 [75]

25   Philosophical thinking can be detected at the core of all scientific thought: even in the case of textual reconstruction. It runs ahead on nimble legs: reason puffs ponderously behind and looks for sturdier legs after it has witnessed this en-

ticing magical image. An infinitely speedy flight across great
expanses! Is it only the greater speed? No. It is flight of imagination, that is, a leaping from possibility to possibility, with
these possibilities for the moment being taken as certainties.
5 Back and forth from a possibility to a certainty and then back
again to a possibility. —

But what is such a "possibility"? A sudden intuition, for
example, "it might perhaps." But how does this sudden intuition *come about*? At times by extrinsic accident: a comparison,
10 the discovery of some analogy or another takes place. Then a
process of *amplification* sets in. The power of imagination consists in the *quick recognition of similarities*. Subsequently, reflection
measures one concept by another and performs tests. *Similarity*
is supposed to be replaced by *causality*.
15   Are "scientific" and "philosophical" thought merely distinguished, then, by the *dosage*? Or perhaps by their *domains*?

19 [76]
    There is no distinct philosophy, separate from science: in both, the
manner of thought is the same. The reason why *unprovable* philosophizing still has some value—more value, in fact, than many
20 a scientific proposition—lies in the aesthetic *value* of such philosophizing, that is, in its beauty and sublimity. It continues to
exist as a *work of art* even when it cannot prove itself as scientific
construction. But isn't this the same in matters of science? —

In other words: it is not the pure *drive for knowledge* that is
25 decisive, but rather the *aesthetic* drive: the inadequately proven
philosophy of Heraclitus has far more artistic value than all the
propositions of Aristotle.

The drive for knowledge is thus controlled by the imagination present in the culture of any people. This fills the philoso-
30 pher with the supreme *pathos for truth*: the *value* of his knowledge is for him the guarantee of its *truth*. All *productivity* and all
driving force are derived from these *prescient* glimpses.

19 [77]

The production of the imagination can be observed in the eye. Similarity leads to the boldest development: but so do entirely different relationships, contrast incessantly to contrast. With this one *perceives* the extraordinary productivity of the intellect. It is a life in images.

19 [78]

In order to think, one must already possess, by means of imagination, what one is seeking—only then can reflection judge it. Reflection accomplishes this by measuring it against common and time-tested standards.

What is really "logical" about thinking in images?—

The sober human being has little need for imagination and hence *has* little imagination.

At any rate, this production of forms, by means of which something then occurs to memory, has something *artistic* about it: *it accentuates this form* and thereby strengthens it. Thinking is accentuating.

There are many more sets of images in the brain than are made use of for thought: the intellect quickly selects similar images: the selected image in turn generates a further profusion of images: but once again the intellect quickly selects one of them, etc.

Conscious thought is nothing but the selection of representations. It is a long way from this to abstraction.

1) The power that generates the profusion of images; 2) the power that selects and emphasizes what is similar.

Feverish people deal in this very way with walls and tapestries; the difference is that those who are healthy also project the tapestry.

19 [79]

A twofold artistic power is present here, the power that generates images and the power that selects among them.

The world of dreams proves that this is correct: here the

human being does not proceed to the point of abstraction, or:
one is not guided and modified by the images that stream in
through the eye.

    If one considers this power more closely, it is not entirely
5 free artistic invention: that would be something arbitrary,
hence something impossible. Intead, these images are the most
delicate emanations of neural activity as viewed on a surface:
these images are related to the underlying neural activity in the
same way that Chladni's sound figures are related to the sound
10 itself. The most delicate oscillation and vibration! Considered
physiologically, the artistic process is absolutely determined
and necessary. On the surface, all thought appears to us to be
voluntary, at our discretion: we do not notice the infinite activity.

15   To conceive of an *artistic process independent of a brain* is bla-
tantly anthropopathic: but the same is true for the will, for
morality, etc.

    Desire thus is nothing but a physiological excess that seeks
to discharge itself and exerts pressure all the way up to the
20 brain.

  19 [80]

    Result: it is only a matter of *degrees* and *quantities*: all human
beings are artistic, philosophical, scientific, etc.

    Our estimation of value refers to quantities, not to qualities.
We venerate what is *great*. To be sure, that is also the *abnormal*.

25   For the veneration of the great effects of what is small is only
amazement at the result and the disproportion of the smallest
cause. Only by adding together a large number of effects and
viewing them as a *unity* do we arrive at the impression of greatness: that is, by means of this unity we *produce* greatness.

30   However, humanity grows only through veneration of what
is *rare and great*. Even something that is merely imagined to
be rare and great, something *miraculous*, for example, has this
effect. Fright is the best part of humanity.

19 [81]
    Dreaming as the selective extension of visual images.
    In the realm of the intellect, everything qualitative is merely *quantitative*. We are led to qualities by the concept, the word.

19 [82]
    Perhaps the human being is incapable of *forgetting* anything. The operations of seeing and knowing are much too complicated for it to be possible completely to efface them again; which means that from this point on, all forms that once have been produced by the brain and the nervous system are repeated frequently in the same way. An identical neural activity generates the same image once again.

19 [83]
    In its specifics, philosophical thought is the same as scientific thought, but it deals with *great* things and concerns. However, the concept of greatness is mutable, partly aesthetic, partly moral. Philosophical thought is a *controlling* of the drive for knowledge. Herein lies its cultural significance.
    But once metaphysics has been cast aside, then humankind will once again gradually begin to perceive other things as *great*. I mean, philosophers will prefer other fields: and hopefully those fields in which they can have a salutary effect on the new culture.
    Philosophy is tied to the *legislation of greatness*, a "name-giving": "that is great," he says, and he thereby elevates the human being. It begins with the legislation of morality: "that is great," the standpoint of the seven wise men, from which, in good times, the Romans never deviated.

19 [84]
    The most delicate sensations of pleasure and displeasure constitute the true raw material of all knowledge: the true mystery is that surface onto which the activity of the nerves, in

pleasure and pain, inscribes its forms: sensation immediately projects *forms*, which in turn generate new sensations.

It belongs to the very nature of sensations of pleasure and displeasure to express themselves in adequate motions: the sen-
5 sation of the *image* is created due to the fact that these adequate motions cause other nerves to experience sensations.

19 [85]

Wisdom and Science.
On Philosophers.
Dedicated to the immortal Arthur Schopenhauer.

19 [86]
10   σοφία and ἐπιστήμη. Inherent in σοφία is discrimination, the possession of good taste: whereas science, lacking such a refined sense of taste, gobbles up anything that is worth knowing.

19 [87]
Darwinism applies to thought in images as well: the stronger
15 image devours the weaker ones.

19 [88]
"In dear despicable Germany!"

19 [89]
What is the philosopher? To be answered using the example of the ancient Greeks?
Thales. Mythologist and philosopher.
20   Anaximander. Tragic world view. Tragedy.
Heraclitus. Illusion. The artistic element in the philosopher. Art.
Pythagoras. Mysticism and philosophy. Religion.
Anaxagoras. Purposes. Spirit and matter.
25   Parmenides. Zeno. The logical. Logic.

Empedocles. Love, hate. Justice and morality of love. Morality.

Democritus. Number and measure, outlook of all of physics. Philosophy of nature.

5 Pythagoreans. Sectarianism.

Socrates. The philosopher and culture. Culture.

Emergence of philosophers and the philosophers' tribunal for the culture of the future.

19 [90]

Whether thinking occurs with pleasure or displeasure is an
10 absolutely essential distinction: anyone who finds it difficult
will be less inclined toward it and will probably also not get as
far: he *forces* himself, and in this realm that is useless.

19 [91]

All natural science is nothing but an attempt to understand
the human being, the anthropological: to be more precise, an
15 attempt constantly to return to the human being by way of the
most lengthy detours. The human being swells up to embrace
the macrocosm, so as in the end to say, "in the end, you are
what you are."

19 [92]

Sometimes a result reached by leaps immediately proves it-
20 self to be true and fruitful, when viewed from the perspective
of its consequences.

Is a brilliant scientific inquirer guided by a correct *hunch*?
Yes, what he sees are precisely *possibilities* that lack sufficient
evidence: but the fact that he considers such a thing possible
25 demonstrates his brilliance. He quickly recognizes what he is
more or less able to prove.

The misuse of knowledge in the eternal repetition of experiments and the gathering of material, whereas the result can
already be established on the basis of a few instances. This is

also true in the case of philology: the completeness of the material is in many cases entirely superfluous.

19 [93]

Even what is moral has its sole source in the intellect, but here the connecting chain of images has a different effect than
5 in the cases of the artist and the intellectual: it provokes an *act*. The sensation of similarity, *identifying*, is certainly a necessary prerequisite. After that, memory of one's own pain. To be good would hence mean: to identify *very easily* and very *quickly*. Thus it is a transformation, similar to that of the actor.

10 By contrast, all righteousness and all justice derive from an equilibrium of egoistic interests: mutual agreement not to harm each other. Hence on wiles. When it takes the form of rigorous principles it appears differently: as *strength* of character. Love and justice opposites: culminate in sacrifice for the
15 sake of the world.

The anticipation of possible sensations of displeasure determines the actions of the just human being: he empirically knows the consequences of injuring his neighbor: but also of his own injury.

20 By contrast, the Christian ethic is the opposite of this: it is based upon identifying oneself with one's neighbor; here being charitable to others is charity to oneself, suffering with others is the same as one's own suffering. Love is bound up with a desire for unity.

19 [94]

25 One honest word by the noble Zöllner was enough to call forth almost unanimous condemnation in our rabble-republic of scholars.

19 [95]

In this book I show no regard for contemporary scholars and thereby give the appearance of considering them insignificant. But if one wants to meditate calmly on serious things, then one cannot let oneself be disturbed by disgusted stares. I now reluctantly turn my eyes toward them so as to tell them that I do not consider them insignificant, but that I wish I did.

19 [96]

It was a great *mathematician* who first introduced *philosophy* in Greece. This is the source of his sense for the abstract, the unmythical. Due to his antimythical attitude he is considered in Delphi to be "wise": — Orphic societies represent abstract thought in allegory.

The Greeks adopt *science* from the orientals. *Mathematics and astronomy are older than philosophy.*

19 [97]

The human being demands truth and adheres to it in his moral interactions with other human beings. This is the basis of all social life. One anticipates the detrimental consequences of mutual lies. This is the origin of the *obligation to be truthful.* The epic poet is allowed to *lie* because in this instance no harmful effects are to be expected. —Hence, where lies are considered pleasing, they are permitted: the beauty and charm of lies, assuming they do no harm. Thus, the priest invents myths for his gods: they justify their sublimity. Extremely difficult to revive the mythic feeling of the free lie. The great Greek philosophers still participate entirely in this justification of the lie.

Where one is incapable of knowing anything that is true, lies are permitted.

Every human being lets himself be continuously lied to every night in his dreams.

Humanity acquires the *aspiration for truth* in an infinitely slow process. Our historical sensibility something completely new in the world. It would be possible for it to completely suppress art.

Speaking the *truth at any price* is *Socratic.*

19 [98]

The Philosopher.
Observations on the Struggle Between Art and Knowledge.

19 [99]

"Ochlocracy of scholars" instead of republic of scholars.

19 [100]

Very instructive when Heraclitus compares his language
with Apollo and the Sibyl.

19 [101]

The senses fool us.

19 [102]

Truth and lie physiological.

Truth as moral imperative — two sources of morality.

The essence of truth judged according to its *effects*.

The effects seduce us into accepting unproven "truths."

The *struggle* of such truths that exist by virtue of their power
makes evident our need to find another way to arrive at them.
Either explaining everything on the basis of truth, or climbing
up to it on the basis of examples, phenomena.

Marvelous invention of logic.

Gradual predominance of the logical powers and limitation
of what it is *possible* to know.

Continuous reaction of the artistic powers and limitation to
what it is *worth* knowing (judged according to its *effect*).

19 [103]

Internal struggle of the *philosopher*.

His universal impulse compels him to bad thought; the enormous pathos of truth, produced by his far-reaching point of
view, forces him to *communicate*, and this, in turn, to logic.

On the one hand, this produces an *optimistic metaphysics of
logic* — which gradually poisons and falsifies everything. Logic,
as sole ruler, leads to lies. For it *is* not the sole ruler.

The other sense of truth derives from *love*, proof of strength.

Expressing *beatifying truth* out of *love*: based upon knowledge arrived at by the individual which he does not need to communicate, but whose ebullient beatitude forces him to do so.

19 [104]

To be completely truthful—marvelous, heroic desire of the human being in the midst of a mendacious nature! *But only possible in a very relative sense!* That is tragic. That is *Kant's tragic problem*! Art now acquires an entirely *new* dignity. The sciences, by contrast, are *degraded* by a degree.

19 [105]

Truthfulness of art: it alone is now honest.

Thus we return, by means of an immense detour, to the *natural* demeanor (that of the Greeks). It has proven itself impossible to erect a culture on knowledge.

19 [106]

Fighting for *a truth* and fighting *for the sake of* **the** truth are two very different things.

19 [107]

Unconscious *inferences* arouse my suspicion: it is probably that transition from *image* to *image*: the last image arrived at then functions as stimulus and incentive.

Unconscious thought must take place without concepts: thus in *perceptions*.

Yet this is the inferential process followed by the contemplative philosopher and the artist. He acts in the same way as everyone else with regard to their personal psychological impulses, but projects them onto an impersonal world.

This thought in images does not initially have a strict *logical* character, but it is still more or less logical. The philosopher then makes an effort to replace this thought in images with conceptual thought. The instincts also appear to be such a thought in images, one that ultimately becomes stimulus and incentive.

19 [108]

The powerful ethical strength of the Stoics is evidenced by the fact that they violate their own principle in the interest of the freedom of the will.

19 [109]

Toward a theory of morality: in politics, the statesman often
5 anticipates the action of his opponent and carries it out first: "If I don't do it, he will." A kind of *self-defense* as the fundamental principle of politics. Standpoint of war.

19 [110]

The ancient Greeks lack a normative theology: everyone has the right to deal with it in a poetic manner and he can believe
10 whatever he wants.

The enormous *quantity* of philosophical thought in the case of the Greeks (along with its continuation as theology throughout the centuries).

Their great powers of logic are evident, for example, in the
15 organization of the cults in individual cities.

19 [111]

The Orphic societies are *rigid* in their phantasma, border on allegory.

Logical — — —

19 [112]

The Stoics' gods only concern themselves with what is *great*,
20 neglecting what is small and individual.

19 [113]

Schopenhauer denies the ability of moral philosophy to influence moral attitudes: just as the artist does not create according to concepts. Interesting! It is true, every human is already an intelligible being (determined through countless genera-
25 tions?). But these moral powers are *strengthened* by the stronger

excitation of certain sensations by means of concepts. Nothing new is created, but the creative energy is concentrated on one side. For example, the categorical imperative has greatly strengthened the sensation of unselfish virtue.

5 Here, too, we see how the individual, morally outstanding human being radiates a power of imitation. The philosopher is supposed to disseminate this power. What is law for the highest specimens must gradually be accepted as universal law: even if only as a barricade against the others.

19 [114]

10 The Stoics interpreted Heraclitus in a shallow manner and misunderstood him. The Epicureans also smuggled laxness into Democritus's rigid principles.

In the case of Heraclitus, the world highly regular, but still no optimism.

19 [115]

15 The procedure of all religion and philosophy and science with regard to the world: it begins with the coarsest anthropomorphisms *and becomes incessantly more refined.*

The individual human being even views the solar system as something that serves him or has a connection to him.

20 In their mythology, the Greeks transformed all of nature into Greeks. They viewed nature merely as a masquerade and disguise, as it were, for human gods. In this they were the opposite of all realists. The opposition between truth and appearance dwelled deep within them. Their metamorphoses are

25 what distinguishes them.

Thales expressed this in his assertion that everything is water.

19 [116]

Does intuition relate to the concepts of the species or to the perfected *types*? But the concept of the species always falls far short of a good specimen, the consummate type surpasses

30 reality.

Ethical anthropomorphisms:	Anaximander: justice.
	Heraclitus: law.
	Empedocles: love and hate.
Logical anthropomorphisms:	Parmenides: nothing but being.
	Anaxagoras: *νοῦς*.
	Pythagoras: everything is number.

19 [117]

World history is shortest when measured according to significant philosophical recognitions, ignoring those spans of
time that were hostile to them. Among the *Greeks* we see a
degree of activity and a creative power found nowhere else:
they occupy the greatest span of time, they truly produced all
the types.

They are the inventors of *logic*.

Didn't language already betray the human being's capacity
to produce logic?

Indeed, it is the most admirable logical operation and distinction. But it did not emerge all at once; instead, it is the
logical result of endlessly long spans of time. Here we should
also think of the emergence of the instincts: developed quite
gradually.

The intellectual activity of millennia deposited in language.

19 [118]

The human being discovers only very gradually how infinitely complicated the world is. At first he conceives it to be
wholly simple, that is, as superficial as he himself is.

He takes himself, the most recent product of nature, as the
standard and believes that the powers, the primordial powers,
are just like those things that enter into his consciousness.

He assumes the *operations of the most complicated mechanisms*, of
the brain, as if all operations had been of this very same sort
since the beginning of time. Because this complicated mecha-

nism produces an intelligent being in such a short time, he
assumes that the existence of the world is something quite recent: it cannot have taken the creator very long, he supposes.

Thus, he believes that the word "instinct" explains something or other, and even projects unconscious purposive actions onto the primordial genesis of things.

Time, space, and the sense of causality seem to have been
given along with the first *sensation*.

The human being is acquainted with the world to the extent
that he is acquainted with himself: that is, its profundity is disclosed to him to the extent that he is amazed at himself and his
own complexity.

19 [119]

It must certainly be possible to demonstrate that at some
time everything present and existent *did not exist* and hence that
at some time it again *will not exist*. Heraclitus's becoming.

19 [120]

It is just as rational to take the moral, artistic, religious needs
of the human being as the basis of the world as it is to discover
it in mechanics: that is, we are acquainted neither with impact
nor with gravity. (?)

19 [121]

We do not know the true nature of *one single causality*.
Absolute skepticism: necessity of art and illusion.

19 [122]

Gravity can perhaps be explained on the basis of the movement of the ether as it revolves, along with the entire solar
system, around some immense heavenly body.

19 [123]

Neither the metaphysical, nor the ethical, nor the aesthetic
significance of existence can be *proven*.

19 [124]

Order in the world, the most laborious and slowest result of terrible evolutions, conceived as the essence of the world— Heraclitus!

19 [125]

It must be *proven* that all constructions of the world are anthropomorphisms: indeed, if Kant is right, all the sciences. To be sure, this is a vicious circle—if the sciences are correct, then we no longer stand on Kant's foundation: if Kant is correct, then the sciences are incorrect.

Against Kant we still can object, even if we accept all his propositions, that it is still *possible* that the world is as it appears to us. On a personal level, moreover, this entire position is useless. No one can live in this skepticism.

We must get beyond this skepticism, we must *forget* it! How many things in this world must we not forget! Art, the ideal structure, temperament.

Our salvation does not lie in *knowing*, but in *creating*! Our greatness lies in supreme semblance, in the noblest fervency. If the universe is no concern of ours, then at least we demand the right to despise it.

19 [126]

Terrible loneliness of the last philosopher! All around, nature stands glaring at him, vultures hover above his head. And so he calls out to nature: Grant oblivion! Oblivion!—*No, he endures his suffering like a Titan—until he is offered appeasement in the supreme tragic art.*

19 [127]

To view "spirit," the product of the brain, as supernatural! Even to deify it. What madness!

19 [128]

Among millions of perishing worlds, just once a possible one! It too perishes! It was not the first!

19 [129]

Pre-Platonic philosophers.	Poetics.
Plato.	Metrics.
Socratic schools.	Rhetoric.

19 [130]

Choephori.	Latin grammar.
Erga.	Greek grammar.
Lyricists.	
Theognis.	

19 [131]

Oedipus.
Soliloquies
of the Last Philosopher.

A Fragment
from the History of Posterity.

I call myself the last philosopher because I am the last human being. I myself am the only one who speaks with me, and my voice comes to me as the voice of someone who is dying. Let me commune with you for just one hour, beloved voice, with you, the last trace of the memory of all human happiness; with your help I will deceive myself about my loneliness and lie my way into community and love; for my heart refuses to believe that love is dead; it cannot bear the shudder of the loneliest loneliness and it forces me to speak as if I were two persons.

Do I still hear you, my voice? You whisper when you curse? And yet your curse should cause the bowels of this world to burst! But it continues to live and merely stares at me all the more brilliantly and coldly with its pitiless stars; it continues to live, as dumb and blind as ever, and the only thing that

dies is—the human being. —And yet! I still hear you, beloved
voice! Someone other than I, the last human being, is dying in
this universe: the last sigh, *your* sigh, dies with me, the drawn
out Woe! Woe! sighing around me, Oedipus, the last of the
5 woeful human beings.

19 [132]

The horrible consequence of Darwinism, which, by the way,
I consider to be correct. All our veneration is based on qualities we take to be eternal: moral, artistic, religious, etc.

We do not come a single step closer to explaining purposive-
10 ness by appealing to the instincts. For precisely these instincts
are already the products of processes that have gone on for an
infinitely long period of time.

The will does not objectify itself *adequately*, as Schopenhauer
claims: it merely appears this way when one takes the most
15 highly perfected forms as one's basis.

This will is also a highly complex end product of nature.
Nerves presupposed.

And even gravity: it is not a simple phenomenon, but rather
itself the effect of movement in the solar system, of ether, etc.

20 And mechanical impact is also something complex.

The world ether as primal matter.

19 [133]

All knowing is a process of reflecting in quite specific forms,
in forms that do not exist at the outset. Nature is acquainted
neither with *structure* nor *size*; rather, only to a knowing being
25 do things appear to be this large or that small. *Infinitude* in
nature: nowhere does it have limits. Only for us is there fini-
tude. Time *infinitely* divisible.

19 [134]

From Thales to Socrates—nothing but projections of the
human being onto nature—immense shadow plays of the hu-
30 man being upon nature, as upon mountains!

Socrates and Plato. Knowledge and good universal. The *beautiful* at the inception. The artist's *ideas*.

Pythagoreans	Number.
Democritus	Matter.
Pythagoras	The human being not a product of the past, rather recurrence. Unity of all living things.
Empedocles	Animals and world of plants understood morally, universal sex drive and hatred. "Will" universal.
Anaxagoras	Intellect as primordial.
Eleatics	
Heraclitus	The creative power of the artist primordial.
Anaximander	Justice and punishment universal.
Thales.	

Prior to that the gods and nature. Religions are only less veiled expressions. Astrology. The human being as purpose. "*World* history."

Kant's thing in itself as category.

The philosopher is the extension of that drive by which we, by means of anthropological illusions, continually relate with nature. The eye. Time.

19 [135]

The philosopher caught in the webs of *language*.

19 [136]

I want to depict and gain a sense for the *incredible development* of the **one** *philosopher* who desires knowledge, the philosopher of humanity.

Most people stand so strongly under the influence of their drives that they do not even notice what is happening. I want to state what is happening and call attention to it.

The *one* philosopher is in this respect identical with all the aspirations of science. For all sciences rest solely on the general foundation of the philosopher.

To bring evidence for the incredible *unity* of all the drives for knowledge: the fragmented scholar.

19 [137]
> *Tasks*:
> The so-called abstractions.
> 5 Forms as surfaces.

19 [138]

Apologia for Art.

> *Introduction.*
> *Necessary lie* and Descartes's *veracité du dieu.*
> Plato *opposed to* art.
> 10   1. Language and concept.
>   2. Forms as surfaces.
>   3. Pathos of truth.
>   4. — — —

19 [139]
Infinity is the primordial fact: The only thing that would have
15 to be explained would be the origin of the finite. But the viewpoint of the finite is purely sensual, that is, a deception.

How can anyone dare to speak of the objective of the earth!

In infinite time and space there are no aims: *what exists, exists eternally* in one form or another. It is impossible to foresee what
20 kind of metaphysical world there ought to be.

Humanity must be able to *stand* without anything of this sort to lean on—enormous task of the artists!

19 [140]
Time in itself is nonsense: time exists only for a sensate creature. The same is true for space.
25   Every *structure* appertains to the subject. It is the registering of *surfaces* by means of mirrors. We have to subtract all qualities.

We cannot conceive things as they are, precisely because we then would not be capable of conceiving them.

Everything remains as it is: which means that all qualities
betray an indefinable and absolute state of affairs. —The relationship more or less like that of Chladni's sound figures to
the vibrations.

19 [141]

5   All knowledge comes about by means of separation, delimi-
tation, restriction; no absolute knowledge of a whole!

19 [142]

Pleasure and displeasure as universal sensations? I don't
think so.

But where do artistic powers appear? Certainly in the crys-
10 tal. The formation of *structure*: but mustn't we then presuppose
the existence of a perceiving being?

19 [143]

Music as a *supplement to language*: music renders many *stimuli*,
and even entire states of stimulation, that language cannot
represent.

19 [144]

15   There is no *form* in nature, because there is no distinction
between inner and outer.

All art is based upon the *mirror* of the eyes.

19 [145]

Beauty is certainly the goal of human *sensual knowledge*, it
transfigures the world. Why do we chase after anything else?
20 Why do we want to transcend our senses? Restless knowledge
leads to desolation and ugliness. — *Contentment* with the world
when perceived artistically!

19 [146]

As soon as one wishes to *gain knowledge of* the thing in itself,
then *it is precisely this world*—knowledge is only possible as a re-

flection and by measuring oneself according to *one* standard (sensation).

We *know* what the world is: absolute and unconditional knowledge is the desire to know without knowledge.

19 [147]

The so-called *unconscious inferences* can be traced back to *all-preserving memory*, which presents us with parallel experiences and hence already *knows* the consequences of an action. It is not anticipation of the effects; rather, it is the feeling: identical causes, identical effects, generated by a mnemonic image.

19 [148]

We far too easily confuse *Kant's* thing in itself with the *Buddhists'* true essence of things: that is, reality either exhibits nothing but *semblance* or an *appearance that is wholly adequate to truth*.

Semblance as nonbeing is confused with the appearance of the existent.

All kinds of superstitions thrive in this vacuum.

19 [149]

The course of philosophy: at first human beings are conceived as the authors of all things—gradually things are explained according to analogies with individual human qualities—ultimately one arrives at *sensation*. Important question: Is sensation a primordial fact of all matter?

Attraction and repulsion?

19 [150]

The historical drive for knowledge—its goal is to comprehend the human being in its development, to eliminate everything miraculous here, as well.

This drive deprives the drive for culture of its greatest strength: acquiring knowledge is a pure luxury, it does not raise the current level of culture one iota.

19 [151]

   To view philosophy like astrology: namely, to tie the fate of
the world to that of human beings: that is, to view the highest evolution of the *human being* as the highest evolution of
the *world*. All the sciences receive their nourishment from this
5 philosophical drive. Humanity first destroys religions, then science.

19 [152]

   The sense of *beauty* connected with procreation.

19 [153]

   Human beings even immediately exploited Kantian epistemology for a glorification of the human being: the world only
10 has reality in them. It is tossed back and forth in their heads
like a ball. In truth, this means nothing other than this: imagine that there is a work of art and a stupid human being to
contemplate it. To be sure, it exists as a mental phenomenon
for that stupid human being only insofar as he himself is an
15 artist and carries the forms about in his own head. He could
boldly assert: outside my brain it has no reality.

   Intellect's *forms* emerged very gradually out of matter. It is
plausible in itself that they are strictly adequate to truth. Where
could such an apparatus that invents something new possibly
20 have come from!

   The primary faculty seems to me to be the perception of
structure, that is, based upon the mirror. Space and time are
merely *measured* things, measured according to a rhythm.

19 [154]

   You should not flee into some metaphysics, rather, you
25 should actively sacrifice yourselves for the *emerging culture*! That
is why I am strictly against dreamy idealism.

19 [155]

   All knowledge is a process of measuring according to a standard. Without a standard, that is, without any limitation, there

can be no knowledge. The same is true in the realm of intellectual forms, as, for example, when I ask about the value of
knowledge per se: I have to adopt some position that is *higher*,
or at least one that is *fixed*, one that can serve as a standard.

19 [156]

5   If we trace the entire intellectual world back to *stimulus* and
sensation, then this sorely inadequate perception explains very
little.

The statement: there is no knowledge without a knower or
no subject without an object and no object without a subject,
10 is entirely true, but utterly trivial.

We cannot say anything about the thing in itself because we
have pulled the standpoint of the knower, that is, of the mea-
surer, out from under our own feet. A quality exists *for us*, that
is, measured according to us. If we take away the standard,
15 then what remains of the quality!

We can prove what things *are* only by means of a measuring
subject placed alongside them. Their properties in themselves
are of no concern to us; they matter only insofar as they have
an effect on us.

20   Now, the question is: How did such a measuring being come
about?

The plant also is a *measuring being*.

19 [157]

The incredible human consensus about things proves the
absolute identity of their perceptual apparatus.

19 [158]

25   For the plant, the world is thus and such — for us, it is thus
and such. If we compare the two perceptual capacities, then
our conception of the world is taken to be the more correct
one, that is, as corresponding more closely to truth. Now, the
human being has evolved slowly and knowledge still is devel-
30 oping: thus, his image of the world constantly is becoming

ever more true and complete. Of course, it is only a *reflection*,
one that keeps getting clearer. The mirror itself, however, is
not something entirely alien and unsuited to the essence of
things, but rather something that likewise developed slowly as
5   the essence of things. We see an effort to make the mirror ever
more adequate: science takes over where the natural process
leaves off. — In this way, things are reflected ever more clearly:
gradual liberation from what is all too anthropomorphic. *For
the plant, the entire world is a plant*, for us, it is a human being.

19 [159]
10   Impact, the influence of one atom upon another, also presupposes *sensation*. Something that is inherently alien cannot
have an effect on something else.
   It is not the awakening of sensation that is so thorny, but
that of consciousness in the world. But still explicable, if every-
15   thing has sensation.
   If everything has sensation, then we have an intermingling
of the smallest, the larger, and the largest centers of sensation. These complexes of sensations, larger or smaller, could
be called "will."
20   We have a difficult time freeing ourselves from *qualities*.

19 [160]
   I consider it false to speak of humanity's unconscious aim.
It is no totality like an anthill. Perhaps one can speak of the
unconscious aim of a city or a people: but what sense does it
make to speak of the unconscious aim of *all the anthills* on earth!

19 [161]
25   Sensation, reflex movements that occur frequently and with
lightning speed, and that then are gradually assimilated, produce inferential operations, that is, the sense of causality. Space
and time are dependent upon the sensation of causality.
   Memory preserves the reflex movements that one experi-
30   ences.

Consciousness commences with the sensation of causality, which means that memory is older than consciousness. For example, the mimosa has memory, but no consciousness. In the case of plants, of course, memory without *images*.

5   But *memory* must be part of the essence of *sensation*; hence it must ⟨be⟩ a primordial characteristic of things. But then the reflex movement, as well.

The inviolability of the laws of nature means: sensation and memory are part of the essence of things. The fact that a sub-
10 stance reacts in a certain way to contact with another substance is a matter of memory and sensation. At some time it *learned* this, that is, the actions of substances are *derived laws*. But then the decision must have been made on the basis of pleasure and displeasure.

15 But if pleasure, displeasure, sensation, memory, reflex movements are all part of the essence of matter, then *human knowledge penetrates far more deeply into the essence of things*.

The entire *logic* of nature is then reduced to a system of *pleasure* and *displeasure*. Everything grasps for pleasure and flees
20 from displeasure, these are the eternal laws of nature.

19 [162]

Memory has nothing to do with nerves, with the brain. It is a primordial characteristic. For the human being carries around with him the memory of all previous generations.

The mnemonic *image* something that is very artificial and
25 *rare*.

19 [163]

It is just as impossible to speak of an unerring memory as it is to speak of an absolutely purposive action produced by natural laws.

19 [164]

Is it an unconscious inference? Does matter *draw inferences*? It
30 has sensations and struggles for its individual existence. "Will"

manifests itself first in *change*, that is, there is a kind of *free will* that modifies the essence of a thing, out of pleasure and flight from displeasure. —Matter has a number of *Protean* qualities, which, depending on the nature of the attack, it stresses, re-
5 inforces, and employs for the benefit of the whole.

Qualities seem to be nothing but particular modified activities of *one single* material. Occurring according to the proportions of measure and number.

19 [165]

We are acquainted with only *one* reality—that of *thoughts*. As
10 if that were the essence of things!

If memory and sensation were the *material* of things!

19 [166]

Thought provides us with the concept of an entirely new form of *reality*: composed of sensation and memory.

19 [167]

The human being in the world actually could conceive him-
15 self as a character **in a** *dream* that itself is part of a dream.

19 [168]

Among the Greeks, the philosopher continues, in bright illumination and visibility, the activity by means of which the Greeks arrived at their culture.

19 [169]

1. No διαδοχαί.
20 2. The various types.

19 [170]

Philosophers are the most distinguished class of intellectual giants. They have no public, they need *fame*. In order to communicate their supreme joys, they need *proof*: in this, they are less fortunate than artists.

19 [171]

On the example of contemporary Germany we see that it is possible for science to flourish in a barbarized culture; likewise, that utility has nothing to do with science (although it may appear to, given the privileging of chemical and scien-
5 tific institutions, and when mere chemists can even become renowned "authorities").

Science provides its own life-sustaining atmosphere. A declining culture (like the Alexandrine) and a nonculture (like our own) do not make it impossible.
10 Acquiring knowledge is probably even a substitute for culture.

19 [172]

It is probably only the isolation of knowledge due to the segregation of the sciences that makes it possible for knowledge and culture to remain alien to one another. In the *philosopher*,
15 knowledge once again comes into contact with culture.

He encompasses all that is known and raises the question concerning the value of knowledge. This is a cultural problem: knowledge and life.

19 [173]

Are the *periods of darkness*, for example, the Middle Ages,
20 actually periods of recuperation, say, times of rest for the intellectual genius of humankind?

Or: are even these *periods of darkness* the results of higher purposes? If books have their own fates, then the disappearance of a book is probably also a fate, with some purpose or other.
25 The *purposes* are what *perplex* us.

19 [174]

In the philosopher, activities are carried on by means of metaphor. The striving for *uniform* control. Every thing strives toward the immeasurable; in nature, individual character rarely is fixed, but instead is constantly expanding. Whether *slowly* or

quickly is an utterly human question. If one considers what is infinitely small, then every development is always *infinitely quick*.

19 [175]
    What does truth matter to human beings!
    The belief that one possesses truth makes possible the high-
5 est and purest life. Human beings need the *belief in truth*.
    Truth appears as a social necessity: by means of a metastasis
it later is applied to all those things for which it is unnecessary.
    All virtues arise from pressing needs. The necessity for truth-
fulness begins with society. Otherwise, the human being lives
10 within eternal occultations. The founding of states arouses
truthfulness. —
    The drive for knowledge has a *moral* source.

19 [176]
    Even the tiniest fragment of the world must reveal how
much it is worth — take a close look at human beings, then you
15 will know what you should think of the world.

19 [177]
    In some instances, necessity produces truthfulness as a so-
ciety's means of existence.
    This drive is fortified by frequent use and then unjustifiably
is transferred by means of metastasis. It becomes a proclivity
20 in itself. Something used for particular instances then becomes
a quality. — Now we have the drive for knowledge.
    This generalization occurs by means of the intervening *con-
cept*. This quality begins with a *false* judgment — to be true means
to be *eternally* true. From this arises the inclination not to want
25 to live a lie: elimination of all illusions.
    But one is chased from one web into another.
    The good human being now wants to be truthful and be-
lieves in the truth of all things. Not only of society, but also
of the world. Hence {he} also {believes} in fathomability. For
30 why should the world deceive him?

Thus he projects his own inclination onto the world and be-lieves that the world *must* also be truthful toward him.

19 [178]

I do not inquire into the purpose of knowledge: it emerged by accident, that is, not according to any rational design. As
5 the extension or the rigidification of a manner of thinking and acting that was necessary in certain instances.

By nature, the human being does not exist in order to ac-quire knowledge.

Two characteristics necessary for different purposes — *truth-*
10 *fulness* — and *metaphor* — produced the inclination for truth. Thus, a moral phenomenon, aesthetically generalized, pro-duces the intellectual drive.

Here instinct is simply habit, frequently drawing the same conclusion and on that basis establishing κατὰ ἀνάλογον the
15 obligation that one must always draw the same conclusion.

19 [179]

Nature immersed the human being in nothing but illu-sions. — That is his true element. He sees forms, he senses stimuli rather than truths. He dreams, he imagines divine human beings as nature.
20 *The human being became a knowing being by accident*, by means of the unintentional combination of two qualities. At some point he will cease to exist and nothing will have happened.

For a long time, human beings did not exist, and even when they have ceased to exist, nothing will have happened. They
25 have no further mission and no purpose.

The human being is an animal full of supreme pathos, and he considers all his qualities to be as important as if they were the hinges on which the world turns.

The similar recalls what is similar and compares itself with
30 it: that is knowledge, the quick grouping of everything that is identical. Only the similar perceives the similar: a physiological

process. Memory is the same thing as the perception of something new. Not thought added upon thought — — —

19 [180]

On Lies.

Heraclitus. Belief in the eternity of truth.
5 Disappearance of his work—one day the disappearance of all
knowledge.
And what is truth in Heraclitus!
Portrayal of his doctrine as anthropomorphism.
The same for Anaximander. Anaxagoras.
10 Heraclitus's relationship to the character of the Greek people.
It is the Hellenic cosmos.
Genesis of the pathos of truth. Accidental genesis of knowledge.
The mendacity and illusion in which human beings live.
15 Lies and speaking the truth—myth, poetry.
The foundations of everything great and vital rest upon illusion. The pathos of truth leads to decline. (There lies what
is "great.") Above all to the decline of *culture*.
Empedocles and the sacrifices. Eleatics. Plato needs the lie for
20 his republic.
The Greeks were separated from culture by *sectarianism*.
Conversely, we are returning to culture in a *sectarian manner*, we
are trying once again to suppress the philosopher's immeasurable knowledge and convince him of the anthropomorphic character of all knowledge.
25

19 [181]

Objective value of knowledge—it does not *improve* anything.
It has no ultimate aims for the world. Its genesis accidental.
Value of truthfulness. —It does indeed improve things! Its
aim is decline. It sacrifices. Our *art* is the likeness of desperate
30 knowledge.

19 [182]

Knowledge provides humanity with a beautiful means for its decline.

19 [183]

That the human being has developed in this particular way rather than in some other is, after all, certainly his own work: It is his *nature* to be so immersed in illusion (dream) and dependent upon surface (eye). Is it then surprising that even his drives for truth also are ultimately reducible to his fundamental nature? —

19 [184]

We get a sense of our own greatness when we hear of a man who refused to lie, even when his life depended on it—even more so when a statesman destroys an empire out of truthfulness.

19 [185]

Our habits become virtues by means of a free translation into the realm of obligation, that is, by incorporating into the concept the notion of inviolability; that means that we make our habits into virtues by considering our own welfare less important than their inviolability—hence, by sacrificing the individual, or at least by *imagining the possibility of such a sacrifice.* — The realm of virtues and of the arts—our metaphysical world —has its inception at the point where the individual begins to regard himself as unimportant. *Obligation* would be especially *pure* if in the essence of things there *were nothing that corresponded to the moral.*

19 [186]

It is not a thought that has an effect on memory, rather, the thought undergoes an infinite number of fine metamorphoses; that is, *to the thought* corresponds *a thing in itself*, which then grasps the analogous thing in itself that exists in memory.

19 [187]
   Individuals are the bridges upon which becoming is
founded. All qualities are originally only *unique actions* that,
when frequently repeated in identical situations, ultimately become habits. The entire being of the individual takes part in
5 every action, and a specific modification of the individual corresponds to a habit. In an individual, everything down to the
smallest cell is individual, that is, it takes part in all experiences
and past events. Hence the possibility of *procreation*.

19 [188]
                    History of Greek Philosophy to
10   Plato
                          Recounted
                        in Its Essentials
                              by
                             F. N.

19 [189]
15 Introduction.
      1. Thales Anaximander Heraclitus Parmenides
         Anax⟨agoras⟩ Empedocles Democritus Pyth⟨agoreans⟩
         Socrates.
      Chapter 1.
20 Chapter 2.

19 [190]
                    History of Greek Philosophy.
      Introduction.
         1.   *Thales.*
         2.   *Anaximander.*
25   3.   *Heraclitus.*
         4.   *Parmenides.*
         5.   *Anax⟨agoras⟩.*
         6.   *Empedocles.*
         7.   *Democritus.*

19 [191]
Introduction on Truth and Lie.
5　1.　*The Pathos of Truth.*
2.　*The Genesis of Truth.*
3.　— — —

19 [192]
The *political* meaning of the early Greek philosophers must be demonstrated, as well as their power to produce *metaphor*.

19 [193]
10　Just as our *theatrical* aptitude has been preserved in only its most vulgar forms, so too our sociability only on the barstool.

19 [194]
Humanity propagates itself by means of impossibilities, these are its *virtues*—the categorical imperative and the demand "Children, you must love one another" are just such impossible
15　demands.
Similarly, *pure logic* is the impossibility by means of which science is maintained.

19 [195]
The philosopher is the rarest form of greatness because human beings arrived at knowledge only by coincidence, not as
20　an original endowment. But for this reason, also the highest type of greatness.

19 [196]
We should learn in the same way that the Greeks learned from their past and their neighbors—for *life*, that is, being highly selective and immediately using all that has been learned

as a pole on which one can vault high—and higher than all
one's neighbors. Thus, not in a scholarly way! Anything not fit
for life is not true history. To be sure, it depends on how high
or how base you take this *life* to be. Anyone who brings Roman
5 history to life by drawing disgusting connections to modern
positions, with their lamentable partisanship and their ephemeral *formation*, commits a greater sin against the past than the
mere scholar who leaves everything dead and mummified. (As
does a particular historian who is frequently mentioned these
10 days, Mommsen.)

19 [197]
    Socrates' behavior at the *trial of the commanders* is remarkable be-
cause it demonstrates his truthfulness in political matters.

19 [198]
    In pursuing knowledge as its aim, our natural science is
heading toward *decline*.
15 Our historical cultivation toward the death of all culture. It
does battle with religions—it destroys all cultures by coincidence.
    This is an unnatural reaction against terrible religious pres-
sure—now taking refuge in extremes. Lacking all moderation.

19 [199]
20 The Germans are not worthy of true artistic creations: for
any silly old political goose, someone like Gervinus, immediately sits down on them and broods with arrogant diligence as
if these eggs had been laid for him alone. The phoenix should
beware not to lay its golden eggs in Germany.

19 [200]
25 This repulsive German culture that now lets even the trumpet fanfares of wartime glory ring out around it.
    Teachers so bad that they could have been produced only by
our famous schools of philology.

19 [201]

Even an upstanding Bible critic like David Strauss begins to speak like a cook in a chemical hash house once the Hegelian haze in which he was enveloped gradually begins to evaporate. Such generally acknowledged "cultivated" Germans can deal
5   with the natural sciences only in the manner of converted students of theology, and they pay attention only when they are convinced that "miracles" have been thoroughly discredited.

Today they are even learning how to take hearty pleasure in their philistinism — the philistine has lost his innocence (Riehl).
10 The philistine and the "cultivated" windbag of our newspaper atmosphere shake each other's hands in brotherhood, and with the same jubilant triumph, the Bonn pseudophilosopher Jürgen Bona-Meyer annihilates pessimism and Riehl, Jahn, or Strauss the Ninth Symphony.

15 Far too few people today sense the way things stand with such specious bibliopolic fabrications, with such Freytag-like novels: our faded gentlemen in the literary branch become enormously grotesque and speak among themselves like the three mighty ones — or they amuse themselves with feeble
20 nymphs in the manner of the painter Schwind.

If you yourselves are not great, then beware of what is great.

19 [202]

I am unaware that the fate of good books is guided by any sort of providence: bad books have almost better prospects of surviving. It appears as a miracle that Aeschylus, Sophocles,
25 and Pindar constantly were transcribed, and apparently it is only by pure accident that we possess any literature from antiquity at all.

19 [203]

If, in our century, Schopenhauer was able to experience that the first edition of his work was pulped, and that it is basically
30 thanks to the diligence of insignificant, indeed, questionable

men of letters that his name gradually resurfaced out of profound obscurity — — —

19 [204]
    Abstractions are *metonymies*, that is, confusions of cause and
effect. However, every concept is a metonymy, and knowledge
5 occurs by means of concepts. "Truth" becomes a *power* only
once we have isolated it as an abstraction.

19 [205]
    A *negating* morality is supremely grandiose because it is won-
derfully impossible. What does it mean when the human being,
in full consciousness, says "No!" while all his senses and nerves
10 say "Yes!" and every fiber, every cell resists.

19 [206]
    When I speak of the terrible possibility that knowledge leads
to decline, then it is by no means my intention to pay a compli-
ment to the present generation: it displays no such tendencies.
But when one observes the development of science since the
15 fifteenth century, then such a power, such a possibility does
indeed become evident.

19 [207]
    The human being who does not believe in the truthfulness
of nature, but instead sees metamorphoses, disguises, masquer-
ades everywhere, who discovers gods in bulls, wise discerners
20 of nature in horses, nymphs in trees — now, when such a person
establishes for himself the law of truthfulness, he also believes
in the truthfulness of nature toward him.

19 [208]
    Every "us," "we," and "I" must be omitted. Also limit the
number of clauses beginning with "that." Every technical term
25 must be avoided as far as possible.

19 [209]

The human being increasingly learned to adapt things to his needs and to acquire knowledge about them. Yet this more complete form of knowledge has not caused him to move farther away from things; in this, the human being does indeed
5 stand closer to truth than do plants.

A sensed stimulus and a glance at a movement, linked together, initially produce causality as an empirical principle: two things—namely, a specific sensation and a specific visual image—always appear together: the belief that the one is the
10 cause of the other is *a metaphor, adopted from* **will** *and act*: an analogical inference.

The only form of causality of which we are aware is that between willing and acting—we transfer this to all things and thereby explain the relationship between two changes that
15 always occur together. The intention, or willing, produces nouns, actions produce verbs. The animal as a creature that wills—that is its essence.

From *quality and act*: one of our *characteristics* leads to action: whereas in reality what happens is that we infer characteristics
20 on the basis of actions: we assume the existence of characteristics because we observe actions of a particular sort.

Thus: the *action* comes first; we connect it with a characteristic.

First the word for the action arises, from it is derived the
25 word for the quality. This relationship transferred onto all things is *causality*.

First "seeing," then "sight." The one who "sees" is taken to be the cause of "seeing." Between the sense and its function we experience a regulated relationship: causality is the transfer of
30 this relationship (of sense to sensory function) onto all things.

It is a primordial phenomenon: to associate with the eye the stimulus sensed by the eye, that is, to associate a sensory impression with the sensory organ. Of course, only the stimulus is given in itself: to sense this to be an action on the part of the eye and call it "seeing" is to draw a causal inference. *Sensing a stimulus to be an activity*, sensing something that is passive to be active, is the first sensation of causality, that is, the initial sensation already produces this sensation of causality. The inner connection of *stimulus* and *activity* transferred onto all things. A word such as "seeing" is *one* word for that interconnection of stimulus and activity. *The eye acts upon a stimulus*: that is, it sees. We explain the world on the basis of our sensory functions: which means, we presuppose a causality everywhere because we ourselves are *constantly experiencing* changes of this sort.

19 [210]

Time, space, and causality are only epistemological *metaphors* with which we explain things. Stimulus and activity connected: we do not know how this occurs; we do not comprehend a single causality, but we have immediate experience of them. All suffering calls forth an action, every action calls forth suffering—this most universal feeling is already *metaphor*. The perceived manifoldness thus already presupposes time and space, succession and coexistence. Temporal coexistence produces the sensation of space.

The sensation of time given along with the feeling of cause and effect, as an answer to the question concerning the speed of various causalities.

Sensation of space first derived by means of metaphor from the sensation of time—or vice versa?

Two *causalities coexisting with* one another—

19 [211]

I am attempting to be helpful to those who are worthy of being introduced to the study of philosophy in an opportune and serious manner. This attempt may or may not be successful, and I am only too well aware that it can be outstripped; and there is nothing I desire more, for the good of that philosophy, than to be imitated and surpassed.

Those who might want to attempt this would be well advised to read Plato and not to place their trust in the guidance of any of those professional academic philosophers.

Above all, they should unlearn all kinds of nonsense and
5 become simple and natural.

Danger of falling into the wrong hands.

19 [212]

Introduction. Types of minds and doctrines necessary as an introduction. They must be simple and easier to grasp.

What philosophy is must become clear, especially philoso-
10 phy's task within a culture.

That it is the *Greeks*, in the age of tragedy, who philosophize. The meaning of *history*: a metamorphosis of plants. Example.

(Ideal and "iconic" history—the last of these impossible.)
15 On the filtering by the common mind. *Schopenhauer*, I, XXVI.

Aversion to compilations.

The questions Schopenhauer poses to philosophy and his criticism of Kant as exemplary. *Schopenhauer*, I 290.

19 [213]
20 Following the method of the ancient historians.

   2. Justify the Greeks.

   3. Thales

19 [214]

                    Philosophy
                       in the
25   Tragic Age of the Greeks.

                    Concise Report
                 on the Ancient Greek
                 Philosophical Masters.

19 [215]

The only way to master manifoldness is by creating categories, for example, to call a whole host of actions "bold." We explain them to ourselves when we place them under the rubric "bold." All explaining and knowing is actually nothing but
5 categorization. —Now with a bold leap: the manifoldness of things is placed under a single heading when we view them, as it were, as countless actions of *one single* quality, for example, actions of *water*, as in the case of Thales. Here we have a transference: innumerable actions are subsumed under one abstraction
10 that is taken to be their cause. What abstraction (characteristic) subsumes the manifoldness of all things? The quality "watery," "moist." The entire world is moist, *hence, the state of being moist is the essence of the entire world*. Metonymy! A false inference. A predicate is confused with a sum of predicates (definition).
15 *Logical thought* practiced little among the Ionians, develops quite slowly. But false inferences are more accurately understood as metonymies, that is, rhetorically, poetically.

All *rhetorical figures* (that is, the essence of language) are *logical paralogisms*. This is where reason begins!

19 [216]

20 We observe how *philosophy* is at first carried on in the same manner in which *language emerged*, that is, illogically.

Then comes the pathos of *truth* and *truthfulness*. Initially this has nothing to do with logic. It merely asserts that *no conscious deception* is being perpetrated. However, those deceptions con-
25 tained in language and in philosophy are initially unconscious, and it is very difficult to become conscious of them. But because of the coexistence of different established philosophies (or religious systems) that shared the same pathos, a curious struggle sprang up. Given the coexistence of inimical reli-
30 gions, each sought to promote itself by declaring the others to be untrue: the same holds for systems.

This caused some people to become skeptical: "Truth is going down the drain!," they sighed.

With Socrates, truthfulness takes possession of logic: it notices the infinite difficulty of correct categorization.

19 [217]

Our sensory perceptions are based on tropes, not on unconscious inferences. Identifying similar thing with similar thing
5 —discovering some similarity or other in one thing and another thing is the primordial procedure. *Memory* thrives on this activity and constantly practices it. *Misapprehension* is the primordial phenomenon.—This presupposes the *perception of structures*. The image in our eye is decisive for knowledge, then
10 the rhythm in our ear. We would *never* arrive at a conception of time based solely on the eye; never arrive at a conception of space based solely on the ear. The sensation of causality corresponds to the sense of touch.

From the very beginning we see the images in the eye only
15 *within ourselves*, we hear the sound only *within ourselves*—it is a considerable leap from this to the assumption of an external world. Plants, for example, have no sensation of an external world. The sense of touch and simultaneously the visual image empirically provide two coexistent sensations; because they
20 always appear together, they arouse the idea of a connection (by means of *metaphor*—for all things that appear together are not necessarily connected).

Abstraction is an extremely significant product. It is an impression that is enduringly retained and rigidified in memory,
25 one that is compatible with very many phenomena and for that reason is very crude and inadequate for each individual phenomenon.

19 [218]

Pathos of truth in a world of lies.

World of lies again in the supreme reaches of philosophy.
30 Purpose of these supreme lies, control of unlimited drive for knowledge.

Emergence of the drive for knowledge out of morality.

19 [219]

Where does the pathos of truth come from in this world of lies? From morality.

The pathos of truth and logic.

Culture and truth.

19 [220]

Every tiny bit of knowledge carries with it a great satisfaction: to be sure, not as truth, but as faith in having discovered the truth. What kind of satisfaction is this?

19 [221]

Culture a unity. Yet the philosopher appears to stand outside of it. He addresses the most distant posterity — fame.

Remarkable that the Greeks philosophized. The beautiful lie.

But even more remarkable that the *human being* ever arrived at the pathos of truth.

The images within him certainly are much more powerful than the nature around him: as in the instance of those fifteenth-century German painters who, despite the nature that surrounded them, created such spidery limbs — dictated by the ancient pious tradition.

Plato desires a new state governed by *dialectic*; he negates the *culture* of the beautiful lie.

19 [222]

No philosophizing is being done in Germany today, and that is why the question What is the philosopher? is incomprehensible to the Germans. That also explains their persistent amazement, which ultimately turns into malice, that someone could live among them as a philosopher without concerning himself with them and yet still address them. Today's Germans can no more endure having someone call out to them than can a ghost.

The desperate awkwardness of being born a philosopher among Germans!

19 [223]

The moral instincts: maternal love — gradually becomes love as such. The same is true for sexual love. Everywhere I recognize *transferences*.

19 [224]

Many things in nature are moist: everything in nature is moist. Moistness is part of the essence of nature: moistness is the essence of nature. So Thales.

19 [225]

Mendacity of the human being toward himself and toward others: prerequisite, ignorance — necessary in order to exist (alone — and in society). The deception of ideation steps into the vacuum. Dreams. The traditional concepts (which hold sway over the old German painters, in spite of nature) are different in all ages. Metonymies. Stimuli, not full knowledge. The eye provides structures. We cling to the surface. The predilection for beauty. Lack of logic, but metaphors. Religions. Philosophies. *Imitation*.

19 [226]

Imitation is the means of all culture; it gradually produces instinct. *All comparing (primordial thought) is imitation. Species* are formed when the first specimens, who are merely similar to one another, rigorously imitate the largest, most powerful specimen. The inculcation of a *second nature* by means of imitation. Unconscious copying is most remarkable in the case of procreation, which is the rearing of a second nature.

Our senses imitate nature by copying it more and more.

Imitation presupposes an act of apprehending and then a perpetual translation of the apprehended image into a thousand metaphors, all of which are effective.

The analogous —

19 [227]

What power compels us to imitate? The appropriation of an unfamiliar impression by means of metaphors.

Stimulus—mnemonic image

connected by means of metaphor (analogical inference).

5   Result: similarities are discovered and revitalized. In a mnemonic image the *repeated* stimulus occurs once again.

Stimulus perceived—then *repeated*, in many metaphors, whereby related images from various categories throng together. Every perception achieves a multiple imitation of the stimulus, but
10 transferred into different realms.

Stimulus sensed

transferred to related nerves

repeated there, in transferred form, etc.

What occurs is a translation of one sense impression into
15 another: some people see or taste something when they hear particular sounds. This a wholly universal phenomenon.

19 [228]

Imitation is the opposite of *knowing* to the extent that knowing does not want to accept any transference as valid, but instead wants to hold onto the impression without metaphor,
20 and without any consequences. To this end the impression is petrified: it is captured and fenced in by means of concepts, then killed, skinned, mummified, and preserved as a concept.

However, there are no "real" expressions and *no real knowing without metaphor*. But the deception about this fact remains, that
25 is, the *faith* in a *truth* of sensory impressions. The most common metaphors, the customary ones, now pass as truths and as standards for measuring the less frequent ones. In principle, the only thing at work here is the difference between habituation and novelty, frequency and rarity.

30 *Knowledge* is nothing but operating with the most favored metaphors, thus an imitation that is no longer felt to be imitation. Hence it cannot, of course, penetrate into the realm of truth.

The pathos of the drive for truth presupposes the observation that the different metaphorical worlds are at odds and
struggle against one another, for example, dream, lie, etc.,
and the ordinary, usual view of things: the one is rarer, the
5 other more frequent. In other words, custom struggles against
the exception, the regular against the uncommon. Hence the
higher esteem for waking reality than for the dream world.

And yet what is rare and uncommon is *more stimulating*—the
lie is felt to be a stimulus. Poetry.

19 [229]

10   In political society a firm agreement is necessary, it is based
on the customary use of metaphors. Every uncommon one
disrupts, indeed, destroys it. Thus, what constitutes political
propriety and morality is using every word in the very same
way the masses use it. To be *true* simply means not to deviate
15 from the common meaning of things. The true is the *existent*,
as opposed to the nonreal. The first convention is the one that
determines what should be considered "existent."

But the drive to be truthful, projected onto *nature*, produces
the belief that nature must also be truthful toward us. The drive
20 for knowledge is based upon this projection.

Initially the word "true" means nothing other than what custom has made into the common metaphor—hence merely an
illusion to which one has become accustomed due to frequent
use, and that hence no longer is felt to be an illusion: forgotten
25 metaphor, that is, a metaphor whose metaphorical nature has
been forgotten.

19 [230]

The *drive for truth* begins with the keen observation of the
opposition between the real world and the world of lies and
how all human existence becomes uncertain if conventional
30 truth is not unconditionally binding: it is a moral conviction
about the necessity of a rigid convention if any human society
is supposed to exist. If the *state of war* is ever to cease, then it

must begin with the fixing of truth, that is, with a valid and binding *signification* of things.

The liar uses words to make the unreal appear real, that is, he misuses the firm foundation.

On the other hand, there exists a drive continually to invent new metaphors, it vents itself in the poet, the actor, etc., above all in religion.

Now, the philosopher also seeks the "real," the *abiding*, in that realm in which religions held sway, in the feeling of the eternal game of mythic lies. He wants truth that *abides*. In other words, he expands the need for firm truth conventions into new areas.

19 [231]

The *oldest form of monotheism* refers to nothing other than the *single* shining firmament and calls it *devas*. Very limited and rigid. What progress the polytheistic religions represent.

19 [232]

The *verbal* arts! That's why the Germans are not able to become writers!

19 [233]

Goethe was able to tell fairy tales, Herder was a preacher.

Faust is the only extended national elocution written in *doggerel* verse.

19 [234]

I would like to treat the question concerning the value of knowledge in the manner of a cold angel who sees through all the shabby tricks. Without anger, but without being hospitable.

19 [235]

All laws of nature are only *relations* between x, y, and z. We define laws of nature as the *relations* to an x, y, and z, each of which, in turn, is known *to us only in relation* to other x's, y's, and z's.

19 [236]

Strictly speaking, knowledge takes only the form of tautology and is *empty*. Every piece of knowledge that is beneficial to us involves an *identification of nonidentical things*, of things that are similar, which means that it is essentially illogical.

5   Only in this way do we arrive at a concept, and afterward we behave as though the concept "human being" were something factual, whereas it is actually only a construction we create by jettisoning all individual traits. We presume that nature operates in accordance with such a concept: but in this both nature
10 and the concept are anthropomorphic. By *omitting* the individual we arrive at the concept, and with this our knowledge begins: in *categorizing*, in the creation of *classes*. But the essence of things does not correspond to this: it is an epistemological process that does not capture the essence of things. Many
15 individual traits, but not all of them, define a thing for us: the uniformity of these traits causes us to subsume many things under a single concept.

We produce beings as the *bearers of characteristics* and abstractions as the causes of these characteristics.

20 That a unity, a tree, for example, appears to us as a multitude of characteristics, of relations, is anthropomorphic in a twofold sense: first, this delimited unity "tree" does not exist; it is arbitrary to carve something out in this way (according to the eye, according to the form); every relation is not the
25 absolute, true relation, but rather is once again anthropomorphically tinged.

19 [237]

The philosopher does not seek truth, but rather the metamorphosis of the world into human beings: he struggles to understand the world by means of self-consciousness. He strug-
30 gles for an *assimilation*: he is satisfied when he has explained something anthropomorphically. Just as the astrologer views the world as serving single individuals, the philosopher views the world as human being.

The *human being* as the measure of all things is also the basic
thought of science. Every law of nature is ultimately a sum
of anthropomorphic relations. Especially number: the dissolution of all laws into multiplicities, their expression in numerical
formulas is a μεταφορά; just as someone who is unable to hear
judges music and sound according to Chladni's sound figures.

19 [238]
  The feeling for *certainty* is the most difficult to develop. Initially one seeks *explanation*: if a hypothesis explains *many things*,
we draw the conclusion that it explains everything.

19 [239]
  Anaximander discovers the contradictory character of our
world: it perishes from its own qualities.

19 [240]
  The world is appearance—but *we* alone are not what causes
it to appear. Viewed from another side it is unreal.

19 [241]
  Our experiences determine our individuality, and they do so
in such a way that after every emotional impression, our individuality is determined down to the very last cell.

19 [242]
  The essence of the definition: the pencil is an elongated, etc.
body. A is B. In this instance what is elongated is also colored.
The characteristics contain nothing but relations.
  A particular body is the equivalent of so many relations. Relations never can be the essence, but only consequences of this
essence. Synthetic judgment describes a thing according to its
consequences, which means *essence* and *consequences* are *identified*,
which means a *metonymy*.
  Thus a *metonymy* lies at the essence of synthetic judgment,
which means it is a *false equation*.

Which means that synthetic inferences are illogical. When we employ them, we presuppose popular metaphysics, that is, a metaphysics that regards effects as causes.

The concept "pencil" is confused with the "thing" pencil.
5 The "is" in the synthetic judgment is false, it contains a transference; two distinct spheres, between which there never can be an equation, are placed next to each other.

We live and think amid nothing but effects of the *illogical*, in lack of knowledge and incorrect knowledge.

19 [243]
10 *The world of untruth*:
    Dream and wakefulness.
    Brief self-consciousness.
    Scant memory.
    Synthetic judgments.
15 Language.
    Illusions and aims.
    The mendacious standpoint of society.
    Time and space.

19 [244]
    Where in the world does the *pathos of truth* come from?
20 It does not desire truth, but rather belief, faith in something.

19 [245]
    Question concerning the *teleology of the philosopher*—who views things neither historically nor emotionally.

    For him, this question expands to become a question of the value of knowledge.
25 Description of the philosopher—he needs fame, he does not think of the *utility* that derives from knowledge, but of the utility that lies in knowledge itself.

    If he were to discover a word that, once uttered, would destroy the world, do you think he would refrain from uttering it?
30 What is the meaning of his belief that humanity needs truth?

19 [246]

What is the value of knowledge as such?

The world of lies—truth is gradually given its due—all virtues arise from vices.

19 [247]

1.   Flight from those who are cultivated and good-natured.
2.   Fame and the philosopher.
3.   Truth and its value as something purely metaphysical.

19 [248]

Main part: systems as anthropomorphisms.

Life in lies.

Pathos of truth, mediated by love and self-preservation.

Imitation and knowledge.

Constraint of the unlimited drive for knowledge by means of deception.

Against iconic historiography.

Religions.

Art.

Impossibility and progress.

Observations of an evil demon on the value of knowledge, scorn. Astrology.

The tragic, indeed, resigned nature of knowledge since Kant.

Culture and science.

Science and philosophy.

Legislation by greatness.

Procreation in the realm of the beautiful.

The logician.

Result: emerged without purpose, accidental, strives for the impossible, moral and historical, disdains life. The phantom venerated as truth has the same effects and must likewise be regarded as something metaphysical.

19 [249]

Metaphor means: to treat as *identical* things that one has recognized to be *similar* in one respect.

19 [250]

Fame deceives itself in this: no one will ever experience the
feeling of creation the way the creator himself experienced it.
5 Hence total appreciation also not possible.

19 [251]

Confidence in a discovered *truth* is displayed in the wish to
communicate it. One can then communicate it in a twofold
way: in its effects, so that the others are convinced of the value
of the foundation by means of a reverse inference. Or by dem-
10 onstrating its genesis from and logical interconnection with
truths that are certain and already known. The interconnection
consists in the correct subordination of particular instances
under general propositions—is pure categorization.

19 [252]

The relation between the work of art and nature is similar
15 to the relation between the mathematical circle and the natural
circle.

19 [253]

Why do we want not to be deceived?

—We want it in art. In many things, at least, we desire ignorance, which is also deception.

20   To the extent that it is necessary for *life*, he does not want to
be deceived, that is, he must be able to survive; in this realm
of needs he wants to be able to feel secure.

He disdains only hostile deceptions, not agreeable ones. He
shuns *being duped*, wicked deception. Thus, at bottom, not de-
25 ception itself, but the consequences of deception, specifically,
the wicked consequences. In other words, he rejects deception
whenever it is possible that the deceit of his confidence will result in deleterious consequences. In such cases he wants truth,

which means, once again, he wants the pleasant consequences. Truth comes into play only as a means to ward off hostile deceptions. The *demand* for *truth* means: do no evil unto human beings by means of deceit. The human being is *indifferent* toward the *pure, inconsequential knowledge of truth*.

Nature also did nothing to prepare him for this. Belief in the truth is belief in certain uplifting effects. —What is the origin, then, of all that moral righteousness attached to the desire for truth? Up to this point everything is egoistic. Or: At what point does the desire for truth become heroic and pernicious for the individual?

19 [254]

Does the philosopher seek the truth?

No, for then he would give more credence to certainty.

Truth is cold, the belief in truth is powerful.

19 [255]

Dominance of art over life—natural side.

Culture and religion.

Culture and science.

Culture and philosophy.

Cosmopolitan path to culture.

Roman and Greek conceptions of art.

Schiller's and Goethe's struggle.

Depiction of the "cultivated person."

False conception of what is German.

Music as vital germ.

19 [256]

A people at the natural preliminary stage {of culture} is unified only to the extent that it possesses a common primitive art.

19 [257]

Due to isolation, certain sets of concepts can become so vehement that they absorb the strength of other drives. Thus, for example, the drive for knowledge.

A nature that has been prepared in this fashion, determined right down to the last cell, then propagates itself in turn and becomes hereditary: intensifying itself until its general constitution is destroyed by this one-sided absorption.

19 [258]

5   Human beings are indifferent to truth: this is demonstrated by tautology as the only accessible form of truth.

Given this, the search for truth can quite correctly be called categorization, that is, correctly subsuming the individual cases under an existing concept. But in this case the concept is our
10 action, as are past ages. To subsume the entire world under the correct concepts means nothing other than to classify things according to the most general types of relation that are of human origin: thus, the concepts only *prove* that we must look under them to find what we previously had hidden under them
15 — thus, at bottom, also tautology.

19 [259]
To be assailed:

Gathering of philologists.
Strasbourg University.
Auerbach in the Augsburg newspaper, national monuments.
20 Freytag, Ingo, scholars, technology.
Gottschall.
Young Germany.
University of Leipzig, Zöllner.
Wastefulness of the theaters.
25 Art endowment in the Reichstag.
Grimm, Lübke, Julian Schmidt.
Jürgen ⟨Bona⟩-Meyer, Kuno Fischer, Lotze.
Riehl, Schwind.
Bungling professors in Berlin.
30 Jahn and Hauptmann.
Gervinus.

Hanslick.
Centralblatt.
Playing music in isolation.
Leipzig, the city in which Wagner was born.
5   Strauss.

19 [260]
The "drastics" are unable to discover unending melody; they
are always at the end and with their drastic accentuations.

19 [261]
Elements of German culture
scholarly
10   religious-emancipating
impulse to imitate foreign nations.

19 [262]
The *laissez aller* in the sciences: every scholar for himself. The
spirit of the entire republic of scholars grows negatively indig-
nant, but does not get inspired.

19 [263]
15   The moderation of morals (religion), learnedness, and science is compatible with barbarism.
The cultural direction pursued by the Germans now has the
audacity to create its own organization, its own tribunal.

19 [264]
How fortunate that music doesn't *speak*—although today's
20   musicians chatter a lot. That is why it is suited to being a germ
of salvation.

19 [265]
In Germany, only three sorts of professionals talk a lot: the
schoolmaster, the preacher, the midwife.

19 [266]

Cultivation—not a vital necessity, but merely a luxury.

Art either convention or *physis*.

Attempt made by our great poets to arrive at a convention. Goethe and the theater.

5 Natural truth—the pathological was too powerful.

They did not achieve a characteristic form.

19 [267]

1. Portrayal of the lonely hopes at Pentecost in Bayreuth. Personal interpretation of the Ninth {Symphony} in relation to Wagner and the symbolic hope for our culture that can be
10 derived from his life. Our gravest fear, that we are not mature enough for such miracles, that their effect will not be profound enough.

2. Silence all around, no one notices anything. Governments believe in the quality of *their* education, as do scholars. Exploit-
15 ing the effects of war. How was it justified? — *Vague antipathy* toward Wagner.

3. The only ones making noise are those who feel immedi- ately threatened, the representatives of today's bad art insti- tutes, journals; they are afraid. *Noisy* antipathy. Can only sub-
20 sist by relying on that vague presentient antipathy.

Presentiment of the *decline* of today's cultivated person.

19 [268]

Plan for 6 Lectures.

Art and our Pentecost.

The cultivated person in all his forms.

25 Genesis of the cultivated person.

Roman and Hellenic conceptions of art and our classical authors.

Music, drama, and life.

Dawn perspectives. The tribunal for higher education. The
30 naive phenomena appear one after the other, the true artist,

the meaning of art, the profound seriousness of a new world outlook.

19 [269]
   Our amazement at Pentecost. It was no music festival. It looked like a dream.
5   Whenever Wagner does injury, he touches on a profound problem.
   Gathering of philologists. Strasbourg.—Teachers and universities and their leaders had no inkling.

19 [270]
   1.2.3.   Characterization of the cultivated person.
10 1.2.3.   Genesis of the cultivated person.
            For them there is no δός μοι ποῦ στῶ.
            The tremendous struggle of Schiller and Goethe.
            They search for the German's talisman.
            Learning from foreign nations among the Greeks.
15   Roman and Hellenic conceptions of art.
   1.2.3.   Wagner recognizes music to be such a δός μοι ποῦ στῶ.
            Ancient saying about music and the state. The next step: music creates its own drama. Then it becomes apparent what spoken drama is: scholarly, unoriginal,
20   fabricated, or drastic. Wagner. Goethe's *Volkslied*, puppet theater, popular verse. Myth. He *creates* for the first time what is German. Consequences of ancient tragedy for all the arts and for life. The "cultivated ones" find themselves in a predicament.

19 [271]
25 How in the world are we supposed to have a literature? We don't even have orators. Goethe, the teller of fairy tales, — — —
   The preacher and the gossip, idealized, produce our principal types of writers: midwife, schoolmaster, preacher, Junker.

19 [272]

Misfortunes of emerging German culture:

    Hegel

    Heine

    The political fever that stressed *nationalism*.

5   The glory of war.

Pillars of developing German culture:

    Schopenhauer—deepens the world outlook of the Goethe-Schiller culture.

19 [273]

Masks of Kotzebue's Bourgeois Comedies.

10   The "*old spinsters*," the sentimental ones:

        Riehl, Gervinus, Schwind, Jahn, Freytag

        talk a lot about innocence and beauty.

    The *young "dotards"* (jaded ones), the historical ones:

        Ranke, the journalists, Mommsen, Bernays.

15   are above it all.

    The *eternal schoolboys*:

        Gottschall, Lindau, Gutzkow, Laube.

    The *impious* from the country:

        Strauss. Philistinism is the true form of impiety.

19 [274]

Bayreuth Horizon Observations.

20   1. Pentecost in Bayreuth. Enormous lack of understanding all around. Gathering of philologists in Leipzig. The war and the University of Strasbourg.

      2. The meek ones.

25   3. The historical ones.

      4. The scholars.   } Characterization of the "cultivated ones."

      5. The journalists.

      6. The natural scientists.

      7.8. Schools. Universities.   } Genesis of the "cultivated ones."

30   9. Their treatment of art.

10. The Phoenicians in the capital cities: as *imitators* of
    that cultivation.
11.12. *Central thesis*: There is *no German cultivation* because there
    still is no *German* artistic style. The tremendous effort
    Schiller and Goethe expended trying to develop a Ger-
    man style. Cosmopolitan tendency necessary. Con-
    tinuation of the work of the Reformation.

Wagner's δός μοι ποῦ στῶ; German music. On its example
we can learn how German culture will relate to other cultures.
Plato on music: culture. It is not "historical," one can sense
what is vital in it. Its profundity overcame everything scholarly
and transformed it into instinctive technique. It revives myth
(*Meistersinger*).

19 [275]
Introduction.
Characterization of the "cultivated person."
Genesis of the "cultivated person."
There is not yet any cultivation. Depiction of the prior
    struggle.
Drama (the drastics, their drastic accentuations are like the
    dramatic accentuations and fermata of opera).
Even the Germans' drinking songs are learned.

19 [276]
"Cultivation" sought to settle down on the basis built by
Schiller and Goethe as if it were a daybed.

19 [277]
  1. The Rohde Fragment.
  2. Heroes' Lament.
  3. Gladly and More Gladly.
  4. Infinite!
  5. Wilted.

6. Things Beckon and Bend.
7. Serenade.
8. Postlude.
9. Death of the Kings.
5   10. Just Laugh for Once.
11. Etes titok.
12. Storm March.
13. From the First New Year's Eve.
14. Misery.
10   15. The Annunciation.

19 [278]
Language is the stable center around which the Greek nation crystallizes.

Homer is the stable center around which its culture crystallizes.

15   Thus, in both instances it is a work of art.

19 [279]
A. Dove comes to the defense of Puschmann, P. Lindau of the Moor.

The great to-do the Germans have made about Gervinus, who is truly ridiculous when it comes to artistic matters.

19 [280]
20   As a dramatist and storyteller, Heinrich von *Kleist* speaks to us as if he were simultaneously climbing a high mountain.

Goethe about Kleist: afraid.

Dramatic art is idle illusion for our public: it has no aesthetic sensibility, but instead is merely pathological.

19 [281]
25   We can conceive of the scholar without culture, the pious person without culture, the philosopher without culture: learnedness stands in contradiction to the unity of cultivation, Christian piety in contradiction — — —

19 [282]

Segregation of the *intellectual* factors from the *intelligible* factors in the nature of the philosopher.

19 [283]

The factors of present-day *culture*.

1. The historical, becoming.
2. The philistine, being.
3. The scholarly.
4. Culture without a people.
5. Customs essentially foreign.
6. The unaesthetic (pathological).
7. Philosophy without praxis.
8. Caste system not according to education.
9. Writing, not speaking.

19 [284]

Previously it was *language* with which people associated things German. Now, in addition, *music*.

Schiller's *tendency cosmopolitan*, and Goethe's corresponding to the Oriental tendency.

What is German must first be created:

Cultivation not on a national basis, but rather *creation of what is German*, not cultivation *of what is accepted as German*.

What is German has to be created: it does not yet exist. To be founded neither on virtues nor on vices.

19 [285]

Factors of the German Past.

Folk art of the Reformation — *Faust*, *Meistersinger*.

Asceticism and pure love, Rome — *Tannhäuser*.

Loyalty and knights, Orient — *Lohengrin*.

Oldest myth, the human being — *Ring of the Nibelungen*.

Metaphysics of love — *Tristan*.

That is our *world of myths*, it reaches up to the Reformation. The belief in it is very similar to that of the Greeks in their myths.

Our primary aim is not *German cultivation*, but instead *creation of what is German*.

5 Instead of the historical—the power to create myths.
Instead of the philistine and meek—metaphysical em-pathy.
Instead of the scholarly—tragic wisdom.
Instead of the unaesthetic-pathological—free play.
Instead of the caste system—the tribunal of education.
10 Instead of writing—thinking and speaking.
Instead of dogmatism—philosophy.
Overcoming the *mix of religions*, the *Asiatic* (in haste and luxury—Phoenician).

Holding *language* and *music* sacred.

19 [286]
15 *Aesthetics in Germany*.
Lessing, Winckelmann, Hamann, Herder.
Schiller, Goethe.
Grillparzer.
Schopenhauer.
20 Wagner.   Fuchs.

19 [287]

Concise Report
on
the Earlier Greek Philosophers.

19 [288]
The metamorphoses of the transmigration of souls.

19 [289]
25   *Extension of the Reformation*.
Scholarliness and scholarly knowledge that was art.
Discovery of the *Volkslied*, Shakespeare, Hamann, *Faust*—: instinctual, without rules—unscholarly.

Simple beauty of sculpture. Strict necessity in drama — : exemplary effects of the ancients, jettisoning the French rules.

19 [290]

Experimenting to find drama, to create a literature — : cosmopolitical imitation.

Full insight into the interconnections of life and art — overcoming the concept "literature" — : Wagner.

Eliminating the practice of **playing music in isolation**. Against the *monastic aspect* of music.

Transition from *scholarliness* to the *necessity* of *art*.

Overcoming the *Roman* conception of art: art as convention, as thesis.

Return to the *Hellenic* conception: art as *physis*.

19 [291]

Even Hellenic art was understood for a long time in a *Roman* manner, I mean, in the manner in which the Romans understood it: as *ornament* that could be placed just anywhere, a greenhouse in contrast to a forest. Refined convention. —

19 [292]

That awful book by *Lotze* in which space is wasted on the treatment of a totally unaesthetic person: *Ritter* (a historian of philosophy whose name is already on the verge of being forgotten) or of that wacky Leipzig philosopher Weisse.

19 [293]

Plautus, Roman art, later Attic comedy. The standard *masque* comedy.

19 [294]

Romantics — in part natural reaction against cultivated cosmopolitanism, in part reaction of music against cold sculpture, in part expansion of the cosmopolitan drive to imitate and sing along. A lot of vision, but too little energy.

Young Germany, like *Kotzebue*, opposed to Schiller-Goethe, represents a Frenchifying Enlightenment accomplished by means of crass imitation.

19 [295]
Not cultivation on a national basis, but instead creation *of the*
5 *German style* in life, knowledge, creativity, speaking, gait, etc.

19 [296]
On German Cultivation.
A Commemorative Volume Dedicated to the Art Connoisseurs
of Bayreuth.

19 [297]
Distinguishing peoples on the basis of their weaknesses,
10 their virtues, when possessing a certain degree of civilization,
together.

19 [298]
On the Creation of a German
Artistic Style.
Before this style exists, the only way to arrive at a certain
15 degree of cultivation is by following the path of cosmopoli-
tanism.
Cultivation is the life of a people under the regimen of art.
Philosophy is not for the people, religion is compatible with
barbarism, as is science.
20 Beginning with the demands of culture after the *war.* 1872.
Strasbourg, inability even to recognize the ridiculousness of
any claim to something that is nationally German. Among us
art is understood in its *Roman* sense, but not even in that sense.
Science is compatible with barbarism.

19 [299]
25 Talent is merely the prerequisite for culture, the main thing
is disciplined training based on models.

Cultivation is not necessarily a matter of *conceptualizing*, but
rather of *perceiving* and making correct *choices*: just as the musician is able to play the correct notes in the dark. The *education* of
a people to *cultivation* is essentially habituation to good models
5 and cultivation of noble needs.

19 [300]
> The Hopeful Ones in Contemporary Germany.
> The Possibility of a German Culture.
> Hopes for a German Culture.
> Commemorative Volume.

19 [301]
10
> The Hopeful Ones.
> Observations on the Alleged Culture
> of Contemporary Germany.

19 [302]
> Speeches of the Hopeful Ones.
> Speeches of a Hopeful One.

19 [303]
15
> Bayreuth's Horizon.
> The Horizon of Bayreuth.
> *Bayreuth Horizon Observations*.

19 [304]
The German speaks little. That is why all dramatists are in
a quandary. Wagner's practice is correct. Short, profound, and
20 with word symbolism, as with runes. The oldest oracle probably three alliterating runes.

19 [305]
Few men will be forgiven for calling their nation barbaric.
But Goethe did; this must be explained.

19 [306]
No culture was ever built in three days, nor has one ever descended from out of the blue: on the contrary, a culture emerges only out of previous barbarism, and there are extended periods of vacillation and struggle in which it remains in doubt.

19 [307]
We call someone "cultivated" when he has become a coherent entity, has taken on form: in this case, the opposite of form is the unstructured, structureless, without *unity*.

19 [308]
What constitutes the *unity* of a *people*? Outwardly, government, inwardly, language and customs. But customs only gradually become unitary, a great deal from communal life, immigration.

19 [309]
Goethe: "to be sure, we have 'cultivated' a great deal."

19 [310]
Culture—dominance of *art* over *life*. The degree of its quality depends first on the *degree of this dominance*, and second on the *value* of this *art* itself.

19 [311]
Moderation of customs by means of religions, laws, etc.
Increase in *knowledge* and thereby less superstition, ignorance, fanaticism, more contemplativeness and tranquility.
Inventions, increased prosperity, commerce with other peoples.
Religion and barbarism are part of this.
Ingenuity, intellect compatible with barbarism. Even art is possible, and yet one can still call this people a barbaric one.
Dominance of art over life.

19 [312]

When among the tumult at the outbreak of the last great war an embittered French scholar called the Germans barbarians and accused them of lacking culture, people in Germany still listened closely enough to take deep offense at this; and it gave
5 many journalists the opportunity to polish brightly the armor of their culture, which had not remained untarnished, and, certain of victory, to flaunt it. They exhausted themselves making assurances that the German people were the most quick to learn, most learned, ⟨most⟩ humble, most virtuous, and most
10 pure people on earth: they even felt sufficiently certain that they could acquit themselves of the charge of cannibalism and piracy. When shortly thereafter a voice was raised on the other side of the Channel and venerable Carlyle publicly praised precisely those qualities in the Germans and, for the sake of these
15 qualities, gave their victory his blessing, then everyone was clear about German culture; and after the experience of success, it was certainly quite innocuous to speak of the victory of German culture. Today, when the Germans have enough time to examine in retrospect many of the words flung at us then,
20 there are probably a few who recognize that the Frenchman was right: the Germans are barbarians, despite all those human qualities. If one felt obliged to wish them, the barbarians, victory, this naturally did not occur because they were barbarians, but rather because the hope for an emerging culture vindicates
25 the Germans: whereas one gives no deference to a degenerate and exhausted culture. It is not the woman who lets her child degenerate, but rather the one who will give birth who is vindicated by the laws. That in other respects they are still barbarians was the opinion of Goethe, who even lived long enough to be
30 permitted to confront the Germans with this truth; and it is to his words that I must allow my observations to refer, because no one else is likely to allow me to do this. "We have," he said one evening to Eckermann — — —

The last statement is particularly apt because, for those who
35 venerate the present, it leaves open the possibility that sev-

eral centuries from now people will say that it has been a long
time since the Germans were barbarians: to be precise, since
the latter half of the nineteenth century. I want now to set
about proving by means of an example that this is not simply
5 an unwarranted assumption, but that the great mass of people
today do indeed—mistakenly—believe that the Germans have
attained a culture. But first we have to define what culture
means. Goethe adds—on the song. Whole piles of war songs
and sonnets, yet not one of them strikes a new note ———

19 [313]
10   The words "barbarian" and "barbarism" are mean, reckless
words, and I do not dare to use them without some prefatory
remarks: and if it is true that the Greeks spoke of the sound of
foreign languages as croaking, and for that reason applied this
same term to frogs, then barbarians are croakers—senseless,
15 ugly chatter. Lack of *aesthetic education*.

19 [314]
   Of course, the Frenchman thought of his civilization that
had been victorious the world over and of the number of
stunted imitations of French civilization that he found in German culture: he said "no culture" because they ⟨have⟩ not pro-
20 duced one and are not even able to imitate skillfully one that
already exists, something that we must grant the Russians, for
example.
   And that was why every threat brought on by the war was
so terrible, because it could have destroyed the covertly grow-
25 ing fruit.
   The *glory of war* almost a greater danger still.

19 [315]
   Introduction.
   Wisdom, science.
   Preliminary mythic stage.

Sporadic-aphoristic.
Preliminary stages of the σοφὸς ἀνήρ.
Thales.
Anaximander.
5   Anaximenes.
Pythagoras.
Heraclitus.
Xenophanes.
Parmenides.
10 Anaxagoras.
Empedocles.
Democritus.
Pythagoreans.
Socrates.   Very simple.

19 [316]

15   *The*
                 Justification of Philosophy
                      by the Greeks.

                 A Commemorative Volume.
                          By
20   Friedrich Nietzsche.

19 [317]

                 Observations of a Hopeful One.

19 [318]

                      The Last Philosopher.

    1. The projections of the human being onto nature.
    2. Greek nature as principle of the world.
25 3. Heraclitus opposed to the Dionysian.
       Empedocles opposed to the sacrifice of animals.
       Pythagoreans sectarianism.
       Democritus the scien⟨tific⟩ voyager.

19 [319]

The original purpose of philosophy has been thwarted.
Against iconic historiography.
Philosophy, without culture, and science.
Altered position of philosophy since Kant.
5   Metaphysics impossible. Self-castration.

Tragic resignation, the end of philosophy.
Only art is capable of saving us.

19 [320]

1. The remaining philosophers.
2. Truth and illusion.
10   3. Illusion and culture.
4. The last philosopher.

19 [321]

Classification of the method by which philosophers arrive at
ultimate insights.
The illogical drive.
15   Truthfulness and metaphor.

Task of the Greek philosopher: controlling.
Barbarizing effect of knowledge.
Life in illusion.

Philosophy dead since Kant.
20   Schopenhauer simplifier, swept away scholasticism.
Science and culture. Opposites.
Task of art.
Education is the way.
Philosophy must produce the need for tragedy.

19 [322]

25   Modern philosophy, not naive, scholastic, burdened with
formulas.

Schopenhauer the simplifier.

We no longer allow invention of concepts. Only in art.

Antidote to science? Where?

Culture as antidote. In order to be receptive to it, one must
have recognized the inadequacy of science. Tragic resignation.
Lord only knows what kind of culture that will be! It is beginning at the end!

19 [323]

January	13 weeks	3. History of metrics.
February		4. Horatian meters
March		after Augustine etc.
		Language viewed metrically.
		5. Hexameter.
		6. Trimeter.
		7. Logaoedic verse.
		8. Doric stanzas.
		9. Composition etc.

19 [324]

Classical philology.

Hesiod and Homer.

Metrics.

19 [325]

Ancient Philosophical Masters
in Greece.

Written for a Young Friend
of Philosophy
by ———

19 [326]

Outlines.

1. Hesiod.

2. The chronometric meter of the Greeks.

3. Greek tragedy.

19 [327]

Five Prefaces to Five Unwritten and
Unwritable Books.

1. On the Future of our Educational Institutions.
2. The Relationship of Schopenhauerian Philosophy to German Culture.
3. On the Pathos of Truth.
4. The Greek State.
5. The Competition Between Homer and Hesiod.

19 [328]

Knowledge of truth impossible.	All
Art and the philosopher.	knowledge
The pathos of truth.	in the service
How does philosophy relate to culture:	of art.
Schopenhauer.	

The unity of a culture.
Description of the muddleheadedness
of the present.
Drama as point of germination.

19 [329]

First stage of culture: the faith in language, as ubiquitous metaphorical designation.
Second stage of culture: unity and coherence of the world of metaphor, under the influence of Homer.

19 [330]

1) The Cultivated Philistines.
2) The Historical Illness.
3) Much Reading and Writing.
4) Literary Musicians (how the genius's disciples deaden his effects).
5) German and Pseudo-German.
6) Military Culture.

7) *Universal* Education — Socialism etc.
8) Educational Theology.
9) Secondary Schools and Universities.
10) Philosophy and Culture.
11) Natural Science.
12) Poets etc.
13) Classical Philology.

Outline of the "Unfashionable Observations."

Basel, 2 September 1873.

[20 = Mp XII 3. Summer 1872]

20 [1]

First, preliminary draft
of
"Homer's Competition."

Begun on 21 July 1872.

20 [2]

5   *For the epilogue.*

Deliberate intellect, sudden and tempestuous emotion.
Ritschl's comparison with Odysseus.
Always trying to bring order into what is disparate.
God in the storm.
10   Jesus in the temple.
Upstanding citizen foretold.
I could not disguise my feelings, only hide them. I am silent,
   others scoff, etc.

[21 = U I 4b. Summer 1872–Beginning 1873]

21 [1]

Autumn: On Aeschylus's *Choephori*.
             On the Chronology of the Pre-Socratic Philoso-
             phers.

Winter: Future of Our Educational Institutions.

21 [2]

5   *The Choephori.*
    Observations on Aeschylus's artistic style.

False enthusiasm and the difficulty of having genuine impact.

1. The sculpturesque element. Must be attributed to the dis-
10   tance from the audience: limited movement. The perspec-
tival element. Masks. Strict hieratic symmetry. Scenery.
Stichometry. Phidias's style anticipated. Why the longevity
of the plastic arts?

2. The musical element. The musicality of language. Every-
15   thing is music, there are nonspoken and spoken passages,
everything sung. The orchestrics also never cease.

3. The mythic element. Comparison with Sophocles. Parti-
tioning of myth. Symmetry, with contrasts. The uncanny,
utilizing the late-afternoon shadows. Rigor of myth in har-
20   mony with the sculpturesque and musical elements.

4. The linguistic artistry. Dialects. "High" style. Syntax corresponding to the $\tilde{\eta}\theta o\varsigma$ of the scene. 954.

I — — —

21 [3]

The sculpturesque element. Unlike Shakespeare, Aeschylus does
not have in mind images of tremendously moving passions,
but rather static, sculpturesque groups.

Movement occurs according to strict symmetry. The number of verses.

21 [4]

Quod felix faustum fortunatumque vertat!

21 [5]

Introduction. *Education through music among the Greeks.*

The Wisdom of the Tragic Age.
Competition. Empedocles.
Love and education. Socrates.
Education through music. Pythagoras.
Art and life. Heraclitus.
Audacities. The Eleatics.

21 [6]

The Philosophy of the Tragic Age.

The Greeks philosophized during that period! Marvelous!

How can we reexperience that age? Reattain its most aston-
ishing vistas? Education occurs when we truly achieve a *vital
empathy* with them.

The "systems" devour one another: but *one* remains.

Each of these philosophers simply saw the world come into
being!

My aim is historical portraiture, not antiquities.

21 [7]

 Birth of Tragedy.
 Bayreuth Horizon Observations.
 Ancient Metrics.
 Pre-Socratic Philosophers.
5 Educational Institutions.

21 [8]

 Conjectures and explanations.
 The mythic element.
 The sculpturesque element.
 The musical element.
10 The metrical element.

21 [9]

 Everything derives from one thing.
 Perishing is a punishment.
 Perishing and coming into being are governed by laws.
 Perishing and coming into being are illusion: the One is.
15 All qualities are eternal. There is no becoming.
 All qualities are quantities.
 All effects magical.
 All effects mechanical.
 Concepts are stable, nothing else.

21 [10]

20 Knowing as such affords no pleasure, just as seeing affords
 no pleasure. How does it come into the world?

21 [11]

 Everything about Socrates false — concepts are not stable,
                              also not important,
                              knowledge is not the
25   source of justice, and
                              not fruitful in the least,
                              negates culture.

21 [12]

Finding something that someone else has lost is primarily a pleasure only for the person who lost it; but to find something that no one has lost and that no one ever possessed—that is, to discover something new—provides the discoverer with un-
5   common joy.

21 [13]

Belief is based on a host of analogical inferences: don't be deceived!

The human being starts to believe when he ceases to know. He wagers all his moral trust on this one throw of the dice and
10 then hopes to be repaid in kind: the dog looks at us with trusting eyes and wants us to trust it.

Knowledge is not as important for the welfare of human beings as is belief. Even for someone who discovers a truth— a mathematical truth, for example—joy is the product of his
15 unconditional faith in one's ability to rely on this truth. If one has belief, then one can do without truth.

21 [14]

What is it that forces the powerful drives to follow the course of common welfare? In general, *love*. *Love for one's native city* contains and controls the agonal drive.
20   Love of one's neighbor overcomes it for the purpose of education. Beauty stands in the service of love: the steadily increasing transfiguration, as described by Plato.

Procreation in the realm of the beautiful genuinely Hellenic.

The growth of *eros* must be depicted—marriage family state.

21 [15]
25   Empedocles. Love and hatred in Greece.

Heraclitus. Cosmodicy of art.

Democritus and the Pythagoreans. Natural science and metaphysics.

Socrates and Plato. Knowledge and instinct.

Anaxagoras. Enlightenment and inspiration.

The Eleatics: logic as the measure of all things—development of the existent determined according to strict logic
beyond atomism.

5   Pythagoras. The ascetic aims of the will. The will *mortifying*
(in nature in the competition between the weaker and the
stronger).

21 [16]

The Philosophers of the Tragic Age
Disclose the World,
10   *as Does Tragedy.*

Unity of the Will.

Intellect only a means for higher satisfactions. The negation
of the will often merely reconstitution of powerful national
unities.

15   Art in the service of the will: Heraclitus.

Love and hatred in Greece: Empedocles.

Limits of logic: it is in the service of the will: the Eleatics.

The ascetic and mortifying element in the service of the will:
Pythagoras.

20   Realm of knowledge: number: atomism and the Pythagoreans.

Enlightenment, struggle against instinct: Anaxagoras, Socrates, Plato.

Characterization of the will: its method of arriving at the
25 rational. Essence of matter absolute logic. Time, space, and
causality as prerequisite for *effects*.

What remains are forces: in the briefest of moments other
forces: in an infinitely brief period of time always a new force,
that is, the forces are not *effective* at all.

30   There is no true *effect* of one force upon another: rather, in
truth, all that exists is a semblance, an image. All matter is

merely the outside: in truth, it is something completely different that lives and is effective. However, our senses are the *product of matter and things*, as is *our intellect*. I mean: on the basis of
the *natural sciences*, one cannot help but arrive at a *thing in itself*.

5   The remnants of the will—when one subtracts from it the
knowing intellect.

21 [17]

It is possible to compose sensation out of matter: as long as
one has first explained organic substances in terms of matter.

The simplest sensation is something infinitely composite:
10 not a primordial phenomenon. Brain activity, memory, etc. are
necessary, along with all kinds of reflex movements.

If one were capable of constructing a sensate being out of
matter—wouldn't one side of nature then be disclosed?

An infinitely complex mental apparatus is the prerequisite
15 for sensation: knowledge is necessary for the postulation of all
matter. But belief in visible matter is purely a sensory illusion.

21 [18]

That nature *proceeds the same way* in all realms: a law that holds
for human beings holds for all of nature. The human being
truly a microcosm.

20 The brain, nature's supreme accomplishment.

21 [19]

Introduction.	Immortality of the great moments.
	The Greeks of the tragic age as philosophers!
	How did they experience existence?
	This constitutes their *eternal* value. Otherwise all
	systems devour one another. Historical portrai-
	ture.
	We rediscover in a metastasis the epic, lyric ele-
	ments, all the requisite elements of tragedy.
	How does one live without religion, with phi-
	losophy? But, to be sure, in a tragic-artistic age.

25 ... 30 (marginal line numbers)

Thales. Contrast between the pre-Socratics and the Socratics. Their attitude toward life is *naïve*. The seven wise men as representatives of the primary ethical virtues. Freedom from myth.

5 The Greek of the tragic age conceptualizes precisely himself and bears testimony. How important! For when considering Greek tragedies we must always supply the Greek character.

21 [20]
Philosophy as the artistic drive in its pupal stage.

21 [21]
The *Universal Artist* and the *Universal Human Being*.
10 The Human Beings of the Tragic Age.

Aeschylus as total artist: his *audience* portrayed in his studio.
We want to become familiar with the Greek whom Aeschylus recognized as his audience. In this instance, we will make use of his philosopher, who *thought* in that age.

21 [22]
15 On the example of Thales, the freedom from myth must be developed.

On the example of Anaximander, the tragedy of reprisal.

On the example of Heraclitus, competition. Game.

On the example of Parmenides, the audacity of necessity 20 and logic.

On the example of Anaxagoras — Not intellect — Matter.

On the example of Empedocles, love and kiss for the entire world.

On the example of Democritus, the attention the Greeks 25 paid to things foreign (and their imitation of what was good).

On the example of Pythagoras, transmigration of souls, rhythm.

21 [23]

Socrates, abstractly human, gives priority to the welfare of the individual, knowledge for the purpose of life. Eradication of the instincts.

21 [24]

First Aeschylus portrayed as pentathlos, then his audience, on the ex-
5 *ample of the types of philosophers.*

21 [25]

Observations on the dedicatory celebration in Bayreuth, May 1872.

Mood: happy and heroic.

We are the fortunate ones and have a foundation, we have a better understanding of good music and of our great poets.
10   Inhabitants of alpine valleys with goiter — they are invalids. Hope for sculpture.

The heroic element in W⟨agner⟩.
Heralds of the empire. Education.
The false "German spirit."
15   Everywhere profound problems where things begin with consternation.
        The mythic element.
        Poetry
            linguistically
20   scenically.
        The musicality of language.
        Healthy and "unhealthy."

22 [1]

First day, 28 September.

Saturday.

With a married couple from Basel whom I did not know but had to *pretend* to know.

5 Telegraphed Lisbeth from Baden: kindness shown me by Herr Haller from Bern, who gave me his card.

Just about to arrive in Zurich, I discover that dear Mr. Götz is on the same train; he tells me about his increased musical activity in Zurich due to the departure of Kirchner, as well as 10 about his opera that is going to be performed in Hannover.

From Zurich, I travel third class in good, humble, company, but cold, as far as Rapperschwyl, so that I lose my courage to ride as far as Chur. In R. I switch back to second class as far as Weesen. Here I locate the coach of the Schwert Hotel and ride 15 with it. Pleasantly comfortable, yet quite empty hotel; I am the only person eating in the dining room.

The entire afternoon clear, golden autumnal transfiguration: the most distant mountain peaks are visible. In the evening, just outside of Zurich, the entire range appeared in the most 20 wonderful steel blue.

At the moment slight headache.

Questionable night, with violent dreams.

Sunday. I wake up with a headache. My window looks out on Wallen Lake: the sun rises beyond its partially snow-covered

peaks. I eat breakfast and take a brief walk to the lake. Then to
the train station, but first I have a look at the Pension Speer,
which sits higher up and appears to be a bit newer. Pure morning air. I ride second class to Chur, but with constantly growing
5 malaise, despite the especially grandiose view—lake, Ragaz,
etc. In Chur, I realize that it is impossible for me to travel on,
ignore the inquiry by the mail coach official, and quickly seek
refuge at the Hotel Lukmanier. There I am given a room with
a good view, but I immediately lie down. I slept three hours—
10 I feel better and have something to eat. An especially agreeable
and intelligent waiter mentions Bad Passug: I remember. The
city of Chur is dominated by Sunday tranquility and an afternoon mood. I follow the road uphill at a comfortable pace;
marvelous view behind me, constantly expanding and chang-
15 ing vista in every direction. After a quarter of an hour a gentle
downhill path, spruce forest, nice shade—for up to that point
it had been quite warm. I can't say enough about the ravine
through which the Rabiusa River rushes. Bridges cross sometimes to the right, sometimes to the left shore. The path leads
20 beyond waterfalls, steadily uphill. At my destination, I mistakenly expect to find a hotel, but instead found only a country
inn, to be sure, with Sunday visitors, families eating heartily
and drinking coffee. First I drink three glasses of water from
the springs: up on a balcony a bottle of Asti and some more of
25 that water. With it I eat some goat cheese, my head already feeling better, and with a fair appetite. A man with Oriental eyes
sitting at my table also receives a glass of my Asti; he says thank
you and drinks with feelings of flattery. Then the hostess hands
me a number of analyses and papers; finally, the host, *Sprecher*,
30 shows me around and lets me have a drink from all the springs;
he shows me the wealth of untapped springs and, noticing
my interest, offers me shares in a cooperative venture to build
a hotel, etc. The valley is very attractive, offering a geologist
unfathomable variety, indeed, marvels. One finds graphites,
35 ocher with quartz, perhaps gold deposits, etc. The stone veins
are strangely bent, diverted, broken, like in the area around

the Axenstein at Vierwaldstätter Lake, only much smaller and
wilder. —Late, toward sunset, I begin my return: the most
distant peaks are aglow. Finally joy and a certain degree of satisfaction set in. A small child with blond hair searches for nuts
5 and is amusing. Eventually an older couple catches up with
me, speaks with me, and listens to my reply. He is an older
man, turning gray, who is or was a master joiner and who 52
years ago, during his apprenticeship, was also in Naumburg
on a warm day. His son has been a missionary in India since
10 1858 and is expected to return to Chur next year so as to see his
father once more. Their daughter has been to Egypt often and
was friends with Pastor Riggenbach in Basel. Upon arriving at
my hotel, I jot down some notes and have something to eat.
An Italian sitting across from me speaks to me: poor commu-
15 nication, since he doesn't speak German. He was in Baden and
wanted to get a few days' rest. Unfortunately, a Jew is depart-
ing tomorrow at the same time as I (5 A.M.): I console myself
with the thought of getting off the train in Thusis.

22 [2]
     Third day. Awakened at four: the mail coach departs at five.
20 Disgusting waiting room. The man at this hour a horrible creature, burping and yawning.

22 [3]

My window in Splügen: the road comes from Chur.

23 [1]

Then the entire group became incomprehensible. Later, people took from these venerable-incomprehensible ones whatever they needed, they looted them; and hence we find, sometimes here, sometimes there, in Plato's academy as well as among the Stoics and in the gardens of the Epicureans, one of Parmenides' arms, a piece of Heraclitus's shoulder, one of Empedocles' feet. In order to understand them as wholes, one must recognize in them the first outline and germ of the Greek *reformer*; their purpose was to pave the way for him, they were supposed to precede him as the dawn precedes the rising sun. But the sun did not rise, the reformer failed: hence the dawn remained nothing but a ghostly apparition. However, the simultaneous emergence of tragedy demonstrates that something new was in the air; but the philosopher and legislator who would have comprehended tragedy never appeared, and hence this art died again and the Greek reformation became forever impossible. It is not possible to think of Empedocles without a sense of profound sadness; he came closest to filling the role of that reformer. That he also failed at this and soon disappeared — following who knows what horrible experiences and what hopelessness — was a pan-Hellenic catastrophe. His soul had a greater capacity for empathy than any other Greek soul; and yet perhaps not enough, for all in all, the Greeks are deficient in this quality. And it was precisely the tyrannical element in their blood that prevented the great philosophers from attaining the profound insight and sweeping vision that Schopenhauer possessed.

23 [2]

Highest form of the human being who has recognized the
5　　　truth, vested with pride.

Loneliness, everything else *vulgus*.

ἱστορίη.

Homer, Hesiod, Archilochus.

Physicians.

10　Gods. Images of the gods.

Mysteries.

Sacrifices.

Comp⟨arison⟩ with Apollo.

23 [3]

Chapter　　I.　　The Greeks as Philosophers.

15
　　　　　　　　　　　　　　　The *sixth century*. The
　　　　　　　　　　　　　　　miracle workers.
　　　　　　　　　　　　　　　Competition. The
　　　　　　　　　　　　　　　Dionysian.

Chapter　II.　　Thales and Anaximander.

　　　　　III.　　Heraclitus.

20　IV.　　Parmenides.

　　V.　　Anaxagoras.

　　VI.　　Empedocles.

　　VII.　　Democritus. What does knowledge of impact mean?

　　VIII.　　Pythagoreans. Numbers as the limits of knowledge.

25　IX.　　Socrates. Abstract truths.

　　X.　　Epilogue. Anthropomorphism: the mutable human
　　　　　　　　　　　　　　　　　　being and water.
　　　　　　　　　　　　　　　　　　Death as punishment.
　　　　　　　　　　　　　　　　　　The artistic game.
30　　　　　　　　　　　　　　　　　Intellect.

23 [4]
Pleasure: stimulus in proportion.
Displeasure: stimulus out of proportion.

Concepts

23 [5]
                    The Hellenic Element in Philosophy.
        Competition.
        Orphic societies.
        Not soul and body.
        The religious.
        Number.
        Philosopher's pride.

23 [6]

Shrove Tuesday	Anaxagoras.
	Empedocles.
By Easter	*Pythagoreans.*
	Socrates.
Easter:	Chapter on the philosopher.
	the Hellenic.

23 [7]
        What is the philosopher?
    1. Beyond the sciences: dematerial⟨iz⟩ing.
    2. This side of religions: de-deifying — disenchanting.
    3. Types: the cult of the intellect.
    4. Anthropomorphic projections.

        What is the purpose of philosophy today?
    1. Impossibility of metaphysics.
    2. Possibility of the thing in itself. Beyond the sciences.
    3. Science as deliverance from miracles.
    4. Philosophy against the dogmatism of the sciences.
    5. But only in the service of a culture.

6. Schopenhauer's simplifying.
7. His popular and artistically plausible metaphysics. The results to be expected from philosophy are the opposite.
8. Against general education.

23 [8]

5   Philosophy has no common denominator; at times it is science, at times art.

Empedocles and Anaxagoras: the former seeks magic, the latter enlightenment, the former against secularization, the latter for it.

10   The Pythagoreans and Democritus: rigorous natural science.
Socrates and the skepticism that then becomes necessary.
Heraclitus: Apollinian ideal, everything semblance and play.
Parmenides: path to the dialectic and scientific *organon*.
Heraclitus is the only one at a standstill.

15 Thales wants to arrive at science,	Anaxim⟨ander⟩ wants to get away from it again.
Likewise Anaxagoras, Democritus	Empedocles
Parmenides' *organon*	Pythagoras.
20 Socrates.	

23 [9]

1. The essential *imperfection* of things:
    of the consequences of a religion
        be they optimistic or pessimistic
    ⟨of the⟩ consequences of culture
25   ⟨of the consequences⟩ of the sciences.
2. The existence of preservatives that do battle with an age for a long time.
    Philosophy belongs among them, essentially not present at all.
30   Tainted and given content according to the age.
3. Early Greek philosophy against myth and for science, in part against secularization.

In the tragic age: Pythagoras, Empedocles, Anaximander in agreement,
hostile from an Apollinian perspective: Heraclitus
Parmenides, dissolution of all art.

23 [10]

Pure truth unknowable: perceptions
                        concepts
                        stimuli,   segregated according
                                     to pleasure and
                                     displeasure, whether
                                     according to numbers,
                                     whether purely intel-
                                     lectual phenomena?
                        Stimulus   the prerequisite for all
                                     perceptions.

Value of philosophy: purges confused and superstit⟨ious⟩
        ideas
        against the dogmatism of the sciences
        to the extent that it is a science, purging and illuminating
        to the extent that it is anti-scientific: it is religious-obscu-
        rantistic.
        Eliminates the doctrine of the soul and rational theology.
        Proof of absolute anthropomorphism.
        Against the rigid validity of ethical concepts.
        Against the hatred of the body.

Harmfulness of philosophy: dissolves the instincts
                                     cultures
                                     mores.

Special business of philosophy for the present day.
        Lack of popular ethics.
        Lack of any sense of the importance of knowledge and of
            discrimination.
        Superficiality of the views on church and state and society.
        Rage for history.
        Talking about art and lack of culture.

23 [11]

Concepts come about through the identification of the non-identical: that is, by means of the illusion that there is some-thing identical, by means of the presupposition of *identities*: in other words, by means of false perceptions.

5   One sees a human being walking: calls it "walking." Then an ape, a dog: once again says "walking."

23 [12]

Three things that should not be confused with Parmenides' doctrine of being:

1) the question: Can we find any content that is present
10   both in thought as well as in being?

2) the primary characteristics, in contrast to the second-ary ones

3) constitution of matter. Schopenhauer.

4) No Buddhistic dream philosophy.

15   He seeks *certainty*. It is true, it is not possible to conceive of nonbeing.

If he declares the senses to be invalid, then he cannot prove being on the basis of sensations of pleasure and displeasure: these must then also be semblance.

20   Thought and being must be the same: for otherwise it could not arrive at knowledge of being.

Thus, in thought there is no movement: a static perception of being. To the extent that thought moves and is infused with other things, it already is no longer being, but merely sem-

25 blance. —

But the dialectic of thought? Isn't that movement?

23 [13]

Concepts can derive only from perception. "Being" is the projection of breath and life onto all things: imposition of the human sense of life.

The only question is: Whether the origin of all perceptions leads us to being: no.

The form of thought, like perception, presupposes that we believe in being: we believe in being because we believe in ourselves. If the latter is a category, then certainly the former as well.

23 [14]

Philosophy and the people. None of the great Greek philosophers was a leader of the people: attempted most consistently by Empedocles (after Pythagoras), but also not with pure philosophy, but instead with a mythicized version of it. Others reject the people from the outset (Heraclitus). Others have a wholly refined circle of educated people as their public (Anaxagoras). Socrates displays the strongest democratic-demagogic tendency: the result is the establishment of sects, in other words, counterevidence. How could lesser philosophers ever be successful where philosophers of this sort were not? It is not possible to base a popular culture on philosophy. Thus, with regard to culture, philosophy never can have primary, but always only secondary, significance. How is it significant?

Control of the mythical. —strengthening the sense for truth as opposed to free invention. *vis veritatis* or strengthening pure knowing (Thales, Democritus, Parmenides).

Control of the drive for knowledge—or strengthening the mythic-mystical, the artistic (Heraclitus, Empedocles, Anaximander). Legislation by *greatness*.

Shattering of rigid dogmatism: a) in religion; b) morality; c) science. *Skeptical* trait. Every power (religion, myth, drive for knowledge) has, when taken to extremes, a barbarizing, corrupting, and stultifying effect as unbending tyranny. (Socrates.)

Shattering of blind secularization (substitute for religion). (Anaxagoras, Pericles). *Mystical* trait.

Result: philosophy cannot create a culture
            but it can pave the way for one
5   or sustain one
            or moderate one.

For us: this is why the philosopher is the supreme tribunal for
      the schools: paves the way for genius: for we have no cul-
      ture. An examination of the symptoms of the age shows the
10   task of the schools to be:
            1) shattering of secularization (lack of popular philoso-
               phy)
            2) control of the barbarizing effects of the drive for
               knowledge (at the same time abstention from fantasiz-
15   ing philosophy itself).
            Against "iconic" history
            against "workaday" scholars.
      Culture can always only issue from the centralizing signifi-
      cance of an art form or a work of art. Philosophy unwit-
20   tingly will pave the way for the view of the world propa-
      gated by this work of art.

23 [15]

                  The Philosopher as Physician of Culture.

23 [16]
      For the introduction to the entire work: description of the
      seventh century: paves the way for culture, mutual hostility of
25 drives. The Oriental element. Centralization of education be-
      gins with Homer.
      I am speaking of the pre-Platonic philosophers, because
      with Plato the open hostility to culture begins, negation. But
      I want to know how a philosophy, one that is not hostile,
30 behaves toward an existing or emerging culture: here the phi-
      losopher is the poisoner of culture.

23 [17]

It is amazing how quickly the Greeks become *free*, compared with the oppressive prejudice of the Middle Ages. Can be compared with Renaissance culture.

Thales, who foretold the solar eclipse, is not thought to be
5 a sorcerer or someone in league with evil demons, rather, he is admired. Only calculation of the exact time imprecise.

Democritus the *freest human being*.

23 [18]
Retrospective on natural science.
Theory of states of aggregation.
10 Theory of matter.
Thus *intermingling of physical and metaphysical* problems.
Becoming and being — it results in absolute difference.

23 [19]
If they are abnormal, then they probably have nothing to do with the people?
15 That's not how it is: the people *need* abnormalities, *even if they do not simply exist for the people's sake.*
Proven by the work of art: the creator of the work understands it, yet one of its sides faces the public.
We want to arrive at knowledge of the side of the philoso-
20 pher that faces the people — and disregard the marvelous side of his nature, that is, the true aim, the question Why?
Today, from the perspective of our contemporary age, it is difficult to arrive at knowledge of this side because our culture possesses no such popular unity.
25 Therefore the Greeks.

23 [20]

Finished

3	Introduction
18	Thales to Parmenides
25	
—	2:1
46	

Consequences ca. 20 pages
proper proportion.

23 [21]

The Philosopher Among Greeks.

What is Hellenic about them. In this regard eternal types. The nonartist in an artistic world. Taken together, they demonstrate the *background* of what is Greek, as well as the *result* of art. Contemporaries of tragedy. The requisite elements for the emergence of tragedy that are scattered among the philosophers.

23 [22]

Freedom as opposed to myth.	Thales and Anaximander. Pessimism and action.
The tragic as game. Genius.	Heraclitus. Competition. Game.
Excess of logic and of necessity.	Parmenides. Abstraction and language. Poet and philosopher. Concept of prose.
	Anaxagoras. Freethinker. Not "intellect—matter."
Love and kiss for the entire world! Will.	Empedocles. Love. Rhetor. State. Pan-Hellenic. Agonal.
The audience. Atom—number. Natural science.	Democritus. Greeks and foreign lands. Freedom from convention.

| Transmigration of souls— dramatic. | Pythagoreans. Rhythm and *metron*. Transmigration of souls. |
| Metastasis of the 5   tragic-artistic drive onto science. | Socrates and Plato. Education. Now for the first time "school." Hostility toward the explanations given by natural science. |

23 [23]

Imagine the philosopher setting out on a journey and arriv-
10 ing among the Greeks—that's how it is for those pre-Platonic
philosophers: they are, as it were, foreigners, astonished foreigners.

Every philosopher is one by virtue of existing in foreign
surroundings: and must first sense what is most familiar to be
15 something foreign.

Herodotus among foreigners—Heraclitus among Greeks.
The historian and geographer among foreigners, the philosopher in his native land. No prophet considered such in his
homeland. Natives in their native land have no understanding
20 for the extraordinary people among them.

23 [24]

The birth of tragedy viewed from another perspective. Con-
firmed by the philosophy of its contemporaries.

23 [25]

The Philosophers of the Tragic Age.
In memory of Schopenhauer.

23 [26]

25   In 415, he was παντελῶς ὑπεργεγηρακῶς, thus he was born
in any case *after* 500. (According to Aristotle, ca. 80 years, if he
was born in 495, that is, 5 years after Anaxagoras.)

Ol. 84   14
Ol. 70   4
          ___
           56

If he was born Olymp. 71, then

5   415
      77
     ___
     492   492
     444   60
     ___   ___
      48   ⟨4⟩32

10   If he took part in the war, then according to Neanthes he
was 77 years old, which means that according to Neanthes,
he was born in 492. If he was born in 492, then according to
Apollodorus, he was in ἀκμῇ in 442, that is, at the age of 50,
and he died in 432 at the age of 60.

15   Here he disputes Neanthes: who expressly claimed that he
lived to be 77: Why? In order to have him take part in that
battle. Yet he still must have been banished by the Agrigentians.

    492 a very fitting date of birth.

    442, ca. Ol. 84 he is 50 years old.

20   He died in 432.

    Apparently he goes to Thurii when he is 50 years old be-
cause he has been banished. He bade farewell to Agrigentum
when he composed his καθαρμοί for Olympia. He is probably
recorded as being in Olympia during that Olymp. 84.

    23 [27]

25   Anaxagoras adopted from Heraclitus the idea that in all be-
        coming and all being opposites are united.
      He probably sensed the contradiction that a body has many
        characteristics and *pulverized* it in the belief that he had
        then dissolved it into its true qualities.

30   Plato: initially a Heraclitean
        resolute skeptic, everything in flux, even thought.

Brought by Socrates to the belief in the permanence of
the good, the beautiful.

These assumed to be existent.

All archetypes partake of the idea of the good, the beautiful, and hence are also *existent* (just as the soul partakes
of the idea of life).

The idea *structureless*.

The question concerning how we can know anything
about the ideas is answered by Pythag⟨oras's⟩ transmigration of souls.

End of Plato: skepticism in Parmenides.

Refutation of the doctrine of ideas.

23 [28]

5.   Art. Concept of Culture. Struggle against science.
6.   Philosophy, marvelous double nature.
7.   Thales.
8.   Anaximander.
9. 10. 11.   Heraclitus.
12. 13.   Parmenides.
14. 15.   Anaxagoras.
16. 17. 18.   Emped⟨ocles⟩.
19. 20.   Democritus.
21. 22.   Pythagor⟨eans⟩.
23. 24.   Socrates.
25.   Conclusion.

23 [29]

Chapter I.   3
Chapter II.   5
Chapter III.   The Philosopher.
Chapter IV.   Thales, Anaximander.
Chapter V.   Heraclitus.
Chapter VI.   Parmenides.

23 [30]

That this entire conception of Anaxagoras's teachings must be correct is most clearly demonstrated by the way in which his successors, *Empedocles* the Agrigentian and Democritus, who promulgated the doctrine of atoms, in their dissenting sys-
5   tems actually criticized and corrected him. The method of this criticism is above all continued repudiation in that previously mentioned spirit of the natural sciences, the law of economy applied to the explanation of nature. The hypothesis able to explain the existing world with the fewest presuppositions and
10 expedients should be given precedence: for it displays the least arbitrariness and prohibits the free play with possibilities. If there are two hypotheses that explain the world equally well, then one must rigorously investigate which of the two best fulfills that demand for economy. Anyone whose explanation can
15 make do with simpler and better-known forces, above all those of mechanics, anyone who derives the existing structure of the world from the smallest possible number of forces, always will take precedence over someone who sees more complicated and lesser-known forces—and these, moreover, in greater num-
20 ber—at work in the construction of the world. Thus, we see how Empedocles endeavors to eliminate the *excessive number* of hypotheses from Anaxagoras's teachings.

The first unnecessary hypothesis to fall is Anaxagoras's *Noûs*, for its assumptions are much too complicated to explain some-
25 thing as simple as motion. After all, it is only necessary to explain two forms of motion, the movement of one object toward another and the movement of one object away from another.

23 [31]

If our current development is a process of separation, even if an incomplete one, ⟨he⟩ then asks: What prevents total sepa-
30   ration? Thus, an opposing force, that is, a latent cohesive motion.

Then: in order to explain that chaos, some power must already have been at work, for this intimate entanglement requires a motion.

Thus, periodic predominance of one or the other power is certain.

5 They are in opposition.

The power of cohesion is still at work, for otherwise there would be no objects at all, everything would be disintegral.

That is what is real: two types of motion. The *νοῦς* does not explain them. Opposed to this, love and hatred: we recognize

10 with certainty that they are in motion, just as we do that the *νοῦς* is in motion.

Then the conception of the primordial condition changes: it is the *most blissful* condition. With Anaxagoras, it was the chaos that preceded the architectonic structure, the heap of stones

15 at a construction site, so to speak.

23 [32]

Empedocles had conceived the thought of a tangential force, caused by reversal, that worked in opposition to gravity (*De coelo*, I, p. 284). Schopenhauer, *World as Will*, II, 390.

He believed the continuity of circular motion in Anaxago-
20 ras's system to be *impossible*. It would produce a *vortex*, that is, the opposite of ordered motion.

If the particles were infinitely intermingled with one another, then one would be able to break bodies apart without the exertion of force, they would not cohere, they would be
25 like dust.

Empedocles calls the forces that press atoms together and give matter its solidity "love." It is a molecular force, a constitutive force of bodies.

23 [33]

Empedocles.

30 In opposition to Anaxagoras.

1) Chaos already presupposes motion.

2) Nothing prevented complete separation.

3) Our bodies would be entities made of dust. How is motion possible if there are not countermotions in all bodies?

4) An ordered, continuous circular motion impossible, only
5 a vortex. He himself presupposes the vortex as the effect of the νεῖκος. How do distant bodies have an influence on one another, the sun on the earth? If everything were in a vortex, that would be impossible. ἀπορροαί. Hence at least two motive forces: which must be inherent in objects.

10   5) Why infinite ὄντα? Does not agree with experience. Anaxagoras meant the chemical atoms. Empedocles attempted to postulate four types of chemical atoms. He believed conditions of aggregation essential and that they were coordinated with heat. Thus, conditions of aggregation by means of repul-
15 sion and attraction; matter in four forms.

6) Periodicity is necessary.

7) Empedocles even wants to apply the same principles in the case of living beings. Here, too, he denies purposiveness. His greatest deed. In the case of Anaxagoras, a dualism.

23 [34]

20   The symbolism of *sexual love*. Here, as in Plato's fable, the longing for oneness is expressed, as is the fact that at one time a greater unity already existed: if this greater unity were reconstituted, then it, in turn, would strive for an even greater unity. The belief in the unity of all living things guarantees that there
25 once was one *enormous living organism* of which we are individual parts: that is the *sphairos* itself. It is the most blissful divinity. Everything was connected only by love, hence supremely purposive. It was torn asunder and split by hatred, dismembered into its elements, and thereby killed, robbed of life. In the
30 vortex, no individual living creatures come into being. Ultimately, everything is separated, and then our period begins (he opposes to Anaxagoras's primordial intermingling a primordial division). Love, blind as it is, throws the elements back together in furious haste, trying to see whether it can bring

them back to life. Here and there it is successful. It continues.
A presentiment arises in living creatures that they must strive
for higher unities as their home and primordial condition.
Eros. It is a terrible crime to kill something living, for with
⁵ this one reverts back to primordial division. At some point,
everything is once again supposed to be one *single living thing*,
the most blissful condition.

The Pythagorean-Orphic doctrine reinterpreted in a natural-
scientific manner: Empedocles consciously masters both vo-
¹⁰ cabularies, that is why he is the first rhetor. Political aims.

Dualistic nature—the agonal and the loving, pitying.

Attempt at a *total reform of the Hellenic*.

All inorganic matter arose from organic matter, it is dead
organic matter. Corpse and human being.

23 [35]
¹⁵ **Conclusion**: Greek thought in the *tragic age*
        is *pessimistic*
        or *artistically optimistic*.
Their judgment on *life* says more.
    Oneness, flight from becoming.
²⁰   *Aut* unity *aut* artistic play.
Profound mistrust of reality
    no one assumes a beneficent deity who has accomplished
    everything in an optimal manner.
    ⎧ Pythagoreans, religious sects.
²⁵   ⎨ Anaximander.
    ⎩ Empedocles.

The Eleatics.

    ⎧ Anaxagoras.
    ⎨ Heraclitus.
³⁰   ⎩ Democritus. The world lacking all moral and aesthetic sig-
    nificance, pessimism of contingency.

If all of them were spectators at a tragedy, the first three would
      see ⟨it as⟩ a reflection of the wretchedness of existence,
      Parmenides as transitory semblance,
      Heraclitus and Anaxagoras as artistic construct and like-
5   ness of the laws of the world,
      Democritus as produced by machines.
   Optimism begins with Socrates, but it is no longer artistic,
      with teleology and the belief in a beneficent deity;
      the belief in the knowing, good human being.
10   Dissolution of the instincts.
   Socrates breaks with all prior *science* and *culture*, he wants to
      return to the ancient civic virtues and to the state.
   Plato abandons the state when he realizes that it has become
      identical with contemporary culture.
15 Socratic skepticism is a weapon that is to be used against the
      previous culture and science.

23 [36]
   What caused the productive experimental physics of antiquity to be broken off after Democritus?

23 [37]
   M. Antonius. Observe the course of the sun and the moon
20 as if you were traveling along with them, and constantly think
about how the elements are transformed into each other. For
these are thoughts that sweep away the muck of earthly existence.

23 [38]
   Antisthenes says: It is kingly to tolerate malicious judgments
25 about good actions.

23 [39]

Democritus.

Greatest possible simplification of hypotheses.

1) There is motion, hence empty space, hence the nonexistent. Thought as a movement.

2) If there is the existent, it must be indivisible, that is, absolutely complete. Division is explainable only if there are empty spaces, pores. Only the nonexistent is an absolutely porous thing.

3) The secondary characteristics of matter νόμῳ, not inherent.

4) Determination of the primary characteristics of ἄτομα. In what respects identical, in what respects different?

5) Empedocles' states of aggregation (four elements) only presuppose identical atoms, and hence cannot themselves be ὄντα.

6) Motion is indissolubly bound up with the atoms, effect of gravity. Epicurus. Criticism: What is the meaning of gravity in an infinitely empty space?

7) Thought is motion of the fire atoms. Soul, life. Sensory perceptions.

23 [40]

Value of materialism and its plight.

Plato and Democritus.

The homeless, noble researcher who turns his back on the world.

Democritus and the Pythagoreans together discover the foundation of the natural sciences.

Pythagoreans.

23 [41]

(10)   *Plan.* What is a philosopher?

What is a philosopher's relation to culture?

In particular to tragic culture?

(20)   *Introduction.* When did the works disappear?
         The sources: a) for the lives; b) for the dogmas.
         Chronology. Confirmed by the systems.
(100)   *Main part.* The philosophers, with quoted passages
         and excursuses.
(20)   *Conclusion.* Philos⟨ophy⟩'s attitude toward culture.

23 [42]

The artist does not perceive "ideas," he derives pleasure from numerical relations.

All pleasure from proportion, displeasure from disproportion.

Concepts constructed according to numbers.

Perceptions that represent good numbers are beautiful.

The man of science calculates the numbers of the laws of nature

the artist perceives them: —in the first case, adherence to
                                        laws,

                                in the second, beauty.

What the artist perceives is something wholly superficial, not an "idea"!

The thinnest veneer around beautiful numbers.

23 [43]

Our perception already modified by concepts.

Concepts are relations, not abstractions.

23 [44]

1. Metaphors relate to actions.
2. Form a system among themselves: stable basic framework—form *numbers*.
3. The core of things, what is essential, expresses itself in the language of number.
4. What is the basis of the arbitrary element in metaphors?

23 [45]
> Philosophy *not for the people*
>> hence *not the basis for a culture*,
>> hence only *the instrument of a culture*.
>> a) Against the dogmatism of the sciences
>> b) against the confusion of images created by mythic religions in nature
>> c) against the ethical confusion caused by religions.

> *According to this, its purpose, by nature it*
>> a) 1. is convinced of the anthropomorphic aspect, is skeptical
>> 2. has discrimination and greatness
>> 3. wings beyond the idea of unity
>> b) is healthy interpretation and an uncomplicated view of nature, is proof.
>> c) destroys the belief in the inviolability of such laws.

> *Its helplessness without culture*, portrayed on the example of the present.

24 [1]

Healthy introspection, without undermining oneself; it is a rare gift to venture into the unexplored depths of the self, without delusions or fictions, but with an uncorrupted gaze. Goethe.

24 [2]

5   Two methodologies are the lamentable instruments for the obstruction and retardation of science; either one approaches and connects things that are heavens apart by applying obscure fancy and comical mysticism; or, by means of pulverizing unreason, one isolates things that belong together, attempts to
10 separate closely related phenomena, attributing to each its own law by means of which it is supposed to be explained.

Since both in knowledge and in reflection no whole can be constructed, etc.

Requirements for a *scientific work of art*: when involved in sci-
15 entific activity, none of the human strengths could be excluded. The abysses of conjecture, a firm perception of the present, mathematical depth, physical exactness, supreme rationality, sharp reason, mobile, yearning fantasy, loving joy in the sensual; we can dispense with none of these for the vital, produc-
20 tive apprehending of the moment; these are the only qualities that can produce a work of art, regardless of its content. — They can appear at any moment, as long as prejudice, the ego-

centricity of the individuals who possess them, and whatever other inhibiting and deadening negations one can name—

For despite the fact that, where science and art are concerned, we live in the most peculiar anarchy, which seems to
5 take us further and further away from every coveted purpose
— — —

24 [3]

On *nature*. It acts out a play: we do not know whether nature itself views this play, and yet it acts it out for us, who stand in the corner. — Its play is constantly new, because it is constantly
10 creating new viewers. Life is its most beautiful invention, and death is the trick it has devised so as to have a great deal of life. Goethe.

24 [4]

People often speak of the *republic of scholars*, but not of the *republic of geniuses*. This is what happens in the latter: — one giant
15 calls to another across the desolate expanse of centuries, without the world of dwarfs that crawls about below ever perceiving more than a mere murmur and ever understanding more than that something is happening. And by the same token, these dwarfs down below incessantly carry on and make a lot
20 of noise, struggle with the things that the giants have dropped, proclaim heroes, who themselves are dwarfs; those giant spirits are not disturbed by any of this, but simply carry on their lofty dialogue between spirits. Schopenhauer.

24 [5]

With their total disregard of my accomplishments and the
25 simultaneous celebration of all that is mediocre and bad, my contemporaries have ⟨done⟩ everything possible to make me have doubts about myself. Schopenhauer.

24 [6]

Genius the cross-bearer of humanity, to deliver it from crudeness and barbarism. Schopenhauer.

24 [7]

Everything forces itself upon me, I no longer reflect on it, everything approaches me, and the immense realm is simplified in my soul, so that I soon am able to solve even the most difficult task. If I could only communicate this gaze and this joy to someone, but it is impossible. And it is no dream, no fantasy; it is an awareness of the essential form with which nature merely plays, as it were, and, while playing, brings forth the manifoldness of life. If I had enough time in the short span of my life, I would venture to extend it to all the domains of nature — to nature's domain in its entirety. G⟨oethe⟩.

24 [8]

I have often said, and I will say it over and over again, that the *causa finalis* of worldly and human affairs is dramatic literature. For otherwise this stuff is of absolutely no use. G⟨oethe⟩.

24 [9]

When making an anatomical discovery, I experience such joy that all my innards are set astir.

24 [10]

Grillparzer in ponderous verse:
> Love of art without artistic sensibility
> Brings princes little profit;
> It opens their ears to artistic prattlers
> And art remains as alone as ever.

24 [11]

There are two types of culture, *Hellenic* and *Roman*: the former, a natural product that in all its structures and elements continually reproduces the essential form in a playful manner, so that the enormous manifoldness is simplified for the observing eye: the latter, a noble convention and decoration, with borrowed, perhaps even misunderstood forms, but which are reinterpreted so as to be splendid and opulent or ornamental.

24 [12]

Once the life of a people has come under the dominance of either the Greek or the Roman mode of art, then we speak of the culture of this people: but what attitude will philosophy assume toward a dominance of art over life that has become rigid
5 and normative if in one instance this art is nature, in the other instance convention? Let's answer this question first by means of an analogy.

24 [13]

My intention is to entertain young men who know Latin and Greek by telling them a simple story about the great Greek
10 philosophical masters.

24 [14]

Lectures on Greek Philosophy.
Part One.

[25 = P II 12b. 54. 55. 52. Winter 1872–73]

25 [1]

I want to begin with the confession that, with regard to Greek tragedy, it has become very difficult for me to arrive at a pure and immediate sentiment that actually touches upon tragedy as a work of art, a sentiment that I would above all like to call "honest." From the very outset, everything today is so disposed that the young person, desiring now finally to be able to peer into such an infinitely renowned world of wonders, will fall into the trap of regarding it with an awe that can only be called dishonest. He anxiously conceals from himself the cool, alienating, and almost embarrassing first impression: for he wants at all costs to love those things whose triumphant song, arising out of antiquity and penetrating into this very moment, resounds around him. Out of this need for love, he unconsciously, with the power of a delicate illusion, transforms this object that had such an alienating effect on him. Perhaps he stares transfixed at those scenes in which he senses an affinity with Shakespeare and judges ancient tragedy in its entirety according to the impression made on him by Aeschylus's Cassandra scene. Or he lingers over the structure of Sophocles' dramas, joyously recognizing in them the same laws that even today the dramatist applies to build and structure his work. Another, in turn, may even experience the contrast to that cooler and more austere mythic world with the fascination of a "sentimentalist": whereas those of lesser character will be

satisfied here as elsewhere with superficialities; that is, they will
in part be entertained by the story, or get bogged down with
individual words and thoughts or meters, or even with corrupt
passages. By contrast, that honest sentiment begins with the
admission of an enormous *defect*, and therefore only with limited awe. The defect is even greater than when we stand before
the rubble of a temple and attempt to reconstruct the impression of entire colonnades on the basis of a few remnants of
columns. For ultimately, what we have before us is nothing but
printed pages, not the reality of that tragedy. We must supply
the Greek character to this, the Greek in the perfected expression of his life, as tragic actor, singer, dancer, the Greek as the
sole exacting artistic viewer. But if we are able to do that, to
re-create the Greek in our thoughts, then we have also almost
created ancient tragedy anew out of ourselves. But precisely
that is the infinite difficulty: where should the modern human
being begin to think like a Greek, when should he cease to do
so? It is, in truth, very difficult to find the proper course once
one has gained insight into that defect. Only analogous phenomena of *our* world, phenomena that almost deserve to be
called Greek, can be of assistance to us now: just as likeness is
always only recognized by like things in like things. Thus, the
better part of our contemporary scholars come to the Greeks
by way of Goethe; others turn to Raphael for help. I rely on
those experiences for which I am indebted to Richard Wagner.
So-called historical-critical scholarship has no way to approach
such alien things: we need bridges, experiences, adventures:
then, in turn, we need people who will interpret them for us,
who will express them. Thus, I believe I am correct when I take
as my point of departure the impression that a performance of
Tristan made on me in the summer of 1872.

 With regard to the *sculpturesque* side of performance, I became aware of a decisive difference between the sculpturesque
performance of our actors in Schillerean and Shakespearean
roles and that of the singers in operas. Wholly independent of
the talent of the performers, an involuntary desire to preserve a

tranquil grandeur, even in the most passionate moments, became apparent in the opera: in essence, one saw noble, moderately affected, for the most part almost static sculpturesque groups. I was pleased to see that modern restlessness had given way
5 here to a tendency toward the sculpturesque. I said to myself that the music and the singing must be the reason why nothing moved as quickly as it did in everyday life and in spoken tragedy. Sung affect is infinitely drawn out in comparison with spoken affect. The accompanying movement must reinterpret
10 the gripping, naturalistic movement as pathos-filled grandeur. And thus I had an inkling of a most fruitful future for our sculpturesque abilities, the task of inventing sublime postures and group configurations that would correspond to such sublime music. And here once again music appeared to me as the
15 redeemer of our contemporary age. And yet, opera was wholly unsuited for bringing about a purification of our sensibility for the sculpturesque: for its singers were instruments in disguise, their movements basically irrelevant and therefore able from the very outset to be determined by conventions. It would
20 be more correct to maintain that the modern human being, seduced by his favorite art form, opera, grew accustomed to the expression of convention in clothing, gestures, etc.: that the aristocratic courts were imitations of the world of opera, and that eventually the entire civilized world was the pale imi-
25 tation of courtly culture.

However, the same thing that in this instance brings about the use of a more static sculpturesque portrayal, the longer duration of the sung sound, apparently also brought about the same kind of portrayal in Aeschylus's dramas: but aside from
30 this increase in sculpturesque stasis, it also brought about yet another circumstance. Tragedy is a religious act for the entire people, that is, for an entire civic community; it thus reckons with a large audience. But this causes the distance between the actors and the audience to be much greater than today. Be-
35 cause of these different viewing conditions, the actor himself had to be introduced in mighty padding and standing on the

cothurn. This is also why the mask took the place of the emotive face. But that is also the very reason why sculpturesque portrayal should be displayed only in grand and static forms. Here the rules governing high style emerged wholly on their
5 own; rigid symmetry was dissolved into contrasts. The restriction to two or three actors was probably also motivated by considerations of sculpturesque portrayal, by the reluctance to try to work with the larger moving group. For here there are too many risks of falling into ugliness. However, that simple
10 sculpturesque portrayal practiced by Aeschylus must have been the preliminary stage for Phidias: for the plastic arts always follow with slow strides behind a beautiful reality. One important problem is why after Socrates the plastic arts did not immediately decline along with the other arts: for one thing,
15 the plastic arts emerge later; for another, they are rescued by the craftsmanlike, but not sophistic, education of the master artists; and third, those creations held to be beautiful are continually copied, so that we experience the beauty of these earlier times even in the works of later ages.

20   The tragic poet must in any case have set down prescriptions for the sculpturesque groups and the movements of his actors: we recognize this in the fact that the number of lines of verse is structured symmetrically, which can be explained only by means of sculpturesque movements. In general, the actor
25 stands while speaking: with each step he marks off groups of verse with an equivalent number of lines. At any rate, his entire demeanor must be subsumed under the concept of orchestrics, and the *chorodidaskolos*—that is, originally the poet—had to think everything through and make prescriptions for the
30 actor. For the Aeschylean period, which was accustomed to a strict hieratic style, we also will have to assume a style that was still frequently influenced by hieratic elements. We would thus have set ourselves the task of understanding Aeschylus as a sculpturesque composer, both in the sculpturesque movement
35 of the individual scene and in the entire sequence of sculpturesque compositions in the work of art as a whole. The main

problem facing this conception would be understanding the sculpturesque use of the *chorus*, its relationship to the characters on stage; and beyond this, the relationship of the sculpturesque group to the surrounding architecture. Here an abyss
5 of artistic powers yawns before us—and the dramatist appears more than ever as the total artist. Cf. Goethe's letter to Schiller, vol. 1, p. 278.

[26 = U I 5b. Spring 1873]

26 [1]

Thales.	Paracelsus. Passage in Homer's allegories. Water in modern chemistry. Lavoisier. Clouds ice. Anaximenes' air (Paracelsus).
5 *Anaximander.*	Becoming as a sign of transience. Not the *infinitum*, but rather the *indefinitum*. The ἄπειρον as cause of the world of becoming? (Emanation theory, Spir.)
Heraclitus. 10	Becoming as *creating*, p. 347 and preceding, Kopp. Two elements necessary for any act of becoming.
Anaxagoras. 15	Circular motion. *Dynamic* theory, penetration of matter, p. 324. Many substances. Becoming now as drawing out, no longer as creating. Penetration to points.
Empedocles. 20	Attraction, repulsion. Affinity. *Actio in distans.* Four elements. Two kinds of electricity, p. 340 Kopp. Love and hatred— sensation as the cause of motion. Boerhave, p. 310 Kopp.

Democritus.	Atoms uniform. Buffon against Newton, p. 311.
	Diversiform, Gassendi.
Pythagoreans.	367 Kopp. The sleeping giant in the ship.
5	Überweg, III, 53. Continuation of atomism, all mechanics of motion is ultimately description of representations.
	Coming into contact. *Actio in distans.*
Parmenides.	Bernardinus Telesius.
10	*Contributions to the History of Physiology* by Rixner and Siber III.
	Descartes's definition of substance, see Überweg, II, 52.
15	Reciprocal impact in the case of absolute dissimilarity of the bodies. III, 53.
	Basic doctrine principle of contradiction, Überweg, III, 81.
	Quidquid est, est: quidquid non est, non est.

26 [2]

Imitation of *nature.*

20   "To god, even the wisest human being is an ape." Heraclitus.
Oedipus the "suffering human being" solves the riddle of the *human being*.

26 [3]

The Eleatics saw the heavens black, as it were, like the inhabitants of the moon.

26 [4]

25 *Cardanus* segregates human beings into
    1) those merely deceived
    2) deceiving deceivers
    3) nondeceived nondeceivers.

26 [5]

Democritus $\left\{ \begin{array}{l} \textit{Sennerti physica Viteb}\langle\textit{ergae}\rangle \text{ 1618} \\ \textit{Magneni Democritus reviviscens Ticino} \text{ 1646} \end{array} \right.$

Empedocles—*Maignani cursus philosoph*⟨*icus*⟩ 1652 and 1673.

26 [6]

The murky waters of metaphysics.

26 [7]

5   Thomas Campanella maintains that space is animate because he shrinks from emptiness and desires fullness.

26 [8]

Observing a series of philosophers one after the other is like
being in a portrait gallery: they are not at home in the house
in which, for the sake of comparison, we give them quarters;
10 that is why they so often appear so arbitrary and like a luxury,
like the creations of characterless artistic hacks. By contrast,
the task should be merely to tell about them in the same way
as they told about their predecessors and about their points of
contact; that is, the *struggle* among them.

26 [9]

15 My aim is to describe a series of great philosophers in the
hope that I can thereby elucidate the nature of the philosopher himself: despite the fact that I will do this in a somewhat
unphilosophical manner, since I will deal only with the philosopher's effects. But I am unable to speak in a more direct
20 manner about their nature, for in their world, the pure drive for
truth is so foreign and inexplicable that I can only hope that
I will at least have demonstrated something by demonstrating
what use this drive serves. Even if it does not exist for the purpose of serving this use, it is still important to recognize that,
25 as long as it exists, it can at least be useful: whereas by nature it
is so strange and inhuman that one is tempted to believe that
it is not only useless, but even harmful. For that drive stands

in contradiction to everything that commonly affords human beings happiness.

26 [10]

> There are only philosophers, that is, friends of truth
>> or *enemies of truth*
>> or skeptics.

26 [11]

I have nothing but sensation and representation.

Thus, I cannot conceive the latter as having arisen from the contents of representation.

All those cosmogonies, etc. are deduced from the sensory data.

We cannot conceive of anything that is not sensation and representation.

Hence also not of the existence of pure time, space, world without the existence of something that senses and represents.

I cannot imagine nonbeing.

> The existent is sensation and representation.

> The nonexistent would be something that is neither sensation nor representation.

The representing being cannot "not imagine" itself, imagine itself away.

The representing being cannot imagine itself either as having come into being or as perishing.

Impossible also the development of matter, up to that representing being.

For the antithesis between matter and representation simply does not exist.

Matter itself is given only as sensation. Every inference about things beyond sensation is prohibited.

Sensation and representation are what cause us to believe in reasons, impacts, bodies.

We can reduce them to motion and numbers.

26 [12]

Motion in *time*

A   B   ·
·   ·

Spatial point A has an effect on spatial point B and vice
versa.

For this it needs a period of time, for every effect must cover
a distance.

Consecutive points in time would merge with one another.

The effect of A no longer strikes the B that existed in the
first moment. What does it then mean to say: B still exists,
just as A still exists, if they collide with one another?

This would above ⟨all⟩ mean that A is unaltered, one and the
same at this and at that point in time. But in that case, A
is not an effective force, for if it were, it no longer could
be the same; for that would mean that it had not had an
effect.

If we take what is effective in *time*, then what is effective in
the tiniest fragment of every moment in time always is
something different.

That means: time demonstrates the *absolute nonpermanence* of
a force.

All laws of space are thus conceived as *timeless*,
which means that they must be simultaneous and immediate.

The entire world with one strike. But then there is no *motion*.

Motion struggles with the contradiction that it is constituted
according to the laws of space and that once we assume
time, these laws become impossible: that means that at
one and the same time it both is and is not.

We can get around this by assuming that either space or time
is = o.

If I take space to be infinitely small, then all the interstices
between atoms become infinitely small; that means that
all punctual atoms would merge at one point.

But since time is infinitely divisible, the entire world is possible as a purely temporal phenomenon, because I can occupy every point in time with one and the same spatial point and hence can place it an infinite number of times. Thus, one would have to conceive *points in time*, as the essence of a body, *to be distinct*; that is, one would have to conceive of one and the same point as being located in particular interstices. There is room for infinite points of time within every interstice: thus, one could conceive of an entire world of bodies, all of them derived from one point, but in such a way that we dissolve bodies into interrupted lines of time.

                ⋮   ⋮

Is now only

                ⋮   ⋮

                .   ⋮

a reproducing being is necessary, one that holds earlier moments in time next to the current ones. Our bodies are imagined in them.

There is, then, no spatial coexistence other than in representation.

All coexistence would be derived and imagined. The laws of space would all be artificial constructs and would not vouch for the existence of space.

The number and the type of sequence of every single frequently placed point would then constitute the body.

The reality of the world would then consist of an abiding point. Manifoldness would arise due to the fact that there would be representing beings who would conceive of this point as being repeated in the tiniest moments of time: beings who assume the point to be nonidentical at different points of time and now consider these points simultaneously.

Translation of all laws of motion into temporal proportions.
The essence of sensation would then consist in gradually
sensing and measuring such temporal figures with more
and more refinement; representation constructs them as
something coexistent and then establishes the development of the world on the basis of this coexistence: pure
translation into another language, into the language of
becoming.

The order of the world would be the regularity of the temporal figures: and yet then one would in any case have to
conceive of time as operating with a constant force, according to laws that we can interpret only on the basis of
that coexistence. *Actio in distans temporis punctum.*

As such we have no means whatsoever for postulating a law
of time.

We would then have a punctual force that would have a relationship with every later temporal moment of its existence, that is, whose forces would consist of those figures
and relationships. In every tiniest moment, that force
would have to be different: but the sequence would take
place in certain proportions, and the existing world would
consist in the *becoming visible of these force proportions*, that is,
translation into the spatial.

In atomic physics one usually assumes unalterable atomic
forces *in time*, thus ὄντα in Parmenides' sense. But these
cannot have an effect.

Rather, only absolutely mutable forces can have an effect,
those that are never the same in any two moments.

All forces are merely a *function of time*.

1) An effect by successive temporal moments is *impossible*: for
two such points in time would merge with one another.
Thus, every effect is *actio in distans*, that is, by means of
a leap.

2) We have absolutely no idea of how such an effect *in distans*
is possible.

3) Fast, slow, etc. in the entire nature of this effect. That means that the forces, as functions of time, express themselves in the relationships to closer or more distant points in time: namely, fast or slow. The force is based on the degree of acceleration. The highest possible acceleration would be based on the effect of one temporal moment on the most proximate one, which means that it would then = infinitely large.

The more slowly this takes place, the greater the temporal interstices, the greater the *distans*.

Hence the relation of distant points in time is slowness: all slowness, of course, is relative.

Time line.

Real: a spatial point.

Relationships among different temporal layers.

Where do the relationships exist.

No motion in time is *constant*.

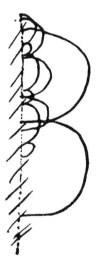

We measure time in terms of something that *remains spatial* and hence we presuppose that between timepoint A and timepoint B there is a *constant* time. But time is by no means a continuum, rather, there are only *wholly different points in time, no line. Actio in distans*.

We can speak only of points in time, no longer of time.
The point in time has an effect on another point in time, thus, *dynamic* qualities must be presupposed.
Doctrine of temporal atoms.

It is possible   1) to reduce the existing world to a theory of punctual spatial atoms,

2) to reduce this, in turn, to a theory of
temporal atoms,

3) the theory of temporal atoms ultimately
coincides with a doctrine of sensation.
The *dynamic point in time* is identical with
the *point of sensation*. For there is no simultaneity of sensation.

26 [13]

Perhaps everyone has experienced in his youth that passionate moment in which he has said to himself: "If only you could
erase your entire past! Then you would stand pure and blank
in the face of nature, like the first human being, so as to live
better and more wisely from that moment on." It is a foolish
and horrible wish: for if the wisher's entire past were really to
be erased from the slate of being, this would be tantamount
to nothing less than extinguishing along with the few miserable moons of his life innumerable earlier generations as well:
whose resonance and remnants ultimately constitute our existence, no matter how much the individual tends to see himself
as something wholly new and unique. Indeed, there is scarcely
a more selfish desire than the wish to destroy entire earlier generations a posteriori just because some individual who comes
later has reason to be dissatisfied with himself. But if someone, overwhelmed by passion, really were to cry out: "A curse
on all generations to which my existence — — —

26 [14]

Marvelous the lack of concern nature displays for culture. It
is attached to too few individuals.

Bakunin, who out of hatred for the present wants to destroy
history and the past. Now, to be sure, in order to eradicate
the entire past it also would be necessary to eradicate human
beings: but he only wants to destroy all prior *cultivation*, our
intellectual inheritance in its entirety. The new generation is
supposed to discover its own culture:

Human beings are worthy only of the art that they themselves create.

Cultivation cannot simply be passed down from generation
to generation. It is much more threatened: it can truly be destroyed for centuries.

It is possible *to destroy cultivation*.

To ruin it is actually quite a simple matter and merely the
work of a few people over a few years.

Nature did not develop such preventive measures

Since *cultivation is so mutable*, it must also be *easy to improve*.

26 [15]

⟨Goethe⟩ on good helpers, 3, p. 59
Eckerm⟨ann⟩, 3, p. 164, *Greek style*.
3, p. 37, due to newspapers, pseudoculture of the masses
3, p. 45, on reforms without God
the degree of what a human being can tolerate determines
his depth and his seriousness, but also his joy.

26 [16]

Public opinion in Germany today almost forbids one to
speak of the deleterious consequences of war, especially of a
war that ends in victory, which is why those writers who possess no opinions other than public opinion are intent upon
competing to sing the praises of the war, especially its service
to culture, art, and morality. Despite all this, let it be said:
of all the deleterious consequences brought about by the recently fought war with France, the worst is perhaps one quickly
spreading and now almost universal illusion that in that war
German culture was victorious over a foreign culture and that
it therefore now deserves more than anything else the laurel
befitting such an extraordinary war. For one thing, even if we
were to grant that this war represented the battle between those
cultures, the measure for the victorious culture would still be a
very relative one, and under certain circumstances it would not

at all warrant either victory celebrations or self-glorification. For it would be a matter of knowing the worth of that subjugated culture; perhaps its worth is small, in which case victory, even if accompanied by the most spectacular military successes,
5 would not provide the victorious culture with just cause for a sense of triumph. On the other hand, in our case, we certainly cannot speak of this at all. Strict military discipline, scientific superiority among the leaders, unity and obedience among the led—in short, essentially qualities that have nothing at all to
10 do with culture—were victorious, and we can only be surprised that culture had so little power to inhibit the development of these military principles: that it was either too impotent or too properly subservient. It is enough that after the war things appear quite different and are viewed quite differently every-
15 where. It is supposed to be culture that was victorious; all the industries, all the sciences celebrate their contribution; and even a gathering of philologists and schoolteachers cannot let this popular topic slip by, and they celebrate their profession as one that contributed to this victory. I will say nothing about
20 the extent to which this is correct. It is only that I see in this the general danger that an extremely ambiguous, immature, non-national culture—in truth, a poor excuse for a culture— suddenly cloaks itself in the robe of triumph. For God's sake, take a look around you and pay attention. Just one more vic-
25 tory of this sort and the German Reich will continue to exist, but the German himself will be destroyed! Even now I barely have the courage to lay claim to any quality as being especially German. German customs, German social life, German institutions and agencies—everything has a foreign tinge to it and
30 looks like an incompetent imitation, whereby it even has been forgotten that it is an imitation at all: everywhere, originality out of forgetfulness. In this time of distress I seek my comfort in the German language, which is for the time being truly the only thing that has been spared all the intermingling of
35 nationalities and the changing times and customs; and it is my opinion that a metaphysical magic that engenders unities out

of diversities, homogeneity out of heterogeneity, must dwell in this language. This is precisely the reason why we must select the strictest warders to watch over this unifying language that guarantees our future Germanness. Our great authors have a
5 holy office as the warders of this language; and our German schools have the fruitful, serious task of educating people, under the eyes of such warders, to use the German language. (New quality of the G⟨erman⟩ language: to incorporate and imitate everything, European mosaic.)

10   Now, the war had the unfortunate effect that even German writers thought it glorified them, and they derived from it as much self-confidence as if the most critical posterity already had acknowledged their immortality. A whole series of new classical authors boldly dared to come out into the light of
15 day: the journals and European newspapers walked ahead of them bearing the coronation crown, and foreign countries were thrown into amazed confusion by the constantly repeated assurance that we possess a great culture and great classical authors. Let's just imagine an educated Englishman who has
20 become acquainted with our great Germans and who now constantly hears from across the Channel that German classical authors and model writers exist once more, as the true advisors and causes of such powerful wars and victories, and that they thereby are placed above those older ones who seldom
25 were presented with the laurels of war. Our Englishman reads, for example, that people are discussing in widely read journals whether David Strauss is the greatest contemporary stylist or whether he has a host of equals: and now his desire to become acquainted with this modern classicism grows to the ut-
30 most and he asks for that work that came into the world four times in the last three months, in large editions, *The Old and the New Faith*.

With this we have said all that had to be said by way of introducing this Englishman, who from this point on will speak
35 for himself: he reads, reads on, is astonished, asks questions, listens, investigates—and ultimately he picks up his pen in des-

peration in order to express in a letter the things that make him
so anxious—he addresses David Strauss directly.

First Letter.

A foreigner has many advantages when entering into a conversation with the famous David Strauss about what is German, especially since he ———

26 [17]

If a modern human being like Strauss has things to criticize
in such a great ancient, then by rights he should do this in no
other pose than on his knees, to cite Goethe, 3, p. 137.

26 [18]

The sudden enrichment of a people holds the same dangers
as a sudden overdose of scientific discoveries. The road from
insight to life, from ken to can, from know-how to art, is
forgotten: a luxurious reveling in knowledge begins. The continuing quiet work of those who produce culture suddenly is
swamped by those who take pride in knowledge: no one wants
any longer to move down the smaller paths in practical matters; instead, everyone egoistically limits himself to being a
know-it-all. And just as people recently feared that the famous
five billion could end up being a curse, the excess of science
appears to be becoming a curse for our culture.

26 [19]

The illusion of a cultural victory.

Necessary to fight against it, outcome improbable due to
that illusion.

What is lacking is the feeling that things are in a sorry state.

26 [20]

On Reading and Writing.

1. Excessive reading.
2. Excessive writing.

3. Style.
4. Oration.

26 [21]
Greek and German.
The Struggle Between the Roman and the Greek.

26 [22]
5   Style. Authors who first write badly and afterward begin to
give their writing structure and to add artifice.
    Authors who merely write badly.
    The haughtiness of hack writers.

26 [23]
    Birth of Tragedy.
10   The Philosophers of the Tragic Age.
    The Future of our Educational Institutions.
    On Reading and Writing.
    The Competition.
    Meter.
15   Greek and German.
    Bayreuth Horizon Observations.

26 [24]
Against David Strauss.
    He is consistent.
        The stylist.
20   The view of art.
        The view of life.
    The philistrious impotence of this cultivation. Resignation
and affected cheerfulness.
    Without any feeling for what is German.

25   By
                  Pacific Nil.

[27 = U II 1. Spring–Autumn 1873]

27 [1]

Strauss's style demonstrates that during his long life he read a lot of *bad books*—I mean above all the works of his *adversaries*.

He ignored the best part of Christianity, the great recluses and saints—in short, its genius—and expresses opinions like those of the village preacher on art or like Kant's on music (who appreciated it only in the form of military marches).

When the French learn to understand German better, they will have a good laugh about the taste of my German countrymen: what kind of scholars, poets, and novelists they are, how haughty and how tasteless! It was impertinent of Strauss to offer the German people a biography of Jesus as a pendant to Renan's much better biography: and he should have just kept his hands off of Voltaire.

Strauss thought he could destroy Christianity by proving that it is full of myths. But the essence of religion consists precisely in the possession of freedom and in the power to create myths. Discrepancies with reason and contemporary science are his trump card. He has no inkling whatsoever of the fundamental antinomy of idealism and of the ultimate relativity of all science and reason. Or: It is precisely reason that should tell him how little reason is able to discover about the essence of things.

27 [2]

He never sees the problems. He constantly takes Christianity, art, in their most trivial and crude democratic form and then refutes them. He believes in modern culture — but ancient culture was a much greater one, and yet Christianity still as-
5 serted its dominance over it. He is no philosopher. He has no sense of style. He is no artist. He is a *schoolmaster*. He displays the schoolmasterly type of cultivation typical of our bourgeoisie.

This confession is a *transgression* of his limitations: the scholar
10 perished by trying to appear to be a philosopher. And yet he is nothing but a creature with a schoolmasterly world view, servile, impoverished, narrow-minded, derivative.

The organization of the text: in the end, two niches for one's edification.

15 He is a bad stylist and an insignificant author, and on top of it all he is not working in his proper field. Moreover, a dotard. What does Goethe say about the *Système de la nature*?

On p. 257 we find the ridiculously feeble dilution of a powerful statement by Proudhon.

20 Strauss's text has no coherence, it is nothing but odds and ends. A gulf yawns between his Darwinism and his ethics; the former should have produced an ethics of the *bellum omnium* and of greater utility and power. The concept of the species as a moral regulative is completely insufficient. He means the
25 concept of the ideal. But how is someone who does not yet adhere to this ethics supposed to formulate such a concept? For the concept of the ideal must first be derived from ethics, hence the concept of the ideal cannot be the moral standard for the human being.

27 [3]
30 The presentation of a biography of Jesus is a lapse on Strauss's part. He had to limit himself to the historical work. — On the other hand, he should not have left out what was actu⟨ally⟩ the true Christianity, the monastic orders.

27 [4]

Against the Writer David Strauss.

27 [5]

If Strauss's "we" are really so numerous, then Lichtenberg's prophecy that our age will once again be called a *dark* age has come true.

27 [6]

For Strauss, Jesus is someone who ought to be thrown into an insane asylum.

27 [7]

To the German Writer David Strauss.
Letter from a Foreigner.

Someone once told me that you are a Jew and as such not in complete command of the German language.

27 [8]

It is comforting when someone grows old and composes his literary testament; we are then allowed to begin forgetting him and to stop reading him—and that is a plus. —The most recent testament bequeaths its wisdom to those who are "intellectually impoverished" because they either never learned anything or read only bad books—for example, only their own. Above all to the intellectually impoverished newspaper readers and concertgoers. A gospel for the Leipzig Gewandhaus.

He goes into his little chamber and plays chamber music— "this is how we live, this is how we live our whole life long."

27 [9]

You should by no means be allowed to glorify Lessing, since you really only intend to glorify *yourselves*. You are completely ignorant of the fact that this marvelous man perished among dull-witted creatures just like you. It was not to his benefit that he had to dabble in the most diverse fields; it prevented him from ever achieving true greatness. Gervinus. Grillparzer.

27 [10]

Jahn, who thinks that the hymn "Ode to Joy" is a failure.

27 [11]

Aristotle is of the opinion that one should destroy everything produced by old men.

27 [12]

Lichtenberg: "I know that famous writers, who were, however, basically shallow minds—a combination that is found quite often in Germany—were, despite all their self-importance, considered by the best minds I could question to be shallow minds."

27 [13]

I had just as little desire to hear a confession about life and philosophical questions from the likes of Strauss as I did from the likes of Mommsen or Freytag or Gervinus.

27 [14]

He is renowned in the same way a traveler in renowned lands becomes renowned: the same amount of labor, invested in a Finnish tale, would have earned him a good name among scholars, but would have offered nothing that a thousand other people don't already have. The stupidity of the theologians made him famous.

27 [15]

Today a great artist would be able to restore Christianity, above all its festivals. Klopstock had an inkling of this privilege of the genius.

27 [16]

They relate to style the same way they relate to art: they relate to art the same way they relate to life: namely, basely, superficially, meekly.

27 [17]

What *courage* to declare oneself a Darwinist, to say "not Christians," and yet in all the serious questions of life to fall timidly back on the most feeble indolence!

27 [18]

The *characterless and apathetic manner* as an expression of *health*.
5   The *ancient* as an expression of *German strength*.
The *image*, drawn specifically from the modern world, as a sign of taste — specifically, of modern taste.
He *plays at* being a *great popular* writer: false notion of popularity.
10   He is to be reckoned among those who after a certain age are incapable of understanding *Kant*.
Classical antiquity does not exist for him.
"The testament of modern ideas!"
Is it really necessary for someone to have a profound under-
15   standing of the field in which he has gained renown?

27 [19]

You call yourself David Strauss, but I have seen through your prank; you want to make the German public think that the real David Strauss is shabby and wretched, that his talents as a writer are inferior and scant. But how badly you have been
20   misunderstood! Everywhere you are being taken seriously: and even your style, that witty caricature, is being praised as something unique.
I want to demonstrate that I have understood you.

27 [20]

Letter   1. The desire to be *naive* and *popular* as an author,
25   indeed, to be a genius. Praise of form.
          2. Archaisms, neologisms.
          3. Mixed metaphors.
          4. Hegel and the newspapers — just like his adversaries.

  5. On Lessing.
  6. The great composers.
  7. Darwinism and ethics.
  8. No philosophy.
  9. Reduced to theology. Everything else should be
     expunged.
  10. He has no concept of Christianity.

27 [21]

Lichtenberg: "One can be satisfied with one's own accomplishment to the point of amazement, and yet someone with experience will laugh at our work." "There are men in the republic of scholars who create a big stir without ever really having accomplished anything. Few people probe into the worth of such men, and if those who knew him expressed their opinion publicly, they would be considered slanderers. The reason for this is that the truly great man has qualities that only the great man can appreciate; the former has those qualities that please only the masses, and they then outvote the sensible people." "It is only all too common that when writing books, intelligent people force their thoughts into a form that is shaped by a particular idea they have of style, just as they strike a pose when they are being painted." Strauss attempts at times to strike a pose like Voltaire's, at other times like Lessing's.

27 [22]

Letters from a Foreigner to the German Writer David Strauss.

27 [23]

It is painful to think that someone can get older without getting *wiser*. In Strauss's case, I continually ask myself: How was he even able to live so long?

The masses are unphilosophical, and Strauss is part of the masses.

His "aristocracy of nature" is wholly inconsistent and coun-
terfeit: he has simply become famous.

27 [24]

The German will soon write a language that is a soulless
word mosaic with European syntax. We continually are losing
more of our language and we should learn to appreciate what
it means to us—everything that is German! We are getting a
German empire at precisely that time when we are on the verge
of ceasing to be Germans. The *abstract European*, who imitates
everything and does it badly—
What are, after all, German customs—for the most part bad
and ossified imitations that no longer are recognized as such.
Moreover, even rigorous thought seems to be disappearing,
for the "classical authors" are slovenly fellows. I no longer have
the courage to claim one single characteristic as especially German. The war has made things decidedly worse. It is almost
forbidden to speak of the deleterious effects of the war: I dare
to do it and say: the most deleterious effect is that the victory
has produced the illusion that German culture has been victorious and that it is therefore worthy of praise.

27 [25]

You tell us that you are old. Well, Lichtenberg says: "I believe that even with failing memory and reduced intellectual capacities one still is able to write well, as long as one just doesn't
leave too much to the spur of the moment, but rather always
makes a note 'for future use' when reading or reflecting. All
great writers certainly proceeded in this manner." —No, you
are no old man, for you leave things to the spur of the moment!
"Popularization always should be done in such a way that
people are elevated by it. If one condescends, then one always
should remember to elevate, even just a little, those people to
whom one has condescended."
"A simple style is preferable, if only because no upstanding
man expresses himself in affected and complicated speech."

"I tend always to feel more affection for the man who writes in a manner that can become fashionable than for one who writes in a manner that is fashionable." "So very much depends on how something is expressed that I believe it possible for the most
5 common things to be expressed in such a way that another person would have to believe the devil had given him that idea."

27 [26]
David Strauss as Writer and Wizard with Words.

27 [27]
Schopenhauer: "That is why such improvers of language, regardless of who they are, must be castigated like schoolboys.
10 Therefore, let every well-meaning and insightful person join me in taking sides with the German language and against German stupidity."

27 [28]
They are *crass empiricists*: our *schools* are wholly inadequate. Our plight cannot get any worse. Police *prohibition* of any *news-*
15 *paper* that contains the slightest grammatical error.

27 [29]
The effects of Hegel and Heine. The latter destroys the feeling for a unified stylistic tone and is infatuated with the motley mixture of colors characteristic of the clown's outfit. His ideas, his images, his observations, his words do not fit together,
20 but he is a virtuoso who has mastered every kind of style in order to jumble them together. With Hegel, the most worthless gray, with Heine, the shimmering of electric kaleidoscopes that place a terrible strain on the eyes, as does that gray, as well. Just think of everything in Hegel and Heine as mimicry.
25 The former a *factor*, the latter a *farceur*.

27 [30]

The horrible destruction caused by Hegelianism! Even those who knew how to free themselves from it, like Strauss, never can be fully cured.

Strauss experienced two misfortunes: first, he fell into the clutches of Hegelianism, and that disoriented him at a time when a serious philosopher should have been giving him direction. And then his adversaries deluded him into believing that his cause was a popular one and he himself a popular writer. As a result of this, he never was able to stop being a theologian and never was permitted to become once more a strict adherent to his scholarly discipline. To be sure, he tried his hardest to jettison Hegel and everything theological: in vain. The first makes itself evident in his tritely optimistic view of the world, which sees the Prussian state as the aim of world history; the second in his angry invectives against Christianity. He has nothing to lean on and throws himself into the arms of the state and of success; his entire manner of thinking is not *sub specie aeternitatis* but rather *decennii vel biennii*. Thus, he becomes a "classical writer for the rabble," like Büchner, etc.

27 [31]

Unusquisque mavult credere quam judicare.

Seneca.

27 [32]

Anyone who knows what pains the ancients took and how the moderns take no pains at all soon makes it a principle never to read this riffraff again.

First one has to have something to say and must believe that one can say it better than anyone else. Hence all its elements must be thought through and found to be coherent.

The first draft has no value other than to establish the general development and the dimensions, the *totum ponere*: to be sure, this is essential for the content: usually the correct tones also are established. At this point, the whole is still full of in-

numerable defects, here and there are provisional partitions or "scaffolds," everywhere you turn there is dust, everywhere the signs of ongoing labor and of problems are visible. All of *this* necessary labor is lacking in Strauss's text: even if one assumes
5 that the *totum ponere* was a success.

The *totum ponere* is a success to the extent that the entire book at least paints a picture of *one* sort of human being, and it paints it in such a way that all the inconsistencies and inadequacies are part of the picture. It is, of course, supposed to portray a faith,
10 not a philosophy, and for that reason it need not be ashamed of its brainlessness, since what counts, above all, is its ethos. This ethos displays courage to the extent that this suits the philistine, that is, in matters of religion, in natural-scientific claims, etc. Otherwise, namely, in his doctrine on life, it is just the
15 opposite, everything that exists is considered rational: a few pious wishes, the abolition of universal suffrage, retention of capital punishment, limitation of the right to strike, and introduction of *Nathan* and *Hermann and Dorothea* in grade school— that's all, for the rest "we live and go our way in bliss!"

27 [33]
20 He misunderstood what it means for the work of great authors to be scantily clad: they merely desired a simple garden house; Str⟨auss⟩'s ponderous design already goes against this, what is lacking is precisely ease and grace. What is superficial and incomplete is far from being simple.

27 [34]
25 Strauss exploits nature's adherence to laws and rationality for the purposes of deception. He does indeed need a complete cosmodicy.

"Ordained by God," that is, "according to nature"!
You coquettish dotard! Flighty schoolmaster!

27 [35]

Lessing has the powerful, restless, eternally playful strength of a young tiger, which is visible everywhere in its bulging muscles.

The new faith cannot move mountains, but it can misplace
5 words. (On his style.)

27 [36]

You will have to admit that I do not turn to the "higher powers" when I do battle with you.

27 [37]

We speak of geological and Darwin⟨istic⟩ processes: in this, we conceive the subject as eternal. It also is wholly impossible
10 to conceive of these processes without it. All the natural sciences unconsciously assume the unity of the subject, its eternity and immutability. Our brain, our eye are already an *extra nos* or *praeter nos*: the world is not a quality produced by the brain, rather, the brain itself is a part of these sensations and repre-
15 sentations. It is not the brain that thinks, but we who think the brain: which in itself has no reality whatsoever. Sensation is the only cardinal fact with which we are acquainted, the only true quality. All the laws of nature can be reduced to laws of motion: wholly without substance. Once this is accomplished,
20 the only thing we have established are the laws of sensation. Nothing at all is thereby gained for the "in itself."

The ideality of the world is not merely a hypothesis, but rather the most concrete, the sole fact. It is senseless to believe that sensation ever will be able to be explained on the basis
25 of motion or, for that matter, on the basis of anything else. Sensation cannot be explained on the basis of something else, since there is nothing else at all.

27 [38]

Where Heine and Hegel have both had an influence—as, for example, in the case of Auerbach (even if not directly)—

and, in addition, due to national reasons a natural foreignness enters the German language, the result is a jargon that is deplorable in every word, every phrase.

27 [39]
Strauss says: "It would be a sign of ingratitude toward my genius if I were not to take pleasure in the fact that, along with the talent for relentlessly incisive critique, I was simultaneously endowed with the ability to enjoy the innocent pleasure of artistic creation." "People have paid me the *unsolicited* honor of regarding me as a kind of classical prose writer." Indeed, you certainly did not solicit it, but instead refrained from doing all that was necessary to become one.

"Our age, which views the formless as sublime" to be applied ironically to Strauss.

Merck: "you don't have to produce such trash any longer; others can do that just as well." Afterword, p. 10. One of my friends assembled a collection of classical stylistic examples from Voltaire.

27 [40]
The "*kingdom of Prussia*" seems to have supplanted the "*kingdom of God*."

27 [41]
The *intentional superficiality*—he can do everything better. Riehlian *House Music*.

It is absolutely essential that we hear powerful, provocative *orators*—instead of bad preachers. Enormous task of art!

It is extremely unreasonable and at least as mad to cling to the *reason* of the universe as one's religion as it is to maintain that one and one are three—a faith.

What Strauss says against the antinomy of infinity is terribly stupid. He doesn't even understand what it is about.

27 [42]

Strauss, p. 10: "We *half-dreamily* think up many things within us that, once we try to express them in the fixed form of words and sentences, *do not fit together*."

27 [43]

The religious reaction: "he sticks himself."

27 [44]

Strauss, p. 11. "In addition, however, we want to find out whether this modern world view serves the same ends for us, and whether it serves them better or worse, as the ends Christianity served for those of the old faith; whether it is better or less suited to serve as the foundation for the edifice of a truly human, that is, moral and thereby happy life." Answer can be found on p. 366: "Anyone who cannot help himself is simply beyond help and is not yet ripe for our standpoint."

It is supposed to be a catechism of *modern ideas*; "he wants to point in the direction in which, in his opinion, we will discover firm ground" — "namely, the modern world view, the laboriously achieved result of continued research into nature and history." Subsequently he opposes the old faith to the new science. *Art* and *philosophy* are ignored.

27 [45]

"Role" p. 35 twice, p. 143.

"No one marches in lockstep down an unknown path along which lie a thousand abysses." But does one then have to pretend to be skipping along?

27 [46]

The philistine who believes himself to be, or acts like, a genius.

27 [47]

Courage and consistency.

Heine, Hegel, sense of style.

totum ponere and his execution.
Lack of philosophy.
Art.
Christianity.
5   He uses aristocratic *genius* the way Bismarck uses social de-
         moc⟨rac⟩y: but Strauss against the social democrats in
         favor of the bourgeoisie, extremely reluctantly.
     He runs like a column of smoke in front of his "we."

27 [48]
     "Thoughts displaying the agility of toads."

27 [49]
10   The philistine who wants to act like a genius.

In moral matters.	To what extent courage and consistency?
In intellectual matters.	Scantily clad in the manner of Voltaire.
	Abstains from philosophy.
	Praises (Kant), recommends, reproaches as genius.
	Classical in art.
In literary matters.	Emancipates himself from Heine, Hegel, but in what way!
	Wants to create a gospel of new ideas.
	Genius in the plan of the book!
	The execution.
	Defects.

     Effect on youth.

27 [50]
     Schopenhauer would say about Strauss: an author who does
not even deserve to be leafed through, let alone studied: ex-

cept for someone interested in measuring the degree of apathy
present today.

27 [51]
    Empedocles says of the Agrigentians: they clung to their de-
sires as though they expected to die the very next day, and they
5 built things as though they never would die. Strauss builds as
though his book were going to die tomorrow, and he behaves
as if it should never, ever die.

27 [52]
    Emergence of the philistine of cultivation. Generally cul-
tivation always only in very exclusive circles. The philistine
10 prop⟨er⟩ kept his distance from it. The scholar formed a transition, he believed in classical antiquity, he regarded artists
as questionable creatures. Hegel was responsible for creating
a great deal of interest in aesthetics at the universities. The
readers of the almanac are the principal public, evening news-
15 paper. In the 1850s the realists, Julian Schmidt. Gradually the
public interested in popular lectures emerges, as a force to be
reckoned with; it has sympathies, expectations, etc. The philistine has no sense of the flaws of culture and of the experimentation done by people like Schiller and Goethe. His point of
20 departure is a vehement chauvinism. The overhasty judgment
of Hegel and his followers produced the belief that we have
reached the zenith.

27 [53]
        1. Whether German culture was victorious?
        2. The cultivated philistine and culture.
25   3. The confession of faith made by such a philistine.
        4. How he lives.
        5. His courage to praise and reproach, and to be optimistic.
        6. Limits of his courage.
        7. A religion for scholars.

8. Politically fashionable, *sub specie biennii*.

9. Contemporary style.

10. Strauss's *totum ponere*.

11. His style in detail.

5   12. Conclusion.

27 [54]

It must be forcefully noted that our universities have absolutely no significance for art. Strauss as a thoroughly unaesthetic person.

27 [55]

What ultimately emerged from this wild brew of philosophy, 10 Romanticism, and experimentation of all sorts was a tremendous certainty in matters of destruction and condemnation, based on extensive practice — and thereby, in turn, a certain confidence on the part of those who are *not culturally productive* in their *own culture* as an absolute standard. What was the posi- 15 tive side of this? A *certain contentedness* that was opposed to all practical experimentation; contentedness with one's own life. Moreover, there were some gifted people who glorified this, the idyllic coziness of the German, of the scholar, etc. These *contented ones* then sought to appropriate the classical writers 20 and arrogantly to reject everything that was still productive and vital; they quietly sat down and invented the age of epigones. Otto Jahn and Mozart. The Ninth Symphony and Strauss. Gervinus and Shakespeare. Everything great was supposed to be understood historically. All vital energy manifested itself in the 25 realm of history, in the rejection and destruction of present-day degenerate impulses, for example, of orthodoxy. Religious liberalism was the prerequisite for everything. The historical impulse made all fanatacism impossible.

    1) It demands no changes, in education, etc.

30   2) It endows the scholar with superiority in matters of taste.

27 [56]

The *philistine* is precisely the ἄμουσος: it is remarkable to see
how *in spite of this* he arrives at the point of wanting to participate in the discussion of aesthetic and cultural issues. It seems
to me that the schoolteacher formed the transition here: he,
who for professional reasons was concerned with classical antiquity and who eventually began to believe that he must therefore also possess classical taste.

27 [57]

David Strauss, the Confessor and the Writer.

Unfashionable Observations
of a

Foreigner.

27 [58]

If polemical treatises are always admired only by those who
share their partisan point of view, then this treatise does not
have the slightest hope of being admired; and David Strauss
himself will be the last person to voice the accusation that in
this instance he is being refuted "amid the loud cheers of the
higher classes" and by means of these cheers. On the contrary, an attack like the one attempted here is likely to benefit
Strauss, and it will not damage its author simply because he has
chosen to remain anonymous. Following this introduction, let
the duel begin: and as witnesses I wish none other than those
people who are partial to Dr. Strauss's book of confessions and
who will be happy if the challenger voluntarily assumes a weak
position from the outset. And what position could be weaker
than that of an isolated foreigner who turns the general *German success* of this book into a reproach of the Germans? And
who views it as the symptom of a degenerate culture?

27 [59]

Arrogance of a confession. Who
is confessing? A partisan group,
the we. Description of this "we."   Strauss as confessor
The cultivated philistine and his   about philistine
5 genesis. Strauss typical.   culture.

The writer.   As writer (he himself
By no means wants to appear   bears testimony to
to be a philistine.   philistine culture).

27 [60]

Was "German culture" victorious? No. But it believes it was.
10   It is easy to see how things stand with *cultivation*
        1) on the basis of these confessions themselves.
            a) from the fact that it ventures a confession at all.
            b) on the basis of the nature of the confessions.
        2) on the basis of the writer's workmanship: more direct.
15   Result. What it was victorious over. Not over French cul-
      ture, but instead over *German culture* and German genius.

27 [61]

Whether German culture was victorious?
The victorious cultivated philistine. His genesis.
Makes confessions.
20   His life, view of art.
      Philosophy presumption.
      His kind of courage.
      Religion of scholars.
      The classical writer.
25   Lightly clad.
      Samples of his style.

27 [62]
> Yes, if we were only dealing with a bad stylist!
> But the entire nation is shouting its approval!
> He speaks like someone who reads the newspapers every day.

27 [63]
> Health.
> The enthusiasm for what is anciently German was a contributing factor.
> The dry philistine is entitled only to sobriety and clarity; but Strauss has heard of the simplicity of genius! And that genius must make use of images, etc.

27 [64]
> 1872. First edition of the *Birth of Tragedy*.
> 1873. Second edition of the *Birth of Tragedy*.
>> Strauss.
>> Future of our Educational Institutions.
>> Pre-Platonic Philosophers.

27 [65]
> The cultural philistine does not know what *culture* is — *unity of style*.
> He is satisfied with the knowledge that there are classical authors (Schiller, Goethe, Lessing) and forgets that they *sought* a culture, but that they are not a foundation upon which one can rest.
> For that reason, he does not understand the earnestness of all the seekers after culture who are still alive today.
> He believes that life, that business must be segregated from the refreshment of cultural leisure. He is not acquainted with the type of culture that constantly makes demands.
> German authors are forced to fall back on the imitation of nature, moreover, of nature either as farmers or as city folk know it; in other words, on the idyll or the satire. They have

no natural relationship to the higher, *purer* forms because their reality is unartistic and lacks any exemplary models.

It is the age of the unstylized *arts of portraiture*, in short, of the *iconic* arts and of *iconic* historiography.

27 [66]

5 For the introduction. For us it is not Strauss's book that is an *event*, but merely his *success*. It does not contain a single thought that deserves to be called good and new.

We have no culture, but only civilization with a few cultural fashions; however, even more barbarism.

10 Even in language we have not yet established a *style*, but only carried out experiments.

A "culture" cannot have been victorious over French culture since we are just as dependent on it as we were before, and no changes have been wrought in French culture itself.

15 "The philistine who does not want to admit to being a barbarian," echoing Vischer's statement about Hölderlin.

You have no culture, not even a bad or degenerate one, for even it would still display a stylistic unity.

German "conversation" like German "oration" is imitated.
20 Our "salon" sociability, our parliamentary orators!

Where is there a foundation upon which one could erect a culture!

27 [67]

Echoing Heraclitus: To the genius (god), even the most intelligent philistine (human being) is an ape.

27 [68]

25 Difficulties in becoming a good writer.
   1) Lack of good oratory and training.
      Corruption of taste by means of public orations.
   2) In the schools, lack of practice in writing and ⟨of⟩ methodological rigor.
30 In spite of this, it is easy to win praise. Esp⟨ecially⟩ among

scholars. They don't look for the productive qualities, but pass judgment according to the *lack of anything offensive* and following a certain pedantic assumption about metaphors, liveliness.

Lessing seems suited for the theatrical dialogue of comedies. Herder pastoral, Goethe joy in telling stories, womanlike.

However, the "lack of anything offensive" has become more and more rare in our newspaper atmosphere: whereas the sensibility for what is offensive is diminishing. It is almost identical with sobriety and dryness, both of which already seem to guarantee that anything offensive will be lacking. Write in the same way that everyone in the world writes; in other words, like the journalists, and they always choose the first, the most convenient word.

Then, the images must be modern, for any others are regarded as old-fashioned.

The didactic element announces its presence in long sentences, the persuasive, brilliant aspect in short sentences.

Who is willing to write a definitive grammar of today's cosmopolitan German style? —That false notion of elegance! Where does it come from?

27 [69]

Hölderlin to Germany:

In silence yet you ponder a joyous work
    To testify of you, and withhold its shape
        That, like you, will be new, uniquely
            Born out of love and as good as you are—

        Where is your Delos, where your Olympia,
        For celebration that would conjoin us all?—
           How shall your son divine the gift that,
               Deathless one, long you have darkly fashioned?

27 [70]

False, p. 106: "people have long known that God, *omnipresent*, is not in need of a special abode."

p. 44: "in this way Schleiermacher, in his characteristic manner, again produces a godly human being."

The didactic by accumulating abstractions, the persuasive by mixing all tones, by "blending."

27 [71]

Next chapter: heaven of heavens — hero worship — Lessing.

27 [72]

Well-laundered rags are indeed clean things to wear, but rags all the same.

27 [73]

Mixed metaphors.

Truncations that lead to obscurity.

Tastelessness and stilted language.

Errors.

Foreword, p. 6: "he assured himself of broad support — against this impugnment."

p. 12.

27 [74]

More refined turns of phrase.

27 [75]

David Strauss,
the Confessor and the Writer.

Unfashionable Observations

by
Friedrich Nietzsche.

27 [76]

The sixth and fifth centuries of the Greeks.
Ethical — Political.

Aesthetic.
Philosophy.

27 [77]
All the natural sciences deal with the laws of sensation.
Sensation is not the work of the sense organs, rather, the
5 sense organs themselves are known to us only as sensations. It
is not the eye that sees, but rather we who see; it is not the brain
that thinks, but rather we who think. Eye and brain are given
to us absolutely only as sensations, in no way differently than
all things *extra nos.* Our body is likewise something outside us,
10 just like everything else, that is, it is likewise only known to us
as sensation, just like other things.

27 [78]
                              Preface.
A book that has gone through six large editions in the space
of a year can still be wholly worthless: but that is precisely why
15 it is important—indeed, necessary—for everyone who recognizes no higher concern than the concern for the people to
know that there really is such a large audience for this book.
Only the success of Strauss's book of confessions, not the book
itself, drove me to make the following observations. It could
20 not help but gradually become unbearable when I found nothing among all those objections to Strauss's book that was conceived in a general enough manner to be able to explain how
such an insignificant book could be such a scandalous success. When Goethe says that the opponents of a brilliant idea
25 beat the coals until they jump around and ignite, then in this
instance, at least, I am certain that I am not opposing a brilliant idea.

27 [79]
New.
   Second Piece: History.
30   *Plato and Predecessors.*

Three Treatises.
2nd Ed⟨ition⟩
   First Piece: *Strauss.*
   Birth of Tragedy.

27 [80]

5   *For the concluding chapter.*
   The age can make no more dangerous change in direction
than moving from self-irony to cynicism.

27 [81]
   History—weakens the ability to act and makes one blind to
the *exemplary*, confuses by means of sheer quantity.
10   *Wasted energy*, invested in what is entirely *past.*
   The *historical illness as the enemy of culture.*
   Exaggeration is a symptom of the barbaric. We exaggerate
the drive for knowledge.
   Only the elderly live in sheer memories.
15   Not respect for history; instead, you should have the courage to *make* history!

[28 = Mp XIII 1. Spring–Autumn 1873]

28 [1]

The scholarly person is a genuine paradox: all around he is faced with the most horrible problems, he saunters past abysses and he picks a flower in order to count its filaments. It is not apathy with regard to knowledge: for he has a burning desire to acquire knowledge and discover things, and he knows no greater pleasure than increasing the store of knowledge. But he behaves like the proudest idler upon whom fortune ever smiled, as if existence were not something hopeless and questionable, but rather a firm possession guaranteed to last forever.

Moreover, at the present time he has begun to work at such a frantic pace that one must imagine scholarship as a factory in which for any delay of mere minutes the scholarly laborer deserves to be punished. He labors, he no longer pursues a calling, he looks neither left nor right and goes through all the matters of life, even those that are questionable in nature, with the half-attention or with the odious need for rest and recreation characteristic of the exhausted laborer. He behaves as if for him life were only *otium*, but *otium sine dignitate*; like a slave who even in his dreams does not throw off this yoke. Perhaps we will have assessed the great mass of scholars correctly if we initially view them as farmers: with a tiny inherited property, diligently occupied day and night in planting the field, pulling the plow, and prodding the oxen.

Pascal believes that human beings pursue their occupations
and their scholarship and science so zealously so as to flee from
those questions that every moment of solitude forces upon
them—those questions about the whence? the how? and the
whither? But it is even more amazing that the most obvious
questions do not even occur to them: What is the purpose of
this labor? What is the purpose of this frantic pace? What is
the purpose of this frenzy? Perhaps to earn one's bread? No.
And yet in the manner of those who must earn their bread.
All scholarship is useless claptrap as soon as the human being
treats it in the same manner he treats tasks of labor foisted
upon him by need and the afflictions of life. Culture is possible
without your scholarship; as is demonstrated by the Greeks.
Mere curiosity is not worthy of such a lofty name. As long as
you do not understand how to mix in the appropriate dose
of crude experience, philosophy, and art to counteract your
scholarly life, then you will be just as unworthy of culture as
you are incapable of it. A future generation will be paralyzed
at the sight of the uniformity of your actual lives and thoughts:
how meager and impoverished is your actual experience of the
world, how bookish your judgments. Some disciplines allow
themselves to be stampeded by herds of scholars, others do
not; and it is precisely the latter that you avoid. Just think of
your scholarly organizations, just look how they are made up of
exhaustion, the need for diversion, and literary reminiscences.
Scholarship itself has entered a period of decline, in spite of
all its methods and instruments: and your great universities
with their impressive apparatuses, their laboratories and spec-
tatories, spectators and laborers—they remind one of arsenals
replete with enormous cannons and other weapons of war: we
are horrified at the preparations, but in actual war no one has
any use for such machines. That's how things are for the great
universities: they stand apart from all culture, but, by contrast,
are open to all the questionable movements of contemporary
nonculture. A professor is a being whose lack of cultivation and
crude sense of taste simply can be taken for granted, as long as

he has not demonstrated otherwise. When I think of the vulgarity of your political or theological views—or even worse,
of the views promoted by Protestant organizations; or when I
think of your philological studies, pursued with the intention
of weakening the classical models; your Indic studies, which
lack any connection with Hindu philosophy; when I think of
the stir that such bad books as David Strauss's cause among you
and that other books have not caused, when I think about how
your professors pursue aesthetics, how in the discipline of art
your universities have only reached the level of men's choruses,
how stolidly you stay away from all productive forces—then at
least I know that you do not deserve any more compassion,
you are the laborers in the factory—but where culture is concerned, you can be viewed only as impediments.

28 [2]

I.   *Introduction.* What is a philosopher capable of accomplishing with regard to the culture of his people?
— He seems to be   a) an indifferent recluse
                     b) a teacher of the hundred most
                        brilliant and abstract minds
                     c) or a hostile destroyer of popular
                        culture.
— With regard to b), the effect is only indirect, but it is
there, as it is with c).
— With regard to a), it certainly seems that, due to the
purposelessness of nature, he will remain a recluse. Still, his work remains for later ages. And
yet we must ask whether he was necessary for his
age.
— Does he have a *necessary* relationship to the people, is
there a teleology of the philosopher?
— In order to answer this, we have to know something
about what we call his "age": this can be a meager
or a very considerable age.
— Primary thesis: he can *create no culture*,

but he can pave the way for one,
   remove impediments,
or moderate and thereby preserve it, ⎫ always
or destroy it.   ⎬ only
                                      ⎭ negating.

A philosopher's *positivis never* have caused the
   people to follow him. For he dwells in the
   cult of the intellect.

With regard to all the *positivis* of a culture, of a
   religion, he has a *disintegrative, destructive* effect
   (even when he seeks to *found* something).

He is most useful when there is *much to be destroyed*, in times of chaos or degeneration.

Every flourishing culture strives to make the philosopher
   unnecessary (or else to isolate him completely).

     This isolation or atrophy can be explained in
     two ways:

     on the basis of the purposelessness of nature
     (at those times when he is needed), on the
     basis of the purposive caution of nature (at
     those times when he is not needed).

II. His destructive and curtailing effects—on what?

III. Now—since there is no culture, he must pave the way
    (destroy)—what?

IV. The attacks on philosophy.

V. Philosophers atrophied.

    Both consequences of the purposelessness of nature,
    which destroys countless seeds: and yet it nevertheless
    successfully brings forth a few great things: Kant and
    Schopenhauer.

VI. Kant and Schopenhauer. The progression to a freer cul-
    ture made in the development from one to the other.

    Schopenhauer's teleology with respect to a future culture.

    His doubly positive philosophy (it lacks a living, cen-
    tral germ)—a conflict only for those who have ceased
    to hope.

How the future culture will overcome this conflict. Olympians. Mysteries. Popular festivals.

28 [3]
  6:100   17
     6

—
5   40   9 green sheets for each chapter.

28 [4]

Everything that is *generally significant* about a scholarly discipline has become either *accidental* or is *entirely absent.*

The study of language, without the principles of style and
rhetoric.

10 Indic studies, without philosophy.

Classical antiquity, without any connection to the practical
endeavor of learning something from it.

Natural science, without any of the healing and repose that
Goethe discovered in it.

15 History, without enthusiasm.

In short, all the scholarly disciplines, without any practical application: hence pursued in a manner different from the
manner in which they have been pursued by genuinely cultured
human beings. Scholarship as breadwinning occupation!

28 [5]

20 You pursue *philosophy* with young, inexperienced people; your
older people turn to history. You have no popular philosophy
whatsoever; instead, you have disgracefully uniform popular
lecture courses. Essay contests proposed by universities for students, about Schopenhauer! Popular lectures about Schopen-
25 hauer! This is lacking in all dignity. It is possible to explain *how
scholarship* could have become what it is today only on the basis
of the development of religion.

28 [6]

On *Schopenhauer*. Ridiculous to imagine him at a present-day
university.

His eudaemonological doctrine, like Horace's, is for experienced men; his other, pessimistic doctrine is nothing for
present-day human beings: at most they will read their own
dissatisfactions into it and when they rediscover them there
believe that they have refuted Schopenhauer. This entire "culture" appears so unspeakably childish, as does the rejoicing
after the war. He is simple and honest: he seeks no empty clichés. What power all his conceptions have, the will, negation,
the portrayal of the genius of the species. There is no disquiet
in his portrayal, but rather the clear depths of a lake when it is
tranquil or experiencing light waves. He is crude like Luther.
He is the most rigorous ideal of a writer that the Germans possess, no one went about it as rigorously as he did. One can see
how dignified he is on the example of his imitator Hartmann.
Infinite greatness to have once again grasped the ground of
existence, no scholarly digressing, no lingering in scholasticism. The study of the others is interesting because they immediately arrive at the place where scholarly knowledge is permitted, but they go no further. He demolishes secularization,
and likewise the barbarizing power of the sciences. He arouses
the most enormous need: just as Socrates was such an arouser
of need. But the latter summoned science; the former religion
and art. People had forgotten what religion was, as they had
forgotten the relationship of art to life. It was pessimism that
made these two things comprehensible again. But just how
profound the new religion must be can be seen in: 1) the fact
that the idea of immortality disappears, along with the fear of
death; 2) the entire segregation of soul and body; 3) the insight
that we cannot escape the misery of existence by means of palliative measures: much more radical; 4) the relationship with a
god is gone; 5) pity (not love of the self, but rather the unity of
all living and suffering beings). Opposite of culture, if religion
no longer should be possible. Tragic resignation.

Schopenhauer stands in contradiction with everything that today *passes for* "culture": Plato with everything that *was* culture at that time. Schopenhauer was catapulted ahead of his time: today, we already have an inkling of his mission. He is the destroyer of those forces that are hostile to culture, he discloses once again the profound foundations of existence. Thanks to him, the cheerfulness of art once again will become possible.

29 [1]

 To speak the truth without a eudaemonological *purpose*;
purely out of a sense of duty. In such instances one frequently
forgets the peculiar *pleasure* that accompanies the expression of
t⟨ruth⟩. The purest instance is the one in which truth is accom-
5 panied by a *much greater displeasure*, even one's own demise —
and in spite of this, one speaks the truth. A statesman decides
the fate of a state with a single word: he speaks the truth and
destroys the state. Kant's speech addressed to duty. A great
human being is worth more than an empire because he has a
10 more salutary effect for all of posterity. The meaning of the
great action—to produce great actions.

29 [2]

 Analysis of the sense of truth commonly found among
scholars. Lie as a defense mechanism, necessary lie possesses a
eudaemonological character: it seeks to rescue the individual.

29 [3]

15 Element of *impossibility* inherent in all *virtues* that make the
human being great.

29 [4]

 1. Truth as duty—pernicious truth. Analysis of the drive for
truth—pathos.

2. The element of impossibility in the virtues.

3. The human being has not sprung from these supreme drives, his entire being evinces a more lax morality; when adhering to the purest morality he leaps beyond his own nature.

4. Lies a part of human nature — dream, for example, self-consciousness (concealing the truth).

5. Language, sensation, concepts.

6. Matter.

7. Art. Necessary lies and voluntary lies. The latter still must be derived from some form of necessity.

All lies are necessary lies. The pleasure of lying is artistic. Otherwise, only truth has pleasure in itself. Artistic pleasure the greatest kind because it speaks the truth quite generally in the form of lies.

Concept of personality, indeed, that of moral freedom as well, are necessary illusions, so that even our drives for truth rest on the foundation of lies.

Truth in the system of *pessimism*. It would be better if thought did not exist at all.

29 [5]

Ika! Ika! Bäh-Bäh-

29 [6]

Benjamin Constant: "The fundamental moral principle, which states that it is a duty to speak the truth, would, if one interpreted it absolutely and independent of any context, make every society impossible."

The Hungarian and the Hegelian professor in Berlin.

Rameau's Nephew. "One gulps down the flattering lie in full draughts, and only swallows drop by drop the bitter truth."

29 [7]

"Truth."

1. Considered as an unconditional duty, truth hostile, destroys the world.
2. Analysis of the common sense of truth (inconsistency).
3. The pathos of truth.
4. The impossible as a corrective for the human being.
5. The foundation of the human being mendacious because optimistic.
6. The world of the body.
7. Individuals.
8. Forms.
9. Art. Hostility toward it.
10. Without untruth there can be neither society nor culture. The tragic conflict. Everything that is good and beautiful depends on illusion: truth kills—indeed, it kills itself (insofar as it recognizes that its foundation is error).

29 [8]

1. What corresponds to *asceticism* with regard to truth? — Truthfulness, as the foundation of all compacts and the prerequisite for the survival of the human race, is a eudaemonistic demand: it is opposed by the knowledge that the supreme welfare of human beings lies rather in *illusions*: that is, that according to the fundamental principle of eudaemonism, truth *and lies* would have to be employed—as, in fact, is actually the case. Concept of the *forbidden truth*, that is, a truth whose function is to *conceal* and *disguise* precisely the eudaemonistic lie. Opposite: the *forbidden lie*, which occurs in the realm governed by permitted truth.

2. Symbol of forbidden truth: *fiat veritas, pereat mundus*. Symbol of forbidden lie: *fiat mendacium! pereat mundus*.

The first thing that perishes from forbidden truths is the individual who expresses them. The last thing that perishes from forbidden lie is the individual. In the first instance, the individual sacrifices itself along with the world, in the second instance, it sacrifices the world to itself and its existence.

Casuistry: Is it permissible to sacrifice humanity to truth? —1) It is probably not possible. I wish to God that humanity were able to die from truth! 2) If it were possible, it would be a good death and a liberation from life. 3) Without a certain amount of *delusion*, no one can firmly believe that he is in possession of truth: skepticism will not be far behind. The question concerning whether it is permissible to sacrifice humanity to a *delusion* would have to be answered in the negative. But in practice ⟨this⟩ happens, since the belief in truth is nothing but a delusion.

3. The belief in truth—or the delusion. Elimination of all *eudaemonistic* components (1. as my own belief; 2. as discovered by me; 3. as the source of other people's good opinions about me, of fame, of popularity; 4. as imperious feeling of pleasure in contrariety).

After we take away all these components, is the expression of truth purely as a *duty* still possible? Analysis of the *belief in truth*: for all possession of truth is basically nothing but the belief that one possesses the truth. The pathos, the sense of duty, originate with *this belief*, not with the alleged truth. This belief presupposes that the individual has an *unconditional* **power** *of knowledge*, thus the conviction that *no cognizant being* ever will progress further in the sphere of cognition: hence its binding nature for the entire range of cognizant beings. The *relation* suspends the pathos of belief, for example, the restriction to what is human, with the skeptical supposition that perhaps all of us err.

But how is *skepticism* possible? It appears to be the truly *ascetic* standpoint of the cognizant being. For it does not believe in belief and thereby destroys everything that benefits from belief.

However, even skepticism contains a belief: the belief in logic. The most extreme position is hence the abandoning of logic, the *credo quia absurdum est*, doubts about reason and its negation. How this occurs in the wake of asceticism. No one

can *live* with these doubts, just as they cannot live in pure asceticism. Whereby it is proven that belief in logic and belief as
such are necessary for life, and hence that the realm of thought
is eudaemonistic. But that is when the demand for lies arises:
namely, when life and εὐδαιμονία are used as arguments. Skepticism turns against the forbidden truths. Then the foundation
for pure truth in itself is lacking, the drive for truth is merely
a disguised eudaemonistic drive.

4. Every natural process is fundamentally inexplicable to
us: in every instance all we can do is establish the scenic backdrop against which the actual drama unfolds. We then speak of
causalities, whereas all we in principle really perceive is a sequence of events. That this sequence always must occur in the
context of a particular scenic backdrop is a belief that is refuted an infinite number of times.

5. Logic is merely slavery in the fetters of language. But language contains an illogical element, metaphor, etc. The first
power effects an identification of the nonidentical and is hence
a product of the imagination. This is the basis for the existence
of concepts, forms, etc.

6. Forms.

7. "Laws of nature." Nothing but relations to one another
and relations to the human being.

8. The human being as the finished and rigidified *measure of
things*. As soon as we conceive him as fluid and vacillating, the
rigidity of the laws of nature disappears. The laws of sensation
—as the core of the laws of nature. Mechanics of motion. The
belief, in natural science, in the external world, and in the past.

9. The truest things in this world—love, religion, and art.
The first of these sees through all dissimulation and disguises,
it penetrates to the core, the suffering individual, and suffers
along with him; the last of these, as practical love, gives consolation for this suffering by telling about another world order
and teaching us to disdain this one. They are the three illogical
powers, which admit to being such.

"on the arid stone desert of the decaying planet earth"

29 [9]

Penzel, recruited by Prussian recruiters, was a common infantryman in Königsberg. Kant prevents him from assuming a professorial post; "(Kant) by regarding him as a vile human being because he so calmly tolerated his position as a soldier." A passage in Luther to the effect that if God had thought of heavy artillery, he would never have created the world.

29 [10]

Analysis of the *Scholar with Respect to His*
Sense of Truth.

1) Habit; 2) flight from boredom; 3) breadwinning occupation; 4) respect from other scholars, fear of their disrespect; 5) sense for the acquisition of something that is his own (it must be "true," otherwise the others will steal it back); tying and untying little knots. — *Limits to their sense of truth*: when an old theory is overturned; when their profession, their education are attacked; when those who are not members of the guild make their views known; hatred of philosophy because it thinks nothing of the scholar. Untruth, if it is universally accepted, is treated by the scholar as truth. Fear of religions and governments. —7) A certain apathy, they do not see the *consequences* and are pitiless. 8) They fail to notice the primary problems of life, and for that reason they concern themselves with the tiniest little problems, that is, in all *important matters they have no need for truth*. That is why a republic of scholars never has existed, but instead merely an *ochlocracy of scholars*. The rare brilliant mind, the friend of truth, and likewise the artist are hated and ostracized.

29 [11]

Doesn't the absolute agreement between logic and mathematics point to the existence of a brain, of a guiding organ whose development is abnormal—to reason? to a soul? —It is only by dint of what is absolutely *subjective* that we are—*human beings*. It is the accumulated inheritance that all of us share.

29 [12]

Natural science is a coming to self-consciousness about all
the things one has inherited, a ledger containing all the fixed
and rigid laws of sensation.

29 [13]

The Scholar.

5   1. *A certain integrity*, almost mere inflexibility when it comes
to the art of dissimulation, since this requires a certain amount
of cleverness. Wherever the dialectical manner of the lawyer
is present, one should have doubts about this integrity and be
wary. It is easier to speak the truth in *adiaphoris*, it is in keep-
10 ing with a certain indolence. For example, it was nothing other
than integrity that objected to the Copernican system because
it went against common sense: common sense and truth are
always one and the same for indolent minds. Even the hatred of
philosophy among scholars is above all hatred of long chains
15 of reasoning and the artificiality of proof: the admiration of
sagacity is combined with fear, and every generation of scholars basically establishes a limit for *permissible* sagacity: whatever
transcends this limit is rejected.

     2. *Keenness of sight for whatever is close by*, with intense myo-
20 pia for whatever is remote and general. The field of vision
is usually quite small, and he must press his eyes very close
to what he is viewing. If the scholar wants to proceed from
one point of investigation to another, he must shift his entire
visual apparatus to that point: he dissects a picture, like some-
25 one using opera glasses, into nothing but blotches of color.
He never *sees* them in connection, but instead only calculates
their interrelation; that is why he has no strong impression of
anything general. For example, a piece of writing that he is incapable of viewing as a whole he judges based on a blotch from
30 the sphere of his studies; he would be the first to maintain, due
to his manner of seeing, that an oil painting is nothing but a
wild mass of splotches.

     3. *Normality of his motivations*, sobriety, insofar as in all ages

the more common characters, and thus the masses, were guided by the same motivations. A mole feels most at home in a molehill. Here he is protected from any artificial and abnormal hypotheses and above all from extravagant ones, and if he is persistent, he digs up, due to his own commonness, all the common motives of the past. To be sure, this is why he is incapable of understanding what is rare, great, and abnormal, that is, what is *important* and *essential*.

4. *Poverty of feeling* even makes them capable of performing vivisections. He has no inkling of the suffering that goes hand in hand with certain kinds of knowledge, and hence is not afraid of venturing into the most dangerous regions. The mule has never known dizziness. They are cold, and that makes them seem slightly cruel, without actually being such.

5. *Low self-esteem*, even modesty. Even in the most paltry area of studies, scholars have no sense of wasted effort, not even of having made sacrifices, they sense in their innermost being that they are creatures never meant to fly, but only to crawl. In this they are often pathetic.

6. *Loyalty* to their teachers and mentors; scholars want to help them, and they know quite well that they can best do this with the truth. They feel gratitude toward them because they know that it is only on account of their teachers that they themselves have been accepted into the hallowed halls of scholarship, into which they would never have gained entrance on their own. Anyone in Germany who can open up a field of study in which inferior minds are able to work will become a famous man; that's how large the swarm will immediately be. Of course, everyone in this swarm is simultaneously the caricature of the master in one sense or another: even his faults appear as caricatures, disproportionately large and exaggerated, exhibited in a much more insignificant individual: whereas the master's virtues exhibited in this same individual appear proportionately small. To that extent it is a deformity, and, as such, if this arises from loyalty, it has a pathetic-humorous effect.

7. *Routine* plodding along that path onto which the scholar has been pushed: a sense of truth stemming from lack of thought and the convenience of following the force of habit. This is especially true of the way they *learn*, which many, based on their experiences in secondary school, pursue as though in the grip of an inescapable necessity. Such natures are compilers, commentators, makers of indexes and herbaria, etc. Their diligence arises almost out of indolence, their thought out of thoughtlessness.

8. *Flight from boredom.* Whereas the true thinker longs for nothing more than leisure, the scholar flees from it because he does not know what to do with it. He finds his comfort in books: that means, he listens to other people thinking and thereby manages to entertain himself and keep himself entertained throughout the long day. He chooses in particular those books that somehow arouse his interest, his personal will, that stir him a little by invoking his likes and dislikes; writings that have to do with the scholar, or with his class, his political or aesthetic or grammatical opinions: once he has his own scholarly discipline, he also has the means to become interested again and again.

9. *Breadwinning.* Truth is served if it is capable of leading to a higher position and a higher income, if it makes one able to procure advancement with one's superiors. But it is precisely only *this* truth that is served, and this is why a line can be drawn between profitable truth and unprofitable t⟨ruth⟩. The latter does not have a beneficial effect where breadwinning is concerned, and since it expends effort and time that could be invested in the former, even works *against* breadwinning. *Ingenii largitor venter*. The "borborygmus of the empty stomach."

10. *Respect* from one's fellow scholars, fear of their disrespect. All of them zealously keep each other under surveillance so that truth, on which so much depends—honor, breadwinning, tenure—is accurately christened in the name of its discoverer. Tribute is paid to the truth discovered by someone else, because one demands the same in the case of the

truth one has discovered oneself. Untruth is noisily exploded
in order that it not be regarded as truth and lay claim to honors and titles that should be bestowed only upon irresistible
truth. Sometimes even real truth is exploded, so that at least
room can be made for other truths that are clamoring for recognition. "Moral idiocies that are called mischievous pranks."
"Exceptions to universally accepted knowledge."

11. The *scholar* out of vanity, a somewhat rarer variation. He
wants to have something all to himself and therefore chooses
curiosities and is pleased if he himself is curiously regarded as
a curiosity. He is usually satisfied with this type of veneration
and does not base his livelihood on such a drive for truth.

12. *The scholar just for the fun of it.* He amuses himself by seeking out and resolving knotty little problems—whereby, so that
he does not lose the feeling of having fun, he must not exert
himself too much. This is why he fails to go into things very
deeply, and yet he oftentimes sees things that the bread-and-
butter scholar, with his dull and laboriously crawling biased
eye, never perceives: at least he enjoys truth and is a dilettante,
and to this extent represents the opposite of the joyless bread-
and-butter scholar, who only accomplishes his work by dint of
force and, as it were, under the yoke of the paying occupation
or the lashings of his own mania for promotion.

29 [14]

There is no drive for knowledge and truth, but only a drive
for belief in truth. Pure knowledge has no drive.

29 [15]

Drives that are easily confused with the drive for truth:

1. *Curiosity*, or even the *search for* intellectual *adventures*. What
is new, rare as opposed to what is old and boring.

2. *Dialectical* drive for the *sport of tracking things down*, joy in
foxily cunning trains of thought: it is not truth that is sought,
but the sly stalking, surrounding, etc.

3. *Drive to contradiction*; the personality seeks to assert itself

in opposition to someone else. As with exhibition fencers, struggle becomes a pleasure, personal victory is the goal.

4. *Drive motivated by servility* to people, religions, governments, to discover *certain* "truths."

5. *Drive motivated by love*, pity, etc. for a human being, class, or humanity as a whole, to find a redeeming, beatifying truth — drive motivating founders of religions.

29 [16]

All drives associated with pleasure and displeasure — there can be no drive for truth, that is, for absolutely inconsequential, pure, dispassionate truth, for there pleasure and displeasure would cease, and there is no drive that does not anticipate pleasure in its own satisfaction. *The pleasure of thinking* does not point to a desire for truth. The pleasure of all sense perception⟨s⟩ lies in the fact that they are achieved by means of *inferences*. To this extent, the human being constantly is swimming in a sea of pleasure. But to what extent can the *inference*, the *logical operation, provide pleasure*?

29 [17]

How is art as lie even possible!

When closed, my eyes see within themselves countless changing images — imagination produces them, and I know that they do not correspond to reality. Thus, I believe in them only as images, not as realities.

Surfaces, forms.

Art includes the joy of awakening belief by means of surfaces: but one isn't really being deceived? For if so, it would cease to be art!

Art's aim is deception — but we are not deceived?

What is the source of the pleasure we take in the attempted deception, in the semblance that is always recognized to be semblance?

Art thus treats *semblance as semblance*, precisely does *not* want to deceive, *is true*.

Pure, disinterested viewing is possible only in the instance of semblance that is recognized to be semblance, that in no way wants to seduce us into belief and to this extent does not stimulate our will at all.

5   Only someone capable of viewing the entire world *as semblance* would be able to look at it without desire and drive — artist and philosopher. This is where drive ceases.

As long as one seeks truth in the world, one is ruled by drives: but such a person desires *pleasure*, and not truth, he wants the
10 belief in truth, that is, the pleasurable effects of this belief.

The world as semblance — saint, artist, philosopher.

29 [18]

All eudaemonistic drives awaken belief in the truth of things, of the world — thus all of science — directed toward becoming, not toward being.

29 [19]

15   Plato as a prisoner of war, offered for sale at a slave market — Why do human beings even want philosophers? — From this we can draw conclusions about why they want truth.

29 [20]

   I.   Truth as a cloak for completely different impulses and drives.
20 II.   The pathos of truth is related to *belief*.
   III.   The drive for lies fundamental.
   IV.   Truth is unknowable. Everything knowable semblance. Significance of art as truthful semblance.

29 [21]

   1. Depiction of the servants of truth.
25 2. Control and limitation of knowledge for the benefit of life, of culture.
   3. Equity among the objects of knowledge, assessment of their importance. What is great.

Must call to mind the principal thing and the principal
problems.
Elimination of the false luster.

29 [22]
The intellectually effective powers are dispersed over the entire past—formation of *colonies*! But the actual homeland falls
into poverty when everyone emigrates. They must be reminded
about what is most needed. Against the *laissez aller* in the sciences.
Everyone is so distracted and remote from each other that
no common bond connects them: the bonding adhesive is provided by our newspaper culture.
Should a youth be allowed to waste his best energy in micro-
scopic investigations and be drawn away from the development
of the self?

29 [23]
All Sorts of Servants of Truth.
At first optimistic astonishment! My goodness, how many
probers of truth there are!
Should the best energies be allowed to be dispersed in this
way?
Control of the drive for knowledge:
classical—antiquarian.
—Pessimistic amazement! But not a single one of them is a
prober of truth!
Price of justice as the mother of the true drive to truth.
Examination of the "servants of truth" according to their
sense of justice.
It is quite a good thing that all of them have been *exiled*: for
they would only cause trouble and do harm everywhere. We
want to call them the proletariat of truth, they serve it against
their will and gasping for breath.
For them, scholarship is a correctional facility, a galley.

Reference to *Socrates*, who calls them all crazy; at home, they have no sense of good and evil.

Neutralization of scholarship by means of cloisters.

Our task: to collect and weld together what has been frag-
mented and scattered, to establish a focal point for the work of German culture, far away from all newspaper culture and popularized scholarly disciplines.

29 [24]

The never-ending experimentation and lack of logical-deductive power that *Zöllner* criticizes also can be seen in the historical disciplines — underestimating the classical as opposed to the antiquarian: the meaning of historical scholarship thereby gets lost, everything is leveled. Just as in the former case the image of the world becomes more and more common and is actually drawn only by the popularizers, in the latter instance the same is true for the image of the past.

29 [25]

Schiller: You go out to capture truth with poles, but it passes right between them.

29 [26]

"*All Sorts of Servants of Truth.*"

1. *Depiction* of the laissez faire of scholarship. Dictatorship is lacking.
2. Consequence: the right adhesive is lacking — (in its place, the adhesive of newspaper culture!)

    in general, ever greater crudeness.

    Atrophy of the image of the servant of truth.
3. That is why many have been able to *sneak their way in. Depiction.*
4. Attitude of German culture toward this: What is the task? (Goethe's attitude toward natural science.)

29 [27]
    Protest against the vivisection of living things, that is, those
things that are not yet dead should be allowed to live and not
immediately be treated as an object for scientific investigation.

29 [28]
    Killing by means of knowledge: it is not even act⟨ually⟩
5 knowledge, but instead merely curious, uneasy prying, that is,
a necessary *means* and *conditio* of science. The wish to contribute
to a discussion although one's contribution is merely disruptive.
    Defienda me Dios de my, "Lord protect me from myself."

29 [29]
10 All remembering is comparing, that is, setting things identical. Every concept tells us this; it is the primordial "historical" phenomenon. Life thus requires the identification of what
is present with what is past; so that a certain violence and distortion always accompany the act of comparing. I designate
15 this drive as the drive for the classical and exemplary: the past
serves the present as its archetype. In opposition to this stands
the antiquarian drive, which strives to conceive of what is past
as past and neither to distort nor to idealize it. The needs of life
demand the classical, the needs of truth the antiquarian stance.
20 The former treats the past artistically and with the power of
artistic transfiguration.
    If one conceives of the other tendency as overpowering,
then the past ceases to function as a model and example because it ceases to be an ideal and has become instead individual
25 reality like the present itself. Then it no longer serves life, but
instead works against this life. One thereby accomplishes in
practice what one would accomplish if one were to burn down
all the art galleries and libraries. The present is isolated, becomes more satisfied with itself, and conforms with its nature
30 and its needs; it demonstrates, in short, what it is, how great or
common it is. —But what utility does the drive for the classical

have for the present? It indicates that what existed at one time
was at least *possible* at one time and will hence most likely also
be possible once again (just as the Pythagoreans believe that
when the stars are in the same position everything will occur in
5 exactly the same way). However, the courageous and bold person thinks about what is possible and impossible: he is fortified
by the past: for example, when he hopes that one hundred productive human beings are capable of founding German culture
in its entirety and discovers that the culture of the Renaissance
10 became possible on a similar basis. But humanity is propagated
by means of what is great and impossible.

29 [30]
    Suppose someone believed that no more than one hundred
productive human beings, educated in the same spirit, would
be needed to put an end to the cultivatedness that is right now
15 fashionable in Germany; how he would be strengthened by the
recognition that the culture of the Renaissance was borne on
the shoulders of just such a band of one hundred men.

29 [31]
    The *evaluation of history and the energy wasted on it*. The anti-
quarian manner, which seeks to eliminate the classical com-
20 pletely or to conceive of it as an entirely individual possibility.
Because a great deal of rational energy is employed in order
to grasp some piece of the past in this manner, one ultimately
believes that rationality also brought about this past. This is
how the superstition of the rationality of history comes about:
25 whereby absolute necessity is understood as a manifestation of
something rational and purposive. But the greatest historical
powers are stupidity and the devil. It diminishes one's courage
to know about all the possibilities that have already existed:
the antiquarian sensibility is paralyzing when it is not intended
30 *to evaluate* (that is, to cull from the past what is classical and
good), but only to comprehend everything as something that
has developed over time; for it perceives even what is sense-

less to be purposive and rational. History deserves only a *grand* treatment; otherwise it just creates slaves.

Now there is, second, a measure of permissible and impermissible retrospection. Vivisection is prohibited; children should be prohibited from lurking where eggs are being laid. The drive for truth, which dissects the moment that has just been experienced, kills the next one. As long as one is acquiring knowledge one is not living.

Furthermore—what dangers accompany the antiquarian sensibility when it takes possession of the multitude and the lesser minds! Ultimately everything breaks down into those who live historically and those who only kill historically. What a fatal curiosity, restlessness, prying, disclosure, eliciting of what has just come into being. No spirit ever can be summoned in the light of day. Every age requires as much history as it can transform, by means of digestion, into flesh and blood; so that the strongest and most powerful age will tolerate the most history. But what happens when weak ages are inundated with it! What digestive problems, what fatigue and lack of energy!

29 [32]

It is possible for a people to kill itself by means of history: something like a human being who denies himself sleep. Rumination is something done by certain animals: but it seems that now and then human cattle have destroyed themselves by means of rumination. If everything that comes into being is considered interesting, worthy of study, then one soon lacks a standard and a feeling for everything that one *ought to* do, the human being becomes basically irrelevant.

29 [33]

The *mythology* with which antiquarian human beings surround themselves—the ideas "that love to reveal themselves in ever purer forms," etc.

29 [34]

The *monumental* disregards the causes. "Effects in themselves," "events that will have an effect at any time" (or that can
come into being at any time, whose causes always are present).

29 [35]

3. Just how is the monumental possible? Or on the utility of
history. Auxiliary concept, what is purely human—or what is
great and uncommon, what repeatedly gives rise to something
great. Aspiration of the antiquarians to drag the uncommon
down to the level of the comprehensible, that is, of the common. That is why they do everything in their power to destroy
what is monumental.

But then the codex of the monumental becomes a constraint
and canon for contemporary artists, one that resists emergence,
resists development: what is great is not supposed to emerge,
it is supposed to exist already.

The antiquarians say: what is great is fundamentally what is
common and universal; they, too, resist the emergence of what
is great (by minimizing it, vituperating it, etc.).

Thus, both historical schools resist what is great: with what
is monumental as well as with what is common. This always
has been the case. What is historically great must assert itself
against both, against the former by forcing its way into the
temple of the monumental, against the antiquarians by finally
becoming once again an object of knowledge and thereby even
becoming "interesting" for the antiquarians.

29 [36]

History pertains to the active human being. It is a disgusting
spectacle to see curious micrologist⟨s⟩ or egoists, or tourists
climbing about on pyramids. Today history is placed on exhibition in the same way as paintings in a gallery: for idlers. In
earlier times one sought strength and consolation in it, now
one wants certainty and support in the real, out of hostility
toward art and toward what is great.

29 [37]

How can we explain the *hypertrophy of the historical sensibility*?
1. *Hostility* toward the fictional, the *mythical*.
2. *Hostility* toward the *problems of life*.
3. It *conceals* or *veils* those who *concern* themselves with it — it
   is *easier* than a work of art.
4. It dissolves and leads to lethargy because it kills or para-
   lyzes the sense of justice and the instincts — in short, all
   that is naive in customs and action — by means of analogies.
5. It is democratic and admits everyone, occupies the weakest minds. It is the ideal of aspiring for truth that comes
   to nothing.
6. That it is not fundamentally guided by productive, powerful instincts is demonstrated, for example, in the history of biblical criticism. Compare with the age of Reformation.

29 [38]

The Historical Sickness.

1. In the case of a Pythagorean constellation one could speak
   of the utility of history. But as things stand, the motivation
   for every action is different.
2. Comparison presupposes setting things identical. Memory
   concept. The classical and the monumental, the "effect in
   itself" an idealizing distortion and generalization, the "universally human" as illusion. The illusion of the monumental
   promotes the continuing procreation of what is great.
3. The antiquarian's resistance to what is great and rare and to
   the monumental. Everything that ever has existed is interesting, rational: paralyzing influence of the antiquarians on
   historical initiative.
4. The modern historian as an amalgamation of both drives,
   hermaphrodite. His mythology. His negative praxis. Influence on art, religion. Dangerous for an emerging culture.
   Vivisection. One *should* not be both, classicist and anti-

quarian, but only one, but that totally. Inefficacy of modern
historians: their consequences manifest in carping criticism
and the Americanizing press. The modern historian lacks
any foundation: he is arbitrary in the monumental, deadly
in the antiquarian, and has no roots in a culture.

29 [39]
Basically, everyone is happy when a day has gone by. It
is ridiculous to take it so seriously that on the very next day
it already is giving rise to historical investigations. For we
thereby forfeit the primary lesson that every day teaches us,
"life must be *suffered* through," "it is a punishment." In principal—that is, precisely in regard to the entire evaluation of
life—no event can teach us anything that is essentially *new*, and
someone who lived a couple thousand years ago can be just as
wise as someone who relies on his knowledge of these past two
thousand years. For the human being who *suffers through* existence, history is nothing: he discovers everywhere the same
problem, a problem that is revealed to him every day. But history is something for the *active*, *imprudent* human being who is
full of hopes, who is not resigned, who struggles—he needs
history as exempla of what one can achieve, how one can be
honored, but especially as a *temple of fame*. It has an exemplary
and fortifying effect.

29 [40]
But now history as a *science*! Here it is thus a matter of *laws*,
people are of little account, courage and enthusiasm no longer
can be achieved here; on the contrary, they are disruptive. Assuming these laws can be discovered, the only result would be
determinism, and the acting human being would be violently reduced once more to a sufferer, without a moral sensation teaching him resignation. In addition, these laws have little value:
because they are derived from the masses and their needs, and
thus are laws that govern the movement of the lower strata, the
loam and clay. Stupidity and hunger always are a part of it, just

as *la femme* is part of every French criminal proceeding. What is the purpose of knowing such laws, since everyone, after all, already has acted in accordance with them for centuries without ever knowing them! The strong and great human being always
5 has had to assert himself against these laws: he is the only person about whom we should even be speaking. The masses are only to be regarded as 1) faded copies of great men on poor paper and printed with wornout plates; 2) as resistance to the great; 3) as a tool of the great. With regard to everything else,
10 they can go to the devil.

29 [41]
Statistics proves that there are laws in history. Yes, it proves how vulgar and disgustingly uniform the masses are. You should have kept statistics in Athens! Then you would have sensed the difference! The more inferior and un-individual the
15 masses are, the more rigorous the statistical law. If the multitude has a more refined and nobler composition, then the law immediately goes to the devil. And way up at the top, where the great minds are, you no longer can make any calculations at all: when, for example, have great artists ever gotten married!
20 You are hopeless, you who want to discover a law in this. Thus, to the extent that there are laws in history, they are worthless, and history itself—that is, everything that has occurred—is worthless.

Moreover, what does the word "law" even mean here? Do
25 these laws somehow have the same status as a law of nature or a law of justice? It does not maintain "thou shalt," but only "that's unfortunately how it was." It is thus the expression of an *inane* factual relation about which no one is still permitted to ask the question Why? "Approximately forty marriages are
30 concluded here each year"—Why precisely this number and not eighty? "It just simply isn't otherwise"! — Very instructive! Thank you very much.

However, there is one movement that takes the great drives

of the masses to be what is important and that views all great
men merely as their expression, as the bubbles that become
visible on the surface of the flood. The masses are supposed to
produce greatness out of themselves, order be produced out of
5 chaos. In the end, of course, the hymn to the great productive
masses is sung; long live history!

Another movement wants to take into consideration everything that has ever been "a historical power" and evaluates
what is "great" according to this standard: what has had a his-
10 torically lasting effect is then called "great." This is tantamount
to confusing quantity and quality. If the coarse masses have
found any thought, any religion whatsoever to be entirely adequate and have bitterly defended it, then the discoverer and
founder of this thought is supposed to be "great." But why!?
15 The noblest and loftiest things have no effect at all on the
masses; and fortunately the historical success of Christianity
does not testify to the greatness of its founder, since it basically would testify *against him*: but here the original impetus
seems to have gotten completely lost, and only the name has
20 remained as a designation for the tendencies of the masses and
of many overambitious and egotistical individuals.

29 [42]

Idolatry of success is quite appropriate for human vulgarity. But
anyone who has studied closely one single success knows what
kind of factors (stupidity, meanness, laziness, etc.) always have
25 played a role, and that they were not the least powerful factors.
It is crazy that success is supposed to have more worth than
the beautiful opportunity that still existed immediately prior
to it! But beyond that, to see in history the realization of what
is good and just is blasphemy against what is good and just.
30 This beautiful world history, to cite Heraclitus's expression, is
"a chaotic heap of sweepings"! What is *strong* always manages
to prevail, that is the universal law: if only it were not so often
also precisely what is stupid and evil!

29 [43]

Luther: "Cicero, a wise and industrious man, suffered and accomplished a great deal."

29 [44]

The Englishman about Berlin: "In Berlin, those who do not appreciate beer halls and wine bars, be they rich or poor, live
5   and die in wretchedness."

29 [45]

The horrible practice of trying to comprehend characters and individuals, and thereby of justifying them on the basis of their vital substance perhaps appears to be based on justice and to aim at being just toward one's contemporaries. This
10 stands in opposition to the fact that we demand the most fatal uniformity precisely in our contemporaries and are least just toward multifarious characters. The most experienced historian is, with regard to his age, "un personnage *haineux*," and is *unjust* or *jaded*.

29 [46]

15 The scholarly class is a kind of clergy and it disdains the layman; they are the descendants of the religious clergy, without this inherited reverence our age hardly would cultivate the scholarly disciplines the way it does. Today we give to scholarship — although more sparingly — what people previously gave
20 to the Church; but the fact *that* we give at all has to do with the power of the Church, whose aftereffect still can be felt today in the scholarly clergy. And especially the pursuit of *history*, as a doctrine that postulates the effect of God or the effect of the rational, is still a disguised theology. Should the notion that
25 history is not scholarship, but instead merely bunk, ever seize the multitude, then their support of it will cease.

29 [47]

The accursed soul of the *people*! When we speak of the *German mind*, we mean the great German minds, people like Luther, Goethe, Schiller, and a few others, not the mythological phantom of the unified mindless masses, in which ——— It would
5   be better to speak of Luther-like human beings, etc. We ought to take care when calling something German: the first thing is the *language*; but to conceive of this as the expression of the character of the people is merely empty rhetoric, and to this day that has never been possible for any people without omi-
10 nous vagueness and figurative language. Greek language and the Greek people! Let someone just try and bring those two things together! Moreover, things stand in much the same way where writing is concerned: the all-important foundation of the language is not *Greek* at all, but rather, as one says today,
15 Indogermanic. Things stand somewhat better where style and the human being are concerned. It always is very dangerous to attach certain predicates to a people: ultimately everything is so intermingled that it is always only later that unity is invented once again on the basis of language, or the illusion of unity
20 arises through language. Yes indeed, Germans! German Empire! That is one thing, speakers of German quite something else. But racial Germans! A characteristically German artistic style has yet to be *discovered*, just as in the case of the Greeks, Greek style was discovered only very late: there was no previ-
25 ous unity, but there certainly was a horrible κρᾶσις.

29 [48]

Against the parallel of history with *youth*, *manhood*, and *old age*: and there is not an iota of truth in it! A span of five or six millennia is absolutely nothing, and above all not a unity, because new peoples constantly emerge and old ones go into
30 hibernation. Ultimately it is not a question of peoples at all, but of human beings; *nationality* is usually only the *consequence* of rigid governmental regulations, that is, a kind of grooming achieved by means of all-encompassing violence and control,

even coercion, to marry one another and to speak and live together.

29 [49]

Expressed in Christian terms: The *devil* is thus the ruler of the world, and that is how things essentially will remain. But now people say, using more cultivated language: the system of egoisms that struggle against one another: whereby people think of the forest that grows so uniformly and regularly because all the trees merely satisfy their own egoism.

29 [50]

1) The *danger* of the *monumental*, which, pulled together from all ages, confuses and debilitates the searching instinct. The same holds true for the knowledge of all relations and social classes: if the farmer had this knowledge, what would he then do with his plow!

29 [51]

A *controlling* of the unlimited historical sensibility is necessary: and in fact one already exists, but one that is not necessary, control by means of the sober, uniformed spirit of the age, which everywhere seeks itself and thinks it finds itself, and which lowers history to its standard. I perceive just such a lowering in the case of Cicero (Mommsen), Seneca (Hausrath), Luther (Protestant Union), etc. Hegel had another way of controlling and stretching history, he, who is truly the person who deserves to be called the German "genius of history"; for he believed himself to be at the culmination and the end of development and therefore in possession of all earlier ages, as their ordering *voῦς*. Every attempt to conceive the present age as the zenith ruins the present because it denies the exemplary significance of the historical. The most horrible formula is Hartmann's, "surrendering oneself to the *world process*."

E. von Hartmann demonstrates on p. 618 where it leads to view history as a *process* (and this explains his enormous suc-

cess). Here the historical view joins forces with pessimism:
now just look at the consequences! The stages in the life of
the individual provide the analogy, the thoroughly unflatter-
ing portrayal of the present leads only to the conclusion that
5 things are going to get worse and that this is the necessary process to which one must surrender oneself. He takes as the basis
for his analogy a rather common human creature whose age
of manhood will attain "solid mediocrity," and a form of art
that, on the average, is approximately the equivalent of "what
10 an evening's farce is, say, to a Berlin stockbroker." Above all,
he takes into consideration "a practical, comfortable accom-
modation in his worldly home that looks out thoughtfully on
the future." Accompanied by a kind of sweet-and-sour imperative: "This work of destroying illusion is merciless and cruel,
15 like the harsh pressure of a hand that awakens to the agony of
reality someone who is sweetly dreaming; but the world must
move forward; the aim cannot be accomplished by dreams, it
must be fought for and achieved, and the path to redemption
passes only through pain." Yet it remains incomprehensible
20 how the process, whose age of manhood was just portrayed,
ultimately "enters into a period of mature introspection in
which it surveys all the stormy, dissolute sufferings of its past
life and grasps the vanity of what it formerly had supposed was
the aim of all its striving." p. 625f. But if humanity is supposed
25 to experience its old age as a kind of Leopardi, then it would
have to be nobler than it is and above all have a different age of
manhood than the one Hartmann grants it. The old man who
would correspond to such a manhood would be extremely repulsive and would hang onto life with disgusting greed, caught
30 up more than ever in the most vulgar illusions.

29 [52]
    Hartmann is important because he deals a deathblow to the
idea of a world process simply by being consistent. In order to
be able to endure it he must base it on the τέλος of conscious
redemption and freedom from illusions and on our willing-

ness to embrace decline. But the end of humanity can occur at any moment due to a geological cataclysm: and that illusion-lessness would presuppose more highly developed moral and intellectual energies: which is wholly improbable: on the con-
5 trary, when they become old, the illusions are likely to become all the more powerful and old age, to conclude with a *return to childishness*. Hence the final result is by no means comforting and certainly could not be called a τέλος. Moreover, the way he describes the stage of manhood, the ability to regard life as
10 a problem steadily decreases and the need for redemption gets smaller and smaller. We want to refrain from all constructions of *human history* and not pay any attention whatsoever to the masses, but instead only to the widely dispersed individuals: they form a bridge above the turbulent stream. They do not
15 further a process; rather, they live conjointly and concurrently, thanks to history, which permits such a collaboration.

It is the "republic of geniuses." The task of history is to mediate between them and thereby continually to incite and lend strength to the production of greatness and beauty. The
20 goal of humankind cannot possibly be found in its end stage, but only in the highest specimens, who, dispersed throughout millennia, conjointly represent all the supreme powers that are buried in humanity.

Moreover: *world* process!! When it's really only a matter of
25 the trifles of the earthly fleas!

Hartmann writes on p. 637: "It would be just as incompatible with the concept of development to ascribe to the world pro-cess an infinite duration in the *past*, since then every conceiv-able development already would have to have occurred, and
30 *this is definitely not the case* (!!!), as it would be to concede to the process an infinite duration in the *future*. Both would annul the concept of *development toward a goal* and would make the world process appear similar to the Danaides' futile attempts to draw water. However, the complete victory of the logical over the
35 illogical must coincide with the *temporal end of the world process*, with *the Last Judgment* (!!)."

One is happy to flee from Hartmann's "world process" to
Democritus's chaos of atoms and to Darwin's doctrine of the
survival of the fittest among countless variations. Here there
is still room for great individuals, even if they are churned out
5 by chance. For Hartmann, the negation of the will is an error
and the affirmation of life one's true duty. In the end, the majorities on the earth are even supposed to vote for annihilation
and the return to nothingness!

Opposed to this our doctrine *that consciousness is promoted* and
10 developed *only by ever loftier illusions.* That is why our "consciousness" is so inferior (by comparison, for example, with that of
the Greeks), because our illusions are *more inferior* and *more vulgar* than theirs. I am incapable of calling this progression to
vulgarity a progression to the "age of manhood." If one were
15 to conceive of a disappearance of all illusions, then consciousness, too, would evaporate down to the level of the plants.
Furthermore, illusions are only the expression for an unknown
state of affairs. Hartmann's goal is to lead humanity to *jadedness*:
then widespread suicide: committed by the majority of human
20 beings! Then the world will topple and sink once more into
the sea of nothingness. Task of the next generation: to lead the
way to jadedness by means of surrender to the world process,
that is, affirmation of the will to life!

Disgusting book, a disgrace to our age! How infinitely more
25 pure, lofty, and moral Schopenhauer's pessimism comes across!
Hartmann's philosophy is the *scowl of Christianity*, with its absolute wisdom, its Last Judgment, its redemption, etc. Specula-
tion with the effect of *monstrous paradoxes*, combined with laissez
faire, was never madder than this. The present day as under-
30 stood by the likes of David Strauss is integrated into the world
process, it finds its place and hence is legitimated. Hence the
success among the *literary masses* (that's the only kind of success there is today: they really know how to incite the public
to buy!).

29 [53]

The *Hegelian* "world process" culminated in a fat Prussian state with a capable police force. That is all disguised theology, in Hartmann's case as well. But we are not capable of conceiving beginning and end: so let's just forget all this
5 crap about "development"! It inevitably sounds ridiculous! The human being and the "world process"! The earthly flea and the world spirit!

29 [54]

We should not concern ourselves at all with the question why human beings exist, why "the human being" exists: but
10 ask yourself why you exist: and if you find no answer, then set aims for yourself, *lofty* and *noble aims*, and perish in the attempt to accomplish them! I know of no better purpose in life than perishing in the attempt to accomplish something great and impossible: *animae magnae prodigus*.

29 [55]

15 1. *Depiction* of the *historical sensibility*, ultimately in its extreme, the world process and the moral law derived from it.
2. Internal *reasons* for this hypertrophy of the historical sensibility.
20 3. *Significance* of *history* for a *culture*.

29 [56]

The historical element in *education*. Young people are whipped onward through the millennia; that did not happen to the Greeks and Romans. Moreover, political history for young men! Who are unable to understand anything about war, about
25 state policy, about trade policy, about questions of power, etc.! That's just how modern human beings walk through galleries and listen to concerts! One thing sounds different from another, they sense, and they then call this a "historical judgment." The mass of material is so great that the only possible

result is stupefaction. Horrible, barbaric things in excess press
their way in, and wherever a more refined consciousness exists,
only one feeling can arise: nausea. In addition, the young person is alienated from his homeland and learns to be skeptical
of all customs and concepts. In every age it was different: "it
does not matter what you are." Depending on the ἦθος, the
human being now will turn toward what is bad or what is
good (that is, great): "Move freely, but always in peril, without
a leash." Fortunately, the sensibilities of youth usually are so
dull that absolutely nothing essential comes of this, except for
an indistinct stupor; a powerful imagination is lacking, and, in
addition, the massive influx is too overpowering, everything is
swamped by the flood.

No one needs such a massive amount of history, as the ancients have demonstrated; indeed, it is extremely dangerous,
as the moderns have demonstrated.

Now the student of history! He has researched a wholly
isolated chapter of the past: now he is a servant of scholarship, of truth; now he no longer needs to be modest, he is
complete! Scholarly arrogance *hinders* higher education. I view
young doctors of history as human beings who in matters of
education cannot even count to three and who usually will
not even count at all: for they are already "productive"! Good
Lord!

29 [57]

To understand everything "objectively," get angry about
nothing, love nothing, "comprehend" everything—that is
what is now called "historical sensibility." Governments are
just as happy to promote such a sensibility as they were to promote Hegelianism; for it makes people submissive and pliant.
But it is above all the press in its entirety that is trained to be
this way: one gets angry and mad only in an "artistic" manner, and besides, one is "jaded" and "understands" everything:
tout comprendre c'est tout pardonner: but one does not "excuse,"
one justifies everything. Himself not bound by anything, the

historical journalist denies all bonds: he lets them stand only
when they have a utilitarian purpose.

It is no longer supposed to be the era of the harmonious
personality, but rather that of "common labor." But that only
means: *before* they are complete, human beings are used in the
factory. But have no doubt, in a short time scholarship will
be just as ruined as the human beings who accomplish this
factory labor. "Solid mediocrity" is becoming more and more
mediocre, one human being wiser than any other human being
only in *one single* respect, and in all other respects dumber than
any previous scholar: in sum, however, infinitely more arrogant. System of carters who have declared genius to be superfluous: one will be able to tell by looking at your buildings that
they were *carted* together rather than *constructed*. To him who
tirelessly mouths "Division of labor!" "In rank and file!," we
have to say clearly and frankly: if you want to further scholarship as quickly as possible, then you will also destroy it as
quickly as possible, just as the hen that you artificially force to
lay eggs as quickly as possible also perishes. Granted, scholarship has been furthered at a quick pace in the last decades,
but look at the scholars, the exhausted hens. They are truly no
longer "harmonious" natures: they can only cackle more than
ever, but the eggs also are smaller than ever. That, then, is also
the reason for the favored "popularization" of history for the
"mixed public." This is so easy for scholars because they themselves—with the exception of their tiny area—are a part of this
"very mixed public," and they bear its needs within them. They
only need to sit down comfortably somewhere in their bath-
robe in order to succeed in opening up their tiny area of study
to those mixed-popular needs: to this act of comfort they af-
fix the designation "a modest condescension of the scholar to
the people," whereas basically the scholar—insofar as he is not
a scholar but actually a plebeian—only descends to his own
level. First create a people—you can never conceive it to be
noble and lofty enough! But it is not easy to conceive your
"mixed public" in all its vulgarity!

29 [58]

For the *conclusion*. If these observations have *annoyed* you,
then the author can tell you that he anticipated this: but he cannot anticipate the object at which you will direct your annoyance: whether against the author or against yourselves. In the
5 latter—certainly less frequent—instance, the best thing you
could do would be to forget the author completely: what does
it matter who has expressed a truth, as long as it was expressed
at all and there are people who take it to heart. I have written
for both groups, and I hope I have written clearly enough.

29 [59]

10 No one in the world speaks about the unconscious, because
by its very nature it is something that is unknown; only in Berlin is there someone who speaks and knows something about
it and tells us what its purpose is. Namely, that our age must be
exactly the way it is if humanity is ever to become fed up with
15 this existence: a belief with which we heartily agree—whereas
E. von H⟨artmann⟩ *knows* it. —What David Strauss accepts as
naive facticity, H⟨artmann⟩ not only justifies on the basis of
the past, *ex causis efficientibus*, but also on the basis of the future,
ex causa finali: H⟨artmann⟩ lets the light of the Last Judgment
20 shine upon our age, and seen in this light, it appears that it is
now approaching humanity's age of manhood, that joyous state
in which there is nothing but solid mediocrity and art of the
type needed in the evening by Berlin stockbrokers, in which
"geniuses are no longer necessary, because that would be tan-
25 tamount to throwing pearls to swine, or even because the age
has progressed beyond that stage suited to genius to a *more significant* stage" (p. 619). We wish we had written that down incorrectly; but in fact, I merely copied it word for word. The moral:
things are in an absolutely sorry state, things will get even sor-
30 rier, but it must be this way, it must come to this, "the Antichrist is clearly ever extending his sphere of influence" (p. 610).
But we are well on our way with all this: "therefore, as laborers
in the vineyards of the Lord, let us strive vigorously onward,

for it is the process alone that can lead to redemption" p. 638.
Have we guessed correctly about H⟨artmann⟩'s intention when
we sense in him an ironic buffoon who once and for all wants
to make the notion of the "world process" look ridiculous? In
5   this sense we seldom have seen a more humorous invention or
read anything so full of philosophical roguishness: but the entire world of literati did not listen very carefully and discovered
in it only its own justification bathed in an apocalyptic light,
so that it failed to see that H⟨artmann⟩ conceived his philoso-
10 phy of the world process as nothing other than a philosophy
for contemporary skulduggery. That is the true charm of all of
H⟨artmann⟩'s inventions: those in the know sense that he does
not mean it seriously at all, except to the extent that is necessary to seduce the unknowing into naive seriousness.

29 [60]

15   Grillparzer: "Every human being has his own particular necessity, so that a million curved and straight lines run parallel to
one another, intersect one another, reinforce and impede one
another, run forward and backward, so that for each other they
take on the character of the fortuitous and thereby make it im-
20 possible — apart from the influences of natural occurrences —
to demonstrate any overarching, wholly comprehensive necessity in events."

Furthermore, only what was already completed, finished,
dead could be studied, because the final, instructive con-
25 sequences become apparent. — History as "world system of
errors and passions." Negative doctrine: something that one
must guard against.

Grillparzer: "There is something peculiar in the blossoming
and withering of nations. In each there is a conspicuous energy
30 that has a beneficial effect as long as there are impediments to
be overcome, but that turns against itself as soon as these have
been overcome."

29 [61]

When a Stoic and an Epicurean come to an agreement, they enter into a conspiracy to murder Caesar.

29 [62]

The facts themselves are viewed as "immediate emanations of the world spirit," and that is why they alone are thought
5 to possess the necessary dignity and profundity, that is why tragic art is supposed to subordinate itself to history! Ridiculous! To history! "What is history other than the way in which the spirit of the human being assimilates what for him are *impenetrable occurrences*; in which he connects things of which only
10 God knows whether they belong together; in which he substitutes the comprehensible for the incomprehensible; in which he projects his concepts of an external purposiveness onto a totality that probably only has an internal purposiveness; and in which he assumes chance when a thousand tiny causes are
15 at work. What is history other than this! What is the world of human beings other than this! However, since what matters to the poet are not the events themselves, but rather their connection and justification, then for God's sake let him at least invent the events himself, if that's what he wishes to do."

29 [63]

20 Just as one says of the actor that his art consists of three stages, "*understanding* a role, *feeling* a role, and perceiving the essence of a role," and that only the combination of all three makes the true actor: it will be said, with slight variation, of the historically great human being: he sees above all what must
25 be accomplished, his mission, as a sum of many individually perceived instances, rarely does he sense the unity of all these instances as his mission, and what is most rare is for him to understand his mission. But the historian follows hot on his heels and can do all three.

29 [64]

The Hungarian and *the Hegelian professor.*

History as "the self-realizing concept, with demonstrable necessity and continuous progress." It thereby takes on "a theoretical aura," it is "the sojourn of God on earth—although this
5 God, for his part, is himself only the product of history." Here I am tempted to agree with the Spaniard Juan Huart⟨e⟩, who says of the Germans that they have a powerful memory and little reason; their reason always is like that of drunkards because the large amount of fluid absorbed by their brains and
10 the rest of their bodies does not permit them to penetrate to the nature of things. One is also reminded of the fact that he attributes to them great inventiveness in clockworks, waterworks, and mechanical contrivances, and that he would be inclined to include such a self-realizing conceptual clockwork in
15 this series.

29 [65]

Grillparzer rails "against the pretense, common in recent times, that literary history has utility even for the practical further development of the literary branches"; indeed, he reckons it "among those dangerous endeavors that, on the one hand,
20 by attempting to increase the mass of superficial knowledge— that is to say, press items—has, on the other hand, the opposite effect of expanding one's field of vision into the immeasurable, so that ultimately it becomes ever more difficult to develop that power of inner concentration without which any action or any
25 deed are impossible. But the lack of this power of concentration is the curse of our age."

"We feel with abstractions," Grillparzer says, "we scarcely know any longer how our contemporaries express their feelings; we let them act in ways in which nowadays feelings would
30 no longer make them act. Shakespeare has spoiled all of us moderns." —Who would believe in the truth of the feelings expressed by someone like Heine! Just as little as I believe in those of someone like E. von Hartmann. But they have

an ironical propensity toward reproduction, in the manner of
great poets and philosophers: although they basically possess
a satirical tendency and ridicule their contemporaries, who, in
philosophy and lyric poetry, are happy to be lied to and hence
5 take a close look with their bespectacled eyes so that they
immediately can discover the historical rubric in which these
new geniuses assume their rightful place: Goethe and Heine,
Schopenhauer and Hartmann! Long live the Germans' refined
"historical" sensibility!

29 [66]
10 Everyone constantly is speaking about the spirit of the
people, about the unconscious, about ideas in history, etc.; but
for the contemporary age it all amounts to nothing. People
only seem to value what issues unconsciously from the deepest fount of the spirit of the people, and in all practical mat-
15 ters they imitate everything—as consciously as possible, and,
unfortunately, as ineptly as possible: English parliamentarian-
ism; French fashions and the petty morality of the English;
and French, indeed, international phraseologies of progress,
as well as the paintings of all ages and nations; and the mod-
20 ern German simply considers everything that is astonishingly
strange to be the most beautiful luxury. Just imagine Freytag
at the victory column: what feelings bloat him! To be sure, as
the scoundrel Hartmann tells us, today things stand with us in
such a way that "since the last century we have been approach-
25 ing that ideal state in which the human race fashions its own
history in full consciousness" (p. 291); we even get an inkling
of that yet more ideal state in which humanity puts an end to
its history and to the world process in its entirety and "flings"
itself, along with the world, "back into nothingness"—perhaps
30 after a telegraphic communication that travels the entire globe
to the effect that this has majority support (see p. 640), and
with the official decree that the demise of the world, including
the outvoted minority, is supposed to take place next Saturday
evening at twelve o'clock sharp. "As of tomorrow, time will

cease to exist": to which the joker Hartmann would cite the
revelation of John, 10:6 (see *Philosophy of the Unconscious*, p. 637).

This same joker calls voluntary collaboration the "fourth and
final" phase of social development: the laborer is to be educated so as to reach maturity; the most important social task of
the present day is to practice this form of education (by means
of associations patterned after the Schulze-Delitzsch model,
better education in the schools, educational associations for
laborers). P. 296: "the ultimate aim of this social development
would be that everyone would be able to lead a comfortable
existence while having a work schedule that would leave him
enough leisure for his intellectual development."

29 [67]

Hartmann and Heine are unconscious ironists, people who
play jokes on themselves: to be sure, Kant denies that anyone
can lie to himself.

29 [68]

"It is difficult to see into the future," *Grillparzer* says, "and
even more difficult to peer without bias into the past. I say
'*without bias*,' that is, without mixing in with one's retrospective
gaze anything that has occurred or become apparent in the
meantime."

Grillparzer: "The fundamental error of all German thought
and aspirations lies in a *weak personality*, which has the consequence that what is real, what subsists, only makes a slight
impression on the German."

29 [69]

Inwardness — outward dishonesty. *Philosophy.*

29 [70]

Polybius says: "Just as an animal becomes unfit when it loses
its eyes, history that is bereft of truth is nothing but a useless story."

"History, the preparation for state administration and the best teacher, who, by reminding us of the misfortunes of others, admonishes us steadfastly to endure the vicissitudes of fortune."

29 [71]

This inflated specimen, the man with the historical fever, relates to the men of historical actions in the very same way the loudmouthed lead articles of the *Kölnische Zeitung* relate to a speech by Demosthenes. A newspaper editor brandishing the Tyrtaean war trumpet is just as comical a thought as Demosthenes composing lead newspaper articles. Anyone who wants to produce something that is sound must have a pre-sentiment rather than a post-sentiment and should not be permitted to look back at all.

29 [72]

Hegel: "When Spirit takes a sudden leap, we philosophers are also at hand." In philosophy it is the spirit of a people, the spirit of an age that arrives at consciousness. Well, then something of the ironical consciousness most likely will ⟨be⟩ found in *Hartmann*.

God is supposed to be "the spirit of humanity that is at work in the spirits of all peoples," religion is supposed to uplift us to the point of enjoying the idea in and of itself. Hegel: "*universal world history*, whose events represent the dialectic of specific *national* spirits (which it stores in bottles), the Last Judgment." "That history (that is, essentially world history) is founded upon a final purpose in and of itself and that this purpose actually is realized and continues to be realized in it (the plan of Providence), that there is *reason* in history, must be determined philosophically for itself and thereby determined to be necessary in and of itself." "History without such a purpose and without such judgment would be only a senseless product of the imagination, not even a child's tale, for even children demand that their stories have some point, that is, at the very

least, a purpose that can be divined and to which the events and actions can be related." Conclusion: every story must have a purpose, hence also the history of a people, the history of the world. That is, since there is "world history," there must
5 also be some purpose in the world process. That is, we demand only those stories that have a purpose: but we have demanded no stories at all about the world process, because we believe it to be humbug even to speak of such a thing. It already is apparent in the fortuitousness of my existence that my life has no
10 purpose; that I am able to establish some purpose for myself is something quite different. But a state has no purpose: it is only we who attribute to it this or that purpose.

29 [73]

On the mythology of the historical. Hegel: "Whatever happens to a people and transpires within it has its primary sig-
15 nificance in the relationship to the state; nothing is further removed from the object that properly belongs to history than the mere particularities of individuals." But the state always is only the means for the preservation of many individuals: how could it possibly be a purpose! The only hope is that inherent
20 in the preservation of so many losers also will be the protection of a few individuals in whom humanity will culminate. Otherwise it has absolutely no sense to preserve so many wretched human beings. The history of states is the history of the egoism of the masses and of the blind desire to exist: this aspiration
25 is only somewhat justified by the geniuses, to the extent that they can exist under such conditions. Particular and collective egoisms involved in mutual struggle — an atomic chaos of egoisms — who would be silly enough to look for purposes in this!

Yet by means of the genius something ultimately comes of
30 that jumble of atoms, and then one thinks more kindly about the senselessness of this activity: almost as if a blind hunter were to fire his gun many hundreds of times until he finally, by chance, kills a bird. "In the end something comes of this," he would say, and then he would go on shooting.

29 [74]

Hegel: "The point of a biography appears to stand in direct
opposition to a universal purpose, but the biography itself has
as its background the historical world with which the individual
is involved." Hence that poor excuse for a title "Demosthenes
and His Age," etc. If there are ten biographies produced by one
and the same age, then what that amounts to is ten times the
same thing: the mere production of books! On the "spirit of
St. Ambrose's age and even—to use Lichter's words—something about the individual particularity of St. Ambrose, insofar
as it is connected with the background of this age."

Otherwise everything would be just fine, if only it weren't
so absurd to speak of "world history": even if we assume that
there is a world purpose, it would be impossible to know it
because we are earthly fleas and not the masters of the world.
Every idolization of abstract general concepts such as state,
nation, humanity, world process has the disadvantage that it
lightens the burden of the individual and lessens his responsibility. If everything is a matter of the state, then very little
depends on the individual: as is amply demonstrated by every
war. Viewed in terms of morality: anyone who *strips* the human
being of his belief that he is something with a fundamentally
higher value than all the means required for his existence makes
him a worse human being. Abstractions are his products, the
means to his existence—nothing more, not his masters. As a
moral creature, he must always be permitted to perish—that is,
to become a martyr—in the struggle against means that, mis-
interpreted as ends, have become overpowering: in order not
to *propter vitam vitae perdere causas*.

29 [75]

Whatever the human being perceives to be interconnected
as *cause* and *effect* he tends to connect as *means* and *intention*.
Schiller: "One phenomenon after another begins to escape the
realm of blind chance and lawless freedom and to integrate
itself as a well-fitting part into a harmonious totality—*which*

exists, of course, only in his imagination." I propose as a general law that we explain the history of nations with a minimum of intelligence and intention, in a wholly material manner, according to an analogy with colliding complexes of atoms. Momentum,
5 senselessness. —Against mythology.

29 [76]
   The need to have contact with great predecessors is certainly the sign of a superior disposition; but Goethe is just as correct when he states that a scoundrel always remains a scoundrel, and that even daily contact with the great sensibility of
10 the ancients does not make a small-minded person one iota greater. But if such small-minded people become acquainted with small-minded and evil deeds from the past and develop a predilection for tracking down in history the effects of all that is small, then with each passing day they will become more
15 impish, sadistic, deceptive, and will practice their nimble evilness to the annoyance of all those who are just and great.

29 [77]
   Goethe once gave expression to the ability of historical knowledge to kill. "If I had known as clearly as I know today how many excellent things have existed for centuries and mil-
20 lennia, I never would have written a single line, but instead would have done something else."

29 [78]
   Goethe: "Our age is so wretched that the poet encounters no useful qualities in the lives of the human beings around him. In order to edify himself Schiller turned to two things: to phi-
25 losophy and history."
   Goethe: "It is not actually my aim to see things more clearly and brightly, up to a certain degree, in the obscure regions of history—it was actually Niebuhr with whom I concerned myself, not Roman history. It is the profound sensibility and dili-
30 gent wisdom of such a man that actually edify us. I don't give a hoot about all those agrarian laws, but the manner in which

he explains them, how he makes complicated relations clear, is what stimulates me, what imposes upon me the duty to proceed in just as conscientious a manner in all the matters that I take on."

Goethe to Lavater: "*I do not like results and abstractions, I do not seek history and details.*"

29 [79]

Goethe: "Schiller appears here, as always, in absolute possession of his sublime nature; he is as great at the dinner table as he would have been in the council of state. Nothing bothers him, nothing confines him, nothing holds back the flight of his thoughts; everything in him that thrives on good intentions always is freely expressed, without deference and without misgivings. He was an upstanding human being, and that is how everyone should be!"

29 [80]

The state of historical cultivation is much like that of scholarship.

Lichtenberg says: "I believe that some of the greatest minds that ever lived had not read half as much and did not know nearly as much as some of our mediocre scholars. And some of our very mediocre scholars could have become greater men if they had not read so much."

Lichtenberg: "Wouldn't things look much better for the human race if we no longer had history, at least no political history? The human being then would act more in accordance with the energies he possesses at any given time; for as things stand today, the example that now and then makes one person better makes a thousand others worse."

Goethe: "Anyone who from now on does not take up some art or handwork is going to be in a sorry situation. Given the quick pace of developments in the world, knowledge no longer helps one advance; by the time someone has taken notice of everything, he has lost himself."

29 [81]

Historical studies gave birth to the opposition between "cultivated" and "uncultivated": how much the productive spirit lost as a result of this! It is inexpressible! He lost the confidence in his people because he recognized their feelings to be
5 falsified and faded. Even if these feelings have become more refined and more noble among a small group of them, that is no compensation for him, for then he addresses himself to a sect, as it were, and no longer feels needed by his people as a whole. He will prefer to bury his treasure because he feels dis-
10 gust at being pretentiously patronized by one class while his heart is full of compassion for all. Religions no longer can survive, nor can the arts, if a thundering god does not succeed at tearing down that wall.

29 [82]

The number of historical publications that appear each year?
15 One would have to take into consideration that almost every piece of scholarship in the area of classical antiquity would have to be included! And what is more, in almost all scholarly disciplines the overwhelming majority of publications are historical, with the exception of mathematics and certain disci-
20 plines in medicine and the natural sciences.

I am always amazed that people don't develop an antipathy toward themselves when they constantly take stock of the past. But the historical fever and the greatest momentary vanity stand side by side.

29 [83]

25 Goethe, nature.

Even assuming it were true — illusion would still be lacking:

in great things
that never prosper without some illusion.

29 [84]

"Scholarship should have an impact on the outside world,"
Goethe says, "only by means of an *enhanced praxis*; for in fact all
the scholarly disciplines are esoteric and can become exoteric
only by having a positive influence on some action. Any other
5 type of impact leads to nothing. —That one also calls the rest
of the world to this vocation and draws its attention to it, as has
been happening in recent times, is an abuse and brings with it
more harm than good."

Goethe: "One of the primary characteristics by which one
10 can, with utmost certainty, distinguish truth from deception is:
the former always has a productive effect and sustains anyone
who possesses and fosters it; by contrast, what is false merely
lies there unproductively and is for all practical purposes dead;
indeed, it must be viewed as a necrosis in which the gangre-
15 nous part of the organism prevents the part that is still living
from undergoing a cure."

29 [85]

"Well done, upon my soul, neighbor Schlehwein! You see,
the dear Lord is a good man; when the two of you ride on the
same horse, someone has to sit behind."

29 [86]

20 "Ask yourself," says *Hume*, "ask any of your acquaintances,
whether they would live over again the last ten or twenty years
of their life. No! but the next twenty, they say, will be better:

> And from the dregs of life hope to rec⟨e⟩ive,
> What the first sprightly running could not give."

25 Misery drives human beings into the future, misery drives
them into a distant past so that they thereby can demonstrate
the relative happiness of the present or console themselves with
the thought that at one time others lived well. It is the drive
to find happiness that prevents human beings from discover-
30 ing the lesson of their day, resignation; since happiness is not

yet there, it obviously must be on the way, they conclude, or must already have been there. Or it is already there by comparison with prior unhappiness, etc. The same thing that drives on each human being drives them all on: they use history in order
5 to become happier in the future.

There are two *modes of viewing the past*; for the first of these, any period of time, any people, any day is sufficient; the second is insatiable because nowhere does it find the answer it seeks: how one can live happily. The wise human being lives ac-
10 cording to the first mode, the historical, unwise, active human being according to the second. Now, there is also a way of pursuing history that prevents human beings from becoming active without making them experience resignation. That is our manner.

15 David Hume: "This world . . . is very faulty and imperfect, compared to a superior standard; and was only the first rude essay of some infant deity who afterwards abandoned it, ashamed of his lame performance; it is the work only of some dependent, inferior deity, and is the object of derision to his
20 superiors; it is the production of old age and dotage in some superannuated deity; and ever since his death has run on at adventures, from the first impulse and active force which it received from him."

Hume: "Were a stranger to drop on a sudden into this world,
25 I would show him, as a specimen of its ills, a hospital full of diseases, a prison crowded with malefactors and debtors, a field of battle strewed with carcasses, a fleet foundering in the ocean, a nation languishing under tyranny, famine, or pestilence. To turn the gay side of life to him and give him a notion
30 of its pleasures—whither should I conduct him? To a ball, to an opera, to a court? He might justly think that I was only showing him a diversity of distress and sorrow."

29 [87]

To enlighten someone about the meaning of life on earth— that is one aim. To make someone, and along with him count-

less future generations, hold onto earthly life (whereby it is
necessary to withhold from him the first observation)—that is
the second aim. The first seeks a sedative for the will, as does
the second: the first finds it in close proximity and is quickly
5 satiated with existence; the second is insatiable and roves far
afield.

In the case of the second, the past actually is supposed to
be viewed only pessimistically—namely, in order to make the
present relatively tolerable. Yet not so pessimistically that it
10 would teach that primary lesson about worthlessness, but rather
in such a way that it is, to be sure, worse than the present, so
that the present-day person would not want to change places,
but still manifests a kind of *progress*—toward nothing other than
the present day—so that it will support the belief that happi-
15 ness can be attained by means of further progress. Thus, the
more an age recognizes its own misery, the darker its picture of
the past will be, and the less it recognizes it, the brighter this
picture will be. And those who are happy, that is, those who
are complacent, will view everything past in a joyous light, but
20 the present in the most joyous light of all. But the greater the
distress of the present is, the stronger will be the drive to gaze
backward: those ages that are joyously active have little need of
history, and for the sedate it becomes a veritable luxury.

In our case, the historical drive is stronger than it ever has
25 been: yet despite this, the firm belief in the happiness of the
present is just as strong. A contradiction! The natural relationship seems to be lacking here.

Think of Livius's aim, of Tacitus, of Mac⟨h⟩iavelli—
flight from the present and consolation—sometimes it suffices
30 merely to recognize that at one time things were *different*, sometimes that it happened *just that way*, sometimes that it was *better*.

Our age, by contrast, is obsessed with *objective* historiography, which means, with history as a luxury: and it betrays the
greatest possible satisfaction with itself.

35 The drive to pursue history has become a *luxuriating drive*:
that is why one should become conscious of distress and

thereby establish a natural relation between history and present-day distress.

How is it that the sense of distress has gotten so *weak*? Due to the *weak personality*.

5   However, the luxuriating historical drive makes it even *weaker*.

29 [88]

There are two modes of viewing the past, and if I call the first of these the historical, the second the ahistorical mode, then my intention is neither to praise the former nor, even
10 less so, to criticize the latter. We simply have to be careful not to confuse the second of these with what is badly historical, that is, with the first in its degenerate or immature form. The ahistorical mode discovers in every moment of time, every experience, under every firmament, and among every people the
15 absolute meaning of human life: and just as all languages express the same human needs, that primordial meaning that lies at the core of what is great and small in all histories appears to the ahistorical observer to be clairvoyantly illuminated from within, so that the manifold hieroglyphs no longer trouble him
20 at all: beggar and prince, village and city, Greeks and Turks— all of them teach us the same lesson about existence. Such a mode of viewing the past is very rare among us: we demand history, just as we give preference to historical peoples and personalities and have only contempt for the rest. In our opinion,
25 the people who live on the banks of the Ganges have become weak and world-weary due to the hot climate and their own indolence; we accuse them of having weak personalities and declare their ahistorical manner of viewing the world to be a symptom of stagnation. But perhaps our demand for historical
30 human beings and peoples is merely an occidental prejudice. It is certain, at the very least, that the wise human beings of all ages thought in just such an ahistorical way and that millennia of historical experiences will not bring us one step *further* along the path of wisdom. But the following investigation is ad-

dressed to the unwise and active human beings, and its purpose
is to ask whether it is not precisely our current manner of pursuing history that is the expression of *weak personalities*: for with
this manner we are, after all, as far as possible from that ahis-
5 torical mode of observation and its attainment of wisdom. —

Let's assume that historical investigations are capable of arriving at truth with regard to something living; for example,
with regard to Christianity: then at least it would have destroyed the *illusion* that surrounds everything living and active
10 like a sustaining atmosphere—namely,

in great things
that never prosper without some illusion.

By eliminating this illusion—for example, with regard to religion—one would have destroyed religiosity itself, that is, its
15 productive temperament, and would be left with nothing but
cold, empty knowledge, along with a feeling of disappoint-
ment.

29 [89]

Anyone who ceases to see the work of a personal god whenever a starling falls from the roof will be much more circum-
20 spect, because then he will not substitute for it mythological
creatures, such as the idea, the logical, the unconscious, etc.,
but instead will attempt to make the existence of the world
comprehensible on the basis of a blind world dominatrix. May
he thus for once ignore the purposes of nature, and ignore even
25 more the purpose that the spirit of a people, or worse, that a
world spirit, must fulfill. He should dare to view the human
being as a pure product of chance, as an unprotected nothing
mercilessly exposed to every kind of ruin: it is just as possible
to break the will of the human being from this position as it is
30 from the position of a divine Providence. The historical sensibility is nothing but a disguised theology, "we are supposed
once more to make marvelous progress!" The human being en-
visions a final purpose. That is why Christianity, which damns
humanity and weeds out rare specimens, is thoroughly ahis-

torical, because it denies that in the subsequent millennia anything came about that is not now and has not been present for the last 1800 years. If, in spite of this, the present age has a thoroughly historical sensibility, it thereby makes it clear that it no longer is held back by Christianity, that it once again is unchristian, as it was a couple of millennia ago.

29 [90]
   I   Historical—Ahistorical.
  II   Monumental—Antiquarian.
 III Effects of hypertrophy.
 IV   Its causes. Hartmann as illustration at the conclusion.
  V   The weak personality. *That is why that drive must be overcome*,
       it is based on a *weakness*.
       (Mythology of history.)
       Measures against the historical fever:
       1) No history?
       2) Disavowal of all purposes: the chaos of atoms.
       3) Goethe, natural science.
       4) Cultivation of the *ahistorical sensibility*: Philosophy—
          Religion—
       Art. Seer: future.

29 [91]
   Many weak human beings do not constitute something terrible: but many stupid human beings do—they represent the ass *in concreto*, a terrible animal. Our age is not stupid.
   Strong human being, take pleasure in your strength.

29 [92]
   When historians such as Ranke become the general rule, they cease being instructive: we were familiar with such statements long before their works were completed: they are reminiscent of the senseless experimentation in the natural sciences that Zöllner laments.

29 [93]
Mirabeau: "Si j'ai dit la vérité, pourquoi ma vehémence en l'exprimant, diminuerait elle de son prix?"

29 [94]
—The path along which the blindness of recent generations is driving us is one at whose conclusion, in the true words of
5   Herr von Stein, "the Jews will be the ruling class, the farmer a rogue, and the craftsman a bungler: where everything will have disintegrated and only the sword will rule."

29 [95]
Niebuhr (*fere*): "History, when understood clearly and fully, is at least useful for one thing: so that we might recognize
10 how even the greatest and loftiest human minds do not know how accidentally their eye has adopted its manner of seeing and forcibly demanded that all others see in this same manner; forcibly, because the intensity of their consciousness is exceptionally great. Anyone who has not recognized and understood
15 this fully and in many individual instances will be enslaved by the presence of any powerful intellect who gives the loftiest passion a specific form: if the reader is immature, the immediate perception of the everyday intellectual life of a *powerful person* brings forth the same liability that the reading of novels has
20 for weak young girls."

29 [96]
"The historian's objectivity" is nonsense. It is taken to mean that all the motives and consequences of an event are observed with such purity that it no longer has any *effect*, that it remains a purely intellectual process: like the landscape for the painter
25 who merely represents it. "Disinterested observation," an aesthetic phenomenon, absence of any stimulation by the will. In other words, "objective" refers to a state of mind in the historian, artistic contemplation: however, it is a superstition to believe that the image things produce in such an aesthetically

attuned person reveals the true essence of these things. Or are
we to suppose that in this state of mind things simply can be
photographed, are we to suppose that it is a purely *passive* state
of mind? On the contrary: it is the truly creative moment of
5   the work of art, a compositional moment of the highest sort:
the will of the individual is asleep when this takes place. The
picture is *artistically true*, but certainly not yet historically true;
it is not the facts, but rather their interweaving and interconnection; this is a fictional invention, one that can be true by
10 accident: but even if it is false, it is nonetheless still "objective."

To conceive history objectively is the silent work of the
dramatist: to think of all things as interrelated, to weave isolated events into a totality: always with the presupposition that
a plan, an interconnection, must be inherent in them: a pre-
15 supposition that is by no means empirical-historical and that
runs counter to all "objectivity" as it commonly is understood.
It is an artistic drive, not a drive for truth, that causes the
human being to spin his web over and subdue the past. The
perfected form of such historiography is simply a work of art:
20 without even a spark of common truth.

Is it permissible for everything to be viewed *artistically*? For
the past I desire above all a *moral* evaluation. Hence, a dis-
quieting confusion of the artistic and the moral realms: which
weakens the moral realm.

25 However, this objectivity is usually nothing but an empty
phrase because the *artistic* potency is lacking. *Histrionic affecta-
tion* of tranquility takes the place of that artistic tranquility: lack
of pathos and moral strength is disguised as an iciness of observation with an air of superiority. In more vulgar instances,
30 banality and commonplace wisdom, which are not exciting in
the least, take the place of artistic disinterestedness. Everything *nonexciting* is sought out —

Now, it is precisely in those instances in which the highest
and rarest things are treated that such vulgar and shallow moti-
35 vations are most revolting, especially when they derive from

the historian's *vanity*. (*Swift*: "Every man's vanity is directly pro-
portional to his lack of intelligence.")

Is the judge supposed to be cold? No: he is supposed to
be unbiased, not to take utility and harm into consideration.
Above all he must truly stand above the concerned parties. I
fail to understand why someone who just happens to have been
born later should for that reason alone be qualified to be the
judge of all those born before him. Most historians stand *below*
the objects they judge!

Today one assumes: anyone who is *totally disinterested* in a particular moment of the past is the one who must be called upon
to portray it. This is the way in which philologists and Greeks
often relate to each other: with total disinterest. This is what
is then called "objectivity": even photography requires light,
in addition to the object and the photographic plate: and yet
people believe that the object and the photographic plate suf-
fice. There is a lack of radiant sunshine: in the best instance
people believe that the light from the oil lamp in the study
will do.

Entirely rash human beings always believe that the popular
views they and their age hold are correct: just as every religion
also believes this of itself. Measuring past opinions and deeds
according to the widespread opinions in which they seek the
canon of all truth is what they call "*objectivity*." Their task is the
translation of the past into the triviality of the present. They
are hostile toward every historiography that does not take these
popular opinions to be canonical: that is supposed to be "subjective"!

Only from the highest power of the present can you interpret the past;
only with the highest exertion will you divine what in the past
is worth knowing. Like for like! Otherwise you are lost, otherwise you will drag the past down to your level. Do *not trust* any
historiography that is not in the hands of the *rarest intellects*; you
will always be able to gauge the quality of their intellect when
they state a general truth. No one can be a great historian and a

blockhead or a nincompoop at one and the same time. Let's not
confuse the laborers: for example, *les historiens de M. Thiers,*
as the French are wont to say with greater naivité. A great
scholar and a great blockhead—that is a possible combination!
5   Thus: *History requires the active human being, history can be writ-*
ten only by the experienced person! The person whose experience of
some things is not greater and superior to the experience of all
other people will also not be capable of interpreting something
from the past. —The voice of the past is always the voice of
10   an oracle; only if you are seers into the future and are familiar
with the present will you be able to interpret the oracular voice
of the past. Today we tend to explain the effect of the Delphic
oracle with the claim that these priests had precise knowledge
of the past; it is time we recognized that only those who build
15   the future have the right to sit in judgment of the past: he is
only a historian by virtue of being a seer. The present is bad
and only a single line.

29 [97]
    1. No view of the past. Animal—Leopardi.
    2. Monumental—Antiquarian.
20   3. "Objectivity."
    4. Hypertrophy due to weakness.
    5. Effects.
    6. Education in history.
    7. Mythology of history.
25   8. Causes.
    9. Hartmann.
    10. Reaction—Chaos of atoms.
    11. Antidotes.
    12. Standard for future historians.

29 [98]
30   The herd grazes past us: it has no sense of the past, leaps,
eats, sleeps, digests, leaps some more, and carries on like this
from morning to night and from day to day, tethered by the

short leash of its pleasures and displeasures to the stake of the
moment: so that seeing this, the human being must sigh and
would like to address it in the manner of Giacomo Leopardi in
"The Night Song of the Shepherd in Asia":

5   Oh, how must I envy you!
           Not only because you appear to be
           almost free of all sufferings,
           forgetting in every moment
           hardship, loss, the worst anxieties —
10   but even more so because you are never tormented
               by boredom!

But we sigh for ourselves because we cannot let go of the
past: whereas it appears to us as if the animal must be happy
because it does ⟨not⟩ get bored, immediately forgets, and con-
15 tinually sees every moment sink back into fog and night. Thus,
it disappears entirely into the present, just as one number disappears into another without remainder, appears in each and
every moment as exactly what it is, without any histrionics and
intentional concealment. By contrast, we all suffer from that
20 obscure and indissoluble remainder of what is past and are
something other than we appear to be, ⟨we⟩ are moved when
we see the herd, or, even closer to home, the child that still
plays — indeed, perhaps only appears to play — between the two
gates of the past and the future without this suffering and in
25 a blindness that is as short as it is blissful; we are reluctant to
disturb its play and awaken it out of obliviousness — because
we know that with the phrase "it was," suffering and strife
begin, and life is inaugurated as an infinite imperfect: finally,
death places its seal on this knowledge that existence is an eter-
30 nal imperfect — as an eternal having-been — by bringing, to be
sure, the long-desired oblivion, but only by simultaneously
suppressing the present and existence.

Thus, we *have to* view the past — that is simply the lot of
human beings: no one will be spared becoming hardened under
35 this hard yoke, and once someone has become very hard, per-

haps he even will reach the point of lauding the lot of human
beings due to this inability to forget, precisely because the past
cannot perish in us and drives us with the disquiet of a ghost to
ascend tirelessly the entire stepladder of all that human beings
5 call great, amazing, immortal, divine.

29 [99]
   I attribute the fact that the common type of historiography
is considered agreeable to the same factor that causes a common discussion to be considered agreeable: it is made up of
politeness and lies.

29 [100]
10   The best view of history is the one that is most productive,
but productive for life. Of what use is it to us rigorously to
gather the causes, to derive from them the fact, and thereby to
mortify it! When viewed in another way it could be vital and
productive: as soon as it appears as the result of a calculation,
15 it no longer has an effect, but merely wastes all its energies trying to explain itself.

29 [101]
   Antiquarian — Monumental.
   All the dangers of both come together in "objectivity."
   The type of human beings who for this reason have come
20   to pursue history —
   This has caused a general hypertrophy.
   Niebuhr — Goethe found no common ground; Niebuhr vic-
       torious. That may have been good, for purely national
       concerns: but now it is high time to go back.

29 [102]
25 Effect on life.
   Natural conditions for the monumental and the antiquarian.
   History as luxury — its effect purely negative.
   These drives are accompanied by *perils for the truth* of history:

that is why people wanted to *extirpate* them: but now history has no meaning.

   A. *Imitation*—do not imitate—result: *assimilation*. Point of view represented by the monumental.

     Veneration, gratitude: result: *loyalty*—motivation of the antiquarian—piety. "This is how it once was," "consolation."

   B. History without any subjective *inducements*, without imitation, piety, distress of the present.

     Highest estimation of the *truthful* a characteristic of the age: Kant—lies.

     Now *pure comprehension*, without reference to life—takes over the degenerate form of the antiquarian (what is dead without veneration) and of the monumental (what is living without imitation).

     Depiction of objectivity.

   C. The drives from which this luxury lives (since natural ones are lacking). Causes of hypertrophy.

   D. Consequences of such historians for history itself. New mythology.

   E. Consequences for the people, art, etc. Politics, religion.

   F. Ultimate consequence for morality—Hartmann.

   G. Remedy: History not a luxury.

29 [103]

What is the significance of history for the formation of a culture?

It *admonishes and dissuades*: it can be used as a *daemon*: but otherwise not at all.

29 [104]

History without imitation (without subordinating oneself to what is great), without piety (without protecting the atmosphere of the living), without the distress of the present ———

29 [105]

Niebuhr writes in 1796 that German literature is clearly entering a period of decline, that Schiller and Goethe are worse than
dead: "Is Voss to remain all by himself?" He gives as the reason for this "the common natural development that universally
5 has manifested itself in all nations." "I am pleased to be able
to share with Baggesen my bitterness over the *Almanac* Schiller
published this year."

29 [106]

Hölderlin: "You certainly will discover that today human organizations, dispositions, which nature appears to have created
10 most distinctly for the purpose of humanity, that everywhere
today these are the least fortunate, precisely because they are
less frequent than in all other eras and regions. The barbarians
who surround us are destroying our best energies before they
can be cultivated, and only the *firm, profound insight into our fate*
15 *can save us from perishing in an utter lack of dignity.* We must seek
out what is exceptional, join forces with it to the greatest possible extent, fortify and heal ourselves in the sensation of it *and
thereby gain strength; we must recognize what is crude, distorted, disfig-
ured, not only in all its pain, but as what it really is, what constitutes its*
20 *character, its specific defect.*"

29 [107]

Hölderlin: "Even I, with all my good will, merely grope in
all my thought and actions to find these singular *human beings*
(the Greeks) in the world, and in all I say and do I am often
all the more clumsy and incongruous because I stand, the way
25 geese do, with flat feet in modern waters and am incapable of
soaring upward into the Greek heavens."

29 [108]

The greatest utility if (in a Pythagorean manner) everything
were to repeat itself: then one would have to be familiar with

the past and the constellation in order to know the precise nature of the repetition. Now nothing repeats itself.

29 [109]
People lament that cosmopolitanism is past: it continues to live in history, as a residue: but its prerequisite, universal piety,
5 has been lost, the desire to be helpful in everything.

29 [110]
Goethe to Sch⟨iller⟩: "You are quite right when you say that in the characters of ancient literature, as in sculpture, an abstraction appears that attains its culmination only by means of what we call style. There are also abstractions based on man-
10 ner, as in the case of the French."

29 [111]
Epic and dramatic treatment of the past. Schiller: "The epic poet merely portrays for us the tranquil existence and the effects things have by their very nature; his purpose already is achieved in every point along the course of development; that
15 is why we do not rush impatiently to a goal, but linger lovingly at every step."

29 [112]
Goethe: "Only inclination can perceive everything that a work of art contains, and only pure inclination can even perceive what it lacks."
20 *Goethe*: "It is humorous to see what actually has made this sort of human being angry, what they believe will make one angry, with what insipidness, emptiness, and vulgarity they view an alien existence, how they shoot their arrows at the superficial aspects of phenomena, of how little they have even
25 the slightest inkling, in what sort of inaccessible fortress the human being resides who is only ever able to take himself and things seriously."

29 [113]

Piety for the past goes so far that the Greeks tolerated the hieratic style, alongside the free and great style, with its pointed noses and smiles: later this was turned into a sign of refined taste. Thus, the antiquarian manner as opposed to the monu-
5 mental.

29 [114]

Antiquarian. — Piety toward the things from which we have emerged and among which we live. Sanctifying power of personality — ancestral household effects and communal institutions attain dignity and arouse enthusiastic investigations. The
10 small, the limited is ennobled — womanlike — the idyllic discovered. Everywhere evidence of an upstanding, loyal, industrious disposition.

Detriments: everything past is taken to be equally important, no relation to life as something *preserving*, not *creative*, the living
15 undervalued in favor of the venerated (hieratic). Lack of judgment, everything past merely lies there like the assorted booty of the hunter. Impedes powerful resolve, lames the person of action, who always offends piety. The venerable "ancient"; *de mortuis nil nisi bene*. The most ancient customs, religions, etc.
20 are justified solely by their age, upsetting all standards of value: because they are the sum of the vast amount of affection the Greeks displayed toward them. Whatever induced the most affection is most venerable: one venerates the amount of love. One forgets to ask what motivated this affection: indolence,
25 egoism, intellectual convenience, etc.

How does the past suffer from this? There is no proportion among things, one person considers this to be important, another that. The p⟨ast⟩ disintegrates: one person looks favorably upon one aspect, but is cold and indifferent to the next.
30 Moreover, what is insignificant is thereby perpetuated.

Gradually the scholarly habit emerges, piety dies out, the mania to collect begins, total confusion of the true human tasks: significant characters get lost in a flood of biographical questions, etc. In sum, the ruin of all that is living, which is constantly plagued by the venerable smell of mustiness.

29 [115]
The human being wants
    to create   monumental
5   to persist in the habitual   antiquarian
    to free himself from distress   critical.

29 [116]
One could raise as an objection against the opposition between the sentimentalist and the naive: that precisely the present day has that frostily clear and sober atmosphere in which
10 myth does not thrive, the air of the historical—whereas the
Greeks lived in the twilight air of the mythical and hence could
make clear contrasts and draw clean lines in their literature:
whereas we seek twilight in art because life is too bright. It is
coherent with this that Goethe understood the position of the
15 human being in nature, and that of surrounding nature itself,
to be more mysterious, enigmatic, and demonic than his contemporaries; but for that sought all the more repose in the
brightness and sharp definition of the work of art.

29 [117]
Schiller used history in the monumental sense, however not
20 as an active human being, but as someone who incited to
action, as a dramatist driving on to deeds. Perhaps we must
now move everything up one position: the ends previously
served by history now are served by drama. *Schiller's hunch* was
correct: spoken drama must overcome history in order to pro-
25 duce the effect history (when portrayed monumentally) originally had. But the historical drama should not be antiquarian
at any price; Shakespeare was correct to let his Romans appear on stage as Englishmen. In drama, the powerful human
being takes precedence: it does not adhere to a statistical law,
30 and this is the reason why it transcends the effect of that his-

tory common today. However, one should not measure it according to the highest artistic expectations; we should make out of drama a *rhetorical* work of art: that is what it truly is in Schiller's case; we should not underestimate the power of elo-
5 quence and should at least let our actors learn how to *speak* eloquently, since it is probably too late for them to learn how to recite something that is poetic. By reserving all the highest effects of tragedy for musical drama, we acquire a position of greater freedom vis-à-vis spoken drama: it can be rhetorical, it
10 can be dialectical, it can be naturalistic, it should have an effect on morality, it should be Schillerean. The *Prince of Homburg* is an exemplary drama. It is once again necessary to speak "naturally" in the highest forms of art: but since today there is not even any natural speech in life itself, we should train our actors
15 in the art of rhetoric and not scorn the French. The road that leads to style must be created, not leapt over: it is impossible to evade hieratically determined "style," that is, convention. Goethe as theater director.

29 [118]

After we abandoned the French school we became helpless:
20 we wanted to become more natural, and we succeeded in becoming more natural by letting ourselves go as much as possible and basically imitating in a sloppy and arbitrary manner what we had earlier painstakingly imitated. We are permitted to think whatever we want, but in principle nothing but pub-
25 lic opinion is permitted. We have acquired the semblance of freedom by breaking the fetters of strict convention and exchanging them for the tethers of philistinism.

The highest and ultimate aim of culture is to be "*simple and natural*": meanwhile, we want to strive to bind and fash-
30 ion ourselves so that perhaps we ultimately can return to the simple and beautiful. There is such an absurd contradiction in our evaluation of the Greeks and our aptitude for their style and life. It has almost become impossible for us to stand even on one of the lowest and most vulgar rungs of style (and that

would be so necessary!) because our knowledge about what is
superior and better is so powerful that we no longer have the
courage even to have the *ability* to accomplish something less
significant. This is the greatest danger of history.

29 [119]

My point of departure is the Prussian soldier: here there is
a true convention, here there is compulsion, earnestness, and
discipline, in matters of form, as well. It arose out of need.
To be sure, far removed from the "simple and natural"! Its
attitude toward history is empirical and for that reason assur-
edly vital, not learned. For some people it is almost mythic. It
has its origin in the strict disciplining of the body and in the
scrupulously fulfilled demands of duty.

Goethe is thus exemplary: his stormy naturalism: that gradually becomes strict dignity. As a stylized human being he has
reached heights never achieved by any other German. Today
people are so narrow-minded as to reproach him for this and
even lament that he ever grew old. Just read Eckermann and ask
yourself whether any human being in Germany ever achieved
as much in such a noble form. To be sure, it is a long way from
this to simplicity and greatness, but we should by no means
ever believe that we can simply ignore Goethe; rather, like him,
we must always begin anew.

29 [120]

Effect of musical drama on the *development* of the *group*, the
extended pose.

29 [121]

In Germany the fear of *convention* has reached epidemic proportions. But before we arrive at a national style, we will have
to have a convention. Moreover, we live in a slovenly-incorrect
convention, as our entire mode of walking, standing, and con-
versing indicates. We seem to desire the form of convention
that requires the least amount of self-overcoming, in which

everyone can be quite sloppy. To be sure, history is extremely dangerous in that it places all conventions *side by side so they can be compared* and thereby calls for a judgment in which the δύναμις is the decisive factor. Just walk through any German
5 city—every convention, when compared with those of other nations, manifests itself in the *negative*, everything is colorless, slovenly, decrepit; everyone does as he likes, but his likes are never powerful and thoughtful, but instead are only prescribed by the comfort that already is indicted as our primary consider-
10 ation when choosing clothing. In addition, we do not want to lose any time, for we are in haste. We sanction only that form of convention that is appropriate to those who are *lazy and in haste*.

It is the same as with Christianity; Protestantism prides itself
15 on having made everything inward: but the essential matter itself thereby got lost. Thus, everything about the German is inward, but we also never see anything of it.

29 [122]

Antithesis between *convention* and *fashion*. It is precisely the latter that is stimulated by the historical sensibility: it grows
20 out of conditions of luxury, seeks what is new—above all what is striking—for its own sake, remains "fashion" as long as it is "new." The Germans are nearly willing, purely for reasons of convenience and their sense of habit, to make a French convention their own convention.

29 [123]

25 Is it true that *lack of style* is inherent in the essence of the German? Or is it a symptom of his immaturity? This is probably how it is: what is *German* is not yet developed in all its clarity. It cannot be learned by looking backward: one must have faith in one's own strength.
30 *The German essence does not yet even exist, it must first come into being; at some time or other it must be born, so that it can above all be visible and honest with itself. But every birth is painful and violent.*

29 [124]

    Remedies: *Schiller's* use of history

               its dangers (the drastics, etc.)

               significance as an *admonisher*, as daemon—indeed, it sends out an admonition about itself.

29 [125]

Goethe: Madame de Stael, "despite her courteous manner, is still boorish enough to act like someone who is visiting the Hyperboreans, whose capitals were old firs and oaks, whose iron and amber were still good enough for utilitarian and ornamental purposes; nevertheless, she still forces one to drag out old carpets as presents for the guest and rusty weapons for her defense."

Goethe: "Moreover, I hate everything that only instructs me without increasing or immediately stimulating my own activity."

29 [126]

Schiller: "I cannot help but believe that the naive spirit, which all the artworks of a certain period of antiquity have in common, is the effect—and consequently also the proof for the effectiveness—of being passed on by means of education and example. Now, the question would be what we could expect from a *school* for art in an age like ours. Those ancient schools were *educational institutions for pupils*, the modern schools would have to be *houses of correction for disciplinants*, and because of the poverty of productive genius they would have to pursue their educational task more in a critical manner than in a relatively constructive one."

29 [127]

Goethe: "An old court gardener used to say: nature can be forced, but not compelled."

Goethe: "How is it possible for something silly, indeed, something absurd to enter into such a felicitous unity with the su-

preme aesthetic grandeur of music? This can happen only by
means of *humor*; for without itself being poetic, it is a type of
poetry, and by its very nature elevates us above the object. The
German so rarely has a sense of humor because his philistin-
5 ism lets him esteem only the kind of silliness that wears the
mask of sentiment or of human reason."

29 [128]
    Schiller to Goethe: "You are truly in darkness as long as you
are working, and the light is merely within you; and when you
begin to reflect, then the inner light passes out of you and illu-
10 minates the objects for you and for others."

29 [129]
    Schiller: "that the Germans have a sense only for the general,
for the commonsense, and for the moral" (nowhere do they betray "a vision for the poetic economy of the totality"). *Goethe*:
"In *Hermann and Dorothea*, as far as the material ⟨is concerned,
15 I did precisely what the Germans wanted, and now they are
utterly satisfied."⟩

29 [130]
    Goethe: "No one despised the material costume more than
he; he knows the inner human costume quite well, and in this
all of us are identical. It has been asserted that he portrayed
20 the Romans splendidly; I don't think this is so. They are nothing but flesh-and-blood Englishmen, and yet they are certainly
human beings, human beings from head to foot, and even the
Roman toga fits them well." "The poet lives at a worthy and
important time and portrays for us its cultivation, indeed, its
25 overcultivation, in the most humorous manner." —
    —Now, I ask you if it would be at all possible to portray
Romans as modern Germans in topcoats with their literati-like,
functionary-like, and lieutenant-like mannerisms. It would be
a caricature: from which we can conclude that they are not
30 human beings.

This is part of the *topic of history*. We tend to cloak ourselves in the attire and customs of foreign ages; as soon as we try to cloak foreign ages and human beings in our attire we make them into ridiculous caricatures.

29 [131]

5   *Goethe*: "But strictly speaking, nothing is theatrical that does not simultaneously appear to the eye to be something symbolic: a significant action that points toward an even more significant one."

29 [132]

Some people believe that "the German lives in isolation and
10 thinks it an honor to develop his individuality in an original way." I no longer can agree with ⟨this⟩: to be sure, a certain freedom of disposition is permitted: but his manner of behaving is uniform and rigidly imperative. Wherever you look there is nothing but an internal without an external, just as
15 Protestanism believed itself to have purified Christianity by reducing it to inwardness and doing away with it. Fashion, an arbitrarily worn manner of dress that distinguishes individuals and that itself immediately becomes a kind of uniformity, has taken the place of custom, that is, of the naturally appropri-
20 ate and suitable manner of dress. Today *fashion* is *permitted*, but *no longer* a divergent kind of thought or behavior. The human being of antiquity, quite the opposite, would have laughed at fashion, but would have approved of an individual way of life, with the exception of clothing. Individuals were stronger and
25 freer and more independent in all those things that are manifested in behavior and life. Our individuals are weak and fearful: an unruly spirit of individuality has retreated into the internal realm and occasionally follows its whims; it resists sullenly and surreptitiously. Freedom of the press has paved the way
30 for these whimsical individuals: now they can even cast their personal little vote in written form without fear of reprisals: where life is concerned, things remain just as they were. To be

sure, the Renaissance displays a different approach, namely, a
return to the strong heathen personality. But even the Middle
Ages were freer and stronger. "*Modernity*" functions by means
of *masses* identical in nature: it is irrelevant whether they are
5 "cultivated" or not.

29 [133]
    The word "virtue" is old in Germany and it has gotten rusty
and somewhat ridiculous: but we also hardly ever see any signs
of strict self-discipline, of the categorical imperative, and of
conscious morality anymore. Most teachers would feel ridicu-
10 lous even having to speak about them! One takes comfort
in having the *matter* itself: but even this seems to me to be
in doubt.

29 [134]
    It is impossible to grasp the wisdom of the mature Goethe
at one go; not as a young person. In such cases it is merely
15 "*jadedness.*"

29 [135]
    One can express one's respect for the German soldier only
by saying "he didn't know what he was singing, he didn't even
hear it"; those songs from the last German war, those marches
from the previous Prussian wars are crude, sometimes even
20 sweetly unsavory vulgarities, the yeast of that "cultivation" that
is praised so highly today. To be sure, only the yeast! But there
have been other types of yeast! Not a trace of true folkish-
ness in it, a true affront to the terms "folk song" and "folk
manner"! Similar to the way in which the Cologne editorialists
25 relate to Tyrtaeus. Shame on you, spinster Cultivation, Luther
would say.

29 [136]
    The Germans' historical sensibility made itself manifest in
the storm of emotions with which Goethe reflected upon

Erwin von Steinach: in *Faust*, in W⟨agner⟩'s *R⟨ing⟩ o⟨f the⟩ N⟨ibelungen⟩*, in Luther, in the German soldier, in Grimm. Feeling and intuiting one's way along, following tracks that almost have disappeared, deciphering the palimpsest, indeed
5 myriopsest—a great deal of error and misinterpretation is possible!

29 [137]
Program. 6th of November 1873.
  1. *Freedom of the cities*—the *conditio*.
  2. Schools and customs under municipal control.
10 3. The absolute teacher destroys (educational Cossack).
  4. The historical sensibility as piety, not as taking into consideration.
  5. The soldier to be used to *prepare the way* for a more serious culture.
15 6. Consequences of the centralization and conformity of opinions to be aggravated to the extreme in order to attain their purest form and thereby provide a deterrent.
  7. The social crisis can be solved only at the level of the city, not at that of the state.
20 8. Elimination of the press by means of municipal eloquence.
  9. The destruction of the large political parties that demand conformity.
  10. Localize the religious problem.
25   Development of a community of the people and its representatives (army, diplomats).
The form of historiography that is called objective is an absurdity: the objective historians are derelict or jaded personalities.

29 [138]
30 In Lichtenberg's day one had no idea that the Germans pursued history in excess. To be sure, he does indeed credit them with having a gift for a higher form of history. Nowadays all

education is founded on history: Is history to blame if German education in its entirety is of so little value?

History purely as an epistemological problem: in its lowest forms only interested in arriving at information, not at insight; in its highest sense lacking any repercussions for life.

Immense investment of energy without sound praxis.

29 [139]

Statistics does not deal with the great active individuals on the stage of history, but only with the supernumeraries, the people, etc.

29 [140]

How easily *objective* historiography reverts to the tendentious! The real trick is to be second and appear to be first.

29 [141]

Platonic education without history. Hartmann.

Progressive haste: where is everyone rushing off to?

Foundation of modern institutes.

The world is becoming more and more utilitarian.

Everything that once bound human beings together is becoming more abstract.

We are experimenting so as to see whether the human being is by nature good or evil.

Institutions are founded on fear and need.

Basically, cosmopolitanism must spread.

The arbitrary delimitations of state and nation gradually lose their mystery and appear much more cruel and wicked. The antitheses are becoming hopelessly extreme. Perishing from fever.

29 [142]
Depiction of the tranquility of the ahistorical world.

Longing for the shelter of the work of art: in it we are at least able to live ahistorically for a few hours.

"The art of silence is one of the verbal arts." Jean Paul.

"It takes a great deal of time for the demise of a world—but nothing but time," Gibbon says.

29 [143]
If happiness were the goal, then animals would be the highest creatures. Their cynicism is grounded in forgetfulness: that is the shortest path to happiness, even if it is a happiness with little value.

29 [144]
Schopenhauer suggests that all genius might be based on the exact recollection of one's own biography. If pure knowledge were the goal—would our age then be the one with the most genius? Is the greatest knowledge about human beings and expertise about things a sign of greatness? Is it the task of every generation to be a judge? It seems to me, on the contrary, that the task is to do something upon which future generations can pass judgment.

29 [145]
Everything historical *measures* itself according to something. What can our age hold up as a standard by which it can measure itself?

29 [146]
   1. Inward.
   2. Just and objective.
   3. Illusion destroyed.
   4. Agedness of the human race.
   5. Mythology.

6. Hartmann.
7. Ahistorical.
8. The most naive stages of history.
9. Limitation of the horizon.

29 [147]

Plan.

1. Ahistorical—Historical.
2. Utility and harm of history. In general.
3. Transition to depiction of the present age.
4. Inwardness.
5. Just, objective.
6. Illusion destroyed.
7. Agedness of the human race. Hartmann. Mythology.
8. Whether ahistorical? Plato.
9. Measure of the historical. Limitation. Mastery.
10. German culture. Value of history for it.
    Style. National variation.

29 [148]

He always expresses things a little more clearly than he actually conceives them.

29 [149]

Continuation of zoology.

Statistics proves that the human being is a herd animal.

29 [150]

Wartburg competition: von der Hagen, *Minnesinger*, II, 2ff. in the year 1300.

Ludus Paschalis *de adventu et interitu Antichristi.* Pezii *thesaur⟨us⟩ Anecdot⟨orum⟩ N⟨ovissimus⟩* 2.

29 [151]

Animal, Human being—Historical, Ahistorical.
Shaping power.

Ahistorical foundation.

State as example. (Forgetting the past and illusion about the past.)

History serves life, it stands in the service of the ahistorical.

29 [152]

What does ahistorical mean?

Passion operates ahistorically.

Also great aims, whether human being or nation.

Excessive valorization — Niebuhr. Leopardi.

29 [153]

1. Theme and theses.			
2.		⎧	Monumental.
3.	History for life.	⎨	Antiquarian.
4.		⎩	Critical.
5. Transition to critique of the present day.			
6.		⎧	inward.
7.	History	⎪	alleged justness, objectivity.
8.	hostile to life.	⎨	no longer mature.
9.		⎪	latecomers.
10.		⎩	world process.
11. Transition to the remedies: Plato. No history.			
12.	⎧ Remedies.		
13.	⎨		

29 [154]

Fictional{,} Mythical.

Love and self-oblivion.

Life as problem.

Right to become mature.

Honesty and the audacity of the word.

The ardor of the sense of justice.

29 [155]

Demonstrate the excess 1) by the fact that everything remains *inward*

2) that nothing becomes *mature* any longer

5   3) the sense of being *latecomers*

4) stage of *self-ridicule*

5) *history itself lames*: alleged objectivity.

Transition: then one is happy to play with the thought: abso-
10 lutely no history. Rousseau.

29 [156]

Historical education as education per se.

Historical objectivity as justice.

Immature.

Irony—Agedness of the human race.

15 World process.

Clever egoism.

Preface.

Introduction.

History for life.

20 History harmful to life.

29 [157]

1. Historical, Ahistorical, and Suprahistorical.

2. History in the service of life.

3. History harmful to life.

4. The ahistorical and the suprahistorical as remedies for
25 life harmed by history.

29 [158]

History hostile to life.

1. engenders the dangerous contrast between inward and outward.

2. awakens the appearance of justice.
3. prevents maturity and completeness.
4. awakens the belief in the agedness of the human race
   and is the *advocatus diaboli*.
5. is suited for service to clever egoism.

29 [159]

Is my reader acquainted with the atmosphere in which the
observer lives? Is he capable of forgetting himself, forgetting
the author, and of letting his soul range widely, as it were,
over the things that we observe together? Is he prepared to be
carried from calm to stormy seas without abandoning the attitude of the observer? Does he love the whistling of the storm
and can he tolerate the outbreaks of rage and contempt? And
to repeat: Is he capable, amid all of this, of thinking neither of
himself nor of the author? —Well, all right then, I believe I
heard him answer "Yes," and I now will no longer refrain from
addressing him.

29 [160]

On the Utility and Liability of History for Life.

Preface.
I.   Historical, Ahistorical, Suprahistorical.
II. History in the service of life.
    a) monumental history
    b) antiquarian
    c) critical
III. History hostile to life.
    a) It engenders the dangerous contrast between
       inward and outward.
    b) It awakens the appearance of justness.
    c) It destroys the instincts and prevents matura-
       tion.
    d) It awakens the belief in the agedness of the hu-
       man race.
    e) It is exploited by clever egoism.

IV.   The ahistorical and the suprahistorical as remedies for
       life harmed by history.

29 [161]
     Chapter on life and history: what scholarship has to say
about it: laissez faire. What is lacking is the appropriate praxis,
5 the art of healing.

29 [162]
     For the conclusion.
     From irony to cynicism.
     Plato's measures for winning over youth for the state.
     Schiller — Correctional facilities.
10   Auxiliary science necessary — applied history, doctrine of
       health.
     Remedies, the ahistorical, the suprahistorical. Praise of art
       and its power to create atmospheres.

29 [163]
                     Outline of the Unfashionable Observations.
15   1873   David Strauss.
             Utility and Liability of History.
     1874   Excessive Reading and Excessive Writing.
             The Scholar.
     1875   Secondary Schools and Universities.
20   Soldier Culture.
     1876   The Absolute Teacher.
             The Social Crisis.
     1877   On Religion.
             Classical Philology.
25   1878   The City.
             Essence of Culture (Original-).
     1879   Nation and Natural Science.

29 [164]
       1 Prelude.
       2 — — —

 3 The Afflictions of Philosophy.
 4 The Scholar.
 5 Art.
 6 Higher Education.
 7 State, War, Nation.
 8 Social.
 9 Classical Philology.
 10 Religion.
 11 Natural Science.
 12 Reading, Writing, Press.
 13 Path to Freedom (as epilogue).

29 [165]
Plato and his predecessors.
Homer.

Skeptical thoughts.

29 [166]
Excellent depiction of the Germans and the French:
Görres, *Europe and the Revolution*, p. 206.
How changeable and blurred the lines of every completed
drawing are. Licht⟨enberg⟩ I, 206.

29 [167]
Cycle of Lecture Courses.
Rhetoric.
Metrics.
History of Poetry.
Prose.
Ancient Philosophy: 1) Pre-Platonic Philosophers and Plato.
                    2) Aristotle and the Socratics.
Choephori.
Hesiod's *Erga.*
Thucydides, B. I.
Lyricists.
Aristotle's *Poetics.*

29 [168]

Romans and Greeks: Attitude of the Romans toward Greek culture. Their judgments about it. The *decorative manner of culture* originates with them.

29 [169]

Three Treatises by Friedrich Nietzsche.

5   Homer and Classical Philology.

On Truth and Lie.

The Foundations of the State. (Competition, war.)

29 [170]

3.

Depiction of the chaotic confusion characteristic of a mythi-
10   cal age. The Oriental. Beginnings of philosophy as something that brings order into the cults, the myths; it organizes the unity of religion.

4.

Beginnings of an ironic attitude toward religion. Renewed
15   emergence of philosophy.

5. etc. narrative.

Conclusion: Plato's state as *super-Hellenic*, as not impossible. Here philosophy reaches its culmination, as the founder of a metaphysically organized state.

29 [171]

20   *Greeks and Barbarians.*

First Part: Birth of Tragedy.

Second Part: Philosophy in the Tragic Age.

Third Part: On Decorative Culture.

29 [172]

It is by no means absurd to think that our memory of the
25   past might also be weaker than it is and that our historical sen-

sibility might slumber just as it slumbered during the highest
acme of ancient Greek culture. Just beyond the present day
darkness would set in: in this darkness, great figures, growing
to enormous size, roam in shadowy uncertainty, influencing
us, but almost like heroes, not like the common reality of the
light of day. All of tradition would be that nearly unconscious
tradition of inherited characters: living human beings, in their
actions, would provide evidence of the fundamental things
they were passing on; history would move about in flesh and
blood, not as a yellowed document and as paper memory. Children hold the customs of their parents and grandparents to be
the past: anything that existed long before that, as architec-
tural remnants, as a temple, as superstition, scarcely influences
those living in the present. Today the farmer lives in a similar
manner, as did every great people of the past. The primary advantage for both is, and was, that the current generation does
not compare and measure itself in such a painstaking way, so
that it can remain unconscious in matters of self-judgment. It
will gain confidence in its strength because its strength will
be applied only to real needs, not to imagined and acquired
ones, and because strength usually will be adequate to need.
It will be spared boredom to a greater extent than a people
that has more history and more cultivation than its productive
energies can support. Not led astray as often in search of the
unattainable goal, disposed to a sense of disgust at whatever
is accomplished, the human being arrives at a tranquility that
is the antithesis of the modern, thoroughly historical world
and its haste. Shouldn't one have to pay the price of living in
the precious picture galleries of all ages, where the viewer's
gaze is constantly reflected back upon himself, forcing him to
make comparisons and ask himself what business he has being
in these rooms at all? And thus even the boldest person may
once utter the curse: "Away with all that is past, into the fire
with all the archives, libraries, art treasures! Let the present
itself produce what it needs, for its only value resides in what
it itself can accomplish. Stop tormenting it with the mummifi-

cation of everything that was once valid and necessary in some distant age, get the skeletons out of here so that the living can take pleasure in their days and their deeds." Yes, if only happiness, freedom from boredom, contentment could be our
5 watchwords: then it would be possible to praise the animal that always lives on the fine line of the present and eats, digests, eats again, sleeps, and leaps without being sullen and bored. "To feel things historically" means to know that one at any rate has been born to suffer and that in the best possible instance
10 the only thing our labor accomplishes is helping us forget this suffering. The demigods always lived only in earlier ages, the present generation is always the degenerate one. It rarely knows what its distinction is; for the past surrounds us like a blackened, darkened wall. Only our descendants are capable
15 of appreciating what it was in which even we were demigods. This is not to say that things are eternally in a state of decline and that everything great recurs in ever smaller proportions: but every age always is simultaneously a dying age and sighs when the autumn leaves fall. Just look at the individual human
20 life: what the youth loses when he leaves childhood behind is so irreplaceable that upon such a loss he would have to wish to abandon life out of apathy. And yet when he becomes a man he again loses something invaluable, and in old age he eventually loses the ultimate possession, so that he now knows life
25 and is ready to lose it. What wasted effort if as youths we were to struggle to achieve those things that constituted happiness and strength during our childhood. The loss can be tolerated, memory continually heaps up one loss after the other, and in the end, when we know we have lost everything, death con-
30 solingly takes away from us even this knowledge, our final inheritance.

29 [173]
    Homer and Classical Philology.   24.
    Competition Among the Greeks.   15.

On Truth and Lie.   20.
The Greek State.   15.

Four Treatises.

29 [174]

Plato.

5 *Youth.*   Plague.
               Critias.
               Plato's artistic qualities.
               Heracliteans.
               Socrates. The Platonic Socrates.
10 *Journeys.*   Aims—the practical ideal.
               Pythagoreans—ideas (inferior conception).
               Dion.
   Academy.   The philosopher in the state. Sophist. Rhetor. Art.
               Literary work—Eros. Dialectics.
15   Second journey.
               Third journey—ideal of the state.
               Dion's end. Other political influences.
               Parmenides. Initial skepticism toward the theory:
                   Plato primarily a legislator and reformer, never a
20   skeptic in this regard.

29 [175]
   Empedocles.
   Democritus.
   Pythagoreans: Struggle against the Eleatics, more in order
                   to protect themselves. Description of their
25   compact.
   Socrates. Moral—dialectical—plebeian.

29 [176]
   "The tendency of human beings to consider little things important has produced much greatness," Lichtenberg says.

29 [177]

History, which certainly does not, either indirectly or directly, make people into better citizens, is only, to cite a statement employed by Bolingbroke in his famous letters _On the Study and Use of History_, "a specious and ingenious sort of idleness."

29 [178]

Aristotle: "There are primarily two things that cause the human being to feel a sense of protective care and attachment: sole possession, and the rarity of the possessed object, which makes it precious to the person who possesses it." This is how the antiquarian human being attends to the past, because it is so completely individual and unique—completely independent of how cheap or precious it is as such; he believes himself in possession of this little possession that sets him apart from all other human beings. The smallest bit of knowledge, as soon as it becomes his property, brings pleasure to the person who discovered it, for example, a correction in a book or manuscript.

29 [179]

What Benjamin Constant says also holds true for critical history: "the fundamental moral principle, which states that it is a duty to speak the truth, would, if one interpreted it absolutely and independent of any context, make every society impossible." Just think of your own life: if the task were to speak openly about one's own past, who would be able to endure it at all? To be able to live requires a great capacity to forget.

29 [180]

Luther: "that if God had thought of heavy artillery, he would never have created the world." The ability to forget is simply a part of all creativity.

29 [181]

Let's just imagine the last human being sitting on the arid desert of the decaying planet earth—

29 [182]

The human being conceals many things within himself with which he should never become familiar: which is why the ancient Spaniard said "Defienda me Dios de my," "Lord protect me from myself."

29 [183]

The antiquarians say: "What is great is fundamentally what is common and universal"; they, too, struggle against the emergence of what is great (by minimizing it, vituperating it, micrology).

29 [184]

Luther: "Cicero, a wise and industrious man, suffered and accomplished a great deal."

One elevates or lowers history according to one's own level: thus, Mommsen lowers his Cicero to the level of a journalist, Luther calls him (see preceding).

29 [185]

The need to *have contact with great predecessors* is certain, etc. Contact with *small-minded ones*, impish (see above).

29 [186]

Goethe: (Anyone who from now on does not take up some art or handwork, etc.).

Piety for the past for the benefit of the hieratic (s⟨ee⟩ a⟨bove⟩).

The art of silence is one of the verbal arts. "It takes time for a world's demise—nothing but time."

29 [187]

For the conclusion: Goethe on Niebuhr, "the historian as the truly worthwhile object, not history itself." This gives some reason for hope (see above).

Schiller praised by Goethe (see above).

29 [188]

Antidotes: 1) *No* history?
             2) Disavowal of purposes, chaos of atoms?
             3) Interest in the historian turned toward history?

Most historians below their objects.

             4) Goethe, nature.
             5) Cultivation of the suprahistorical and ahistorical. Religion, pity, art.

29 [189]

Niebuhr in defense of Machiavelli: "There are ages in which one must hold every human being sacred: others in which one can and should treat them only as masses; it is a matter of being acquainted with the age."

29 [190]

"Since losing his simple, great character, the German is by nature pseudorhetorical and denigrating, and the last thing he is is fair: no, he is even less loving."

29 [191]

Desired result:

To reveal *character* in cultivation, not decorative, but rather organic cultivation.

Then the Germans will perhaps yet succeed in accomplishing what the Greeks accomplished with regard to the Orient — and thereby finally discover what is "German."

29 [192]

To take possession of oneself, to organize the chaos, to jettison all fear of "cultivation" and be honest: summons to γνῶθι σαυτόν, not in the brooding sense, but in order really to know what our genuine needs are. From that point boldly toss aside everything foreign and grow from within your own self, do not make yourself fit the mold of something outside yourself.

Art and religion are suited for the organization of this chaos:
the latter provides love for the human being, the former love
for existence

with this, contempt ———

29 [193]

Planting the seeds of tradition, progressive motion, oak trees
for one's grandchildren. Finding organization to make existence possible for the first generation and then taking charge
of the education of the people. Like a planet, without rest,
without haste.

The tranquility of those who are working. The tranquil gaze
into the future only possible when we no longer sense ourselves to be so ephemeral, so like a wave.

29 [194]

The ahistorical powers are called forgetfulness and illusion.
The suprahistorical, art, religion, pity, nature, philosophy.

29 [195]

Learning a *trade*, necessary return to the smallest sphere,
which he idealizes as much as possible, for the individual in
need of cultivation. Struggle against abstract production by
machines and in factories.

Evoking scorn and hatred toward everything that today is
considered "cultivation": by holding up to it a more mature
form of cultivation.

29 [196]

"And what is to become of us," the historians will reluctantly
reply. "What is to become of the *science* of history, our famous,
rigorous, sober, motherly science?" "Get thee to a nunnery,
Ophelia," Hamlet says; but to which nunnery do we wish to
ban this science and the historical scholar? This is a riddle that
the reader must himself address and solve if he is too impatient
to wait for the slow appearance of the author's own solution in

a herewith promised later set of observations "On the Scholar"
and his thoughtless integration into modern society.

Conclusion: There is a society of hopeful ones.

29 [197]
The Afflictions of Philosophy.
5   External: natural science, history (example: instinct. Has become concept).

Internal: the courage to live according to a philosophy has
broken down.

The other sciences (natural science, history) are able only to
10 explain, not to give orders. And when they do give orders, they
are only able to refer to their *utility*. But every religion, every
philosophy has somewhere within it precisely a sublime *breach
with nature*, a striking lack of utility. Is that all there is to it? —
Just like poetry, which is a kind of nonsense.
15   Human happiness is predicated on the belief that somewhere there exists for the human being an *incontrovertible* truth,
cruder ones (for example, the welfare of one's family as the supreme motivation), more refined ones, the belief in the church,
etc. He refuses to listen when someone argues against it.
20   At times of tremendous instability the philosopher ought to
be a *brake shoe*: can he still perform this function?

The *mistrust* of rigorous scientific investigators toward every
deductive system, *vid*. Bagehot.

29 [198]
The Afflictions of Philosophy.
25 A. The demands made on philosophy in the distress of the
present age. Greater than ever.

B. The attacks on philosophy greater than ever.

C. And philosophers weaker than ever.

29 [199]
To turn *philosophy* purely into a science (as Trendelenburg
30 does) is to throw in the towel.

29 [200]

The defectively developed *logic*! It has been stunted by historical studies. Even Zöllner complains. Praise of Spir. And of the English.

29 [201]

What kind of people still become philosophers today?

29 [202]

5   "Who the deepest has thought loves what is most alive."

Hölderlin.

    A mystery are those of pure origin.
Even song may hardly unveil it.
For as you began, so you will remain,
10   And much as need can effect,
And breeding, still greater power
Adheres to your birth
And the ray of light
That meets the new-born infant.   Hölderlin.

29 [203]

15   On *religion*. I notice an exhaustion, people have grown weary of its meaningful symbols. All the possibilities of Christian life, the most serious and the most insipid, the most harmless and the best thought through, have been tried out; it is time for imitation or for something else. Even ridicule, cynicism,
20   hostility have been played out—what one sees is an ice field when the weather is warming, everywhere the ice is dirty, broken, without luster, covered with puddles, dangerous. Here the only attitude that to me seems appropriate is deference, but total abstinence: in this way I honor that religion, even
25   though it is a dying one. The only thing one can do is soothe and assuage; we must protest only against the bad, thoughtless cooks, especially if they are scholars. —Christianity has been entirely turned over to critical history.

29 [204]

If for once I can indulge my wishes, then I think that I could have been relieved of the terrible effort of educating myself if I had found a philosopher as educator whom I could have obeyed because I trusted him more than myself! Then I would try to guess the maxims of his education, for example, his views on harmonious and partial education: and his own methods. It would be extremely difficult, and we, who are accustomed to laxness in matters of education and to taking things easy, would often lose heart. —But as things stand, without such educators, one often senses that one's strengths are in conflict with one another, revolting, even one's intellectual drives. To be sure, scholars believe that it is not easy to do enough for scholarship: not enough for scholarship, that is true, but more than enough for themselves, too much: that is also true. I see nothing but intellectual cripples: their partial education has turned them into hunchbacks. —What do harmonious and partial mean? Do we have any reason to be afraid of partial education? On the contrary, the *pars* is merely supposed to become the center for all the other strengths, the sun in the planetary system. But wherever a great strength is present, it is necessary to balance it out with counterweights. Kleist—philosophy (he was lacking Schopenhauer).

29 [205]

The philosopher is a philosopher first for himself, and only then for others. It is impossible to be a philosopher for oneself alone. For as a human being he has relationships with other human beings: and if he is a philosopher, he must also be a philosopher in these relationships. I mean: even if he rigorously isolates himself from others, as a recluse, even by doing this he provides a lesson, sets an example, and is a philosopher for the others as well. It makes no difference how he behaves: the fact that he is a philosopher means that he has one side that always faces other human beings.

The philosopher's product is his *life* (first, before his *works*).

It is his work of art. Every work of art first faces the artist and then other human beings. —What effects does the philosopher have on nonphilosophers and on other philosophers?

State, society, religion, etc., all of them can ask: what has philosophy done for us? What can it do for us today? The same is true for culture.

Question concerning the cultural effects of philosophy in general.

Transcription of culture—as a single temperament and key composed of many initially hostile forces that now make it possible to play a melody.

29 [206]

In the Middle Ages inimical forces are more or less held together by the church: when this bond tears, each of these forces rises up against the others. The Reformation declared many things to be ἀδιάφορα—hereafter, the gulf steadily widens. Ultimately, only the crudest forces determine almost everything on their own, beginning with the military state. Attempt by the state to organize everything anew out of itself and be the bond for those inimical forces. Concepts of a state culture, as opposed to a religious culture. Now power is evil and desires what is useful more than it desires anything else.

We find ourselves in the ice-filled stream of the Middle Ages, it has begun to thaw and is rushing on with devastating power.

29 [207]

By all means *revolution*: but whether it will produce barbarism or something else depends on the intelligence and humanity of the following generations:

the lack of ethical philosophy among the educated classes has, of course, penetrated in even more obvious forms into the uneducated classes, who always were nothing but a crude imitation. In them, everything is doomed. No new great thought can be seen far and wide. Only that at some time everything will begin anew.

29 [208]

I cannot imagine Schopenhauer at a university: the students would flee from him and he, in turn, would flee from his fellow professors.

29 [209]

When I think about the strong, joyful generations that have
5   lived—whatever became of the energies possessed by the age
of Reformation!—then our manner of living appears to me
like the beginning of winter high in the mountains, the sun
is rarely seen, everything is gray, every simple joy moves the
observer—what fleeting happiness! Life is so difficult. And on
10 top of it all the memory of warm summer days.

29 [210]

Alas, this span of time! We at least want to deal with it
grandly and voluntarily. For such a small gift we should not
make ourselves the slaves of the givers! What is most amazing
is how limited the thought and imagination of human beings
15 are, they never perceive life as a totality. They are afraid of the
words and opinions of their neighbors—alas, only two more
generations and no one will still have these opinions that are
dominant today and that seek to make you their slaves.

29 [211]

Every philosophy must be able to do what I demand, concen-
20 trate the human being—but no philosophy can do this today.

29 [212]

Two tasks: to defend the new against the old and to link the
old with the new.

29 [213]

For the *plan*.

The philosopher has *two sides: one faces human beings*, the other
25 we never see, since here he is a philosopher for himself. We

observe first the philosopher's relationship to other human beings. Consequence for our age: nothing comes of this relationship. Why is that? *They are not philosophers for themselves.*

"Physician, heal thyself!" That is what we must shout out to them.

29 [214]

Alas, we human beings of this age! A winter's day is upon us, and we live high up in the mountains, in peril and in need. Every joy is short-lived, and every ray of sunshine that looks down at us from the mountains is pale. Then music sounds—at the sound of this, the wanderer is deeply moved; everything was so wild, so isolated, so bleak, so hopeless—and now suddenly there is a sound of joy, of pure, thoughtless joy! But already the early evening fog creeps in, the sound dies out, the wanderer's footsteps crunch in the snow; the face of nature at evening, which always comes so soon and is reluctant to leave, is cruel and dead.

29 [215]

The floating gossamer of old men's summer—*Strauss* as confessor.—

29 [216]

If the working classes ever discover that they easily could surpass us in matters of education and virtue, then it is all over for us! But if this does not occur, then it is really over for us.

29 [217]

Begin with the painter and ⟨with⟩ the connoisseur of art standing in front of the painting—Goethe.

29 [218]

We not only call someone "irrational" who pursues an irrational aim, but also someone who applies inappropriate and disproportionate means to attain a rational aim: hence, both

someone who seeks to bail out the entire sea as well as someone
who shoots at sparrows with buckshot. Nature is full of this
second type of irrationality. Even in the highest realm of nature
known to us, in the human being, nature does not prove itself
to be any more intelligent with regard to its means, regardless
of how extraordinary its aims and intentions are. The way in
which it employs rare gifts for the well-being of humanity is
just as admirable in its irrationality as it is amazing to utilize the
rare for the well-being of the common: for the well-being of
the common lies in its elevation, its augmentation into something rare, its reminting as something uncommon and new. I
am asking about the teleology of the philosopher, one of the
rarest creations produced in nature's workshop: What is the
purpose of his existence? For the well-being of a people and
an age, perhaps also for all peoples and all ages. And how is
he employed for that purpose? Like the most indifferent play-
thing, which one either ignores or picks up, throws around or
steps on, as if thousands of them simply could be found on the
street. Isn't it necessary for human beings to have hope and
work against the irrationality of nature? Yes, it would be necessary if it were only possible! Because nature exerts its effects
precisely in human beings and by means of human beings,
and because a people as a whole displays precisely that duality
of nature, that marvelous rationality of aims and that no less
amazing irrationality of means. There can be no doubt that the
artist creates his work for other human beings. Nevertheless,
he knows that no one will ever understand and love his work
the way he does. But this high degree of knowledge and love
is necessary so that a lower degree can be produced: this lower
degree is the aim nature pursues with the work of art, it wastes
its means and energies, and the expenditure far exceeds what
it brings in. And yet this is the natural relationship, everywhere. Cutting expenditures and increasing profits a hundred-
fold would be much more sensible. Less effort, less pleasure
and knowledge in the artist himself, but a tremendous increase in pleasure and knowledge in art's receptive audience —

that would be a more advantageous arrangement. If we could
switch their roles: the artist would have to be the weaker human
being and the receptive audience, the listeners, the viewers, the
stronger human beings. The power of works of art would have
5 to grow with their resonance among the people: just as speed
increases by the square of the distance. Is it senseless to wish
that art could have its weakest effect at the outset, ultimately
its strongest one at the conclusion? Or at least that as much is
taken as is given, that cause and effect are equally strong?
10   That is why it oftentimes seems as if an artist, and sometimes even a philosopher, only lives *by chance* in his age, scattered wanderers or recluses left behind.
    But wherever we discover a relationship between a philoso-
pher and a people, we also sense the following aims of nature,
15 the following vocation of the philosopher.

29 [219]
    1. What the philosopher has been in different ages.
    2. What he would have to be in our age.
    3. Picture of the fashionable philosophy of our day.
    4. Why he cannot accomplish what, according to n⟨o⟩. 2,
20   he ought to be able to accomplish: because a stable cul-
       ture is lacking. The philosopher as recluse. Schopenhauer
       demonstrates how nature exerts itself: it still falls short.

29 [220]
    Wisdom independent of scientific knowledge.
    The lower, unlearned classes are now our only hope. The
25 learned, educated classes must be abandoned. And along with
them the priests, who understand only these classes and who
themselves belong to them. Those human beings who still
know what distress is also will be able to sense what wisdom
can mean for them.
30   The greatest danger is if the unlearned classes are contami-
nated with the yeast of present-day education.
    If a Luther were to appear today, he would rise up against

the disgusting attitude of the propertied classes, against their stupidity and thoughtlessness, which even prevents them from sensing any danger.

Where shall we seek the people!

5   The level of education gets lower by the day because the haste increases.

29 [221]

We must seriously consider whether the foundations for the development of a culture even exist at all. Can philosophy function as such a foundation? — But it *never* had such a function.

10   My confidence in religion is boundlessly slight: one can see the receding floodwaters after an enormous flood.

29 [222]

For the *beginning*. Everywhere *symptoms* that education *is dying out*, being completely extirpated. (Laissez faire of the scholarly disciplines.) Haste, receding floodwaters of religion,

15   national conflicts, scholarship fragmenting and disintegrating, the contemptible economy of money and pleasures among the educated classes, their lack of love and greatness. It becomes clearer and clearer to me that the learned classes are definitely part of this movement. They are becoming less thoughtful

20   and less loving by the day. Everything stands in the service of approaching barbarism, art as well as science—where else shall we turn? The great deluge of barbarism is at the door. Since we really have nothing to defend and all of us are in this together—what can be done?

25   Attempt to warn those powers that actually exist, join forces with them and subdue in a timely fashion the classes from which the threat of barbarism comes. However, every alliance with the "educated people" must be rejected. They are the greatest enemy because they interfere with the work of the

30   physician and employ lies to deny the malaise.

29 [223]
On the Vocation of the Philosopher.

We must reproach nature for its lack of expedience: we
notice it in the case of the question: why does a work of art
exist? For whom? For the artist? For the other human beings?
5 But an artist does not need to make visible an image that he
sees and then show it to others. At any rate, the artist finds
happiness in his work, just as his understanding of his work is
greater than the happiness and understanding of all the others.
This disproportion strikes me as inexpedient. The cause should
10 be proportionate to the effect. This is *never* the case with works
of art. It is stupid to create an avalanche only in order to remove a little snow, or to kill a human being in order to swat
the fly on his nose. But that's how nature proceeds. The artist
bears witness against teleology.

15 The philosopher even more so. For whom does he philosophize? For himself? For others? But the first would be senseless
wastefulness on the part of nature, the second once again inexpedient. The philosopher always has utility only for the few,
not for an entire people: and his effect on these few is not as
20 strong as on the author himself.

For whom does an architect build? Is the manifold, unequal
reflex, this repercussion in many souls, supposed to be nature's
intention? I think he builds for the next great architect. Every
artwork seeks to continue to procreate and to this end seeks
25 receptive and creative souls. The same holds true for the philosopher.

Nature proceeds in an incomprehensible and clumsy way.
The artist, like the philosopher, shoots an arrow into the teem-
ing multitude. It probably will hit something. They do not take
30 aim. Nature does not take aim, and it misses the mark countless times. Artists and philosophers perish because their arrows
do not hit their mark. Nature is just as wasteful in the realm
of culture as it is in planting and sowing. It accomplishes its
purposes in an inefficient and general manner. It expends too
35 much energy for purposes that are out of proportion. The re-

lationship between the artist and his connoisseurs and fans is
like the relationship of heavy artillery to a flock of sparrows.

Nature always works for the common good, but it does not
always employ the best and most skillful means. There can
5 be no doubt that by producing the artist, the philosopher, it
sought to help the others: but how relatively small and how
accidental is its effect when measured against the causes (the
artist, the work of art)! Its predicament is even worse in the
case of the philosopher: the path from him to the object on
10 which he is supposed to have an effect is entirely accidental. It
fails countless times. Nature is wasteful, yet not out of extravagance, but rather out of inexperience: we must assume that if
nature were a human being, it never would cease to be annoyed
with itself.

29 [224]

15   I hate it when one leaps beyond this world by condemning
it wholesale: art and religion have their origin in it. — Oh, this
is how I understand this flight: up and away into the peace of
the One!

Alas, the lack of love in those philosophers who always are
20 thinking only of the chosen ones and have so little faith in their
own wisdom. Wisdom must shine upon everyone, like the sun:
and a faint ray of light must even be able to shine down upon
the lowliest soul.

A **possession** promised to human beings! Philosophy and
25 religion are a longing for *property*.

29 [225]

I find the thought amusing that someday soon human beings
will be fed up with reading: and with writers as well; that some
day the scholar of a future generation will come to his senses,
write his testament, and ordain that his corpse be burned along
30 with his books, especially his own writings. And if the for-
ests are becoming increasingly sparse, won't the time soon
come when libraries should be treated as paper firewood and

kindling? After all, most books are the products of smoking
brains, so they might just as well revert to smoke again. I
believe, moreover, that a generation that has the good taste
to heat its furnaces with its libraries will for that very reason
5 also have the good taste to select a small number of deserving
books that will be permitted to survive. To be sure, it would be
possible that a century later precisely our present age would be
considered the darkest period of the past because nothing of it
has survived. How fortunate we thus are to have been able to
10 get to know this age of ours on the basis of the volumes of material it turns over to the printing presses every day: if it makes
good sense at all for someone to occupy himself with an object,
then it is in any event good fortune if he can occupy himself
with it so thoroughly that he no longer has any doubts about
15 it. But it *does make* good sense; for one thereby is able to *become
acquainted* with many things *oneself*, and it is precisely the bad
literature of an age that permits us to see ourselves in its image:
because it portrays the average morality dominant at that particular moment, etc.; that is, it does not portray the exception,
20 but the rule. Whereas the truly good books are usually produced by contemporaries who have nothing in common with
the contemporary age except their contemporariness. That is
why they are not as useful for the attainment of self-knowledge
as the bad books.
25   Based on examples from bad books and newspapers I now
want to demonstrate that we are all dilettantes in philosophical
matters and that we have no ph⟨ilosophy⟩.

29 [226]
Reading and Writing.
Thought and speech opposed to them: what influence does
30 excessive reading and writing have on them?

29 [227]
Some things become enduring only when they have become
weak: up to that point they are threatened with the danger of

a sudden demise: today Christianity is so vigorously defended because it has become the most comfortable religion; now it has prospects for immortality, after having won over to its side the most abiding thing in the world, human indolence
5 and complacence. Thus, philosophy also is now valued higher than ever, for it no longer torments people, and yet it gets their tongues wagging. The forceful and strong things are in danger of suddenly perishing, of being broken and struck by lightning. The plethoric person is overcome by stroke. Our
10 philosophy today certainly will not die of a stroke.

29 [228]
Moving: a festival in high, snow-covered mountains during winter.

29 [229]
The Path to Freedom. Thirteenth Unfashionable Observation.
Stage of observation. Of confusion. Of hatred. Of con-
15 tempt. Of connection. Of enlightenment. Of illumination. Of struggle for. Of inner freedom and free thought. Attempts at construction. Of integration into history. Of integration into the state. Of friends.

29 [230]
The Philosopher.
20 1. Chap.　Medicinal morality.
　　2.　　An excess of thought ineffectual. Kleist.
　　3.　　Effect of philosophy, then and now.
　　4.　　Popular philosophy (Plutarch, Montaigne).
　　5.　　Schopenhauer.
25 6.　　The clerical controversy between optimism and pessimism.
　　7.　　Primitive times.
　　8.　　Christianity and morality. Why does it fail to achieve the power of the ancients?

9.   Young teachers and educators as philosophers.
10.   Veneration of ethical naturalism.
Immense operations, but they amount to nothing.

29 [231]

I never would let a professional position rob me of more
than a quarter of my energy.

29 [232]

I do not consider myself inordinately fortunate to have been
born among the Germans, and I perhaps would view life with
more satisfaction if I were a Spaniard.

30 [1]

On the Utility and Liability
of History.

30 [2]

I.

The herd grazes past us: it cannot distinguish yesterday from
5 today, leaps about, eats, sleeps, digests, leaps some more and
carries on like this from morning to night and from day to
day, tethered by the short leash of its pleasures and displeasures to the stake of the moment, and thus it is neither sullen
nor bored. It is hard on the human being to observe this, since
10 he considers himself better than the animal and yet covets its
happiness: for what he desires is to live neither in boredom nor
sadness, like the animal: and yet he desires this to no avail and
without hope.

Oh, how must I envy you!
15 Not only because you appear to be
almost free of all sufferings, —
forgetting in every moment
hardship, loss, the worst anxieties —
but even more so because you are never tormented
20 by boredom!

We sigh for ourselves because we cannot let go of the past
and must constantly drag its chain along behind us; whereas

it appears to us as if the animal is happy because it does not
get bored, immediately forgets, and continually sees every moment sink back into fog and night. Thus, it disappears entirely
into the present, just as one number disappears into another
5 without remainder, appears in each and every moment as exactly what it is, without any histrionics and intentional concealment. By contrast, we all suffer from that obscure and indissoluble remainder of what is past and are something other than
we appear to be: so that we are moved by the sensation of lost
10 paradise when we see the grazing herd, or, even closer to home,
the child that still plays between the two gates of the past and
the future in a blindness that is as short as it is blissful. Who
would dare disturb its play and awaken it out of obliviousness!
We know, of course, that with the phrase "it was," suffering
15 and strife begin and life is inaugurated as an infinite imperfect:
when death finally brings the much longed for oblivion, but
only by simultaneously suppressing the present and existence,
it places its seal on that knowledge—namely, that existence is
an eternal having-been, an eternal imperfect, something that
20 constantly contradicts, negates, and consumes itself.

Thus, we *have to* view the past and suffer under it—that is
simply the lot of human beings. No one will be spared becoming hardened under this hard yoke; and once someone has
become very hard, perhaps he even will reach the point of
25 lauding the lot of human beings due to this inability to forget,
precisely because the past cannot perish in us and drives us
like an injected drop of foreign blood to ascend tirelessly the
entire stepladder of all that human beings call great, amazing,
immortal, divine.

30 But if we have to view the past, there is at least a choice
between two different modes of dealing with it, and I wish
to call these clearly and frankly the *historical* and the *ahistorical*: however, no one should think it is my intention to praise
the former by giving it this designation or even that I want
35 to criticize the latter, the ahistorical, by giving it this designation. This would be nothing other than the confusion of the

ahistorical mode with the bad historical one, under which we should, however, simply understand the historical mode in a state of immaturity or degeneration. On the contrary, it is *sui generis* and *sui juris*; to be sure, it has just as much legitimation
5 as the historical mode, although individual ages and peoples, depending upon whether they are caught up in the one or the other, always accept only one of them as valid, find the other to be incomprehensible, and at most accept it only as a curiosity; just as, for example, the ahistorical mode of viewing history is
10 by and large foreign and incomprehensible to our contemporary age, and that is why we tend to view it as reprehensible or at the very least as a little crazy. {"}Just ask yourself,{"} David Hume demands of us, {"}or all of your acquaintances whether they would like to relive the last ten or twenty years of their
15 lives. No! But the next twenty will be better, they will say{"} —

> "And from the dregs of life hope to rec⟨e⟩ive,
> What the first sprightly running could not give."

Those who answer in this way are the historical human beings; a glance into the past drives them on toward the future,
20 inflames their courage to go on living, kindles their hope that justice will come, that happiness is waiting just the other side of the mountain we are approaching. For the historical human beings believe that the meaning of existence lies in the *process*, they look backward only to understand the present by obser-
25 vation of the prior process and to learn to desire the future even more keenly. But that question, whose first answer we have just heard, can also be answered differently: of course, in the end perhaps only once again with a "No!" We do not want to relive those ten years a second time. But with what justifi-
30 cation? With the justification of the a(supra)historical human being who does not seek salvation in a process, but rather in every human being and every experience, and who, moreover, believes he recognizes in every experienced period of time, in every day, in every hour why we live at all: so that for him the
35 world is complete and has arrived at its culmination in every

individual moment. What can ten new years possibly teach
that the past ten, if they were to be experienced once more,
could not!

Suprahistorical human beings have never agreed whether the
substance of this doctrine is happiness or resignation, virtue
or atonement; but, contrary to all historical modes of viewing
the past, they do arrive at unanimity with regard to the statement: the past and the present are one and the same, that is,
in all their diversity, they are identical, and as the omnipres-
ence of imperishable types they make up a stationary formation of unalterable worth and eternally identical meaning. Just
as the hundreds of different languages conform to the same
constant types of human needs, so that anyone who understood these needs would be able to learn nothing new from
these languages, the suprahistorical human being illuminates
the entire destiny of peoples and individuals from the inside,
clairvoyantly divining the primordial meaning of the changing
hieroglyphs and gradually even evading this constantly rising
flood of written signs. For, given the infinite superabundance
of events, how could he possibly avoid being satiated!

Such a mode of viewing the past is rare and considered offensive among us, for we demand precisely insatiability in viewing occurrences and call those peoples who continue to live
with this insatiable drive and, as one says, continually "make
progress," the "historical" peoples in the honorable sense; indeed, we feel only contempt for those who think differently—
the Hindus, for example—and we tend to attribute their mode
to the hot climate and their general indolence, but above all
to their so-called "*weakness of personality*": as if to live and think
ahistorically must always be a sign of degeneration and stagnation. It torments our scholars when they are unable to reconstruct a Hindu tale: they themselves lose confidence in
their derivation of literary genres on the basis of occidental
schemes and even begin to have doubts in such generalities
as, for example, whether a philosophy as powerful and elabo-
rate as Sankhya philosophy is pre- or post-Buddhistic: because

of such doubts and failures they then take revenge on such wrongheaded, indolent, and stagnant peoples by means of this disdain. The historical human beings do not notice how ahistorical they are, nor how their occupation with history does
5 not stand in the service of knowledge, but rather in the service of life. Perhaps the Hindus, in turn, perceive our craving for the historical and our esteem of "historical" peoples and human beings to be an occidental prejudice, or perhaps even a mental illness: "Haven't all those men, whom you yourselves
10 call wise," they will say, "lived just as ahistorically as we do? Or was Plato not an ahistorical human being? To cite as evidence against you just one of your much lauded Greeks, and not entire generations. And do you seriously believe that by means of a millennium of historical things someone *cannot help*
15 *but* move one giant step closer to the goddess of wisdom than someone who has experienced nothing of these things? Perhaps your present manner of pursuing and demanding history is itself nothing but an expression of the so-called 'weak personality'; at the very least, to us it seems that precisely your
20 strong personalities, your great men of history, display precious little of that specific 'historical sensibility,' of that 'historical objectivity,' of that learnedness with regard to historical dates, names of battles, and the spirits of peoples that has become obligatory: and they had no reason to hide such qualities,
25 since they lived among you and not among us."

But let us leave the Hindus to their bickering: even if they might be wiser than we are, today we want to rejoice in our unwisdom and make things easier for ourselves by playing the roles of "active and progressive people." For our aim is
30 to reflect on the utility of history, specifically, on whether we already have derived from it the *greatest possible utility* that can be derived from it. Long live the occidental prejudice for the historical: but let's just make certain that we, with our belief in progress, also make some progress within that "prejudice,"
35 namely, by progressing to some point or other where we have not already been.

But we will be able to derive the greatest possible utility
from history only if we are able to arrive at the best possible
understanding of the harm that it could inflict upon us. For
if, as is well known, one cannot just suffer, but even can per-
5 ish from every hypertrophied virtue, then the knowledge that
history also can be detrimental—indeed, that it is possible to
suffer and perish from it—scarcely will detract from history's
dignity. Should one, then, for that reason beware of the hypertrophy of every virtue? Should one renounce the utility of his-
10 tory just because one is exposed to the danger of suffering from
it if it happens to hyertrophy? Or does it perhaps even incite
the courageous person to recognize that one can be destroyed
by and in history? Isn't it ultimately the aim of every form of
heroism to discover the greatest possible profit in destruction?
15 Decide as you will, have doubts about the hypertrophy of history, deny completely that history is a virtue—you thereby will
betray how far and how profoundly you think, indeed, whether
you think at all: but meanwhile, we want to discuss the extent
to which history (that is, with the indulgence of my readers:
20 every type of occupation with history) can also be *detrimental*.

30 [3]

Concise writing. It is difficult to write concisely, Winckelmann
says, and also not possible for everyone; for in a more expan-
sive manner of writing it is not as easy to be taken at one's
word. That person who wrote to someone: "I did not have the
25 time to make this letter more concise" recognized exactly how
demanding the concise manner of writing is.

30 [4]

Without any pathos. Almost no periods. No questions. Few
metaphors. Everything very terse. Tranquil. No irony. No cli-
max. Stress the logical, but very concisely.

30 [5]

30 What is wisdom? In contrast to science. | Preface. Is there
any striving for wisdom today? No. | Main section. Is a

striving for truth necessary, a need? —No. But perhaps it will soon be a need. When? Depiction. | Afterword.

30 [6]

Education runs contrary to the nature of a human being. What would happen if one were to allow nature to develop on its own, that is, by means of purely accidental influences: it still would be educated, *accidentally* educated and shaped, but according to the boundless irrationality of nature, among countless specimens one beautiful specimen. Apart from that, innumerable destroyed seeds, destroyed either by the conflict of internal forces or by external influence. Destruction due either to inner conflict (while the forces grow stronger) or from without, due to a lack of life-giving oxygen, etc.

Preference of our age for powerful biases because they at least still betray nature's energy for life: and the prerequisite is indeed nature's *energy*. One should never even include weaker natures in the educational plan; they will not be of much significance either in a positive or a negative way.

30 [7]

There are two maxims with regard to education: 1) The educator quickly should recognize the strength of an individual and then direct all his energies toward developing this strength at the expense of all the lesser strengths: so that education then becomes precisely the supervision of that strength. 2) The educator should draw on *all* the existing strengths and bring them into a harmonious relationship, hence strengthen the weaker ones, precisely those ⟨in need of⟩ a transfusion, weaken those that are overpowerful. But what should one then take as a standard? The happiness of the individual? The utility that he renders to the community? The partial ones are more useful, the harmonious ones happier. Immediately this question arises anew: a large community, a state, a people: should it especially cultivate a partial strength or many strengths? In the first case, the state will tolerate the partial development of individuals

only if the partial characteristics are consistent with *its* aims,
that is, it will educate only a *portion* of the individuals according
to their strength, in the case of the others it no longer will pay
attention to strength and weakness, but rather see to it that the
5 one particular characteristic, regardless of how weak it initially
was, will in any event undergo *development*. If the state desires
harmony, then it still can achieve this in two ways: either by
means of the harmonious development of all individuals, or by
means of a harmony among the partially developed individu-
10 als. In the latter case it will have to produce a single temperament out of nothing but conflicting, powerful forces, that is,
it must prevent those who are strong in their partial exclusivity
from being hostile to one another, from immediately destroying one another; it must unite them all by means of a common
15 *aim* (church, the welfare of the state, etc.).

Athens is an example of the second type, *Sparta* of the first.
The first type is much more difficult and artificial, it is more
often exposed to degeneration, it requires a supervising *physician*.
20 In our age everything is confused and unclear. The modern
state is becoming ever more Spartanic. It would be possible for
the greatest and noblest strengths to dry up and die out due to
atrophy and transfusion. For I have noticed that it is precisely
the sciences and philosophy itself that are paving the way for
25 this. They no longer are bulwarks because they no longer are
permitted to have their own *aim*; that is, because no commonwealth has adopted their essence as part of its own aim. Thus,
what would be needed would be the establishment of a *cultural
state* — in opposition to the mendacious states that now go by
30 this name — as a kind of *refugium* for culture.

30 [8]
In the state, the happiness of the individual is subordinated
to the general welfare: what does that mean? Not that the mi-
norities are utilized for the welfare of the majorities. Rather,
that the individuals are subordinated to the welfare of the *highest*

individuals, to the welfare of the highest specimens. The highest individuals are the creative human beings, be they morally
the best individuals, or individuals who otherwise are useful
in some larger sense, thus, the purest types and the improvers
5 of humankind. The aim of the commonwealth is not the existence of a state at any price, but rather its aim is that the highest
human beings be able to live in it and be creative. That is also
the basis for the foundation of states, except that people often
had a false idea about who the highest specimens were: often
10 the conquerors, etc., hereditary rulers. If the existence of a
state no longer can be upheld in such a way that the great individuals still are able to live in it: then what comes into being
is the horribly rapacious, indigent state: in which the *strongest* individuals take the place of the *best* ones. The task of the
15 state is not to ensure that as many people as possible live well
and ethically within it: the number is irrelevant: but rather to
ensure that it is fundamentally possible to live well and beautifully within it: to ensure that it provides the basis for a *culture*.
In a word: a nobler form of humanity is the aim of the state,
20 its purpose lies outside of itself, it is merely the *means*.

Today we are lacking anything that could unite all the partial strengths: and thus we see that everything is at odds with
everything else and all the noble strengths are engaged in a
war of mutual destruction. This can be demonstrated on the
25 example of philosophy: it *destroys* because there is nothing to
hold it in check. The philosopher has become a being who is
detrimental to the community. He destroys happiness, virtue, culture, and ultimately himself. — In contrast to this, philosophy
must be an *alliance* of unifying *forces, as the physician of culture*.

30 [9]
30 *Beginning!*   What nonsense! Harmonious development!
Should one violently force someone who has a talent for sculpture to take up music, as Cellini repeatedly was forced by his
father to play that dear little horn and make that damned piping

——— make the shoemaker into a tailor? Of what value is the dilettantish learning of such a person! —The *weak* natures often are mistaken for the harmonious ones. Quite the opposite, harmony exists when everything is related to a center, to a cardinal force, not when numerous weak forces are operating in concert.

The aesthetic human being is supposed to be the harmonious one? He is not even aesthetically useful, he is flat. Yet Raphael certainly is harmonious.

30 [10]

What is eloquence?

Making oneself understood? But the painter, the hieroglyph, the gesture also seek to do that.

Making oneself understood by means of words?

For the purposes of this definition, it is irrelevant whether written or spoken words.

But then this includes both poetry and prose. To be sure, there is also rhetoric *in* poetry, but poetry is not a part of rhetoric.

But to make oneself understood? It is not solely the appeal to the power of understanding? After all, there is no rhetoric in mathematics.

To stimulate an alien intellect and will by means of words? But even the hothead, the drunkard does that.

To accomplish this with deliberation?

But even the deceiver, the liar does this. Is it possible to pay heed to morality when formulating this definition? No provision for dissimulation.

To accomplish this with artistic deliberation?

Yet the actor also does this and is clearly not an orator (even when he plays the role of an orator he is something other than a real orator).

But the purpose certainly is not an artistic one?

Only the means? Architecture must be called to mind.

To accomplish by means of words and with artistic deliberation that someone thinks and feels about something the way
one wants them to.

But is the actual "accomplishment" part of the definition?

5   No. Even if the aim is not accomplished, rhetoric still is
present.

The orator endeavors, by employing words and gestures,
with artistic deliberation, to make those he is addressing think
and feel the way he wants them to.

10   *Yet does one not seek* this even in the case of *dialectics*?

How does one use words to have an effect on understanding?
How to have an effect on feelings?

What distinguishes the orator from the passionate speaker,
from the deceiver? From the actor?

15   Basically, poet and orator are one and the same. What is the
basis of the distinction later made between them?

Is it an art, a skill? The orator certainly is an artist. But the
oldest orators know nothing of art? They *inherited* it as living
praxis.

20   The most important thing is: formulating the *topic*.

Then: organization, outline, structure.

Then: color, ornament, etc.

The orator in contrast to the *scholar*.

The application of the *strategies of dialectics* to *oratory*.

30 [11]

25   One difficult problem is honesty and the artistic element:
just think of Cicero and the Roman principle of decoration.

30 [12]

Poetics. Rhetoric. Ancient philosophy. Mythology. State.
Ethics.

30 [13]

An Essay on *the Greeks*.

30   State. Ethics. Religion. Philosophy. Poetics. Rhetoric.

30 [14]
> Chap. I.
> The alleged world day and the eradication of pessimism.
> From where? Nonhumans. The word "philosopher" refuses
>   to cross my lips.
> Modern human beings worship *strength*.
> Depiction of weakness everywhere.
> The mutual hostility, because the bond is missing.
> The atomistic element.
>
> Hartmann not even to be mentioned.

30 [15]
THE AFFLICTIONS *of* PHILOSOPHY

A.   Distress of the age, demands made of the philosopher.
> 1. Haste.
> 2. No building for eternity (modern houses).
> 3. Exhausted religion.
> 4. Medicinal morality. Naturalism.
> 5. Weakened logic (by history, natural science).
> 6. Lack of educators.
> 7. Useless and dangerous *complexity* of needs, duties.
> 8. Volcanic ground.

B.   Attacks on philosophy.
> 1. Mistrust of the more rigorous methods.
> 2. History strips systems of all that is valid.
> 3. The church has a monopoly on popular influence.
> 4. The state demands that one live in the moment.

C.   Picture of the philosopher.
> 1. Exhausted — excess of thought ineffectual (Kleist).
> 2. They discover the point where the scholarly begins.
> 3. Clerical controversy.
> 4. Primitive times.
> 5. Lack of morally great models.

> 6. Conflict between life and thought tolerated every-
>   where.
> 7. Defective logic.
> 8. The senseless education of students.
5 > 9. The life of philosophers and their genesis.
>
> D. Philosophy—whether it can serve as the foundation of a
>   culture? Yes—but no longer today: it is too refined and
>   exaggerated, one can no longer rely on it. In fact, phi-
>   losophy has allowed itself to be drawn into the current of
10 >   present-day education: it by no means controls it. At best
>   it has become a scholarly discipline (Trendelenburg).
>   Portrait of Schopenhauer. Opposition between his eudae-
>   monological praxis (the worldly wisdom of overripe ages,
>   like that of the Spaniards) and his merely intuited pro-
15 >   found philosophy. He condemns the present from two
>   perspectives. For the moment I see no other possibility
>   for praxis than Schopenhauer's worldly wisdom, wisdom
>   for the more profound needs.
>   Anyone who does not want to live in this contradiction
20 >   must fight for an *improved physis* (culture).

30 [16]

Is Herr Ulrici wise? Does he even hang around in the entou-
rage of wisdom as one of its fans? No: sadly, no; and it is not
my fault, after all, if he is not a wise man. It would be so uplifting to know that we Germans possess a wise man of Halle,
25 a wise man of Munich, etc.: and we are especially loath to let
Carrière, the inventor of real idealism and wooden iron, slip
away: if he were just a little more wise we would be happy to
take him seriously. For it is truly a disgrace that this nation does
not have a single wise man, but only five thought merchants:
30 and that E. von Hartmann can reveal what he knows: that at
the moment there are absolutely no philosophers in Germany.

30 [17]
    Effects of Kantian philosophy. Kleist.
    Simplicity of the ancients.
    One should have a philosophy only to the extent that one is
capable of living according to this philosophy: so that every-
5 thing does not become mere words (as in Plato, "Seventh Letter").

30 [18]
    What effect has philosophy today exerted *on philosophers*?
— They live just like all other scholars, even like politicians.
Schopenhauer is, of course, an exception. They are not distin-
10 guished by any set of customs. They live for money. The five
thinkers of the *Augsburger Allgemeine*. Just look at the lives of
their highest specimens, Kant and Schopenhauer — are those
the lives of wise men? It remains scholarship: they relate to
their work as do performers, hence in Schopenhauer's case the
15 desire for success. It is *comfortable* to be a philosopher: for no
one makes demands of them. The first night of Diogenes. They
occupy themselves with nothing but *apices*: Socrates would demand that one bring philosophy back down to the level of
human beings; either there is no popular philosophy, or only
20 a very bad popular philosophy. They manifest all the vices of
their age, above all haste, and simply let fly with their writing.
They are not ashamed to teach, even when they are very young.
    What noticeable effect has philosophy had among the dis-
ciples of the philosophers, I mean *among the educated people*? We
25 lack the best matter for conversation, a more refined ethics.
Rameau's Nephew.
    Proliferation of aesthetic points of view for the consider-
ation of greatness, of life.

30 [19]
    The word philosophy, when applied to German scholars and
30 writers, has caused me some difficulties of late: it appears to me
inappropriate. I wish one would avoid this word and from now

on speak, in plain German and forcefully, only of commerce in thought. But let me explain how I arrived at this notion.

30 [20]

I have the impudence to speak to the "nation of thinkers" of German commerce in thought (so as not to have to say "phi-
5 losophy"). "Where does this nation live?" the foreigner will ask. Where those five thinkers live to whom an exceptionally public forum recently called our attention, referring to them as the quintessence of contemporary German philosophy: Ul-rici, Frohschammer, Huber, Carrière, Fichte. Regarding the
10 last of these, it is easy to say something nice: for even that wicked he-man Büchner did so: "According to the younger Fichte, all human beings have a guiding spirit that accompa-nies them from the day of their birth: only Herr Fichte has none." But even regarding the other four men, that fanati-
15 cal friend of the material would even concede to me that in them something phosphoresces that does not phosphoresce in the younger Fichte. Thus: one lacks a spirit and the other four phosphoresce: wholesale: all five philosophize, or, to ex-press it in plain German, they engage in commerce in thought.
20 Yet they are the ones called to the attention of foreigners so that they might recognize that we Germans are still the nation of thinkers. There were good reasons for not including E. von Hartmann in this list: for he actually possesses what the younger Fichte would like to have: indeed, by dint of this some-
25 thing he has been able to lead the nation of those five think-ers, the Germans, around by the nose in a rather unmannerly manner: as a result, it appears that he no longer believes in the nation of thinkers, and probably—which is even worse— not even in the five thought merchants. But only those who
30 believe in them are beatified today: that is why Hartmann is absent among the famous names of the German Reich. For he has spirit, and today the "Reich" belongs only to those who are poor in spirit.

30 [21]

Professors of philosophy no longer practice skills, not even debate. Logic as it is being taught today is wholly useless. But the teachers, after all, are much too young to be able to be anything but scholarly trainees: how in the world could they
5 educate anyone, and educate them to wisdom, at that?

30 [22]

Virtue, an old-fashioned word. One need only think of young secondary school teachers when they tried to play the part of ethical educators!

30 [23]

The same holds true for the scholarly disciplines as for trees:
10 one can cling only to the stout trunk: not to the uppermost limbs, for then one plunges down and usually even breaks off the limbs. This is how things stand with epistemology.

30 [24]

What reflection, what intimacy with the soul there was dur-ing the time of Diderot and Frederick the Great! Even *Minna*
15 *von Barnhelm*, built completely on the foundation of French social discourse, is too refined for us today. We are crude natu-ralists.

I wish someone would show how in our glorification of ethi-cal naturalism we have become complete Jesuits. We love the
20 natural as aestheticians, not as ethicists: but there are no ethi-cists. Just think of Schleiermacher.

30 [25]

The most important thing about wisdom is that it prevents human beings from being ruled by the moment. It is conse-quently not newspaperish: its purpose is to gird human beings
25 equally well to face all the blows of fate, to arm them for all time. There is little about it that is national.

30 [26]

Even Montaigne is an ethical naturalist in comparison with the ancients, but a boundlessly richer and more thoughtful one. We are thoughtless naturalists, and we are fully aware of it.

30 [27]

Sympathy for primitive conditions is truly the fancy of the age. What nonsense that the doctrine of evolution even can be taught as though it were a religion! The satisfaction lies in the fact that it contains nothing stable, nothing eternal and inviolable.

30 [28]

Ethical *celebrities* are lacking; the ability to recognize them is decidedly lacking. On the other hand, the theory of strength haunts us. An example: one person says Hegel is a bad stylist; another that he is so rich in original and popular turns of phrase. But that applies solely to the material: the stylist does not reveal himself in the beauty of the marble, but in how he sculpts it. The same holds true in the realm of ethics.

30 [29]

Philosophers always have sought tranquility of the soul: today they seek unconditional unrest: so that the human being becomes identical with his profession, with his occupation. No philosopher will put up with the tyranny of the press: Goethe permitted only weeklies and pamphlets to appear.

30 [30]

There is an art of keeping things distant simply by means of the words and names one ascribes to them: a foreign word often makes foreign to us something with which we are otherwise intimately familiar and know quite well. When I say "wisdom" and "love of wisdom," then I definitely sense something more native, more effective than when I say "philosophy": but as I said, the art sometimes consists precisely in not letting things get too close. So often there is something shameful

in the words of one's native language! For who would not be
ashamed to call himself a "wise man" or even only "someone
who is becoming wise"! But a "philosopher"? That crosses
people's lips so easily: about as easily as people use the title
5 "doctor," without ever thinking of the presumptuous confession to being a teacher, to thinking, that is inherent in this
word. Let us then assume that the foreign word "philosopher"
is prompted by shame and modesty: or could it be the case that
no love of wisdom exists at all and that the foreign designa-
10 tion, much as in the case of the word "doctor," is intended only
to conceal the lack of content, the emptiness of the concept? It
is sometimes extraordinarily difficult to demonstrate the presence of a thing: it is so amalgamated, translated, hidden, so
diluted and weakened, whereas the names are persistent, and
15 seducers to boot. Is what we now call "philosophy" really love
of wisdom? And are there any true friends of wisdom today
at all? Let us dauntlessly replace the word "philosophy" with
"love of wisdom": then it will surely become apparent whether
they mean the same thing.

30 [31]
20 Lack of familiarity with Plutarch. Montaigne placed above
him. The most effective author (according to Smiles). Would a
new Plutarch even be possible? We all live, after all, in a naturalistic morality that lacks any style; it is too easy for us to think
of the figures of antiquity as declamatory.

30 [32]
25 Christianity manifested higher forms: but the greater portion has regressed. It is so difficult today to return once more
to the simplicity of the ancients.

30 [33]
The Jesuits weakened and softened the demands of Christianity in order merely to continue asserting its power. Protes-
30 tantism began with the declaration of *adiaphora* on a large scale.

30 [34]

Gracián displays a wisdom and intelligence in his life experience with which nothing of today can be compared. We are doubtless the microscopists of the real, our novelists know how to observe (Balzac, Dickens), but no one knows how to
5   demand and explain.

30 [35]

The predilection for mysticism among our philosophers is surely simultaneously a flight from tangible ethics. Here there are no more demands, nor are there geniuses of goodness, of transcendental pity. If imputability is transferred to essence,
10 then the antique moral systems become meaningless.

30 [36]

Philosophers want to flee from scholarship: they are pursued by it. We see what {philosophy's} weakness is. It no longer leads the way: because it itself is merely scholarship, and it is gradually turning into nothing but the guarding of borders.

30 [37]

15 24   Introduction.
     8   Inward.
     8   Objective.
     8   Hartmann.
     8   Antidotes.
20 56

30 [38]

Outline of the "*Unfashionable Observations.*"
     1. The Cultivated Philistine.
     2. History.
     3. Philosopher.
25   4. Scholars.
     5. Art.

6. Teachers.
7. Religion.
8. State, War, Nation.
9. The Press.
10. Natural Science.
11. Nation, Society.
12. {Social} Relations.
13. Language.

[31 = Mp XIII 5. Autumn–Winter 1873–74]

31 [1]

Morning is past and midday
scorches with heated gaze our heads{.}
Let us sit together in the leaves
and sing songs to friendship,
5   which was born of life's red dawn:
it will be red of evening for us,
yet at midday it is merely a tone:
tell me, didn't the morning skies
promise us more beautiful gains ———

31 [2]

10   Pericles speaks of the Athenian festivals, of the beautiful
and costly household furnishings, the daily sight of which dis-
pels a gloomy disposition. We Germans suffer greatly from
this gloomy nature; Schiller hoped that the influx of beauty
and greatness, of aesthetic edification, would have an influ-
15 ence in the realm of moral edification. Wagner hopes, quite to
the contrary, that the Germans' moral strengths one day finally
will be devoted to the realm of art so as to demand seriousness
and dignity in this realm, as well. He understands art in the
most rigorous and serious manner possible: he thereby hopes
20 ultimately to experience its cheering effect. With us things are
rather topsy-turvy and unnatural; we create the greatest difficulties for those human beings who seek to cheer us by means

of art by demanding of them moral genius and greatness of
character. Because we make the development of the most tal-
ented artists so difficult, and because they have to squander
all their energy in this struggle, we nonartists, in turn, have
become extremely lax in the moral demands we place upon
ourselves: complacency dominates in our principles and views
of life. Because we take life so lightly, we lose the proper need
for art. When life, as in Athens, is constantly suffused in responsibility, commitments, initiative, and effort, then people
also know how to honor and crave art, the festival, and cultivation in general: so that it will cheer them. And that is why the
Germans' moral weakness is the primary cause of their lack of
culture. To be sure: they work extraordinarily hard, do everything in haste, their hereditary diligence appears almost to be
a force of nature. In which their moral weakness is revealed!

31 [3]
    Preference of our age for powerful biases because they at
least still betray energy for life: but energy must be present
before something can be created. If only weakness is present,
then all effort is directed at conservation at any price: it produces, at any rate, no creation that could give one pleasure.
Comparable to the consumptive who gasps for life and in each
and every moment is forced to think of health, that is, of survival. If an age has many individuals of this sort, it ultimately
venerates strength, even when it is crude and hostile: Napo-
leon as a healthy yellow tiger in the *Marwitz* letter.

31 [4]
    Anyone who is familiar with the morality of the ancients will
be amazed at how many things that today are treated medically
were understood then in moral terms; how many disorders of
the soul, of the mind, that today are entrusted to the physician
were then entrusted to the philosopher; in particular, how the
nerves today are soothed by means of alkalies or narcotics. The
ancients were much more moderate, intentionally moderate,

in their daily lives: they knew how to abstain from and how to deny themselves many things in order not to lose their self-control. Their maxims about morality always are derived from the living examples of people who had lived according to these
5 maxims. I have no understanding for the strange and faraway things modern moralists talk about: they conceive the human being as a marvelously spiritualistic being, they seem to consider it improper to treat the human being in such a nakedly ancient manner and to speak of his many necessary but base
10 needs. Modesty even has reached the point that one is tempted to believe the modern human being has only the semblance of a body. I believe that the vegetarians, with their prescriptions for eating more simply and eating less, have done more good than all the recent moral systems taken together: in this
15 case a little exaggeration is of no account. There can be no doubt that future educators once again will begin prescribing human beings a stricter diet. People believe that modern human beings can be made healthy by means of air, sun, living quarters, travel, etc., including all the medical stimulants and
20 toxins. But everything that is difficult for the human being no longer seems to be prescribed: the order of the day seems to be that one should be healthy and ill in a pleasant and comfortable manner. Yet it is precisely the continued lack of moderation in *small* matters, that is, the lack of self-discipline, that ultimately
25 makes itself manifest as universal haste and *impotentia*.

31 [5]

Some things become enduring only when they have become weak: up to that point they are threatened with the danger of a sudden and violent demise. In old age one's health continually improves. For example, today Christianity is so vigorously
30 defended, and will continue to be defended for a long time, because it has become the most comfortable religion. Now it has prospects for immortality, after having won over to its side the most abiding thing in the world, human laziness and complacence. Thus, philosophy also is now valued higher than

ever and has won its most adherents: for it no longer torments
people, indeed, many are entertained by it, and all of them
are allowed to open their mouths and jabber on without suffering any consequences. The forceful and strong things are
in danger of suddenly perishing, of being broken and struck
by lightning. The plethoric person is overcome by stroke. Our
philosophy today certainly will not die of a stroke. Especially
now that philosophy has become a historical discipline, it has
guaranteed its own innocuousness and permanence.

31 [6]

[+ + +] whereas the philosopher, as the knowing representative of this connection, is no longer recognized, is no longer
believed, but rather is considered a swindler, someone who
promises more than he can deliver. 3) The most rigorous line
of thought in philosophy is on the verge of being transformed
into a relativistic system, more or less like the $\pi\acute{a}\nu\tau\omega\nu\ \mu\acute{\epsilon}\tau\rho o\nu$
$\ddot{a}\nu\theta\rho\omega\pi o\varsigma$. Then philosophy will be finished: for there is nothing more insufferable than such border guards, who never
know how to say anything other than "You can't go on in
this direction!" "You're not allowed to go that way!" "He lost
his way!" "We cannot know anything with absolute certainty!"
etc. This is absolutely infertile ground. —So, then philosophy is finished? —When he was a very young child, Emperor
Augustus, annoyed by the croaking frogs at his country estate,
commanded them to be silent: they are said to have been silent
from that day on, as Suetonius tells us. —

31 [7]

If philosophers today were to create the *polis* of their dreams,
it certainly would not be a Platonopolis, but rather an Apra-
gopolis (city of idlers).

31 [8]
Toward the Depiction of the Contemporary Age.

Where religion is concerned, I notice an exhaustion, people
finally have grown weary of and exhausted by its meaningful
symbols. All the possibilities of Christian life, the most seri-
5 ous and the most insipid, the most harmless and thoughtless as
well as the best thought through, have been tried out; it is time
for the invention of something new, or else we repeatedly will
fall back into the same vicious circle: to be sure, it is difficult
to break out of this whirlpool now that it has been spinning
10 around for a couple of millennia. Even ridicule, cynicism, hostility toward Christianity have been played out—what one sees
is an ice field when the weather is warming, everywhere the ice
is broken, dirty, without luster, covered with puddles, dangerous. Here the only attitude that to me seems appropriate is def-
15 erence, but total abstinence: in this way I honor that religion,
even though it is a dying one. Our job is to soothe and assuage,
as in the case of the seriously, terminally ill; we must protest
against only the bad, thoughtless quack physicians (who are
usually scholars). —Christianity soon will be ripe for critical
20 history, that is, for dissection.

31 [9]
One must also keep in mind that a great deal of philosophy already has been inherited, indeed, that human beings
are nearly saturated with it. What conversation, what popular
book, what scholarly discipline is not full of applied philoso-
25 phy! How countless are the deeds that likewise demonstrate
that the present-day human being has inherited an infinite
amount of philosophy. Even the human beings of Homer's
time displayed this inherited philosophy. It seems to me that
human beings would not cease to philosophize even if all the
30 professorial chairs were left unoccupied! What hasn't theology
already gobbled up! Ethics in its entirety, it seems to me. A
world view like the Christian one must gradually subsume,
combat, embrace all other forms of ethics, it must come to

terms with them—indeed, it must destroy them if they are stronger and more enduring.

31 [10]

I am thinking of the first night of Diogenes: all ancient philosophy was aimed at simplicity of life and taught a certain absence of needs, the most important remedy for all thoughts of social rebellion. In this respect the few philosophical vegetarians have accomplished more for humanity than all the more recent philosophies taken together; and as long as philosophers do not muster the courage to advocate a lifestyle structured in an entirely different way and demonstrate it by their own example, they will come to nothing.

31 [11]

The same holds true for the scholarly disciplines as for trees: one can cling only to the stout trunk and the lower limbs, not to the uppermost branches and crowns; for then one plunges down and usually even breaks off the limbs. This is how things stand with philosophy: woe to the young people who seek to cling to its *apices*!

[32 = U II 5a. Beginning 1874–Spring 1874]

32 [1]

Is everything we call Christian truly Christian? Or, to put the
question in a more comprehensive and simultaneously more
critical way: What aspects of our present-day life are actually
even Christian at all, what aspects, by contrast, are only called
5 Christian out of force of habit or out of cowardice? And is
there anything that we no longer even call Christian ⟨and⟩ that
is avowedly unchristian? To answer the last question first, I cite
by way of example science in its entirety: it is now unchristian
and insists on being called unchristian.

32 [2]

10   Cicero.

Ornament.
Honesty.
Decorative culture.
Can be learned even today from the example of the Greeks.
15 Cicero's moral deficiency explains his aesthetic deficiency (in
honesty)?
All modern ages suffer from this deficiency: our style con-
ceals.
We must struggle to come to terms with the Greeks in the
20 manner of Cicero. Leopardi.

The *strength* and honesty *of his character* are evident in the artist. But his taste is not so refined that he is capable of imitating
Demosthenes: although he enters into an intense competition
with him. (W⟨agner⟩ and Beethoven.) As an artist he is honest
⁵ and gives freely of whatever pleases him. But what pleases him
most is not what is best, but what is Asiatic. That was genuinely Roman.

Ponders civilizing possibility.

The segregation of "*form*" essential for Roman culture; "con-
¹⁰ tent" is hidden or covered by it. The imitation of a mature foreign culture can be clearly discerned. But the Greeks also did
this. The result is a new creation. Roman eloquence was at the
height of its power and for that reason was capable of assimi-
lating something foreign. Initially, everything pompous, bru-
¹⁵ tal, and seductive in Asiatic rhetoric; then Rhodic, then Attic
art: thus backward, toward the progressively more simple.

32 [3]

Epos (language genesis of culture)—Hesiod's *Erga.*
Lyric (along with metrics)—fragments.
Drama (state and art)—*Choephori*, *Oedipus rex.*
²⁰ Orators (Greeks and Romans)—Demosth⟨enes'⟩ *de corona.*
Philosophers (struggle against religion)—*Phaedo.*
Historians (struggle against the mythical)—Thucydides.

32 [4]

Greek and Barbarian.

1. The Birth of Tragedy from the Spirit of Music.
²⁵ 2. Plato and His Predecessors.
3. Cicero and Demosthenes.

Unfashionable Observations.

Strauss.
History.
³⁰ Reading and Writing.
One-year Volunteer.

Wagner.
Secondary Schools and Universities.
Christianness.
Absolute Teachers.
5   Philosopher.
Nation and Culture.
Classical Philology.
The Scholar.
Newspaper Slavery.

32 [5]

10 1874 Thuc{ydides} I *Persians. Gorgias.* *Pro corona.*	Orator. Epos
1875 Thuc{ydides} II *Trachinian Women.* Ar{istotle} *Ethics.* Oration	Drama.
1876 Thuc{ydides} 3 *Antigone.* Ar{istotle} 15 *Politics.* Oration.	Lyric.
1877 Thuc{ydides} 4 *Oed{ipus at} Col{onus}.* Plat{o} *Republic.* Oration.	Mythology.
1878 Thuc{ydides} 5 *Frogs. Leges.* Oration.	
1879 Thuc{ydides} 6 *Birds.* Theophr{astus} 20 *Charact{ers}.* Oration	Historians

32 [6]

Work on history.
Tragedy.
Novella.
Morality and Medicine.   On Greek literature.

32 [7]
25   *The Philosophers.*
Diogenes Laertius.
The διαδοχαί.
Language.

32 [8]

If Goethe is a displaced painter and Schiller a displaced orator, then Wagner is a displaced actor. In par⟨ticular⟩, he supplements it with music —

32 [9]

Wagner discovered that his audience had very different back-
grounds, different in its views on acting, different in its views on music. He took his audience to be unitary and thought its outbursts of approval stemmed from a common root, that is, he presupposed that the total effect was composed of equal por-tions of individual effects. So and so much pleasure in music,
just as much pleasure in acting, just as much pleasure in drama.

Then he finds out how a great actress can throw this calcu-lation off — but at the same time his ideal is enhanced — *what* heights of effect can be achieved if an equally grandiose music, etc. is attained?

32 [10]

He seems to have considered immoderation and unbridled-ness to be natural.

Goethe likewise never doubted his own *ability* to create what-ever pleased him. His taste and his ability ran parallel. Pre-sumptuousness.

Wagner wanted to create whatever had a powerful effect on him. He never understood anything about his models other than what he also was able to imitate. Character of the actor.

Wagner has a legislative nature: he has an overview of many relationships and does not get caught up in trivialities; he orga-nizes everything on a large scale and cannot be judged by the isolated detail — music, drama, poetry, state, art, etc.

The music does not have much value, ⟨n⟩or does the poetry, nor does the drama; the acting is often mere rhetoric — but everything forms a totality on a large scale and at the same level.

Wagner the thinker ranks just as high as Wagner the composer and the poet.

32 [11]

Wagner's first problem: "Why isn't the expected effect realized, since *I* experience it?" This drives him to a critique of his
5 public, of the state, of society. He posits between artist and his public the relationship of subject to object—totally naive.

Wagner's talent is a growing *forest*, not an individual tree.

32 [12]

He has a sense for *unity in diversity*—that is why I consider him a *bearer of culture*.

32 [13]

10 Some of his harmonies have something pleasantly jarring, like turning a key in a complicated lock.

On the whole, Wagner is predictable and rhythmic, however his details often are violent and unrhythmic.

Wagner grew so accustomed to being simultaneously sensi-
15 tive to distinct art forms that he is entirely insensitive to modern music: so that he rejects it in theory. The same is true for literature. This gave rise to much discord with his contemporaries.

32 [14]

Every art has a stage at which it is rhetoric. Fundamen-
20 tal difference between poetry and rhetoric or between art and rhetoric.

Its origin in *Empedocles* characteristic. Something halfway between.

Actor and orator: the first presupposed.

25 Naturalism. Reckons with affect. With a large audience.

Enumerate all the ways in which rhetoric corresponds to immoral art.

Emergence of literary prose as an aftereffect of rhetoric. It is rare for an artist truly to *highlight his subjectivity*: most artists hide it behind an acquired manner and style.

Honest art and *dishonest art*—primary distinction. So-called objective art is commonly nothing but *dishonest* art. Rhetoric is 5 more honest for the simple reason that it acknowledges *deception* as its aim. It by no means seeks to express subjectivity, but rather only ⟨to be in accord with⟩ a specific ideal subject, the powerful statesman, etc., as he is conceived by the people.

Every artist begins in a dishonest way, namely, by speaking 10 with the voice of his master (Sophocles, Aeschylus's bombast). Most frequently contrast between insight and ability eternal: then artists take sides with taste and remain eternally dishonest. Cicero *the decorative human being of a world empire*. He believes himself to be a perfected human being and the delight of nature, 15 hence his sense of glory. His political actions are mere decoration. He exploits everything, sciences and arts, purely according to their decorative power. Inventor of "pathos as such," of beautiful passion. Culture as a concealing decoration.

Task: to explain psychologically the development of such a 20 character.

32 [15]

One of Wagner's characteristics: lack of restraint, immoderation; he climbs up to the last rungs of his strength, of his emotion.

Wagner's cheerfulness is the sense of security felt by some- 25 one who has returned home to limitation from the greatest perils and indulgence: all the human beings with whom he has contact are such limited extracts from the course of his own life (at any rate, they have no other significance for him); that is why in this regard he can be cheerful and superior, for here 30 he can *play* with all needs, all concerns.

The other characteristic is a great theatrical talent that is displaced, that breaks through to courses other than just simply the next best: for he lacks the stature, the voice, and the self-contentedness to be an actor.

None of our great composers was as bad a composer as Wagner when he was 28 years old.

In *Tannhäuser* he attempts to motivate a series of ecstatic states in one individual: he seems to believe that the natural
5 human being is revealed only in these states.

In the *Meistersinger* and in parts of the *Ring of the Nibelungen* he returns to self-control: here he is greater than when he ecstatically lets himself go. Limitation suits him well.

A human being who is disciplined by his artistic drive. He
10 finds an outlet for his weaknesses by attributing them to the modern age: natural belief in the goodness of nature when left to take its course.

He measures state, society, virtue, people, everything by the standard of his art: and when in a state of dissatisfaction he
15 wishes that the world would perish.

Wagner's youth is that of a many-sided dilettante who seems destined to come to nothing.

Absurd as it seems, I often have had doubts about whether Wagner has musical talent.

20 His character gradually divides: Sachs-Wotan appears alongside Siegfried, Walter, Tannhäuser. He learns only late in life how to understand the adult male. Tannhäuser and Lohengrin are the monstrosities of a young man.

He ran away from his position because he no longer wanted
25 to be subservient.

32 [16]

As an actor he wanted to play the human being only at his most effective and most real: experiencing extreme affect. For his extreme nature saw weakness and untruth in all other states. For the artist, the peril of portraying affect is extraordi-
30 nary. The intoxicating, the sensual, the ecstatic, the impulsive, being moved at any price — these are horrible tendencies!

32 [17]

The music for Beckmesser is superlative: it could not possibly better express someone who is beaten and tormented. One has genuine pity, as when a hunchback is ridiculed.

32 [18]

Richard Wagner in Bayreuth.

5   1. Causes of his failure. Among them above all his tendency to arouse consternation. Lack of sympathy for Wagner. Difficult, complicated.
     2. Wagner's dual nature.
     3. Affect, ecstasy. Perils.
10   4. Music and drama. Coexistence.
     5. The presumptuousness.
     6. Late manhood — slow development.
     7. Wagner as writer.
     8. Friends (arouse new misgivings).
15   9. Enemies (awaken no esteem, no interest for the object under attack).
    10. The consternation explained: perhaps elevated?

Motto: ———

32 [19]

The longing for tranquility, loyalty — out of the unrestrained,
20 limitless — in *The Flying Dutchman*.

32 [20]

Wagner has a domineering character, only then is he in his element, only then is he secure, moderate, and stable: the inhibition of this drive makes him immoderate, eccentric, obstreperous.

25 Wagner is a born actor, but in the very same way that Goethe was a born painter without the hands of a painter. His talent seeks and finds outlets.

Now, just imagine these suppressed drives working in concert.

32 [21]

It is entirely possible that Wagner will destroy the Germans' interest in occupying themselves with the separate, individual arts. Perhaps in his wake we even will be able to formulate the image of a unified education, one that cannot be achieved by
5 simply adding together separate skills and areas of knowledge.

32 [22]

We should never forget: Wagner's art speaks a *theatrical* language; it has no place in the chamber, in the *camera*. It employs a populist manner of speaking, and it cannot conceive even the most noble things without making them much more coarse. It
10 is supposed to have an effect for the future and cement together the chaos of the people. For example, the "Imperial March."

32 [23]

A great many mistakes occur when the person passing judgment takes his partial art (household art) as his point of departure.

32 [24]

15 His relation to music is that of an actor: that is why he can, as it were, speak from within the souls of diverse composers and create entirely distinct yet coexistent worlds (*Tristan*, *Meistersinger*).

32 [25]

One should not be unfair and demand from an artist the
20 purity and unselfishness that someone like Luther, etc., possessed. And yet a purer nature emanates from Bach and Beethoven. The ecstatic element in Wagner is often violent and not naive enough; moreover, staged too forcefully by means of exaggerated contrasts.

32 [26]

25 His flight back to nature, that is, to affect, is suspicious for the simple reason that nothing is more effective than affect.

The possibility of an art that is pure improvisation is false: in contradistinction to German music, this is nothing but a naive standpoint. Wagner's organic unity lies in the drama, but that is why it does not (frequently does not) permeate the music,
just as it does not permeate the text. The latter retains the impression of being improvised (which is something good only in the case of consummate artists, not in the case of developing artists: but it is always deceptive and awakens the impression of richness).

32 [27]

A truly organic link between music and language is possible: in the song. Often even in entire scenes. To bring music and drama into such a relationship is an ideal. Model, the dance of the ancient chorus. But the aim immediately is set much too high: for we have no style in matters of movement, no development of orchestics that is as rich as the development of our music. But to force music to serve the purpose of a naturalistic passion causes it to dissolve, confuses it, and later makes it incapable of responding to the common challenge. There is no doubt that an art such as Wagner's is immensely pleasing to us, that it points toward an infinitely remote development of art. But the German sense for form! As long as the music does not degenerate and lack form! In the service of the kind of gestures appropriate to Hans Sachs, music must degenerate (Beckmesser).

32 [28]

There is something comical in it: Wagner cannot convince the Germans to take theater seriously. They remain cold and contented—he gets so agitated that one would think the salvation of the Germans depended on it. Today in particular the Germans believe they are occupied with more serious things, and it strikes them as a kind of amusing fanaticism that anyone would devote himself to art in such a solemn manner.

Wagner is not a reformer, for up to now everything has re-

mained as it was. In Germany everyone takes his own matters
seriously and laughs at someone who lays claim to a monopoly
on taking things seriously.

Influence of the monetary crises.

5   General instability of the political situation.

Doubts in the prudent control of the G⟨ermans'⟩ destiny.

Age of artistic agitation (Liszt, etc.) past.

A serious nation does not want to let its frivolity dissipate,
the Germans won't let this happen in the theater arts.

10   Main thing: the significance of art such as Wagner's is not
compatible with our relations in society and on the job. Hence
our instinctual aversion to what is inappropriate.

32 [29]

For a German, Wagner is too immodest; just think of Luther,
our generals.

32 [30]

15   As a writer, Wagner does not reflect a true image of himself.
He does not compose: he has no conception of the totality: in
the details he digresses, is obscure, rather than harmless and superior. He does not know how to be cheerfully presumptuous.
He is incapable of any charm, delicacy, and dialectical rigor.

32 [31]

20   How did Wagner acquire his followers? Singers who became interesting as actors and who found an entirely new pursuit, perhaps because they had weaker voices. Musicians who
studied under the master of performance: the performance
must be so brilliantly executed that it does not distract from the
25 awareness of the work itself. Orchestra musicians in the theater
who previously were bored. Musicians who aimed at the in-
toxication or enchantment of the audience in a direct manner
and who learned the tonal effects of the Wagnerian orchestra.
All sorts of dissatisfied people who hoped to profit from every
30 revolution. People who are enthusiastic about every form of

so-called "progress." Those who were bored by previous music
and now found that their nerves were more powerfully agitated. People who let themselves be swept away by everything
that is audacious and bold. —He soon had the virtuosos on
his side, as well as a part of the composers; —hardly anyone
can get along without him. Literary people with all sorts of indistinct needs for reform. Artists who admire his independent
way of life.

32 [32]

The "false omnipotence" gives rise to something "tyrannical" in Wagner. The feeling of having no *successors*—that is why
he seeks to disseminate his ideas of reform as widely as possible
and to procreate, so to speak, by means of adoption. Striving
for legitimacy.

The tyrant acknowledges no individuality other than his own
and that of his confidants. Wagner faces a great danger when
he refuses to acknowledge Brahms, etc.: or the Jews.

32 [33]

Wagner is a modern human being and is incapable of en-
couraging and fortifying himself by means of faith in god. He
does not believe himself to be in the hands of a beneficent
being, but he believes in himself. No one is completely honest
with himself anymore when he believes only in himself. Wagner gets rid of all his weaknesses by imputing them to his age
and his adversaries.

32 [34]

The tyrant's sensibility for the *colossal*.

He is treated with absolutely no piety, the genuine musician
views him as an intruder, as illegitimate.

32 [35]

It is fortunate that Wagner was not born into a higher class,
as a nobleman, and that he did not become a politician.

32 [36]

It is extremely difficult for a human being who feels himself capable of such intense raptures and self-abandonment to remain modest; for only the knowing person is called upon to be modest, someone who is unconsciously inspired is unlimited.
5 The cult of genius also plays a role, nourished by Schopenhauer.

32 [37]

One should not agitate Wagner even more by means of failure; that would provoke him all too much.

32 [38]

Today he is probably the most unabashed admirer of the
10 small German virtues and limitations, for he sees that they are being overwhelmed and enters into a conspiracy with them against what is victorious today.

32 [39]

He did not steer clear of thinking about political possibilities: which contributed to his unfortunate relationship with
15 the K⟨ing⟩ o⟨f⟩ B⟨avaria⟩, as well, who: first, refused to have his works performed; second, half squandered them by means of provisional performances; and third, gave him an extremely unpopular reputation because people generally attributed the King's excesses to Wagner. His association with the revolution
20 was just as unfortunate: he lost his wealthy patrons, aroused fear, and yet could not help but appear to the socialist parties to be a renegade: all of this without any benefit for his art and without any higher necessity, and what is more, as a sign of his lack of political insight, for he had absolutely no understand-
25 ing of the political situation in 1849.

Third, he insulted the Jews, who possess most of the money and own most of the newspapers in Germany today. When he first did this, he had no reason for it: later on it was merely revenge.

Whether he was correct to place so much faith in Bismarck will become evident in the not too distant future.

32 [40]

In his value judgments on the great composers he employs expressions that are much too exaggerated; for example, he
5 calls Beethoven a saint. It is also a bit too much to portray the addition of words in the Ninth Symphony as an act of major significance. He arouses suspicion with his praise as well as with his criticism. He lacks all delicacy and charm, as well as pure beauty, the radiance that reflects a wholly balanced soul:
10 but he seeks to discredit them.

32 [41]

His talent as an actor manifests itself in the fact that he *never* lives a personal life. As a writer he is a rhetor who lacks the power to persuade.

32 [42]

The end of grand rhythmical periods, the persistence of
15 measured phrases does, to be sure, give an impression of in-finity, of the sea: but it is an artistic trick, not the regular law Wagner would like to make it out to be. First we chase after them, seek out periods, constantly are deceived, and ultimately we throw ourselves into the waves.

32 [43]
20 The road from dance to symphony cannot be left untrav-eled: what remains other than a naturalistic counterpart to un-rhythmic real passion. But art can do nothing with unstylized nature. Excesses in *Tristan* of the most questionable sort, for example the outbursts at the end of the second act. Immodera-
25 tion in the beating scene in *Meistersinger*. Wagner senses that in matters of form he possesses all the crudeness of the Germans and prefers to fight under Hans Sachs's banner than under that of the French or the Greeks. But our German music (Mozart,

Beethoven) assimilated Italian form, as it did the folk song, and that is why its finely ordered wealth of lines no longer is in conformity with rustic-bourgeois boorishness.

32 [44]

Wagner's art is soaring and transcendental; of what use is it for our poor German vulgarity! There is something in Wagner's art that resembles flight from this world; it negates this world, it does not transfigure it. That is why it does not have a directly moralizing, indirectly quietistic effect. We see him occupied and active only in his efforts to win a place for his art in this world: but what do a Tannhäuser, Lohengrin, Tristan, Siegfried matter to us! But that seems to be the fate of art in an age like the present one, it saps away part of the strength of moribund religion. Hence the alliance between Wagner and Schopenhauer. It indicates that perhaps someday culture will exist only in the form of cloisterlike isolated sects: that reject the surrounding world. Here the Schopenhauerian "will to life" receives its artistic expression: this dull drive without a purpose, this ecstasy, this despair, this tone of suffering and desire, this accentuation of love and of ardor. Rarely a cheerful ray of sunshine, but many magic tricks that give artificial light.

The strength and weakness of Wagner's art lie in this artistic attitude: it is so difficult to return from it to life in its simplicity. Improvement of the real no longer is the goal, but rather destruction of or delusion about the real. Its strength lies in its sectarian character: it is extreme and demands of the human being an unconditional decision. —Whether this art and Schopenhauerian philosophy actually are capable of improving a human being? With regard to truthfulness, certainly. If only truthfulness were not so interesting—so entertaining!, aesthetically enticing! —in an age in which lies and convention are so boring and uninteresting!

32 [45]

His artistic strength ennobles the uncontrolled drive and confines it, concentrates it (into the desire to structure this work in its most consummate form). It ennobles Wagner's entire character. It constantly strains to reach ever higher goals, as high as he possibly can see: these goals continually become better, but ultimately also more clearly defined and thereby nearer. Thus, the Wagner of today appears to have nothing in common with the Wagner of "Opera and Drama," with Wagner the socialist: the previous goal appears to be higher, but in fact it is merely farther away and less clearly defined. His current view of existence, of Germany, etc., is more profound, although it is much more conservative.

32 [46]

The simplicity in the design of the dramas betrays the actor.

32 [47]

Shakespeare and Beethoven taken together—the boldest, craziest thought.

32 [48]

Shaking off guilt and injustice—because he constantly is growing, he quickly forgets every injustice: at the newly attained stage it already appears to him to be unimportant and healed over. Can console himself about everything, like Schopenhauer.

32 [49]

The passage from *Goethe* about the presumptuous human being can be found on 27, 507.

32 [50]

Whether in Wagner's case one could speak of magnificent "nude figure music"?

He has in mind the image of the inner person becoming

visible, of the process of emotions that can be seen as motion;
this is what he wants to represent: to grasp the will directly in
an extremely Schopenhauerian fashion.

Music as a likeness of his life due to its successive character.

32 [51]

5   Danger that the motivations for the movement of the music
lie in the movements and actions of the drama, that it is *guided*.
It is not necessary for one of the two to guide the other—in
the consummate work of art we have the feeling of a necessary
coexistence.

32 [52]

10   For Wagner the error of opera as an artistic genre is that
it turned a *means of expression*, music, into an end, and that it
turned the end of expression into a means.

Thus, for him music is a means of expression—very characteristic for the actor. Then one has to ask in the case of a
15 symphony: if the music here is a *means of expression*, then what is
the end? It hence cannot lie in the music itself: however, what
is in essence a means of expression must have something that
it is supposed to express: Wagner believes this to be the drama.
Without this he considers music to be nonsense: it evokes the
20 question: "Why are you making all that noise?" That is why
he considered the Ninth Symphony to be Beethoven's greatest
act, because by supplementing it with words he endowed music
with its fundamental meaning of being a means of expression.

Means and end—music and drama—older doctrine.

25   *General idea* and *example*—music and drama—newer doctrine.

If the latter is true, then the general idea by no means can
be dependent upon the example, that is, absolute music is justified, even the music that accompanies drama must be absolute music.

30   Now, to be sure, that is really only a metaphor and an image
—it is not really true that drama is only an example for the

general idea of the music: genus and species, in what sense? As the movement of sounds over against the movement of figures (to refer here only to mimical drama).

However, the movements of a figure also can be the general idea: for they express inner conditions that are much richer and more nuanced than the resulting movements expressed by the external person: which is why we so frequently misunderstand gestures. Moreover, all gestures are infinitely conventional—the wholly autonomous human being is a figment of the imagination. But if we abandon the movement of the figure and speak instead of the motive feeling, then the music ought to be what is more general, the motive feeling of such and such a person the particular. But the music is nothing other than the motive feeling of the composer expressed in sounds, and hence in any case the motive feeling of a particular individual. And that's how it always was (if we ignore the completely formalistic doctrine of sound arabesques). Then we would arrive at an absolute contradiction: a wholly particular expression of feeling as the music, wholly determinate—and on the other side the drama, a succession of expressions of wholly determinate feelings, of the dramatic figures, through words and movements. How can these ever be compatible? Of course, the composer himself can identify empathetically with the dramatic events and reproduce them as pure music ("Coriolan Overture"). But this likeness then would relate only to the drama as a generalization, all the political motivations, reasons, are left out and only the irrational will speaks. In every other sense dramatic music is bad music.

But what about the desired *simultaneity* and the most precise parallelism of all the events in the composer and in the drama! Here the music disturbs the dramatist, for it requires time in order to express something, oftentimes an entire *symphony* just to express one single dramatic sentiment. What is the drama supposed to do during this time? For this Wagner employs dialogue, *language* in general.

But then a new power and a new difficulty arise: language. It speaks in concepts. These, too, have their own *temporal* laws: in short

the mime alone expresses the	
5 fundamental feeling	each ⟨expresses it⟩ in
conceptual world	different temporal units.
music	

Verbal drama is governed by the power that requires the most time, the concept. That is why the action frequently is sta-
10 tionary, sculpturesque groups. Especially in antiquity: the stationary, sculpturesque figures express a condition. The mime thus is influenced by the verbal drama in significant ways.

Now, the composer requires entirely different temporal units and it actually is impossible to impose upon him any laws at
15 all. For one composer an emotion put to music will have a long duration, for another a short duration. How ridiculous to demand that conceptual language and the language of sound must run parallel to one another!

And yet language itself contains a musical element. The in-
20 tensely felt statement has a melody that is also an image of the most general volitional impulse. This melody can be artistically exploited and interpreted in an infinite number of ways.

The unification of all these factors seems to be impossible: one composer will reproduce individual moods aroused by the
25 drama and have no idea what to do with the major portion of the drama itself: that is probably the reason for recitative and rhetoric. The poet will not be able to help the composer, and therefore he also will have no idea what to do: he wishes to create only as much text as can be sung. But he has only a
30 theoretical awareness of this, not an inherent one. Above all, the actor as singer must do a great many things that are undramatic, open his mouth wide, etc.; he needs conventional mannerisms. Of course, everything would change if the actor were simultaneously composer and poet.

35 He employs gesture, language, language melody, and in addition to this the *accepted symbols* of musical expression. He

presupposes a form of music whose state of development is extremely rich, one that already has established a more stable, recognizable, and recurrent expression for a host of emotions. By means of these musical quotations he reminds the listener
5 of a particular mood that he is supposed to imagine the actor experiencing. Then the music truly has become a "means of expression": for that reason it stands artistically at a lower level, because it is no longer inherently organic. Now, the master composer still will be able to interweave these symbols in an
10 artistic fashion: but since the actual interconnection and plan lie beyond and outside the music itself, it cannot be organic. But it would be unfair to reproach the dramatist for this. He is permitted to exploit music as a means for the benefit of the drama, just as he exploits painting as a means. Such music,
15 pure in itself, is comparable to allegory in painting: the actual meaning does not dwell in the image itself, and that is why this meaning can be extremely beautiful.

32 [53]
Dangers of *dramatic* music for music.
Dangers of musical drama for the dramatic poet.
20 Dangers for the singer.

32 [54]
Everything great, especially when it is new, is dangerous: usually it acts as though it alone were legitimate.
One has to consider precisely what kind of age an art is creating for itself here: entirely unrestrained, breathless, impious,
25 greedy, formless, unstable in its very foundations, almost desperate, nonnaive, thoroughly conscious, ignoble, violent, cowardly.

32 [55]
Wagner reproduces most effectively as an actor, he takes up residence in alien souls (of composers).

32 [56]

Art gathers together everything with which it still is able
to stimulate modern Germans — character, knowledge, everything is brought together. An enormous attempt to assert
itself and to dominate — in an age that is hostile to art. Poison for poison: all the exaggerations are directed polemically
against the great powers hostile to art. Religious, philosophical
elements included, longing for the idyllic, everything, everything.

32 [57]

Wagner values simplicity of dramatic design because it has
the most powerful *effect*. He gathers together all the *effective*
elements in an age that, because of its insensitivity, requires
extremely crude and powerful measures. The magnificent, intoxicating, confusing, the grandiose, the horrible, noisy, ugly,
enraptured, nervous, everything is legitimate. Inordinate dimensions, inordinate measures.

The irregularity, the overdone splendor and ornament, give
the impression of wealth and luxury. He is aware of what still
has an effect on our human beings of today: yet at the same
time he still idealized and had a very high opinion of "our
human beings of today."

32 [58]

It was Wagner's peculiar form of ambition to compare himself to the great figures of the past: to Schiller-Goethe, Beethoven, Luther, Greek tragedy, Shakespeare, Bismarck. It was
only with the Renaissance that he felt no particular affinity.
But he invented the German spirit, in contrast to the Romanic
spirit. Interesting characterization of the German spirit according to his model.

32 [59]

A kind of Counter-Reformation: transcendental reflection
has been severely weakened, beauty, art, love of existence se-

verely vulgarized, due to the repercussions of the Protestant spirit. Idealized Christianity of the Catholic sort.

32 [60]

Language intensified to the point of most forceful expression—alliteration. Likewise the orchestra. The most important thing is not the clarity of the language, but rather the intoxicating power of *divination*.

32 [61]

—Wagner attempts a renewal of art on the only basis that still exists, that of theater: here a *mass* is truly still aroused and makes no pretensions as in museums and concert halls. To be sure, it is an extremely crude mass, and to this very day it has proven impossible to regain control of the theatrocracy. Problem: should art forever go on living in a sectarian and isolated way? Is it possible to put it in control? This is where Wagner's significance lies: he attempts to establish a *tyrannis* with the aid of the masses of theater goers. There can be little doubt that if he had been born an Italian, Wagner would have achieved his goal. The German has no respect for opera and always views it as something imported and un-German. Indeed, he refuses to take seriously the theater as a whole.

32 [62]

War.

The victor usually becomes foolish, the vanquished malicious.

War simplifies. Tragedy for men. What are its effects on culture?

Indirect effects: it barbarizes and thereby makes more natural. It is a hibernation of culture.

Direct effects: Prussian experiment with one-year flies: tie certain reductions in one's duties to cultural requirements.

Instructive about life.

Abbreviated form of existence.

The Greeks made Sophocles into a general, and this then led to his defeat.

Scientific war. — Indifferent to the individual and his duty. Acting in accordance with one's duty versus humanity — a wonderfully instructive conflict. The "state" does not conduct wars, but only the sovereign or the minister; we should not be deceptive with words.

The meaning of the state cannot possibly be the state itself, even less so society: instead, only individuals.

Nature operates the same way war does: indifferent to the value of the individual.

I am certain that in the not too distant future many Germans will feel about this in just the same way I do: the need to experience their education free of politics, national questions, and newspapers. Ideal of an educational sect.

32 [63]

I consider it impossible to emerge from the study of politics as a person of action. The horrible insignificance of all the political parties, including those with church affiliations, is obvious to me. I long for relief from politics: and the exercising of the immediate duties of the citizen on the local level. I consider a representational constitution to be superfluous in Prussia: indeed, to be infinitely detrimental. It injects us with the political fever. There must be circles like the monastic orders, except with a broader content. Or like the class of philosophers in Athens. Education by means of state-run educational systems is to be disdained.

32 [64]

If someone is not connected to another person either by old debts of gratitude or by some cooperative association and yet nevertheless desires his assistance — and this is precisely the situation we are in — then he has to prove two things: above all, that his request will bring the other person some advantage, or at least no disadvantage; and second, that this person will be able to count with absolute certainty on his gratitude. If he does not succeed in allaying all doubts with regard to these two points, he has no reason to be angry if that person denies his request.

32 [65]
Wagner's nature.
His work of art.
Struggle against his age.
The justified resistance.
Attempt to make a surprise attack.

32 [66]
The significance Wagner ascribes to art is not *German*. Here even a decorative art is lacking. All public decorum for art is lacking. In essence either scholarly or completely common. Here and there the isolated desire for beauty. Music stands entirely alone. But even music has not been capable of creating any organization: not even of preventing the importation of theater music.

Anyone who applauds in the theater today will be ashamed of having done so tomorrow: for we have our family altar, Beethoven, Bach—they cause the memory to pale.

32 [67]
On the Age.
Nature is not good—counterdogma against false, feeble opinions and secularization.

The meaning of life does not lie in the preservation of institutions, or in their progress, but instead in individuals. They are supposed to be crushed.

When someone takes upon himself the work of justice, then existence gives him a lesson about his own significance.

Life should not be arranged in the most comfortable and tolerable manner possible, but rather in the most rigorous manner possible. We must cling to its metaphysical meaning in every possible way.

The great instability of things makes it easier for us to learn this lesson. Nothing should be *shown mercy*, the truth must be
5 stated frankly, no matter what the consequences.

Our task, to rise up again out of all the obfuscations and half-truths and to stop deceiving ourselves about the nature of existence. For all of humanity has now *fallen victim to shallowness* (including the religious parties, of course. Even the ultramon-
10 tanists, for they underhandedly defend a mythic expression as *sensu proprio* true and want to retain their external power).

Goethe's Hellenism is, first, historically false, and second, too weak and effeminate.

The danger of enervation is not present: justice is one of the
15 most serious responsibilities, and pity a great stimulus.

If it were our task to pass over life to the greatest possible extent, then we would not be at a loss for recipes, Goethe's in particular.

It is lovely to *observe* things, but horrible to *be* them.
20 *We must take upon ourselves the voluntary suffering for truthfulness*, the personal agonies.

Suffering is the meaning of existence.

The many evasions in which we are enveloped—in that sense, our ignorance of our own nature—also deceive us about
25 the meaning of life: *the same courage that it takes to know oneself also teaches us how to regard life without evasions*: and vice versa.

32 [68]

Metaphysics of culture.

We must promote everything that lends this life a metaphysical meaning.
30 Religion no longer possible in all its purity, but only displaced.

What motivates our drive for education, for knowledge, etc.? The advantages they bring in the struggle for existence?

Immortality of genius, of the drive for genius.

32 [69]

The sensibility of Bach and Händel is German.

32 [70]

The Germans could not tolerate particularism. Submissive, cowardly, and inwardly rich.

Will they be able to tolerate unity! Arrogant, inwardly hollow.

32 [71]

German Culture.

Up to now no one has established great goals for German culture.

Danger of the political sensibility.

As a powerful nation we have an enormous responsibility: to take the lead! It is absolutely impossible for us to crawl into our shell like a snail.

Having political supremacy without true human supremacy is the greatest detriment.

We must seek to compensate for our political supremacy. Power is something to be *ashamed* of. It must be used in the most beneficial way.

Everyone thinks that the Germans now can lie back and enjoy their moral and intellectual superiority.

People seem to think that now is the time for something new, for the state. In earlier times for "art," etc. This is a disgraceful misunderstanding; the seeds are present for the most marvelous development of humanity. These seeds are supposed to perish for the benefit of the state! But what is a state!

The age of scholars is past. They must be replaced by the philalethes. Enormous power.

The only way to correctly employ the *power* the Germans wield today is to grasp the enormous *responsibility* that it entails. An enervation of these cultural tasks would transform this power into the most terrible tyranny.

32 [72]

The Age.

—Destruction of the Enlightenment.

—Reestablishment of the metaphysical meaning of existence.

5   —Hostility toward Christianity because it fails to recognize this.

—Against thoughts of revolution.

—Not directed toward *happiness*: the "truth"; not in comfortable repose, but heroic and hard.

10   —Against the overestimation of the state, of national interests. J⟨acob⟩ B⟨urckhardt⟩.

Schopenhauer has been *misunderstood*.

Loveless or merely short-lived in its love.

32 [73]

Education of the Philosopher.

15   Made insensitive to national sentiments by means of journeys at an early age.

Know human beings, read little.

No drawing-room culture.

Take the state and one's duties lightly. Or emigrate.

20   Not scholarly. No universities.

Also no history of philosophy; he should seek truth for himself, not in order to write books.

32 [74]

Let's assume there were at present a rather weak generation of such philosophers—but a better one would *not be able to tol-*
25 *erate our universities.*

32 [75]

University philosophy
        in the service of the theologians
                        of history (Trendelenburg).
The philosopher as scholar among scholars.

No model.

He should not hold any position.

How can one examine young people in philosophy.

Their youth and their education {is sacrificed} for their oc-
5 cupation.

32 [76]

1) There are not nearly as many {philosophers} as the state
needs — hence *decline in quality*, too *young*, etc.

2) They are integrated into institutions of *scholarship*.

3) They are supposed to instruct every youth who *desires* in-
10 struction, and at *specified* times, and even in specific disciplines.

4) They are controlled by theology.

5) By the aims of the state, as well.

6) They are supposed to be learned and be familiar with the
history (and the *judgments*) of a scholarly discipline.

15   7) Is there any reason for introducing *young people* to philosophy (or ruining them) prior to all experience in life? For
examining them in it?

Greek youths had more life experience.

8) *Can they* actually say: Follow me and leave everything else
20 behind? No state or university would permit that.

9) They do not stand in the midst of life and for that reason
they lack any experience. So many hostile conditions exist there
that the entire generation is, in addition, genuinely crippled.

From this comes: *contempt for philosophy*.

25   Noticing this, they become angry and refuse to recognize
the true philosopher no matter what. They work insidiously in
their little niche, comradery, etc.

With the exception of a few scholars worthy of respect: yet
even they are nothing but scholars and as such cannot serve as
30 models; their historical studies could be done better by philologists: thus, Greek philosophy is still in need of being rescued
from the curse of being boring: just read {Diogenes} Laertius,
as well as his predecessors.

Their salary, as well, is not actually an honorarium, not payment in honor of their work; rather, they are bought off for making certain concessions: thus, it is not, in fact, a privilege granted by the state with no strings attached.

32 [77]

For Chapter IV.

5 *Distinct from Rousseau's human being.* He does not seek worldly happiness, nor does he strive to achieve it for his fellow human beings.

⟨Distinct from⟩ *Goethe's* ⟨human being⟩. He does not want to deceive himself about life; he also does not want to live solely 10 for himself, in a noble egoism.

Contradiction with the age due to his truthfulness
 against the goodness of nature
 against the Enlightenment
 against degenerate Christianity
15 against thoughts of revolution
 against the overestimation of the state
 against the historical
 against haste.
Establishment of *Metaphysical Meaning.*
20 *The distorted images of Schopenhauer's human being*
 in the direction of Mephistopheles, without goodness
 in the comfortable direction toward Goethe, fascination
 with the discovery of *new* and *different* things, without consequence.
25 Absence of anything *heroic.* Conclusion.

32 [78]

What are the reasons for the *suffering inherent in truthfulness*?
 One destroys one's earthly happiness.
 One must be hostile toward the human beings one loves.
 One must expose and renounce the institutions with
30 which one has sympathetic ties.
 One frequently will be unjust in one's striving for justice.

One cannot show mercy toward individuals and suffer
    with them.
How often our sentiments are impure, clouded by hatred
    and scorn.
5   It often will appear as though one is protecting institu-
    tions and hence one will be considered an ally of every-
    thing contemptible.

The *disposition of truthfulness*
    pure, impersonal
10 not cold and scientific
    always renouncing itself
    without carping and sullenness
    with consciousness of the sufferings that arise from it.

32 [79]
    Belief in a God and a Redeemer is nothing but mythologi-
15 cal frills and has nothing to do with the essence of a religion.

32 [80]
                    Chapter V. *German Culture.*
    Every great power entails a great *guilt.*
    Therefore great responsibilities, great goals.
    One is by no means permitted simply to live for oneself and
20 let others live for themselves.
    Completely wrong to say that the Germans now have politi-
    cal interests, previously they had aesthetic interests.
    The Germans sought an ideal in their Luther; German
    music, higher than everything we know about culture.
25 The search for this should cease because they now have
    political power? Precisely power (because of its maliciousness)
    should lead them to this more intensely than ever.
    It must *employ* its power to achieve its lofty cultural aims.
    Secularization to be combated.
30 The struggle against the Catholic Church is an act of en-

lightenment, nothing loftier; and in the end it merely makes it disproportionately strong: which is wholly undesirable. Of course, in general it is correct. If only the state and the churches would devour each other!

5   The adoration of the modern state can lead to the sheer destruction of every culture.

The metaphysical meaning of existence is also the meaning of every culture.

In opposition to this, people have set themselves the task of
10   elegance and prettification!

32 [81]
Schopenhauer's teleology among the Germans.
Genius and the meaning of life.
Truthfulness as the bridge to culture.
Such human beings need art.

32 [82]
15   Persians: shoot well, ride well, borrow nothing, and never lie.

32 [83]
Common enemies of culture and of metaphysical meaning—Enlightenment, revolution, nature, etc. That is why they belong together.

20   End of enlightened education, which is hostile to the metaphysical: and of the Renaissance, which was not really acquainted with antiquity, like Goethe.

Music stands in full bloom. How infinitely high above Goethe Beethoven stands!

25   Their meaning understood by Schopenhauer.
Problem of modern culture.
Question: Whether it is national?
What the Germans now long for as their national culture: elegance.

30   Dubois-Reymond.

33 [1]

If for Goethe literature was a kind of compensation for his thwarted desire to be a painter, if one can speak of Schiller's dramas as a displaced populist oratory, then it also may be correct to assume that Wagner's natural gift was a theatrical one that was prevented from attaining satisfaction by pursuing the most traditional means and that discovers its compensation and salvation in the merging of all the other arts to form a great theatrical ideal.

33 [2]

The audience that sits in our theaters has been educated in different and unequal ways for the different arts of the theater; the degree of its knowledge about and feeling for music is different than for acting, and different again for dramatic literature. At a very early age Wagner observed what had an effect on this audience, and he presupposed as an explanation of these effects that this audience's expressions of approval and disapproval always issued from its innermost depths, from the single root of its essence, so to speak. He thus sought the source of these effects beyond the different educational backgrounds of the individuals, in their vital core. For example, he instinctively assumed that when viewing an opera no listener would be able to distinguish his enjoyment of the music from his enjoyment of the drama and of the theatrical artistry,

and that the effect achieved by the opera as a whole was composed of the combination of individual effects, whereby each
art form contributed the very same amount. Later on this calculation was thrown off by a great actress; Schröder-Devrient
5 was able, purely on the basis of her acting, to enhance insignificant music and a superficial, marionette-like drama till they
had the effect of great tragedy; but immediately Wagner's ideal
itself also was enhanced, and his calculation was squared away
by posing the question: what heights can effect achieve if the
10 grandeur of the music, indeed, if the entire drama, is on a par
with the skills of such an actress.

33 [3]

Wagner could have said of himself what Goethe says about
himself: "I never have known a human being who is more presumptuous than I am; and the very fact that I say this indicates
15 that it is true. I never thought that something had to be attained, I always thought I had everything; a crown could have
been placed on my head and I would have thought it a matter of course. And yet in this respect I was merely a human
being like any other, except that I attempted to work through
20 whatever lay beyond my powers, to merit what lay beyond my
merits, and it was this alone that distinguished me from someone who is truly insane." In much the same way Wagner never
doubted in his ability to accomplish whatever pleased him; his
taste and his abilities grew side by side. He wanted to create
25 whatever had a powerful effect on him. At every stage of his
life he never understood anything about his models other than
what he was also able to imitate.

33 [4]

Wagner has a legislative nature. With one glance he has an
overview of many relationships and does not get caught up
30 in trivialities. He organizes everything on a large scale; one
always will judge him incorrectly if one judges him according
to a detail, not only with regard to music and drama, but also
with regard to his views of the state and of society.

33 [5]

About his earliest works one could say that the music does not have much value, nor does the poetry, nor does the drama; the acting is often nothing but naturalistic rhetoric, but everything forms a totality and at the same level and derives its greatness from this. It would be possible for Wagner the thinker to rank just as high as Wagner the composer and the poet.

33 [6]

Wagner's earliest problem is: why isn't the expected effect realized, since I experience it? This drives him to a critique of his audience, of the state, of society. His instinct initially led him to presuppose between artist and public the relationship of subject to object. His experience shows him that this relationship is unfortunately an entirely different one, and he becomes a critic of his age.

33 [7]

Wagner's talent is a growing forest, not an individual growing tree. His greatest strength is his ability to sense unity in diversity, both outside himself, as an artist, and within himself, as an individual. By nature his eye is focused on the relationship of the arts among themselves, on the interconnection of state, society, and art.

33 [8]

In the sequence of some of Wagner's harmonies I sense something pleasantly jarring, like turning a key in a complicated lock. One is surprised by the predictable way in which the jarring element is resolved.

33 [9]

In Wagner what is predictable and rhythmic manifests itself only in structures of the greatest dimension, in the details he is often violent and unrhythmic.

33 [10]

Wagner grew so accustomed to being simultaneously sensitive to distinct art forms that he often proves to be entirely insensitive or unjust to individual art forms. During the period of his greatest theoretical rigor he even denied the legitimacy of those individual art forms, and much of the discord with his contemporaries dates from that time.

33 [11]

One of Wagner's characteristics is lack of restraint and immoderation. He always climbs up to the last rungs of his strength, of his emotion, and believes that it is only here that he is in uninhibited nature. His other characteristic is an extraordinary theatrical talent that is impeded and displaced, and that has to break through to courses other than just simply the next best: for he lacks the stature, the voice, and the necessary limitation to be an actor.

33 [12]

Wagner's cheerfulness is the sense of security felt by someone who has returned home to limitation from the greatest perils and indulgence. All the human beings with whom he has contact are such limited extracts from the limitless course of his own life (at any rate, they have no other significance for him); that is why he can interact with them in a cheerful and supremely good-natured manner, since all their sufferings, needs, and concerns, in comparison with his own, are nothing but marvelous games.

33 [13]

None of our great composers was still such a bad composer as he when he was 28 years old.

33 [14]

In *Tannhäuser* he attempted to motivate a series of different ecstatic states as the expressions of a single individual. He

probably believed at that time that the natural and free human
being is revealed only in these states. In the *Meistersinger* and
in parts of the *Ring of the Nibelungen* he returns voluntarily to
self-control and self-limitation. In this he is greater than in the
5 earlier phase, when he ecstatically let himself go.

33 [15]

   Wagner is a human being whose moral nature is disciplined
by the constantly growing demands of his artistic drive. His
character gradually divides, like a limb divides into branches:
Sachs and Wotan appear alongside Tannhäuser, Walter, Sieg-
10 fried. He learns how to understand the adult male, but he
learns this very late in life. Wagner's youth is that of a many-
sided dilettante who seems destined to come to nothing. But in
the last few years even I have two or three times sensed within
me the absurd doubt about whether Wagner has any musical
15 talent at all.

33 [16]

   He measured state, society, youth, the talents of peoples,
and absolutely everything by the standard of his art: when in a
state of dissatisfaction he probably wished that the entire modern world would perish. He finds an outlet for his weaknesses,
20 once he has recognized them, by attributing them to the modern ⟨world⟩. He believes in the goodness of human nature,
assuming it is left to take its course, and he ascribes all evil
to servitude and repression. ⟨In order⟩ to be free as an artist
as well, he ran away from his position in Dresden; for he re-
25 fused to be subservient any longer, and he used the revolution
to make it impossible for himself to be the conductor of the
court orchestra.

[34 = U II 6. Spring–Summer 1874]

34 [1]

Schopenhauer as Educator and Taskmaster
of the Germans.

Spring 1874.

34 [2]

Siegfried, the emerging philosopher.

34 [3]

Decline in *religiosity* since antiquity.

A couple of centuries from now it probably no longer will occur in its pure form, but only encrusted.

Weariness with its symbols.

34 [4]

Schopenhauer's human being:

suffers voluntarily

shows no mercy

tragic—for now and again he cannot help but be unjust, he cannot help but injure those people he loves

he lives truthfully—and thus, like life, he has an effect on others, liberating and preaching the metaphysical meaning of life.

34 [5]

What is his task with regard to culture?

He combats every enfeeblement of existence. He cannot seek elegance.

Due to his truthfulness, he comprehends the meaning of
5 culture: continually to produce human beings who understand life metaphysically.

34 [6]

How does one promote the genesis of the philosophical genius? Journeys, freedom from national interests. Not by means of philosophy professors.

34 [7]

10 Depiction of the age: the question concerning whether it is hopeless has no meaning for Schopenhauer. By being *truthful* he produces originary nature and the meaning of life. There is no *hope* for earthly happiness: it is enough if human beings, thanks to this truthfulness, admit to themselves that this was
15 *never* possible. For the individual the meaning of life is always the same, in every age. It is *supposed* to be hopeless where happiness is concerned: but he can hope that he himself will learn better to comprehend the meaning of life. —Above all, for him the purification of culture means truthfulness with regard
20 to true needs, but not beauty and luster of life.

34 [8]

Schopenhauer educated himself *against* his age, and in the struggle with its consciousness he struggled against himself. In this way he strives to return to his own core, to that center where his genuis is, and he gains knowledge of humanity
25 in its supreme strength. It is from this standpoint, as genius and transfigurer of the world, that he speaks about existence, about the world—and cites its worthlessness, even the worthlessness of the genius. —He is exemplary in the manner in which he discovers and thereby transcends himself. Everyone

is basically a genius insofar as he is *unique* and has an entirely
new perspective on things. He *increases* nature, he creates with
this new perspective.

34 [9]
How the Persians were educated: to shoot with a bow and
5 to tell the truth.

34 [10]
                          Plan.
Introduction to the fourth chapter. See left.
Then the depiction of the age.
The three images.
10 The degenerate forms of the Schopenhauerian human being.
     J⟨acob⟩ B⟨urckhardt⟩, etc.

34 [11]
A certain kind of stoicism among the Germans, based on
phlegm, p. 392, *Parerga* II.

34 [12]
The freedom of the will in one's *esse* — to become conscious
15 of it? Perhaps it is fortunate that most people do not become
conscious of it (since their *esse* is so evil).

34 [13]
I am far from believing that I have understood Schopenhauer correctly; on the contrary, it is only myself that I have
come to understand a little better by means of Schopenhauer;
20 that is why I owe him the greatest debt of gratitude. But in
general it does not seem very important to me to fathom completely and bring to light, as one does today, the actual teachings, understood comprehensively and rigorously, of any particular philosopher: this kind of knowledge is, at any rate, not
25 suitable for human beings who seek a philosophy for their life,
rather than merely a new form of learnedness for their mem-

ory: and ultimately it seems to me improbable that something
of this sort ever can really be fathomed.

34 [14]

Now, how does one return from such moments of sublime
isolation to so-called life? How can one even endure it? It is a
feeling as though one had just been wide awake: and immediately thereafter dreams descend upon the soul with hundreds
of twists and turns, like a swarm of snakes: and once seized
by the dream that feeling reverts to its opposite, namely, as
though we had just been dreaming and now have awakened.

34 [15]

What we call *culture* consists of the influence and collaboration of the state, the moneymakers, those in need of form, and
the scholars. They have learned to get along with one another
and no longer are feuding among themselves. A great clamor
and apparent success.

Except that the true test never has been faced: the great
geniuses usually stand in a feud against it. Just think of Goethe
and the scholars, Wagner and the state theaters. Schopenhauer
and the universities: people obviously refuse to admit that the
great human beings are the apex for whom everything else
exists. — The conditions for the development of genius in no
way have *improved*, but instead have *grown worse*. Universal loath-
ing for original human beings. Among us Socrates would not
have been able to reach the age of 70.

34 [16]

Now, I do not have much faith in the permanence of this
modern world. Many things can happen. For that reason we
do not want to conceal anything, but instead want to speak
the truth, as long as that is not prohibited, out of belief in
the metaphysics of culture. In any case, a number of things
must happen and change over the course of time. Whether an
institution can be found? — In any case, concepts must first

be cleansed and a number of institutions improved. Humanity must learn to deal with its most noble products in a more solicitous manner.

34 [17]

It is extremely difficult for human beings to support origi-
5 nality.

34 [18]

That the production of great individual specimens
the enormous work and restlessness of the human being
It requires overcoming even more than it does insight,———

34 [19]

Thus, if I now express once more very briefly what Schopen-
10 h⟨auerian⟩ philosophy, as an educator, meant and still means
to me, then I do this in ———

34 [20]

No one has the right to use the same terms Schopenhauer himself uses to portray his experiences—terms that are and should remain his own manifest property—when describing
15 what one learns in such moments of sublime isolation; and yet it infuriates one even more to come across those words, which are simply inaccessible to everyday life and to everyday minds, in dry, sparse excerpts—for example, in outlines of the history of philosophy. On the contrary, it should be a universal law:
20 every person has the right to speak about his inner experiences if and only if he is able to find his own words with which to describe them. For it goes against all propriety, and in principle even against all honesty, to treat the language of great minds as though it were not someone's property and were simply found
25 lying around on the street somewhere.

34 [21]

For Schopenhauerian philosophy warns us against nothing
more vehemently than against the derogation and obfuscation
of that deaf, pitiless — indeed, evil primordial trait of existence:
never does it arouse the terrifying sensation of the sublime
5 more than when it transports us to the icy purity of the highest alpine air so as to let us read the primordial granite characters inscribed there by nature. Anyone who cannot endure
such heights and whose knees tremble should quickly flee back
down to the comforts of his constructed transfigurations.

34 [22]

10 That is why they rave in their hostility against anyone who,
like Schopenhauer, recognizes their need and sits like a gad-
fly on their neck; in such moments they gesticulate and make
faces so crude and unrestrained that the mask of "elegance"
and "beautiful form" often falls off. But if an entire army of
15 such gadflies descends upon them, then nothing at all remains
of their "culture": for as soon as they no longer keep themselves in check and lose their artificial self-control, they cease
to have any power whatsoever: because as soon as the ugly content is laid bare, they are no longer able to pull the wool over
20 anyone's eyes.

But everything depends on bringing this ugly content of the
human being to consciousness — — —

Now, it is precisely this *content* at which those truthful human
beings direct their gaze — — —

34 [23]

25 The superior goodness and humanity of our souls and the
superiority of the modern intellect.

Not that we really believe in it: but we are supposed to *appear* to believe in it.

The intention of that pseudoculture is directed at an erro-
30 neous conclusion: "beautiful form" is supposed to vouch for
the "good content"; it is supposed to appear as though the

modern human being is totally happy and satisfied with himself; hence that since previous ages were very dissatisfied with themselves, he has not only surpassed them in intellectual strength, but also in natural goodness and humanity.

5   Quite the opposite, one gives one's own greedy selfishness free reign, to the point of a wanton depravity unknown to almost any other age—but always armed with all of modern science—and one learns how to explain and transfigure everything that happens in a philosophical, in a moral manner.

10   In general, "transfiguration" is today the preferred way of dealing with things that are not above reproach: state, war, money market, inequality of human beings.

34 [24]

Every moment of life wants to tell us something, but we do not want to hear what it has to say: when we are alone and quiet
15   we are afraid that something will be whispered into our ear— and hence we despise quiet and drug ourselves with sociability. The human being evades suffering as best he can, but even more so he evades the meaning of endured suffering; he seeks to forget what lies behind it by constantly setting new goals.
20 When the poor and tormented person rages against the fate that tossed him onto this, the most rugged shore of existence, he is evading the profound eye that looks at him questioningly from amid his suffering: as if it wanted to say: "Hasn't it been made easier for you to comprehend existence? Blessed
25 are the poor!" —And when those who seem to be more happy are actually consumed by unrest and flight from themselves, so that they never have any insight whatsoever into the natural, evil character of things—of the state, for example, or of labor, or of private property—then who could possibly envy them!

34 [25]
30   If we think, for example, of the brutal law of "labor" under which all of humanity, with a few exceptions, languishes ———
Thus everywhere people speak with ———

34 [26]

The drive that makes those who are poor and oppressed rebel against their oppression is identical with the drive that makes the state or those who are wealthy so inhuman: they want to avoid *being used* at any price. The state is afraid of this
5 attitude; it seeks to stamp it out as thoroughly as possible by means of its culture; statecraft must entertain and seduce. The state girds itself with the "cultivated people."

Description of my "cultivated person." He can be found in all classes, at all levels of education. Profound desire for re-
10 birth as a saint and a genius. Insight into our common suffering and deception. Strong sense for what is identical and for those whose sufferings are identical. Profound gratitude toward the few redeemers.

34 [27]

All action must gradually be tinged with the conviction that
15 we must atone for our life. "The blessing of labor!": that is the sweet habit, the joy of having completed something, and so on. But the meaning is: to preserve one's life, but not out of mere joy of living: on the contrary, everyone is gladly prepared to die at any moment. But the lesson is not in our hands: we
20 cannot simply conclude it in any way we choose.

34 [28]

But really: how hollow and hungry a soul must have become to let itself be contented with the disgusting fodder they now throw at your feet.

34 [29]

And it is really of almost no consequence whether someone
25 demonstrates good or bad "taste": at least as long, that is, as he only deals with art as someone who "tastes" it, art is, and will remain, a rather contemptible thing and is not suited to earnestly active and suffering human beings. When I hear the clamor for "beautiful form," for "elegance," that is constantly

being intoned by our literary artists, then it hardly sounds different to me than if an Indian were to clamor to be tattooed or desire to have a ring through his nose.

34 [30]

The ancients sought happiness and truth — let's just restrict
ourselves to seeking untruth everywhere and unhappiness in
things.

34 [31]

He wants to attain knowledge about everything.

He abandons himself and does not consider himself very important.

He does not merely want to be entertained, like Goethe's
human being.

He no longer hopes, like Rouss⟨eau's⟩ human being (since what
he hopes for is ineffable and has nothing at all to do with a
change in human institutions. It matters very little whether
human beings behave one way or another).

Finally, he *tells* human beings this and no longer withholds it.
Retroactive effect of truthfulness on his development.

New ideal of the theoretical human being. He is involved with
the state, etc., only for the purpose of *play*. This is the supreme
human possibility — to reduce everything to play, behind
which earnestness stands.

Music — Schopenhauer recognizes its essence.

Dream in which waking life begins to play a role.

34 [32]

Schopenhauer reminded us of something that we almost
had forgotten, something that, in any case, we wanted to forget:
that the life of the individual cannot have its meaning in
something historical, in his disappearance into some category,
and in the large and changing configurations of nation, state,
society, or in the smaller ones of community and family. Anyone
who is purely historical has not understood life as a lesson

and will have to learn this lesson all over again. The human
being is only too happy to make things easy on himself and believe that he has satisfied existence by concerning himself with
those large vehicles and by constantly remaining on the surface. He does not want to penetrate to the depths. But all these
generalities alienate you from yourself, even when they bear the
name of churches, of scholarly disciplines. The riddle of existence is expressed in you: no one can solve it for you, only you
alone. The human being flees from this task by surrendering
himself to things. —If he ever reverses his manner of viewing
things, if he ever sees himself in all his misery, then he also
comes to recognize the mendacity of all these generalities. He
no longer pins his hopes on them: on the contrary, the only
thing he hopes for is that all human beings will understand
the lesson of life correctly. He will have to be involved with
the state, etc., but without passionate impatience: nothing can
come to him from the outside. For him everything increasingly
becomes play. He has a presentiment of a most blissful period
in which nations will only play at being nations and states will
only play at being salespeople and scholars—above all of this.
There is music that explains this: how everything can be only
play, can be fundamentally only blissfulness. That is why it is
the transfiguring art, metaphysical through and through.

34 [33]
    The world cannot possibly be better than the human being:
for how does it exist—only as human sensation.

34 [34]
    What could we possibly admire in ourselves, what would re-
main firm for us! Everything is insignificant. Being truthful
with oneself is the highest thing we can expect from ourselves:
for most people deceive themselves. We achieve our zenith by
means of a sincere self-contempt: we see that the objects and
products of such human beings are something contemptible
and no longer allow ourselves to be deceived by the masses.

Pessimism. — Profound self-contempt: Christianity too nar-
row.

Why should destruction be a negative occupation! We are
clearing away all our fears and temptations.

34 [35]

5   The ancient philosophers sought the happiness of the individual: alas, they could not find it because they sought it. Schopenhauer seeks unhappiness: and the supreme consolation is
that someone like him cannot actually find unhappiness because he is seeking it: seeking has very different rewards.

34 [36]

10 Chapter 3/4. He is the *genius of heroic truthfulness*. The chapter
on his dangers has demonstrated how he educated himself.
Yet *by what means* did he accomplish this?
    By means of his aspiration to be *truthful*.
    That is a *disintegrative*, destructive aspiration; yet it makes the
15 individual *great* and *free*. Perhaps he will perish outwardly
from it, not inwardly.
    Chapter 4. Schopenhauer as *liberating destroyer* in his age. Noth-
ing deserves to be shown any mercy. Everything is incomplete and rotten.
20 Chapter 5. He takes exactly the same stance toward *German culture*. The liberating destroyer.
    Chapter 6. Continuation of his work. For this it is necessary to
educate a generation of philalethes. How will they be educated?

34 [37]

25 Every philosopher is a philosopher first for himself, and
only then for others: it is impossible for him to escape this
duality of relations. Even if he were rigorously to isolate himself from his fellow human beings, precisely this isolation
would have to be a law of his philosophy: it would become his
30 public lesson, his visible example. The most peculiar product

of any philosopher is his life; it is his work of art, and as such
it faces both the person who created it and all other human
beings. State, society, religion—indeed, even agriculture and
horticulture—all of them can ask: "What does this philoso-
5 pher mean to me? What can he offer us, how can he be useful,
how detrimental to us?" —Now, this is exactly what *German
culture* asks with regard to Schopenhauer.

I call him an educator of the Germans even in this important
respect. After the war with the French it became clearer to me
10 by the hour just how much the Germans are in need of just such
an educator: although someone who saw things more clearly
would not even have needed these most recent lessons. "We
have to learn from the French"—but what? "Elegance!" That
seems to be the sole lesson the Germans have drawn from that
15 war and brought home with them. Prior to this, that call was
heard quite infrequently: although there were enough literary
people who looked with envy toward Paris. Renan's elegance,
for example, first awakened Strauss's pen, and it recently awakened the pen of the theologian Hausrath [. . .]

34 [38]
20   4. So much about Schopenhauer as an

                                        educator of human beings.
    5.   of Germans.
    6.   of philosophers.

34 [39]
This activity of the philosopher does not stand alone, it is part
25 of a cycle.
Culture. Main character.
Pseudoculture.
    Pressed into the service
        of moneymaking
30   of the state.
    Beautiful form, deceiving.
Fundamental attitude out of which true culture grows.

34 [40]

That is an ideal; it makes the individual feel ashamed. How
    does he enter into a natural, *active* relationship with it? How
    can the path to education be found?

His attitude is *exploited* by secularized culture, its aims are nearer
5   and do not place such a burden on the individual.

The metaphysical meaning of true culture must be *ascertained*.
    First doctrine of education.

The production of genius is the *practical* task.

34 [41]

An ideal.

10 Objection: it forces one to live in a dual way, no linking ac-
    tivity is found.

Those who are more consequential retreat to a lower aim.

Counterargument: it is part of a circle of ideals, culture.

That lower aim is not a step along the way, but rather another
15   hostile standpoint.

Two dangers in cases where the image is very great:

    1) the great aim is abandoned (aberrant culture)
    2) the aim is retained, but no activity found that links us
       with it. The weaker natures are defeated: that is why Scho-
20   penhauer is suited only for the most active.

Significance of aberrant culture.

Attempt to derive *responsibilities* from its comprehensive con-
    cept.

In individual moments one stands within it.

25 It is necessary to find the lower step on which we actually can
    stand, where we will not get dizzy.

34 [42]

But these are regressions and characteristics of philosophical
originality and youth: and it must be possible to live in a more
manly, more persistent way, without these blinding intervals of
30 darkness and light, waking and dreaming: in such a way that my
gaze is reflected back at me coldly and brightly from the nature

of things onto my own nature, not onto something new and
different, but rather only onto a single example that is of little
significance and that gradually disappears when less attention
is paid to it. Once this ego is fused with us and we no longer—
5 or almost no longer—suffer as individuals, but instead as conscious living beings in general, then that transformation that
the entire play of becoming never can imagine also has occurred, and the human being toward which nature presses then
has been born so that nature can observe itself in his mirror.

34 [43]
10   Beginning.
     It is precisely this problem that is in need of being consid-
ered in more detail: how was it possible for Schopenhauer to
endure living in his age without attempting in some way or
other to become its reformer?
15 And didn't the weakness of the modern age weaken his image
of life?
     Against 1) He is the liberating destroyer. The freethinker.
     Against 2) As genius he takes action against the weakness
                    of the age and thereby becomes acquainted with
20   nature in all its power.

34 [44]
                         Final chapter.
How do we educate the philosopher?
The one who makes justice into his banner!

34 [45]
     Odysseus sacrificed so that the shades — — —
25 Let us make a similar sacrifice to the spirit of Schopenhauer,
by saying: *Philosophia academica delenda est.*

34 [46]
     Ils se croient profonds et ne sont que creux.

34 [47]

(II) Chapter.

Amazement that Schopenhauer could come into being and
exist at all.

Dangers: coming from Kant.

5   Isolation.

Climate of German cultivation.

Innermost conflict: La Trappe and genius. (His
greatness lies in this feeling of limitation, it has
nothing to do with his age: an eternal conflict.)

10 Example: Transition from Kant to Schopenhauer in life.

Overcoming the scholar.

Overcoming the Romantic.

Supplementing the classical ideal.

Inciting contempt for his age.

15 (III) Chapter. Was he *successful*?

Where success is to be expected: a) with regard to philosophy, the university.

Chap. IV   b) knowledge and correction of his age.

20   Chap. V   c) applied to German situation: genesis of genius.

34 [48]

As writer: honest

cheerful

manly (never old) and not emotional, he never com-
25   plains.

[35 = Mp XIII 3. Spring–Summer 1874]

35 [1]

There is an ethical aristocracy into which no one can gain entrance who was not already born into it and born for it.

Now, it is worth observing how people act in this ethical aristocracy.

5   They reproach Schopenh⟨auerian⟩ ethics for not having an imperativistic form, indeed, for openly rejecting such a form.

35 [2]

But the sphere of truth does not coincide with the sphere of the good.

35 [3]

We should esteem in particular the profundity that expresses
10 itself forcefully, harshly, coarsely, imperatively: whereas among the Germans it usually is found in its nebulous, meek, blurred form. Courageous scholars are a rarity. Active and harsh thinkers are even more rare in Germany.

35 [4]

Aristippus said that the most noble utility he derived from
15 his worldly wisdom was that it gave him the ability to feel at ease in any society—

Ariston said—a bath and an oration that do not purify and cleanse are good for nothing.

35 [5]

Philosophy
in
Affliction.
Preliminary and Fragmentary Remarks.

35 [6]

5   Goethe: "Friends, just do everything with seriousness and with love, for these two emotions suit the Germans so well, whereas so many other emotions disfigure them."

35 [7]

It is horrible to think that when one speaks to the Germans about their lack of culture, the only thing they hear is that they 10 are being reproached for their lack of elegance.

35 [8]

Schopenhauer among the Germans. What is the significance of the fact that he appeared here and not somewhere else? What is the significance of Schopenhauer's youth among a people in which philosophy is perishing? What meaning does philoso-15 phy have among the Germans?

He could just as well have been born among the Italians: see Leopardi

Leopardi: "only it (the thought of beauty) is capable of
mollifying
20   the severe guilt of fate
that fruitlessly gives us human beings
so much to endure on this earth;
and only through this thought of beauty can life
at times appear to noble souls, not merely to vulgar
25   ones,
to be sweeter than death."

35 [9]

There are probably not many who sense the image of the Schopenhauerian human being to be an ideal and who embrace it.

35 [10]

A mystical ideal and a dangerous one, to boot! "This
Schopenhauerian human being"—the timorous and ordinary people will say; "of what concern is he to us?"—

35 [11]

Schopenhauer is simple and honest: he seeks no empty clichés and no fig leaves, but instead openly says to a world that is deformed by dishonesty: "behold, this is once again the human
10 being!" What power all his conceptions have, the will (which connects us with Augustine, Pascal, the Hindus), negation, the doctrine of the genius of the species; there is no disquiet in his portrayal, but rather the clear depths of a lake when it is tranquil or experiencing light waves when the sun is shining upon it. He
15 is crude like Luther. He is the most rigorous example of a German prose writer, no one has taken language and the responsibility it imposes upon us as seriously as he did. One can see, *e contrario*, how much dignity and greatness ⟨he⟩ possesses by looking at his imitator Hartmann (who is actually his *adversary*).
20 His greatness is extraordinary, to have once again peered into the heart of existence, without scholarly digressions, without tiresome lingering and entanglement in philosophical scholasticism. The study of the one-quarter-philosophers who followed him is attractive for the sole purpose of seeing how they
25 immediately arrive at the place where scholarly pro and con, brooding, contradiction, but nothing more is permitted—and where, above all, one is not permitted to *live*. He demolishes secularization, but likewise the barbarizing power of the sciences; he arouses the most enormous need, just as Socrates was
30 an arouser of such need. People have forgotten what religion was, as they have the significance that art has for life. Schopen-

hauer stands in contradiction with everything that today passes
for culture: Plato with everything that *was* culture in Greece at
that time. Schopenhauer was catapulted ahead of his time.

35 [12]

5.

5	The philosopher as the true opponent of secularization, as
the destroyer of every apparent and seductive happiness and of
everything that promises such happiness among human beings,
of states, revolutions, wealth, honors, scholarly disciplines,
churches — for the salvation of us all, this philosopher must be
10	reborn an infinite number of times; the single fragile embodi-
ment of this philosopher in Schopenhauer is not enough. But
for all future ages he remains one thing: the most important
educator and soother of those few human beings who are born,
to any degree whatever, with that heroic sense of truthfulness
15	and at the same time, as its instrument, with acumen and far-
sightedness. Certainly, many other, different forms of that very
same basic attitude, which is hostile to the world and unfashionable, are possible: popular forms, more figurative forms,
more loving forms, more telling forms — and precisely our age,
20	caught up in the most hasty, most unreflected secularization,
and simultaneously at the threshold of the most horrible perils
for all worldly happiness, may bear within it more than just a
few of these possibilities. To find one single word that describes
this entire, yet possible, cycle of revelations — who possibly
25	could achieve that without calling forth misunderstandings?
But nevertheless, I want to say the word "culture" and have it
be understood in the sense of that entire developing cycle.

The aim of this future culture is not of this world, and yet
the greatest expressions of past cultures likewise point toward
30	an ineffable outcome and were hostile to the world and to be-
coming. Doesn't every true work of art wrest from itself a confession that gives the lie to Aristotle's claim? Isn't it nature that
imitates art? Doesn't it, with the restiveness of its becoming,
merely haltingly repeat, in an inadequate language and in ever

new attempts, what the artist expresses in all its purity? Doesn't
nature long for the artist so that he can redeem it from its imperfection? It was Goethe who said, with arrogant profundity:
"I have often said, and I will say it over and over again, that
5 the *causa finalis* of worldly and human affairs is dramatic literature. For otherwise this stuff is of absolutely no use." Doesn't
every culture seek to lift the individual human being out of the
pushing, shoving, and crushing of the historical stream and
make him understand that he is not merely a historically lim-
10 ited being, but also an absolutely extrahistorical and infinite
being with whom all existence began and will end? I refuse to
believe that this creature who crawls through life with somber
diligence, learns, calculates, plays politics, reads books, bears
children, and then lies down to die is a human being—that
15 can be only an insect larva, something contemptible and transitory that is nothing but surface. To live in such a manner is
tantamount to a bad way of dreaming. Now, the philosopher
and the artist call out a few words, words from the world of the
wakeful, to the person dreaming in this way; will they awaken
20 the restless sleeper? Rarely: for him these sounds usually contain nothing that could destroy his dream, he simply weaves
them into it, thereby increasing the muddle and commotion of
his life.

Thus, there is a kind of *aberrant culture* that is deferential to
25 the world and to becoming and that takes great pains to con-
fine the human being strictly to the realm of his historical existence. By means of it we are supposed to be able to accomplish
the task of liberating the intellectual energies of a generation
to such an extent that they can be of most use to existing insti-
30 tutions, to the state, commerce, the church, society: but only
to that extent: like a forest stream that is partially diverted by
means of dams and sluices so that its diminished energy can
drive mills, whereas its full energy would sweep the mill away.
This liberating is at the same time, and to a greater degree, a
35 shackling. If the great historical powers acknowledge the form
of culture that is hostile to the world and dare to try to reconcile

themselves with it, by reconciliation they always understand
only this damming and diversion of the stream onto their mills.
If they succeed at this, as the modern state has succeeded at
it, afterward one perceives the fiercest and most verbose effort
5 to win special, individual privileges for this weakened culture
that has been drafted into service and made deferential to the
world, as though it and only it deserved to be called culture:
and it is this misused culture itself that crows the loudest, because it knows that it is guilty and has deviated from its true
10 nature. Thus, Christianity, one of the most amazing individual
manifestations and expressions of that inexhaustively expres-
sive culture that is hostile to the world, gradually has been
used in a hundred ways to drive the mills of world powers, and
for that reason it became hypocritical and dishonest down to
15 its very roots; and even its final event, the German Reformation, would have been nothing but a sudden and quickly extin-
guished flare-up if the worldly states, led by the papal and the
German states, had not borrowed fresh fuel and flames from its
conflagration. If today Christian theologians still act as though
20 modern state culture must be reconciled with Christianity, their
words are just empty phrases: for Christianity no longer exists
in any other form than in the form of that state culture.

And today's *art*? It is supposed to justify nothing other than
our modern way of life, as a faithful copy of its hasty and over-
25 wrought secularization, as a means for ever greater diversion
and dispersion, inexhaustible in its alternation of stimulating
and piquant sensations, like a spice shop of the entire Occi-
dent and Orient, with something for every taste, regardless of
whether he has a hankering for the fragrant or foul-smelling,
30 for sublimity or peasantlike coarseness, for Greek or Chinese
cuisine, for tragic drama or dramatized obscenities. And it
is really of almost no consequence whether someone demonstrates good or bad "taste." At least as long, that is, as he only
deals with art as someone who tastes it, art is, and will remain,
35 a rather contemptible thing and will not be suited to earnestly
active and suffering human beings. When I hear the clamor for

"beautiful form," for "elegance," that is constantly being intoned by our literary artists, then it hardly sounds different to
me than if an Indian were to clamor to be tattooed or desire to
have a ring through his nose.

5   The Germans appear without exception to have brought
home similar desires from their last war with France. For many,
that war was their first trip into the more elegant half of the
world; what better way for the victor to appear unbiased than
by not disdaining to adopt his "culture" from those he has
10 vanquished. Craftspeople, in particular, are constantly being
encouraged to compete with our cultivated neighbor; the German house is to be furnished and decorated in a way similar
to the French house; by means of an academy founded along
the lines of the French model, even the German language
15 is supposed to acquire "sound taste" and be purged of the
dubious influence exerted upon it by Goethe. For some time
now our theaters—not merely in words, like that Berlin acade-
mician Dubois-Reymond, but in actions—have demonstrated
that they are motivated by the same drive for "sound taste"
20 and for French elegance. Even the elegant German scholar has
been invented: and we can certainly expect that everything that
up to now refused to submit to that law of elegance—German
music, tragedy, and philosophy—will gradually be written off
as "un-German," or, as one would probably say today, as "hos-
25 tile to the state." Deference to the state has elegance—may God
bless them both! —Or, to speak plain German, may the first of
these go to the devil if it wants to inculcate us with the disgusting notion of elegance. Truly, it would not be worth lifting a
finger on behalf of German culture if the German saw the cul-
30 ture he still lacks, but still is supposed to acquire, as nothing
other than agreeability—or, to express it more clearly, a certain sensibility of the dance master and the wallpaper hanger—
or if in his language he was only prompted by academically
sanctioned norms and the demand for gentility. But the last
35 war and the personal comparison with the French hardly can
have called forth any loftier aspirations; on the contrary, the

German seems anxious to escape those ancient obligations imposed upon him by his wonderful talent, his peculiar natural
inclination for seriousness and profundity; for once he would
prefer to play the role of the buffoon or the ape; he would pre-
5 fer to learn those arts and manners that prettify life, not those
that transfigure and illuminate it. I can conceive of no greater
violation of the German spirit than to treat it as though it were
so much wax, so that one day it might be able to be molded into
the shape of elegance. And if it is unfortunately true that a large
10 proportion of Germans would like to be shaped and formed
in this manner, then until they have finally listened to us we
should not cease to tell them: "That German spirit no longer
dwells in you. To be sure, it is hard, harsh, and resistant, but it is
a most precious material, one with which only the greatest art-
15 ists are permitted to work, because they alone are worthy of it.
You are made of a soft, doughy material; make out of it whatever you choose and in particular whatever you can, create with
it elegant puppets and national idols and then take up elegant
postures of prayer before them — Richard Wagner's words will
20 still remain true: 'The German is awkward and clumsy when he
tries to be genteel; but he is sublime and superior to all when
he catches fire.'" And elegant people have every good reason
to beware of this German fire, for otherwise it might devour
them some day, along with all their puppets and idols. —

25   But so as not to speak solely about the Germans: everywhere
and in general that pseudoculture, that culture deferential to
the world and to becoming, has reached the point that outwardly it demands gentility and the newest fashions, inwardly
the hastiest knowledge and exploitation of the ephemeral, in-
30 deed, of the momentary: and nothing else! Consequently, it is
embodied in the pernicious essence of the journalist, the slave
of the three M's, Moment, Majority Opinion, and Modish-
ness; and the more closely connected one is with that culture,
the more one will begin to resemble the journalist. Now, what
35 is most worthwhile about philosophy is precisely that it constantly teaches the doctrine that opposes everything journal-

istic in order to prevent human beings from considering the
moment too important and being swept away by it. Its intention, by contrast, is to set the human being on a foundation
firm enough to resist all the blows and surprises of fate and
to steel him against everything unexpected. As such, it is the
greatest enemy of that haste, that breathless seizing of the moment, that impatience that plucks all fruits from the branch
when they are still too green, from that rat race and chasing that
now cuts furrows into people's faces and places its tattoo, as it
were, upon everything they do. They storm about in indecent
anxiety as though they were under the influence of a potion
that no longer lets them breathe easily: so that the resulting
lack of dignity makes itself all too painfully evident, and now
a deceitful elegance becomes necessary to disguise the disease
of this undignified haste. For this is how that modish greed
for "beautiful form," as it is called, is connected with the *ugly
content* of the contemporary human being: the former is supposed to conceal, the latter supposed to be concealed. "To be
cultivated" now means not to let others notice how wretched
and base one is, how predatory in striving, how insatiable in
acquiring, how selfish and shameless in enjoying. That is how
this whole horrible cycle comes into being: the more money,
the more cultivation; or, expressed differently: the more desire
and wildness, the more dissimulation and polish. Anyone who
wants to affirm existence at any price must act as though he
himself is the tasty and charming fruit of that tree and as
though existence itself were worthy of being affirmed; for he
thereby seduces others into sharing his belief. As long as the
wealthy are experts in the trick of "beautiful form," the poor
also will endeavor to become rich.

   When I point out to people the absence of a German culture,
I have frequently met with the objection: "But this absence is
wholly natural, for up to now the Germans have been too poor;
just let our fellow countrymen become rich for once, and then
they will also have a culture!" Even though faith is supposed
to bring happiness, *this particular* kind of faith makes me un-

happy, because I sense that the German culture in whose future
one thereby expresses faith—a culture of wealth, of polish,
and of genteel dissimulation—is the most hostile antithesis to
that German culture in which I have faith. To be sure, anyone who has to live among Germans suffers horribly under the
infamous drabness of their lives and their senses, under their
formlessness, their dumbness and numbness, their coarseness
in delicate relations, and even more under their envy and a certain furtiveness and uncleanliness of character. He is pained
and insulted by their rampant pleasure in the false and counter-
feit, in the badly imitated, in the translation of good foreign
things into bad native ones: but it is thoroughly disgusting to
think that all these diseases and weaknesses can never principally be cured, but always only cosmetically covered over—by
just such a "culture of luxury" of the sort that inhumane wealth
has displayed in all ages in order to lend itself the appearance
of humanity. This sort of culture is hung like a veil over the vulgar and animalistic face of a wild lust for existence: woven of
pseudoreligion, pseudo-arts, pseudosciences, pseudophilosophies, [+ + +]

35 [13]
Schopenhauer once made the statement that it is always best
to lag behind one's time when one sees that it itself is regress-
ing.

35 [14]
That is why I tend to see and distinguish two things as the
roots of this entire contemporary culture that is deferential to
the age and to becoming: first, the opulent gravitation of this
society toward moneymaking and possessions; and second, the
clever selfishness of the modern state. Earthly happiness: in
both instances this is the bait with which culture is lured into
the trap; the rich and powerful human being, the free personality, the cultured state—these are the promises with which our
contemporaries are supposed to be deceived. That it is in fact

a matter of *deception* immediately comes to us like a revelation
once we have descended for just one single moment into that
cave in which we can find the roots of the genuine culture that
is hostile to the world.

5   Human beings of greater profundity have always felt compassion with animals precisely because they suffer from life
and yet do not possess the strength to turn the sting of suffering against themselves and understand their existence metaphysically; and the sight of senseless suffering arouses pro-
10 found indignation. That is why at more than one place on this
earth the conjecture arose that the souls of guilt-laden human
beings were trapped inside the bodies of these animals, and
that that suffering whose senselessness at first glance arouses
indignation acquires sense and significance as punishment and
15 penance when viewed against the backdrop of eternal justice.
Could one conceive of a harsher punishment than to live in
the manner of an animal, subject to hunger and desires, and
yet without arriving at any insight at all into the nature of this
life, as a beast of prey, for example, who is driven through
20 the desert by its gnawing torment, is seldom satisfied, and this
only in such a way that this satisfaction turns into agony in the
flesh-tearing struggle with other beasts, or from nauseating
greediness and oversatiation. To cling so blindly and madly to
life, for no higher reward, far from knowing that one is pun-
25 ished or why one is punished in this way, but instead to thirst
with the inanity of a horrible desire for precisely this punishment as though it were happiness—that is what it means to
be an animal. And if all of nature presses onward toward the
human being, then it senses that he is necessary for its salva-
30 tion and that in him existence holds before itself a mirror in
which life no longer appears senseless but appears, rather, in
its metaphysical meaningfulness. But where does the animal
cease, where does the human being begin! As long as someone
desires life as he desires happiness, he has not elevated his gaze
35 above the horizon of the animal, the only difference being that
he desires with more awareness what the animal craves out of

blind instinct—which means that we spend the greatest part of our lives in the state of animality, we ourselves are those creatures who seem to suffer senselessly.

But there are moments when the clouds break and when we, along with all of nature, *press onward toward the human being.* In this sudden brightness we gaze with a shudder around and behind us: here we see the refined beasts of prey run, and we run in their midst. The tremendous mobility of human beings on the great earthly desert, their founding of cities and states, their waging of wars, their ceaseless gathering and dispersing, their confused mingling, their imitation and deceit of one another, their mutual outwitting and trampling underfoot, their cries in distress and their joyous cheers in victory—all this is a continuation of animality, as if human beings were intended to regress and be cheated out of their metaphysical disposition; indeed, as if nature, having yearned and labored for human beings for so long, now recoiled from them in fear and preferred to return to the unconsciousness of instinct. Alas, nature needs knowledge, and it is horrified at the knowledge it actually needs; and so the flame flickers unsteadily, trembling, as it were, out of fear of its task, and seizes upon a thousand things before seizing upon that thing on whose account nature even needs knowledge in the first place. All of us know in individual moments how the most extensive arrangements of our own lives are made only in order to flee from our true task; how we want to hide our heads somewhere, as though our hundred-eyed conscience would not find us there; how we hasten to sell our soul to the state, or to moneymaking, to scholarship, to social life, just so that we will no longer have it; how even in our daily work we slave away without reflection and more ardently than is necessary to make a living—because it seems to us more necessary not to stop and reflect. Haste is universal because everyone is fleeing from himself; universal, too, is the timid concealment of this haste, because we want to appear satisfied and deceive the most perceptive observers about our wretchedness; universal, as well, the need for new-sounding

word bells with which life can be adorned and lent an air of fes-
tive noisiness. Everyone knows from his own experience how
unpleasant memories suddenly force themselves upon us and
how we then make an effort to drive them out of our heads by
5 means of violent gestures and sounds—but the general structure of our life indicates that we always find ourselves in such
a state: What is it that assails us so often, what mosquito is
this that refuses to let us sleep? Ghostly things are occurring
around us, every moment of life wants to tell us something, but
10 we do not want to hear this ghostly voice. When we are quiet
and alone we are afraid that something will be whispered into
our ear; and hence we despise quiet and drug ourselves with
sociability. The human being evades suffering as best he can,
but even more so he evades the interpretation of the endured
15 suffering; he seeks to forget what lies behind it by constantly
setting new goals. When the poor and tormented person rages
against the fate that tossed him onto this, the most rugged
shore of existence, then he also is only trying to deceive himself: he does not want to look into the profound eye that looks
20 at him questioningly from amid his suffering, as if it wanted to
say: "Hasn't it been made easier for you to comprehend existence?" Those who seemingly are more happy, who are consumed by unrest and flight from themselves in order never to
have to admit at all the natural, evil character of things, of the
25 state, for example, or of labor, or of private property [+ + +]

[36 = U II 7b. May 1874]

36 [1]
Introduction to Plato. 1874.
Ancient Metrics.
Diogenes Laertius.
On Homer.

36 [2]
5   1874.
Schopenhauer.
The Scholar.
1875.
Two Unfashionable Observations.
10   1876.
One Unfashionable Observation.

36 [3]
To be read:
2 Greek literature.
1 Encyclopedia.
15   1 Metrics.

[37 = U II 7c. P II 12a, 220. P II 12b, 59.58.56. End of 1874]

37 [1]

Abarten; degenerare (son from father)
abätzen (the pasture) *depascere*
abbesolden
eine Sache zu grün *abbrechen* = to be overhasty
er *bricht* sich nichts *ab* = denies himself nothing
die Zeit wird den Aberglauben schon *abbringen*
abbrüchig (dative) = disadvantageous
Licht *abdäuben* (mute)
davon lässt sich nichts *abdingen*
alles, was man uns *abdringt*
Aberglauben und *Abdünkel*
einem etwas *abeilen* (quickly take away)
es gehet *gegen den Abend*
auf wahrscheinliche Vermuthungen ein *Abenteuer* wagen
abenteuernd
euer ganzes *aberweises* Jahrhundert
in *Abfall* und Verachtung kommen
die Regel muss einen *Abfall* leiden
nach ihm *abgeformt*
abgeführte und arglistige Köpfe
Fehl, *Abgang* und Gebrechen
abgängige Kleider (worn out)
er *gab* einen Begleiter *ab*
das Feuer *abgehen* lassen

uns, denen nichts *abgeht*
abgelebte Tage
unser *abgesagtester* Feind
dir will ich leicht *abgewinnen* mit
5   zerlumpt die Segel, Rippen *abgewittert*
er *gewöhnte* ihn von den Ausschweifungen *ab*
da wird ein Todter geschwind noch *abgegossen*
Abglimmen des Lichtes bei heiteren Abenden
das Glück war mir *abgünstig*
10   dass er ihnen nichts *abhaben* konnte
Spiess abhag abziehn = to abandon the siege
er hält gar nichts ab = aus
ich kam mir selbst *abhanden*
ich *hange* ganz von ihrem Willen ab
15   die Natur macht den Menschen *abhängig zur Erde*, das
       Gemüth wie eine schwere Bleiwage nach der Eitelkeit
       abhängig
bei *abgehellter* Luft
helfet mir das Marter *ab*
20   Abhub (*ablatio ciborum*)
ich lasse mir nichts *abheucheln*
den Zeugen vor Gericht *abhören*
allem Laster *abhold*
abkarten
25   abkaufen
sich von der Welt *abkehren*
das Jahr *klingt ab*, der Wind geht über die Stoppeln
abgeklaubte Formeln
als er seines Frostes ein wenig *abgekommen* war
30   *abkräftige* Kranke
er will sich keinen Heller von dem Gelde *abkürzen* lassen
nach *abgelegter* Reise
einen Besuch in der Nachbarschaft *abzulegen*
einen Brief von Basel *ablassen*
35   das Pferd *läuft* von der Strasse *ab*
ihm den Vortheil, den Preis *ablaufen*

du weisst dass bei Licht seine Augen immer mehr *ablegen*
    ablenken
aller Wein muss erst *abliegen*, bevor man ihn trinken kann
ein versetztes Pfand *ablösen*
5   die Handgriffe *abmerken*
den Streit gütlich *abmachen*
was aber *windfällig* und *wipfeldürr*, mag man wohl abhauen
du kannst dich wohl von dem Schreiben einen Augenblick
    abmüssigen
10   die Regel aus der Analogie *abnehmen*
Bergleute müssen manchen Schurf vergebens werfen und
    viel Schächte abteufeln
ich bin nicht in Abrede, dass
dass ich sie nicht recht gemahlet, sondern allein auf ein
15   Papier schlecht abgerissen
einen *Absagbrief* wider alle Zeitungsschreiber
das Glück *sagt* ihm *ab* und widerstehet ihm
eine Neigung, welche mit ihrem Alter einen starken *Absatz*
    machte
20   ein glücklicher Abschied aus dieser Welt
wie leichtfertig hat jener Fürst seinen Dienern das
    abgebrochen und *abgeschatzet*
pfui welch ein *Abscheu*, welch ein Schreckbild!
aus der *Abschilderung*, die man mir von ihm gemacht
25   ich nehme keinen *Abschlag* an, keine vorläufige Bezahlung
jeden Gewaltstreich *abschlagen*
worauf kann er wohl sein Absehen richten? (haben)
seinen Vortheil schnell *absehen*
Tag und Nacht *setzen* so entschieden von einander *ab*
30   alte *abgesetzte* Wörter
er *setzte* einen grossen Streit *ab*
in gewisser *Absicht*, in *Absicht* der Wirkungen.

37 [2]
Ebenmaass
echt is correct, not *ächt*

ehe is false: must be written *eh*
mit *ehester* Gelegenheit
augenfällig und eindrücklich
zu wilden und einöden Orten
5 er hat ein grosses Stück am Eis gebrochen.

37 [3]
Value of writing Latin.
Translating.
Amount and kind of reading.
On stylistic models.
10 Utility of anthologies.
Extent of writing.
Speaking and hearing.
The logical proposition.
On ornament.
15 Overall tone.
Development of a text—ideas.
Persuading—instructing and other aims.
artem tegere.
Joy of writing as counterweight to reading.
20 Whether shorter or longer texts should be composed first?
One must have a feeling for the overall proportion.
The ancients did not write well by nature.
On quotations (should not disrupt the tone).
Abstinence from newspapers (writing while reading).
25 The simple comes last and is most difficult.
What is individual must first be expressed, then it must be
      broken.
Punctuation, dashes, etc.
Preservation of language tied only to artistic treatment.

37 [4]
30 Translating: but creating verses corrupts one's language.
Never shy away from being clearer than the author.

"Reading between the lines" must be rendered by means of more overt allusions.

Sometimes one sees too many of the *bare bones* in Aristotle (although *leanness* is certainly *appropriate*).

5   Perspectives on the future of language; the time has come for lifelong labor on it.

Take the unfortunate idea of an academy as the point of departure —

Our ways and means for arriving at culture are hostile to the
10   strength and health of culture.

The problem of literary prose; necessary at a certain time as the only thing that still preserves language; but accompanied by an enormous loss.

The struggle for prose (written and oral prose).

15   The immoral conditions of the individual literary genres, for example, the audience's impatience at dramatic performances: likewise the intellectual limitations that are necessary for every specific art form.

On reading: we are an age whose culture is perishing from
20   the means for arriving at culture.

Keller. Auerbach. Heine. Grimm.

Auerbach can neither tell a story nor think; he just acts as though he can. By contrast, he is in his element when he can flounder around in a meek, garrulous emotion; but
25   we do not like being in his element.

When *effective*, a good text will cause one to forget that it is a literary work; it is effective in the same way as the words and actions of a friend; who would want to have something published about that!

30   The decline of cultivation manifests itself in the impoverishment of language; the German used in newspapers is already a κοινή. One can improve language *outwardly* (second and third centuries A.D.).

37 [5]

The poverty of language corresponds to the poverty of opinions: just think of our literary journals: how few dominant
views! When a judgment about a book is expressed, one thinks
at first that one is dealing with nothing but specialists: now I
5   see what's *behind it*.

The disadvantages that are tied to the unity of a nation as
to the unity of a church; blessing of struggle. In the competition among nations the refractory, divisive character of the
Germans dries up inside and becomes outwardly pugnacious,
10 lavish, self-indulgent, greedy.

Woe to all who now aspire to achieve a beautiful style: be
what you appear to be and write that way!

Five-year Pythagorean prohibition on reading.

Goethe's use of dictation: its advantage, closer to spoken
15 language.

"Beautiful style" is an invention of the flashy orators.

"Why should one take such pains with language!" Clarity is
enough, as Epicurus believed. Must show what gets lost due
to this principle of clarity. Does the human being consist of
20 nothing but logic?

37 [6]

All intercourse among human beings is based on the ability
of one person to read the soul of another; and the common
language is the voiced expression of a common soul. The more
intimate and sensitive that intercourse becomes, the richer the
25 language; which either grows—or wastes away—along with
that shared soul. To speak is essentially to ask my fellow human
being whether he shares with me an identical soul; the oldest
statements seem to me to have been questions, and I suspect
that accentuation is the echo of that oldest form by which
30 the soul posed questions to itself, but in a different medium.
Do you recognize yourself? —This feeling accompanies the
speaker's every statement; he attempts to enter into a mono-
logue and dialogue with himself. The less he recognizes him-

self, the more he falls silent, and in this forced silence his soul becomes more needy and smaller. If one could force human beings to keep quiet from now on: one could make them revert to horses, seals, and cows; for in these creatures one recog-
5 nizes what it means not to be able to speak: namely, the same thing as to possess a torpid soul.

Now, many human beings, and sometimes the human beings of entire ages, do, in fact, have something of the cow about them; their soul lies torpid and indifferent within them. Re-
10 gardless of whether they are leaping, grazing, or staring at each other, the only thing they have in common is this miserable remnant of a soul. Consequently their language *cannot help but* be impoverished or become mechanical. For it is not true that need is the cause of language, the need of the individual; on the
15 contrary, at most the need of an entire herd, of a tribe; but in order for this to be experienced as something held in common the soul already must have developed further than the individual; it must undertake journeys, *want* to find itself again, it must first *want* to speak before it speaks; and this wanting is not
20 something individual. If one were to imagine a mythological primal being with a hundred heads and feet and hands as the primal human being: then it would speak with itself; and only after it had noticed that it was able to speak with itself as with a second, third, indeed, hundredth creature, would it let itself
25 be divided into parts, the individual human beings, because it would know that it never could completely lose its unity: for unity does not exist in space, like the multitude of these hundred human beings; rather, when they speak, this mythological monster senses itself to be once more complete and one.

30 And does the marvelous sound of a language really have the ring of a language that is born of need? Isn't everything born of pleasure and extravagance, free and with the signs of reflective profundity? What does the apelike human being have to do with our languages! A people that has six grammatical cases
35 and verbs that are conjugated in a hundred ways has a fully shared and overflowing soul; and any people that created such

a language for itself effuses all of posterity with the fullness
of its soul; in a later age the same forces manifest themselves
as poets and composers and artists, orators and prophets; but
when these forces still were in the exuberant fullness of their
5 early youth, they produced creators of languages: they were
the most productive human beings of all time, and they were
distinguished by that quality that distinguishes composers and
artists of all ages: their souls were more grand, more loving,
more communal, and living more or less in all places rather
10 than in one single gloomy corner. In them the shared soul
spoke with itself.

37 [7]

Are *many* languages of use for a future writer? Or foreign
languages at all? In particular for a German writer? The Greeks
depended upon themselves and did not make an effort to learn
15 foreign languages: but they did make an effort to learn their
own. In our case it is just the opposite: German studies have
only gradually established themselves, and the *way* they are
pursued has something foreign and scholarly about it. Much
is done for the teaching of Latin style; but in German one
20 teaches the history of the language and literature: and yet this
history has meaning only as the means and instrument of a
practical exercise. In earlier times the ability to read German
meant little or nothing. But it means a lot to arrive at a judgment about the *corrupt state* of present-day language and hence
25 to seek assistance from the past. The stock of words and expressions that everyone now has at his disposal must be perceived
and sensed to be *exhausted*; in actuality, language is much richer
than this stock would lead one to believe; likewise, knotty syntax is exhausted. One must hence treat language in an artistic
30 manner in order to avoid disgust; similar to the way in which I
no longer can endure Mendelssohnian phrases; I desire a more
powerful, more exciting language. To be sure, today it is much
more difficult to write than it used to be; one has to create one's
own language. This is no external desire, as if one were tired

of a certain manner of dress and desired a new fashion. For in
the languid character of our language it is easy for me to recognize our languishing Germanness, our vanishing individuality.
At times the struggle is nothing but a rebellion against the destruction of that better and stronger Germanness in which we
still believe. The last thing *we* need would be a set of stylistic
axioms that concentrated on what is correct and conventional:
whereas for the others it hardly is necessary anymore, since they
already involuntarily dwell inside it, I mean in the confines of
what is correct and conventional. Anyone who still wants to
promise that the German language will have a future must create a movement *against* our present-day German. We will have
to put up with a lot of unfortunate and tortured things; the
first aim is that we *exert* ourselves, that we invest blood and
energy in our language. "Beautiful" and "ugly" are words that
should be of no concern to us today, there is no such thing as
good "taste." An end to all meekness, complacency.

   In other words: the impoverishment and paling of language
is a symptom of the stunted shared soul in Germany; whereas
the great uniformity in words and phrases could appear to be
just the opposite, the counterpart to political unity, the attainment of a shared soul. One would at least be able to say: a unity
develops due to shrinkage and expansion; it is the first type that
we now have. As proof of the fact that we do not have the second type it is enough to recognize that our greatest and richest
minds are absolutely incapable of making themselves comprehensible to their fellow Germans. They are involuntarily made
into exiles. Further proof is supplied by the type of writers and
artists who are in conformity with the present-day shared soul
and who are comprehensible; for example, the likes of Strauss,
Auerbach, etc.

37 [8]
   How can one possibly consider style and the manner of presentation to be so important! It is really only a matter of making
oneself understood. —But, admittedly, that is no easy matter,

and it is very important. Just think ⟨what⟩ a complex creature the human being is: how infinitely difficult for him to truly *ex*press himself! Most human beings remain trapped inside themselves and cannot get out; but that is slavery. To be able to
5 speak and write means to be liberated: I admit that this is not always for the best; but it is good for it to become visible, for it to take on word and color. Anyone who cannot express himself, who slavishly prattles, is a barbarian. —To be sure, "beautiful style" is nothing but another cage, a gilded barbarism.
10   I demand from a book *harmony* as unity and moderation; that determines the choice of words, the type and number of metaphors, the development and conclusion.

[38 = Mp XII 5. End of 1874]

38 [1]

Prometheus and his vulture were *forgotten* when the old world of the Olympians and their power were destroyed.

Prometheus expects his redemption to come from human beings.

5   He did not betray his secret to Zeus, Zeus perished because of his son.

Lightning bolts in possession of Adrasteia.

Zeus wanted to destroy human beings—by means of war and women and their singer, Homer: *in summa*, Greek culture, spoil life for all future generations; he wanted to make them insensitive to the Greeks by means of imitation and envy.

To rescue them from this end, his son made them unknowing and fearful of death and caused them to hate Hellenism; he thereby destroyed Zeus himself. Medieval times to be compared with conditions prior to Prometheus's act of giving them fire. This son of Zeus seeks to destroy human beings as well.

Prometheus sends Epimetheus to help them, and he takes in aged Pandora once more (history and memory). And humanity really is revived, and Zeus along with it, the latter from a *fable* in mythology. Fabulous Greekdom seduces to life—until, better recognized, it *leads away* from life again: its foundation is recognized to be horrible and inimitable. —

(Prometheus deprived human beings of their awareness of

death, everyone considers himself an immortal individual and
actually lives differently, as a link in the chain.)

Period of *distrust* toward Zeus and his son; toward Prometheus, as well, because he sent them Epimetheus.

5   Inauguration of chaos.

Prometheus is instructed by Epimetheus about his mistake
when creating human beings. He *accepts* his own punishment.

The vulture no longer wants to eat. Prometheus's liver grows
too large.

10   Zeus, his son, and Prometheus speak with one another. Zeus
releases him, Prometheus is supposed to pulp human beings,
create a new form, the individual of the future. Means by
which one produces a material, a pulp. To relieve the pain of
humanity when being pulped the son grants music.

15   Thus: concession to Prometheus, human beings shall come
into being again; concession to Zeus and his son, first they
must perish.

38 [2]

On the structure of the whole: the vulture speaks to himself and says: I am Prometheus's vulture and due to the most
20 unusual circumstances I have been *free* since yesterday. When
Zeus gave me the task of eating Prometheus's liver he wanted
to get rid of me, for he was jealous because of Ganymede.

38 [3]

All religion is somewhat detrimental to the human being.
What would have happened if Prometheus had not been de-
25 ceptive at Mecone! State of things under the son when the
priests devour everything.

38 [4]

"Oh, what an unfortunate bird I am, I've become a myth!"

38 [5]

Due to Christianity human beings have become so shade-
like, like the Greeks in Hades. Drink blood. (Wars.)

38 [6]

When Prometh⟨eus⟩ created human beings he forgot that
the strength and experience of human beings are separated by
a temporal gulf: all wisdom has a tinge of senility.

38 [7]

The gods are stupid (the vulture blabbers like a parrot);
when Zeus created Achilles, Helen, and Homer he was short-
sighted and was not familiar with human beings; the real result
was not the destruction of human beings, but instead Greek
culture. Whereupon he created the world conqueror in the
form of man and woman (Alexander and Roma, science); his
son Dionysus {created} the overcomer of the world (foolish-
fanciful, bleeds himself, becomes a fanatical Hades shade on
earth, establishment of Hades on earth). The overcomers of
the world embrace the idea of the world conqueror—and with
that things seem to be over for human beings. Zeus nearly perishes from this, but Dionysus-overcomer as well. Prometheus
sees how all human beings have become shades, ruined to
the core, fearful, evil. Out of pity he sends them Epimetheus
along with seductive Pandora (Greek culture). Then things get
completely ghostly and disgusting and pulplike among human
beings. Prometheus despairs [+ + +]

Notes

[19 = P I 20b]

19 [1] For a planned treatise on the "philosopher" or the "pre-Platonic" (Nietzsche's preferred designation for "pre-Socratic") Greek philosophers. The various titles Nietzsche used for this project display a development and a multitude of complementary perspectives: see 19 [13, 36, 85, 98, 131], and the comprehensive titles in 19 [316, 318]. Parallel to this, Nietzsche developed the themes of truth and value, the struggle between art and knowledge, the value of lies, and the historical development of Greek philosophy. Out of these thoughts emerged the treatises "Philosophy in the Tragic Age of the Greeks" and "On Truth and Lie in an Extra-Moral Sense." The entries in this notebook display a distinctly unified character.

3, 9–10   *There ... another]* This idea of geniuses as a spiritual bridge or mountain range far above the masses is derived from Schopenhauer's "republic of geniuses." See Arthur Schopenhauer, *Der handschriftliche Nachlaß*, ed. Arthur Hübscher (Frankfurt: W. Kramer, 1966–75), 3: 188. Nietzsche returns to this idea frequently in his early writings. See, for example, section 9 of "History," p. 151, and 24 [4] and 29 [52].

19 [4]

4, 1   *Preface ... Schopenhauer]* Many of the entries in notebook 19 are notes for the planned treatise on the "philosopher." Nietzsche intended to dedicate this work to Schopenhauer. Some of the ideas presented in "Schopenhauer as Educator" developed out of these early reflections on the character of the philosopher.

4, 1–2 *entrance … sheep*] Cf. *Human, All Too Human*, vol. 2, no. 408, where Nietzsche returns to this idea of entering the underworld and sacrificing sheep to Schopenhauer. The allusion is to Homer, *Odyssey*, 11.23–50, where Odysseus sacrifices a black sheep to the gods to ensure his safe return to Ithaca before descending to the underworld.

19 [7]

4, 12 *opinionator of the public*] Nietzsche coined the phrase *öffentlich meinende* in analogy to *öffentliche Meinung* ("public opinion"), suggesting that the press creates and disseminates opinions. Nietzsche returned to this idea in section 1 of "Strauss," p. 5.

4, 19 *saecular*] One of the meanings of the Latin word *saeculum*, "age," or "century," from which the English word "secular" is derived, is "spirit of the age," or "fashion." This is the meaning to which Nietzsche is alluding here.

19 [10]

5, 3 *The will … imperishable*] The immortality of the will is a fundamental principle of Schopenhauer's philosophy.

5, 11–12 *procreating … beautiful*] An allusion to Plato's *Symposium*, 206b, in which Diotima defines love as procreating in the realm of the beautiful. In 206c–206e she goes on to explain that this notion applies to both the physical realm, as "begetting," and to the spiritual realm, as "creativity." These two forms of procreation in the beautiful, she asserts, bring the human being as close as possible to a form of immortality. Nietzsche returns repeatedly to this thought throughout these early notebooks, whereby he tends to emphasize the aspect of artistic or spiritual creativity.

19 [14]

6, 10 *The seven wise men*] A group of pre-Socratic statesmen and philosophers, ca. 620–550 B.C. Authorities differ on the names and number, but commonly included are Bias, Chilon, Cleobulus, Periander, Pittacus, Solon, and Thales.

19 [18]

7, 21 *voûs*] *nous*, "mind," or "intellect."

19 [19]

7, 24 *historical-critical atmosphere*] This is the earliest remark on

David Strauss in Nietzsche's notebooks. Prior to the appearance of Strauss's *Der alte und der neue Glaube* (The old and the new faith) in 1872, against whose popularity Nietzsche protested in the first essay in *Unfashionable Observations*, David Strauss was known primarily as a religious scholar. By identifying him with historical-critical studies, Nietzsche is suggesting that religious scholarship, not the pseudo-philosophizing of *Der alte und der neue Glaube*, is his proper domain.

19 [20] Cf. 19 [27]

19 [22]

8, 28 *To ... sublime!]* Cf. 19 [33].

19 [26]

9, 26 *peuple publicum]* Nietzsche combines the French term *peuple*, meaning "people," or "everyone," with the Latin *publicum*, "public," or "belonging to the commonweal." The implication is that German popular philosophers do not take up higher issues of the common good, but simply address themselves to the base concerns of the masses.

19 [27] Cf. 19 [20].

19 [28]

10, 20 *laissez aller]* "let it be," "leave it alone."

19 [32] Cf. section 1 of "Strauss," p. 9.

19 [33]

11, 17–18 *intellectual ... centuries.]* See note to 19 [1].

11, 23 *Holding ... sublime!]* Cf. 19 [22].

19 [34]

12, 6 *morality."]* Kant, preface to the second edition of *The Critique of Pure Reason*, B xxx; based on the translation by J. M. D. Meiklejohn (London: George Bell, 1893), p. xxxv.

12, 17 *seven wise men]* See note to 19 [14].

19 [36]

13, 28–29 *excessive knowledge]* Nietzsche's neologism, *Vielwissen* (literally: knowing much) is derived from the derogatory term *Vielwisser*, signifying a pundit or someone who makes pretense to great knowledge. Hence the derogatory attribute "excessive" in my rendering.

19 [37]

15, 13–14 *torch … crest.]* In the opening scene of Aeschylus's *Aga-memnon*, the first play in his *Oresteia*, Agamemnon's return from defeated Troy is signaled by the approaching light of torches.

19 [39]

16, 17–18 *mores … morality]* Nietzsche's words are *Sitte* and *Sitt-lichkeit*. The former is usually translated as "custom," the latter as "morality," but the context requires a rendering that under-scores the connection of these two concepts.

19 [40]

16, 27 *free poetic]* Nietzsche's neologism is *freidichtend*, an adjective formed in analogy to *freidenkend*, "freethinking."

19 [41]

17, 13–14 ἀγάπη … ἔρως] *agape … eros*; the former refers to nonsexual, "Platonic" love, the latter to erotic or sexual love.

19 [43]

18, 9 πάθος] *pathos*; the Greek word has a broader meaning than "pathos," encompassing "experience," "suffering," and "pas-sion," as well.

19 [53]

21, 16–17 *Heraclitus's fate]* According to Diogenes Laertius, *Lives of the Eminent Philosophers* (9.6), Heraclitus was plagued by fanatic followers, and he deliberately made his writings more obscure so that none but adepts could understand them.

21, 25–26 *procreation … beautiful!]* See note to 19 [10].

19 [55] These remarks refer to Nietzsche's *Birth of Tragedy*, which was received unfavorably by the scholarly community, espe-cially by his fellow classical philologists. Cf. 19 [58].

19 [56]

22, 4 *age of the seven wise men]* See note to 19 [14].

19 [57] Plans for university lecture courses.

22, 9 *Choephori]* The second play in Aeschylus's *Oresteia*, usually translated into English as *The Libation Bearers*.

19 [58]

22, 11 *my book]* *The Birth of Tragedy*, first published in 1872. Cf. 19 [55].

22, 17–18 *ignore … again]* Nietzsche was working on a second edition of *The Birth of Tragedy*. In a letter to his mother dated

3 January 1873, he notes that he has finished the corrections for this second edition. However, this edition was not printed until 1874, and it was not available for sale until 1878.

22, 17–19 *neutral manner … castrati*] Instead of *die Philologie*, with its grammatically feminine article, Nietzsche writes simply *Philologie*. "Neutral" thus implies here "genderless," or "neutered," and it thereby ironically anticipates the accusation that contemporary philologists are castrati.

22, 19–20 *textual reconstruction*] *Conjekturen*. In the discipline of classical philology, this term refers to the reconstruction of faulty or missing text passages based on educated conjectures. Nietzsche is implying that his fellow philologists are workaday, myopic scholars incapable of imaginative thought.

19 [59]

22, 21 *Διαδοχαί*] *Diadochai*, "successions" or "successors." This term refers to the idea that the early Greek philosophical schools had a strict organization and were led by masters who determined their own successors. The oldest histories of philosophy, such as those of Aristotle and Theophrastus, were attempts to reconstruct the order of succession in these philosophical schools. Nietzsche began to work on a detailed examination of the pre-Socratic philosophers in 1873–74, presumably as a supplement to his university lecture course that dealt with these thinkers.

19 [61]

23, 16–17 *Apollinian … oracles*] Apollo was the Greek god of oracles.

19 [62]

23, 23–30 *poetic artistry … poeticizing … poeticizes … poetry*] Nietzsche's words, *Dichtkunst*, *dichten*, and *Dichtung*, most commonly mean, respectively: "poetic composition" or "literature" in general; "to compose poetry" or "to write literature"; and "poetry." The verb *dichten* also has the more general sense of invention, creative thought, and this is one of the significations Nietzsche has in mind here. The notion of philosophy as a kind of poetry goes back to the German Romantic thinkers Friedrich Schlegel and Novalis, and it was central to Schopenhauer's conception of philosophy, as well.

19 [67]

25, 21 *being]* *Sein,* which means "being" in the ontological sense of existence or the existent per se.

19 [68] Cf. 19 [138].

25, 25–26 *Thales ... right]* Thales held that water is the basic element from which all things derive and to which they return. To him is also attributed the claim that water is a highly plastic medium, an idea to which Nietzsche is referring here.

19 [74]

27, 22 *philological reconstruction]* *philologischen Conjektur.* See note to 19 [58].

19 [75]

27, 26 *textual reconstruction]* *Conjektur.* See note to 19 [58].

19 [78]

29, 22–23 *representations]* *Vorstellungen.* This is a fundamental term in Schopenhauer's philosophy, occurring in the title of his major opus, *Die Welt als Wille und Vorstellung* (The world as will and representation), and is commonly translated as "idea," "ideation," or "representation."

19 [79]

30, 9 *Chladni's sound figures]* The German physicist Ernst Friedrich Chladni (1756–1827) created his sound figures by attaching a string to a sand-covered flat and recording in the sand the sonic vibrations of the string.

19 [83]

31, 24 *seven wise men]* See note to 19 [14].

19 [85] Nietzsche returned to this title in 1875; cf. 6 [4] from that period, in Vol. 12 of this edition.

19 [86]

32, 10 σοφία ... ἐπιστήμη] *sophia,* "wisdom"; *episteme,* "knowledge," or "science."

19 [88] Cf. the "Preface" to "The Relationship of Schopenhauerian Philosophy to a German Culture," the fourth of Nietzsche's "Five Prefaces to Five Unwritten Books," in Vol. 1 of this edition.

19 [94]

34, 25 *Zöllner]* Johann Karl Friedrich Zöllner (1834–82), an astronomer and physicist, published a controversial book entitled *Über die Natur der Kometen* (On the nature of comets) in which he severely criticized his colleagues in the natural sciences for their unscholarly and unscientific practices. Nietzsche was well acquainted with Zöllner's book, which he first read in November 1872 and subsequently reread several times. Nietzsche, whose *Birth of Tragedy* was being panned by mainstream philologists, closely identified with Zöllner and his status as a critical outsider. See Nietzsche's letter to Erwin Rhode from November 1872.

19 [96]

35, 5–6 *a great … Greece]* Thales, who was considered by many, including Aristotle, to be the first philosopher.

35, 8 *Delphi]* City in ancient Greece on the slopes of Mount Parnassus and site of the Delphic oracle of Apollo.

35, 8 *Orphic societies]* Societies that performed rites of mystical worship in the name of Orpheus. They emerged around the same time as the development of philosophy in Greece.

19 [99]

36, 3 *Ochlocracy]* "mob rule."

19 [100]

36, 4–5 *Heraclitus … Sibyl]* See Heraclitus, fragment 92, in *Die Fragmente der Vorsokratiker, griechisch und deutsch*, ed. Hermann Diels and Walther Kranz, 3 vols. (Berlin: Weidemann, 1934–37), vol. 1.

19 [107]

37, 16 *Unconscious inferences]* Johann Zöllner and Hermann von Helmholtz (1821–94), with whose works Nietzsche was familiar, defended a theory of perceptions based on unconscious inferences.

37, 20 *perceptions]* *Anschauungen*. This word, derived from the verb *anschauen*, meaning "to look at," is commonly translated either as "intuitions" or "perceptions." The latter rendering is most relevant in the present context. This emphasis on visual perception is evoked in the word "contemplative" (*beschaulich*, which has the same stem as *anschauen*) in the very next line.

37, 24 *projects]* *überträgt*. The first usage in these writings of a term that is central to Nietzsche's arguments about the anthropomorphic and metaphorical nature of knowledge and truth. The verb *übertragen* can mean "to project," "to transfer," or "to translate"; likewise the noun derived from this verb, *Übertragung*, can mean "projection," "transference," or "translation." My rendering of the term varies according to what is appropriate in the given context, but I have supplied a note for each occurrence in an attempt to highlight the consistency of Nietzsche's terminology.

19 [111]

37, 16 *Orphic societies]* See note to 19 [96].

19 [113]

39, 3 *categorical imperative]* Kant's ethical doctrine, which states that one should always act as though one's action were to become a moral law or imperative that would serve as a model for the actions of others.

19 [115]

39, 26 *Thales … water]* See note to 19 [68].

19 [116]

40, 6 *voûs]* *nous*, "mind," or "intellect."

19 [118]

41, 5 *projects]* *überträgt*. See note to 19 [107].

19 [119]

41, 15 *Heraclitus's becoming]* Heraclitus postulated that all existence is in a constant state of flux.

19 [129] Titles of planned lectures.

19 [130] Titles of planned lectures.

43, 6 *Choephori]* See note to 19 [57].

43, 7 *Erga]* Poem by Hesiod, commonly called *Opera et Dies* (Works and days).

43, 9 *Theognis]* Late sixth-century to early fifth-century Greek elegiac poet.

19 [132]

44, 13–14 *The will … claims]* Schopenhauer's thesis in *Die Welt als Wille und Vorstellung* (The world as will and representation) is that the phenomenal world is made up of (more or less adequate) representations of the underlying, metaphysical will.

19 [134]

44, 28 *projections]* See note to 19 [107].

45, 12 *Eleatics]* An ancient Greek school of philosophy centered in Elea in the fifth and sixth centuries B.C. Its greatest representatives were Parmenides and Zeno.

19 [138] Cf. 19 [68]

46, 8 *Necessary lie]* Plato develops the theory of the necessary lie in *The Republic*, 3.414b.

46, 8 *veracité du dieu]* "truth of God." Cartesian philosophy was based on the "truth"—the absolute necessity—of God's existence and God's truthfulness, i.e., that God cannot lie or deceive.

19 [140]

47, 3 *Chladni's sound figures]* See note to 19 [79].

19 [147]

48, 5 *unconscious inferences]* See note to 19 [107].

19 [164]

52, 29 *unconscious inference]* See note to 19 [107].

19 [169]

53, 19 διαδοχαί] "diadochai." See note to 19 [59].

19 [177]

55, 19 *transferred]* *übertragen.* See note to 19 [107].

56, 1 *projects]* *überträgt.*

19 [178]

56, 14 κατὰ ἀνάλογον] *kata analogon,* "by means of analogy."

19 [180] See note to 19 [1].

57, 19 *Eleatics]* See note to 19 [134].

19 [185]

58, 13 *translation]* *Übertragung.* See note to 19 [107].

19 [188] Preliminary title of "Philosophy in the Tragic Age of the Greeks." Cf. 19 [214, 287, 325].

19 [190] With Nietzsche's estimates of the approximate number of pages.

19 [194]

60, 13 *categorical imperative]* See note to 19 [113].

19 [197]

61, 11 *Socrates' … commanders]* Socrates was a member of the coun-

cil given the task of passing judgment en bloc on ten command-
ers who had failed to rescue the men lost in a naval engagement.
Since such trials en bloc were unconstitutional, Socrates protested and was the only member of the council who voted
against the proposal. See Plato, *Apology*, 32b.

19 [199]

61, 21 *Gervinus*] Georg Gottfried Gervinus (1805–71), a German
critic and literary historian associated by Nietzsche with the
"cultural philistines" and hence a frequent object of Nietzsche's
ire.

19 [200] Cf. "The Relationship of Schopenhauerian Philosophy to
a German Culture," the fourth of Nietzsche's "Five Prefaces to
Five Unwritten Books," in Vol. 1 of this edition.

61, 26 *wartime glory*] The Prussian victory over the French in 1871.

19 [201]

62, 13 *Bona-Meyer ... Riehl, Jahn*] Nietzsche viewed the cultural historian, music historian, and composer Wilhelm Heinrich Riehl
(1823–97) and the classicist, archeologist, and music theoreti-
cian Otto Jahn (1813–69) as anti-Wagnerian defenders of traditional music. Cf. notes to 27 [41] and 27 [55]. Jürgen Bona Meyer
(1829–97), author of *Über Fichtes Reden an die Deutsche Nation* (On
Fichte's *Addresses to the German Nation*) (1862) and *Arthur Schopenhauer als Mensch und Denker* (Arthur Schopenhauer as man and
thinker) (1872), was a philosophy professor in Bonn.

62, 16–17 *Freytag-like novels*] The novelist Gustav Freytag (1816–
95) was one of the standard-bearers of the German bourgeoisie,
and his novels were enormously popular in Nietzsche's day.

62, 19–20 *feeble nymphs ... Schwind*] The Austrian history painter
Moriz von Schwind (1804–71) was especially renowned as an
illustrator of fairy tale cycles and of the legends of the German
Middle Ages, populated by nymphs, giants, dwarfs, etc.

19 [209]

64, 16 *nouns*] *Above*: abstractions.

64, 13–29 *transfer ... transferred ... transfer*] *übertragen ... Übertragung ... übertragen*. See note to 19 [107].

19 [212]

66, 12 *metamorphosis of plants*] An allusion to Goethe's scientific investigations into the metamorphosis of plants. Nietzsche is transferring Goethe's biological model to the realm of history.

66, 15–16 *Schopenhauer, I, XXVI]* The reference is to the "Vorrede" (preface) to the second edition of *Die Welt als Wille und Vorstellung* (The world as will and representation). Here, as elsewhere, Nietzsche is citing from Julius Frauenstädt's edition of Schopenhauer's *Sämmtliche Werke* (Leipzig, 1873–74).

29 [215]

67, 8 *Thales]* See note to 19 [68].

67, 8–9 *transference]* *Übertragung*. See note to 19 [107].

19 [222]

69, 26–27 *no ... ghosts]* According to German superstition, a ghost takes flight if one calls out its name.

19 [223]

70, 3 *transferences]* *Übertragungen*. See note to 19 [107].

19 [224]

70, 6 *Thales]* See note to 19 [68].

19 [225]

70, 9 *ideation]* *Vorstellungen*. See note to 19 [78].

19 [226]

70, 25 *translation]* *Übertragung*. See note to 19 [107].

19 [227]

71, 10–13 *transferred ... transferred ... transferred]* *Übertragung ... übertragen ... Übertragung*. See note to 19 [107].

19 [228]

71, 18 *transference]* *Übertragung*. See note to 19 [107].

19 [229] Cf. "On Truth and Lie in an Extra-Moral Sense," in Vol. 1 of this edition.

72, 18–20 *projected ... projection]* *übertragen ... Übertragung*. See note to 19 [107].

19 [230] Cf. "On Truth and Lie in an Extra-Moral Sense."

19 [231]

73, 14 *devas]* Sanskrit for "god," etymologically related to the Latin *deus*; the term refers to the oldest known Hindu divinity. Nietzsche was acquainted with this primordial form of Hindu monotheism from *Die Religion des Buddha und ihre Entstehung* (The religion of Buddha and its genesis) (Berlin, 1857), by the German historian and journalist Carl Friedrich Koeppen (1808–63), which treats the concept of *devas* on p. 3. Schopenhauer also refers to this divinity in bk. 4, ch. 48 of *Die Welt als Wille und Vorstellung* (The world as will and representation).

19 [237]

75, 5 μεταφορά] *metaphora*, "metaphor."

75, 6 *Chladni's sound figures*] See note to 19 [79].

19 [242]

76, 5–6 *transference*] *Übertragung.* See note to 19 [107].

19 [248]

77, 24 *Procreation … beautiful.*] See note to 19 [10].

19 [253] Cf. "On Truth and Lie in an Extra-Moral Sense," in Vol. 1 of this edition.

19 [258] Cf. "On Truth and Lie in an Extra-Moral Sense."

19 [259] From about this entry onward, Nietzsche's literary projects assume an increasingly polemical character. The people and incidents named here are frequent critical targets and function for Nietzsche as examples of the German cultural malaise. Cf. 19 [274].

80, 17 *Gathering of philologists*] The twenty-eighth meeting of German philologists took place in Leipzig from the third to the sixth of October, 1870, just a few months after the outbreak of the Franco-Prussian War in July. Nietzsche is apparently reacting to the patriotic sentiments voiced by some scholars at this meeting. Cf. 26 [16].

80, 18 *Strasbourg University*] The old Strasbourg University, which had operated from 1702 to 1789, was newly founded in 1872, at an initial cost of fourteen million marks, after the Prussian victory over the French and the annexation of Alsace-Lorraine by the German Empire. Nietzsche viewed the refounded University of Strasbourg as an institution that would propagate the cultivated philistinism he so despised, the object of his attack in the first essay in *Unfashionable Observations*. It also represented to him the missed opportunity to establish a true educational institution, like the one he advocated in "On the Future of Our Educational Institutions" (see Vol. 1 of this edition), which would contribute to the regeneration of the German spirit. See Nietzsche's letter to Erwin Rohde dated 28 January 1872.

80, 19 *Auerbach … monuments]* The novelist Berthold Auerbach (1812–82) published an appeal "To the German Nation" in the Augsburg *Allgemeine Zeitung*, calling for a German monument. Cf. section 11 of "Strauss," p. 65.

80, 20 *Ingo]* The protagonist in Gustav Freytag's historical novel *Ingo und Ingabran*, published in 1872, the first volume in his six-volume novel cycle *Die Ahnen* (The ancestors). This cycle relates the history of Germany from the fourth century A.D. to the Revolution of 1848 by tracing the lineage of a single family descended from the Vandal prince Ingo.

80, 21 *Gottschall]* Rudolph von Gottschall (1823–1909), German author, dramatist, critic, and literary historian. Gottschall reviewed and commented extensively on the poetry and dramas of emerging young German writers in his *Blätter für literarische Unterhaltung* (1865–88, Leipzig) and his monthly *Unsere Zeit* (1865–87).

80, 22 *Young Germany]* A group of liberal writers who defended democratic principles and fed revolutionary sentiments in the years prior to the Revolution of 1848. The group included such figures as Heinrich Heine, Ludwig Börne (1786–1837), and Karl Gutzkow (1811–78).

80, 23 *Zöllner]* See note to 19 [94].

80, 26 *Grimm, Lübke, Julian Schmidt]* Of the two Grimm brothers, Jakob (1785–1863) and Wilhelm (1786–1859), the reference is most likely to Jakob, author of the first comprehensive text on German grammar, *Grammatik* (1819). Wilhelm Lübke (1826–93) was a German art historian, best known for his *Geschichte der Renaissance Frankreichs* (History of the Renaissance in France), a work Nietzsche used in his lectures, especially in Basel. Julian Schmidt (1818–86), a German editor and literary historian, was best known for his then-standard three-volume *Geschichte der deutschen Literatur im neunzehnten Jahrhundert* (History of German literature in the nineteenth century) (1855), which covered the explosion in German letters in Weimar and Jena at the turn of the nineteenth century, the period of the restoration, and then contemporary literature.

80, 27 *Kuno Fischer, Lotze]* Kuno Fischer (1824–1907), the most prominent neo-Kantian historian of philosophy, was best known for his interpretations of Kant's theory of space. Following a Romanticized Hegel, he understood the historical development of philosophy as a progressive process of the self-realization of the human spirit. His *Anti-Trendelenburg* (1870) was his response to a controversial polemical attack by the neo-Aristotelian philosopher Trendelenburg. See note to 29 [199]. (Rudolph) Hermann Lotze (1817–81) likewise was a German philosopher who developed a distinctive post-Hegelian teleological idealism that assimilated ethics to metaphysics, especially in his three-volume *Mikrokosmus* (Microcosm). He first became prominent as a physiologist and articulate critic of vitalism. A man of immense learning, he earned doctorates in both medicine and philosophy at the University of Leipzig (1834–38). Nietzsche, following his philosophical exemplar Schopenhauer, who was a bitter opponent of Hegel and his philosophy, frequently attacked Hegel's thought and his neo-Hegelian disciples. For Bona Meyer, see note to 19 [201].

80, 30 *Hauptmann]* Moritz Hauptmann (1792–1868), German violinist, composer, and musical theorist. For Jahn, see note to 19 [201].

81, 1 *Hanslick]* Eduard Hanslick (1825–1904), an Austrian writer and music critic whose elegant literary style gained him a wide reputation, as did his numerous controversies with other critics. Hanslick rejected the accomplishments of Wagner and Liszt while advocating the music of Schumann and Brahms. He also rejected the importance of the emotions in music, emphasizing formalism instead.

81, 2 *Centralblatt]* *Literarisches Centralblatt für Deutschland*, a journal of German literary and intellectual affairs published from 1850 to 1944. Nietzsche's close friend, the classical philologist Erwin Rohde (1845–98), submitted an announcement of Nietzsche's *Birth of Tragedy* to the *Centralblatt* in early 1872, but the editors refused to publish it.

81, 3 *Playing music in isolation]* Nietzsche fashions the obscure phrase *Abseits-Musikmachen*. He is apparently arguing against the isolation of music as an art form, or against its subordination to the other arts (as to the spoken word in traditional opera), in favor of the primary status afforded it in Wagner's *Gesamtkunstwerk*, his "total work of art." Cf. 19 [289], where this isolation is associated with the monastic — that is, the solitary — element in music.

19 [262]

81, 12 *laissez aller]* "let it be," "leave it alone."

19 [266]

82, 2 *physis]* "nature."

19 [267]

82, 7 *lonely … Bayreuth]* Nietzsche was with friends in Bayreuth from 18 to 23 May 1872 to celebrate the laying of the cornerstone for Wagner's festival theater.

19 [269]

83, 3 *Pentecost … festival]* See note to 19 [267].

83, 7 *Gathering … Strasbourg]* See notes to 19 [259].

19 [270]

83, 11 δός μοι ποῦ στῶ] A reference to Archimedes' famous statement "Give me a point at which I can stand and I will move the earth." Nietzsche conceives of the German cultural renewal as the attempt to find such a fulcrum, still represented for Nietzsche at this time by Wagnerian opera.

19 [273] This satirical note contains a nearly complete catalogue of the figures with whom Nietzsche associated the German cultural decline he so vehemently lambastes in the first three essays of *Unfashionable Observations* and whom he associated with Strauss's "cultural philistinism."

84, 9 *Kotzebue's Bourgeois Comedies]* See note to 19 [294].

84, 14 *Bernays]* Jakob Bernays (1824–81), German classical philologist.

84, 17 *Lindau … Laube]* Paul Lindau (1839–1919), German theater director, dramatist, and journalist. Heinrich Laube (1806–84), German author and editor.

19 [274]

84, 21 *Pentecost … Bayreuth]* See note to 19 [267].

84, 22–23 *Gathering … Strasbourg]* See notes to 19 [259].

85, 8 δός μοι ποῦ στῶ] See note to 19 [270].

19 [275]

85, 20 *fermata]* In music, the holding of a tone or rest longer than its written value, at the discretion of the performer.

19 [277] List of Nietzsche's musical compositions.

86, 6 *Etes titok]* The derivation of this title could not be ascertained.

19 [279]

86, 16 *A. Dove … Puschmann.]* The German historian and essayist Alfred Wilhelm Dove (1844–1916) published a "Neujahrswort an die deutsche Geistesarbeit" (New Year's greeting for the German brain work) in January 1873 in the journal *Im neuen Reich* in which he attacked the physicist Friedrich Zöllner (see note to 19 [94]) and praised the book by the psychiatrist Theodor Puschmann (1844–99), which attempted to prove that Richard Wagner suffered from megalomania. Nietzsche came to Wagner's defense and counterattacked Dove in his response "Ein Neujahrswort an den Herausgeber der Wochenschrift *Im neuen Reich*" (A New Year's greeting for the editor of the weekly *Im neuen Reich*).

19 [284]

87, 17–19 *created … Cultivation … creation … cultivation]* In these lines, as throughout this entry, Nietzsche is playing on the nuances of the German words *bilden* and *Bildung*, which can mean both "creation," formation of something new, and "education," "cultivation" of what already exists. Nietzsche's valorization of the former meaning and his ridicule of the latter becomes the basis for his attack on David Strauss and the "cultivated philistines" in the first of the *Unfashionable Observations*.

19 [285]

88, 3 *cultivation … creation]* Bildung … Bildung. See note to 19 [284].

19 [286]

88, 16 *Winckelmann, Hamann]* Johann Joachim Winckelmann (1717–68), German art historian. Johann Georg Hamann (1730–88), German Protestant theologian and philosopher.

88, 18 *Grillparzer]* Franz Grillparzer (1791–1872), Austrian poet and dramatist.

88, 20 *Fuchs]* Johann Nepomuk Fuchs (1842–99), German composer and music critic.

89, 1–2 *Simple … rules]* Nietzsche is alluding to the two major tendencies that shaped the culture of German classicism in the last quarter of the eighteenth century: Winckelmann's glorification of ancient sculpture for its "noble simplicity" and the resistance to the rule-governed drama of the French.

19 [290]

89, 7 *playing music in isolation]* See note to 19 [259].

89, 11 *thesis]* Nietzsche is referring to the meaning of this word in Greek metrics (the accented syllable) and in music (the accented note). The implication is that Roman art was concerned primarily with formal, structural characteristics.

89, 12 *physis]* "nature."

19 [292]

89, 18–20 *Ritter … Weisse]* Heinrich Ritter (1791–1869), German historian of philosophy; Christian Hermann Weisse (1801–66), German philosopher.

19 [294]

90, 1 *Kotzebue]* August von Kotzebue (1761–1819), a German dramatist and popularizer of melodramatic and sentimental poetic drama who was in repeated conflict with Goethe and the Weimar Romantics. He served as the political envoy of Czar Alexander in 1817, for which he was maligned as a spy in the pay of a reactionary power. Two years later he was assassinated.

19 [295]

90, 4 *cultivation … creation]* Bildung … Bildung. See note to 19 [284].

19 [298]

90, 20 *war]* The Franco-Prussian War of 1870–71.

19 [305]

91, 23 *Goethe]* Gespräche mit Eckermann (Conversations with Eckermann), 3 May 1827.

19 [307]

92, 6–7 *"cultivated" … coherent entity]* "gebildet" … Gebilde. Nietzsche is once again playing on the various meanings of the verb *bilden*. The word *Gebilde* suggests the idea of a harmoniously structured whole.

19 [309]

92, 13 *deal."]* Goethe, *Gespräche mit Eckermann* (Conversations with Eckermann), 3 May 1827. Cf. 19 [312] and sec. 1 of "Strauss," 10.

19 [312] Preliminary draft for section 1 of "Strauss," pp. 5–10.

93, 1 *war]* The Franco-Prussian War of 1870–71.

93, 32–33 *"We ... Eckermann]* Goethe, *Gespräche mit Eckermann* (Conversations with Eckermann), 3 May 1827. Cf. 19 [309] and section 1 of "Strauss," p. 10.

94, 8 *Goethe ... song]* Goethe, *Gespräche mit Eckermann* (Conversations with Eckermann), 3 May 1827.

19 [313]

94, 15 *aesthetic education]* A reference to Schiller's renowned aesthetic treatise, *Über die ästhetische Erziehung des Menschen* (On the aesthetic education of the human being).

19 [315]

95, 2 σοφὸς ἀνήρ] *sophos aner*, "wise man."

19 [318]

95, 23 *projections] Übertragungen.* See note to 19 [107].

19 [323]

97, 14 *Logaoedic verse]* An ancient metrical verse form consisting of single long syllables that alternate first with double short then single short syllables.

97, 15 *Doric stanzas]* In Greek tragedy, a Doric dialect was prominently used in the choral song, while the speeches were in Attic dialect.

19 [330] This entry was added to the notebook at a later date.

[20 = Mp XII 3]

20 [1] Cf. "Homer's Competition," the fifth of Nietzsche's "Five Prefaces to Five Unwritten Books," in Vol. 1 of this edition.

20 [2] Autobiographical notes; cf. 11 [11] and 28 [6, 8, 9] in Vol. 10 of this edition.

100, 7 *Ritschl's ... Odysseus]* Friedrich Wilhelm Ritschl (1791–1838), Nietzsche's dissertation advisor and academic mentor, apparently compared Nietzsche with Odysseus.

[21 = U I 4b]

21 [1] Nietzsche's planned publications for fall 1872 and winter 1872–73.

101, 1 *Choephori]* See note to 19 [57].

21 [2]

101, 9 *The sculpturesque element] Das Plastische.* This term refers to the static forms of Greek sculpture, those elements that in *The Birth of Tragedy* Nietzsche identified with the Apollinian aspect of Greek tragedy.

101, 12 *Stichometry]* Designation for the practice in antiquity of counting the number of lines to determine the length of a literary work, whereby the line length of a verse of dactylic hexameter, or about sixteen syllables, was taken as a standard. The sum of the lines was noted at the end of the papyrus scroll to protect against interpolations.

101, 16 *orchestrics]* Nietzsche is thinking of the original Greek meaning of this word, "to dance," and its association with the chorus in ancient Greek drama. In *The Birth of Tragedy*, he connected this dimension with the Dionysian aspect of tragedy.

102, 2 *ἦθος]* ethos, "ethos." In antiquity "ethos" was understood in the sense of "character," the disposition, habits, etc. of an individual.

102, 2 *scene. 954]* Nietzsche is referring to line 954 in *The Libation Bearers*, but line numbers vary according to the edition. The intended reference is most likely the response of the chorus after Orestes, avenging his father's murder, kills his mother Clytemnestra and her lover Aegisthus.

21 [4]

102, 9 *Quod felix faustum fortunatumque vertat!]* "May it turn out pleasant, propitious, and prosperous," a popular Roman religious formula.

21 [5] Draft for "Philosophy in the Tragic Age of the Greeks, in Vol. 1 of this edition. Cf. also 21 [6, 15, 16, 19, 21, 22].

102, 16 *Eleatics]* See note to 19 [134].

21 [6] Draft for "Philosophy in the Tragic Age of the Greeks." Cf. also 21 [5, 15, 16, 19, 21, 22].

21 [7] Nietzsche's planned publications for fall 1872 and winter 1872–73. Cf. 21 [1].

21 [8]

103, 6 *Conjectures] Conjekturen*. See note to 19 [58]. In this instance, it is not clear from the context whether Nietzsche is using the term with its more specific philological meaning or in a more general sense.

103, 8 *The sculpturesque element]* See note to 21 [2].

21 [14]

104, 23 *Procreation ... beautiful]* See note to 19 [10].

21 [15] Draft for "Philosophy in the Tragic Age of the Greeks," found in Vol. 1 of this edition. Cf. also 21 [5, 6, 16, 19, 21, 22].

104, 26 *Cosmodicy]* Nietzsche coins the word "cosmodicy" (*Cosmodicee*) in analogy to the Leibnizian notion of "theodicy," the system of natural theology that seeks to vindicate divine justice by giving evil a role in divine creation. Cf. Nietzsche's use of this term in section 7 of "Strauss," p. 41.

105, 2 *Eleatics]* See note to 19 [134].

21 [16] Draft for "Philosophy in the Tragic Age of the Greeks," found in Vol. 1 of this edition. Cf. also 21 [5, 6, 15, 19, 21, 22].

105, 17 *Eleatics]* See note to 19 [134].

105, 29 *effective]* Nietzsche's adjective, *wirklich*, means "actual" or "real." But it is derived from the verb *wirken*, "to have an effect," and in the context of this entry the literal meaning, "effective," is germane. Nietzsche intends the pun, with its implication that only what is effective is real. In section 5 of "Philosophy in the Tragic Age of the Greeks" (see Vol. 1 of this edition), he attributes to Heraclitus this belief that reality is composed only of effects and effectivity, and in this context he cites Schopenhauer's reflections on the relationship between the German verb *wirken* and the noun *Wirklichkeit*, "reality." See Schopenhauer, *Die Welt als Wille und Vorstellung*, ed. Julius Frauenstädt (Leipzig, 1873–74), 1: 10.

106, 2 *is effective]* Or "is real." The verb is *wirken*. See previous note.

21 [19] Draft for "Philosophy in the Tragic Age of the Greeks." Cf. also 21 [5, 6, 15, 16, 21, 22].

107, 2 *seven wise men]* See note to 19 [14].

21 [21] Draft for "Philosophy in the Tragic Age of the Greeks," found in Vol. 1 of this edition. Cf. also 21 [5, 6, 15, 16, 19, 22].

21 [22] Draft for "Philosophy in the Tragic Age of the Greeks." Cf. also 21 [5, 6, 15, 16, 19, 21].

107, 27 *rhythm]* Pythagoras conceived existence in terms of the recurrence of set patterns. This is what Nietzsche is referring to here with the term "rhythm." This Pythagorean notion is a possible model for Nietzsche's idea of eternal recurrence. Cf.

Nietzsche's allusion to this Pythagorean doctrine in section 2 of "History," p. 99.

21 [24]

108, 4 *pentathlos]* A contestant in a pentathlon, a contest consisting of five different events. Nietzsche uses the term metaphorically here, alluding to five distinct areas in which the tragic poet, according to Nietzsche, must display mastery: poetry, music, dance, acting, and stage direction. See "Greek Musical Drama," the first of Nietzsche's "Two Public Lectures on Greek Tragedy" (Vol. 1 of this edition), where this notion of the tragic poet as *pentathlos* is developed in more detail.

21 [25]

108, 6 *dedicatory … 1872]* See note to 19 [267].

[22 = N I 3a]

22 [1] Cf. Nietzsche's letter to his mother dated 1 October 1872.

109, 5 *Lisbeth]* Nietzsche's sister, Elisabeth Förster-Nietzsche (1846–1935).

109, 7 *Götz]* Hermann Götz (1840–76), German composer.

109, 9 *Kirchner]* Theodor Kirchner (1823–1903), German composer.

22 [2] Cf. Nietzsche's letter to his mother from 1 October 1872.

[23 = Mp XII 4]

23 [1] Notes for "Philosophy in the Tragic Age of the Greeks," in Vol. 1 of this edition; cf. also 23 [2, 3, 5, 6, 7, 8, 9, 11, 12, 14, 16, 22, 23, 24, 27, 28, 29, 30, 31, 32, 33, 34, 35, 36, 39, 40, 41]; title: 23 [15, 21, 25].

23 [2]

114, 6 *vulgus]* "rabble," "common people."

114, 7 ἱστορίη] *historie,* "inquiry," or "history."

23 [5]

115, 6 *Orphic societies]* See note to 19 [96].

23 [7]

115, 21 *projections] Übertragungen.* See note to 19 [107].

116, 1 *Schopenhauer's simplifying]* Cf. Nietzsche's claim in section 4 of "Wagner" that Wagner is a "simplifier of the world," pp. 274–75.

23 [8]

116, 13; 19 *organon]* "instrument."

23 [12]

118, 7–8 *Parmenides' doctrine of being]* Parmenides drew a strict distinction between being and nonbeing and argued that being
is not accessible through the senses, by means of perception,
but only by means of thought. Perception is the realm of semblance, or nonbeing; thought the domain of being. The world
of being, Parmenides claimed, is absolutely stable and immu-
table and hence opposed to the principle of becoming. Parmenides thus objected to the Heraclitean doctrine that everything is subject to incessant flux and change. In this sense,
Plato's notion of archetypes or eternal ideas is an extension of
Parmenides' doctrine of being.

118, 22 *perception]*   *Anschauung.* See note to 19 [107].

23 [13]

118, 27 *perception]* Throughout this entry, this is the rendering for
Anschauung. See note to 19 [107].

118, 27 *"Being"]* See note to 23 [12].

118, 28 *projection]*   *Übertragung.* See note to 19 [107].

23 [14]

119, 22 *vis veritatis]* "the power of truth."

23 [18]

121, 12 *Becoming and being]* See note to 23 [12].

23 [22]

123, 1 *Rhythm]* See note to 21 [22].

123, 2 *metron]* "measure."

23 [23]

123, 16 *Herodotus among foreigners]* Herodotus was banished from
his native city of Halikarnassus and traveled widely to foreign
lands.

123, 18–19 *No ... homeland.]* See Matthew 13: 57: "And they took
offense at him. But Jesus said to them, 'A prophet is not without honor except in his own country and in his own house.'"

23 [26] Dates from Empedocles' life. Nietzsche follows the information given by Diogenes Laertius, *Lives of the Eminent Philosophers,* 8.51–77.

123, 25 παντελῶς ὑπεργεγηρακώς] *pantelos hypergegerakos*, "in extreme old age." See Diogenes Laertius, *Lives of the Eminent Philosophers*, 8.52, where this statement about Empedocles is attributed to Apollodorus.

124, 13 ἀκμῇ] *akmei*, "the prime of life."

124, 17 *Agrigentians*] Inhabitants of Agrigentum, a city on the south coast of Sicily and the birthplace of Empedocles.

124, 21 *Thurii*] A pan-Hellenistic colony founded in 444–443 B.C. under Pericles.

124, 23 καθαρμοί] *Katharmoi*, "Purifications," a poem in which Empedocles, assuming the role of a divine prophet, speaks admonitions to the citizens of his native Agrigentum.

124, 23 *Olympia*] Site of the temple and Sacred Grove of Zeus Olympius. The Olympic Games were held here during the Festival of Zeus.

23 [30]

126, 23 *Noûs*] *Nous*, "intellect," or "mind." Anaxagoras taught that an all-powerful intellect is the source of the world and its sensible structure.

23 [31]

126, 28 *process of separation*] Anaxagoras viewed the process by which the world developed as a vortex whose motion separated light things, which moved to the periphery, from heavy things, which remained close to the center.

127, 8; 11 *voûs*] *nous*, "intellect," or "mind." See note to 23 [30].

23 [32]

127, 18 *De coelo, I, p. 284*] Aristotle's *De caelo* (*De coelo* is an alternate spelling). Nietzsche's exact reference is unclear, since he is apparently citing volume and page number of a specific edition. Section 284 in book 2 of *De caelo* does, however, deal with the question of motion and primordial forces, and this could be the passage to which Nietzsche is referring.

127, 18 *Schopenhauer, World as Will, II, 390*] Nietzsche's reference is to volume 2 of *Die Welt als Wille und Vorstellung* (The world as will and representation) in the Frauenstädt edition of Schopenhauer's works (Leipzig, 1873–74).

23 [33]

128, 6 *νεῖκος]* *neikos,* "hatred," or "strife." In Empedocles's doctrine, the principle of separation.

128, 8 *ἀπορροαί]* *aporroai,* "stream," or "emanation."

128, 10 *ὄντα]* *onta,* "existent things."

23 [34]

128, 20 *Plato's fable]* In *Symposium,* 189e–192b, Plato relates how an originally hermaphroditic human being was split into two halves by Zeus. He attributes human love to the desperate longing each half of this formerly whole being feels for its amputated mate.

128, 26 *sphairos]* "sphere"; here in the sense of "celestial sphere."

23 [35]

129, 20 *Aut … aut]* "Either … or."

129, 27 *Eleatics]* See note to 19 [134].

23 [37]

130, 19 *M. Antonius]* The citation is from Marcus Aurelius (who is sometimes known under the name Antonius) and taken from his *Meditations,* 7.47.

23 [38]

130, 24 *Antisthenes]* This statement is attributed to Antisthenes by Diogenes Laertius, *Lives of the Eminent Philosophers,* 6.3.

23 [39]

131, 9 *νόμῳ]* *nomoi,* "established by convention."

131, 11 *ἄτομα]* *atoma,* "atoms."

131, 15 *ὄντα]* *onta,* "existent things."

[24 = U II 7a]

24 [1]

134, 4 *Goethe.]* See Goethe's "Das Sehen in subjektiver Hinsicht, von Purkinje" (Vision in subjective regard, by Purkinje), a review essay of a book with this title published by the physiologist and pathologist Johannes Purkinje (1787–1869) in 1819. See the "Sophien-Ausgabe" of *Goethes Werke* (Weimar: H. Böhlau, 1887–1919), pt. 2, vol. 11, p. 271.

24 [3]

135, 12 *Goethe.]* From Goethe's essay "Die Natur" (Nature); see the "Sophien-Ausgabe" of *Goethes Werke* (Weimar: H. Böhlau, 1887–1919), pt. 2, vol. 11, p. 6.

24 [4] Cf. section 9 of "History," p. 151.

135, 23 *Schopenhauer]* Nietzsche borrows this description of the republic of geniuses from Schopenhauer, *Der handschriftliche Nachlaß*, ed. Arthur Hübscher (Frankfurt: W. Kramer, 1966–75), 3:
188.

24 [5]

135, 27 *Schopenhauer]* See Schopenhauer, *Der handschriftliche Nachlaß*, ed. Arthur Hübscher (Frankfurt: W. Kramer, 1966–75), 4,
pt. 1: 295.

24 [6]

135, 29 *Schopenhauer]* The source for the reference to Schopenhauer could not be ascertained.

24 [7] See Goethe's letter to Charlotte von Stein dated 15 June 1786.

24 [8] See Goethe's letter to Charlotte von Stein dated 3 March
1785. Cf. section 5 of "Schopenhauer," p. 213.

136, 12 *causa finalis]* "final purpose"; "ultimate aim."

24 [9] See Goethe's letter to Charlotte von Stein dated 27 March
1784.

24 [10] Franz Grillparzer, *Sprüche und Epigramme* (Sayings and epi-
grams), no. 1450 (dated 1856), *Sämtliche Werke*, ed. August Sauer
(Vienna, 1907–39), 12: 272.

24 [14] Title for "Philosophy in the Tragic Age of the Greeks."

[25 = P II 12b]

25 [1] Postscript for *The Birth of Tragedy*.

138, 18–19 *Aeschylus's Cassandra scene]* See *Agamemnon*, the first play
in Aeschylus's *Oresteia*, lines 1072–1330. Here Cassandra has a
vision of her own death and the murders that are about to occur
in Agamemnon's house.

138, 24 *"sentimentalist"]* Nietzsche is alluding to the distinction
Schiller drew in *Über naive und sentimentalische Dichtung* (On naive
and sentimentalist poetry) between the naive poet, who responds to things in an immediate and natural way, and the sentimentalist poet, who approaches them with deliberation and
reflection. Schiller considered the sentimentalist mode characteristic of modern poets in general, including himself.

139, 21–22 *likeness … like things]* An allusion to the famous statement by Pythagoras that only the like recognizes the like.

139, 32 *sculpturesque]* See note to 21 [2].

141, 1 *cothurn]* High, thick-soled boot worn by actors in ancient Greek tragedy.

141, 27–28 *orchestrics]* Nietzsche is thinking of the original Greek sense of this word, which derives from the verb *orcheisthai*, "to dance." See note to 21 [2].

141, 28 *chorodidaskolos]* "chorus master."

142, 6–7 *Goethe's ... 278]* Nietzsche is citing the volume *Goethes Briefwechsel mit Schiller* (Goethe's correspondence with Schiller) (Stuttgart, 1870), a book he had in his personal library. The allusion is to Goethe's letter to Schiller dated 27 December 1797.

[26 = U I 5b]

26 [1]

143, 6 *infinitum ... indefinitum]* "infinite ... indefinite."

143, 7 ἄπειρον] *apeiron*, "the unlimited." In Anaximander's philosophy, the unlimited is understood as the fundamental potentiality from which all delimited, dimensional reality emerges. This position is rejected by Plato and Aristotle and the concept of *apeiron* is narrowed to the signification "infinite," which for them has the negative connotation of "indeterminate" and "chaotic," a connotation that is not present in Anaximander's understanding of the term.

143, 8 *Spir]* Afrikan Spir, *Denken und Wirklichkeit* (Thought and reality), vol. 1 (Leipzig, 1873). Nietzsche was profoundly influenced by this book, which he borrowed from the university library in Basel on 13 March 1873. Spir (1837–90) provided Nietzsche with support for his own epistemological position. See 26 [11].

143, 9–144, 4 *p. 347 ... Kopp ... p. 324 ... p. 340 Kopp ... p. 310 Kopp ... p. 311 ... 367 Kopp]* Nietzsche's references are to *Geschichte der Chemie, Teil II* (History of chemistry, part II) (Braunschweig, 1844), by Hermann Franz Moritz Kopp (1817–92). Nietzsche borrowed this book from the university library in Basel on 28 March 1873.

143, 19–20 *Actio in distans]* "Action at a distance."

144, 5–17 *Überweg, III, 53 ... Rixner and Siber ... Überweg, II, 52 ... III, 53 ... Überweg, III, 81]* Friedrich Überweg, *Grundriß der Geschichte der Philosophie von Thales bis auf die Gegenwart* (Outline of the history of philosophy from Thales to the present), 3 vols. (Berlin, 1867). These volumes were in Nietzsche's personal library. On Rixner and Siber, see Überweg, 3: 24, where their *Contributions to the History of Physiology* is mentioned in connection with Descartes, epistemology, and the philosophy of matter.

144, 7 *representations] Vorstellungen.* See note to 19 [78].

144, 9 *Telesius]* Bernardino Telesio (1509–88), an Italian philosopher and scientist whose early scientific empiricism influenced Francis Bacon, Galileo, Tommaso Campanella, and Thomas Hobbes. Telesio rejected dominant Aristotelian notions about the nature of matter and initiated the Renaissance reaction against reasoning without reference to concrete data.

144, 18 *Quidquid est, est: quidquid non est, non est.]* "Whatever is, is; whatever is not, is not."

26 [2]

144, 20 *ape."]* Heraclitus, fragment 83, in *Die Fragmente der Vorsokratiker*, ed. Diels and Kranz, vol. 1.

26 [3]

144, 23 *Eleatics]* See note to 19 [134].

26 [4]

144, 25–28 *Cardanus … nondeceivers.]* Quoted in Überweg, *Grundriß der Geschichte der Philosophie von Thales bis auf die Gegenwart*, 3: 23. The reference is to Hieronymus Cardanus (1501–76), an Italian philosopher and scientist.

26 [5] Cf. Überweg, *Grundriß*, 3: 25.

145, 1 *Sennerti physica Viteb⟨ergae⟩ 1618]* The probable reference is to Daniel Sennert, *Epitome scientiae naturalis* (Outline of the natural sciences), published in Wittenberg in 1618. Sennert (1572–1637), a German physician and scientist, was a disciple of Democritus's theory of atomism.

145, 2 *Magneni Democritus reviviscens, Ticino 1646]* Jean Chrysostôme Magnen, *Democritus reviviscens; sive, vita et philosophia Democriti* (Democritus restored to life, or The life and philosophy of Democritus). Jean Chrystôme Magnen (?–?) was a seventeenth-century French professor of philosophy and medicine.

145, 3 *Maignani cursus philosoph⟨icus⟩ 1652 and 1673]* Emmanuel Maig-

nan, *Cursus philosophicus* (The course of philosophy). Emmanuel
Maignan (1601–76) was a Spanish philosopher and scientist.

26 [7] Cf. Überweg, *Grundriß*, 3: 28.

145, 5 *Campanella]* Tommaso Campanella (1568–1655), Italian Renaissance philosopher.

26 [8] For "Philosophy in the Tragic Age of the Greeks," in Vol. 1
of this edition.

26 [9] For "Philosophy in the Tragic Age of the Greeks," in Vol. 1
of this edition.

26 [11] In these reflections, Nietzsche is following thoughts articulated by Afrikan Spir in *Denken und Wirklichkeit* (Thought and
reality). See note to 26 [1].

146, 6; 8 *representation]* *Vorstellung.* See note to 19 [78].

146, 19 *imagine]* *vorstellen.* The verb functions here in its more
literal sense, "to imagine," but the Schopenhauerian notion of
"representation" is evoked, as well. Imagination is the representation of images to oneself. Nietzsche plays on the ambiguity of these terms throughout this entry.

26 [12] According to Karl Schlechta and Anni Anders, *Friedrich Nietzsche: Von den verborgenen Anfängen seines Philosophierens*
(Friedrich Nietzsche: On the hidden beginnings of his philosophizing) (Stuttgart: Fromann, 1962), this entry represents
Nietzsche's attempt to integrate the positions of the Italian mathematician and physicist Ruggero Boscovich (1711–87),
Afrikan Spir, and Johann Zöllner into his own epistemological
theory.

148, 16–18 *representation … imagined]* *Vorstellung … vorgestellt.* See
notes to 19 [78] and 26 [11].

149, 13 *Actio in distans temporis punctum]* "Action at a distance at a
point in time."

149, 25 *ὄντα]* onta, "existent things."

149, 32 *actio in distans]* "action at a distance."

26 [14]

151, 27 *Bakunin]* Nietzsche probably became familiar with the
ideas of the Russian political writer and revolutionary agitator
Mikhail Alexandrovitch Bakunin (1813–76) through discussions
with Richard Wagner.

26 [15]

152, 11 ⟨*Goethe*⟩ … *p. 59]* Goethe, *Gespräche mit Eckermann* (Conversations with Eckermann), 18 May 1824. Here and in the subsequent citations, Nietzsche's page references are to the edition *Eckermann: Gespräche mit Goethe* (Leipzig, 1868), which was part of Nietzsche's personal library.

152, 12 *Eckerm⟨ann⟩ … style]* Goethe, *Gespräche mit Eckermann* (Conversations with Eckermann), 3 May 1827.

152, 13 *3 … masses]* Goethe, *Gespräche mit Eckermann* (Conversations with Eckermann), 2 January 1824.

152, 14 *3 … God]* Goethe, *Gespräche mit Eckermann* (Conversations with Eckermann), 4 January 1824.

26 [16] Nietzsche's initial draft for section 1 of "Strauss," pp. 5–6.

152, 19 *war]* The Franco-Prussian War (1870–71).

153, 17–19 *gathering … victory]* See note to 19 [259].

154, 30–32 *work … Faith]* Strauss's book was so popular that it went through four printings in just the first few months subsequent to its appearance.

26 [17]

155, 9 *Goethe, 3, p. 137]* Goethe, *Gespräche mit Eckermann* (Conversations with Eckermann), 28 March 1827, in which Goethe discusses August Wilhelm Schlegel's criticism of Euripedes. On the edition Nietzsche cites, see the note to 26 [15].

26 [18] Cf. section 1 of "Strauss," p. 8.

155, 12 *ken to can] Kennen zum Können*. Nietzsche is playing on the similarity of these two words, which literally mean "knowledge" and "ability."

155, 12 *know-how to art] Kunde zu Kunst*. It is impossible to evoke the rhetorical playfulness of Nietzsche's German here, which is structured around the phonic similarity and consistent alliteration of the pairs *Kennen-Können* and *Kunde-Kunst*.

155, 18–19 *the famous five billion]* After its defeat in the Franco-Prussian War, France was forced to pay reparations in the amount of five billion francs to the German Empire over a span of three years.

26 [19] Outline for section 1 of "Strauss."

26 [20] Cf. 29 [226] and 32 [4] (List of *Unfashionable Observations*).

26 [22] For the planned *Unfashionable Observation* on "Reading and Writing." Cf. 26 [20].

26 [23] List of publications that already had appeared, currently were being written, or were planned.

26 [24] Outline for "Strauss."

156, 22 *philistrious]* Nietzsche coins the adjective *philiströs*, formed from the noun *Philister* (philistine), instead of using the common adjective *philisterhaft*.

156, 26 *Pacific Nil]* Pacific = Friedrich (which is etymologically related to the German word *Friede*, "peace," hence "pacific"); Nil = Nietzsche.

[27 = U II 1]

27 [1] Draft for "Strauss." Most of the material in this group of writings is devoted to the preliminary work on this piece, the first essay in *Unfashionable Observations*.

157, 11–12 *a biography … biography.]* Strauss's *Das Leben Jesu* (Life of Jesus) was first published in 1835–36. This work gave rise to considerable controversy because Strauss, applying a rigorous historical criticism, sought to demonstrate that the Biblical tales about Jesus are nothing but fictions and hence cannot be drawn on in an attempt to reconstruct the life of the historical Jesus. In 1864, one year after the appearance of Ernest Renan's *Vie de Jésus* (Life of Jesus), Strauss published a revised edition of his life of Jesus under the title *Das Leben Jesu für das deutsche Volk bearbeitet* (Life of Jesus revised for the German people). In this revised version, to which Nietzsche explicitly refers here, Strauss no longer addressed himself to theologians, but to the lay public, to the entire German people.

157, 13 *Voltaire]* Strauss gave a series of lectures on Voltaire that subsequently were published under the title *Voltaire: Sechs Vorträge* (Voltaire: six lectures) (Leipzig, 1870).

157, 18–19 *the fundamental antinomy of idealism]* One of the central tenets of Kantian idealism is that human perception and knowledge are bound up solely with the phenomenal world and hence cannot penetrate to the "thing in itself," the noumenal, metaphysical world that is the site of all essential truth.

27 [2]

158, 17 *Goethe … Système de la nature]* The *Système de la nature* was a materialistic, deterministic treatise, published in 1770 by Baron d'Holbach under the pseudonym J. B. Mirabaud. Goethe relates the disillusionment and revulsion he felt upon first reading this treatise in *Dichtung und Wahrheit* (Poetry and truth), bk. 3, chap. 11. Cf. section 7 of "Strauss," p. 44.

158, 18 *p. 257]* The page reference is to Strauss's *Der alte und der neue Glaube: Ein Bekenntnis* (The old and the new faith: a confession) (Leipzig, 1872).

158, 22 *bellum omnium]* Abbreviated form of *bellum omnium contra omnes*, "the war of all against all."

27 [3]

158, 30 *biography of Jesus]* See note to 27 [1].

27 [5]

159, 2–3 *Lichtenberg's prophecy]* The source for this reference could not be ascertained.

27 [8] Cf. 15 [7] in Vol. 12 of this edition.

159, 14–15 *"intellectually impoverished"]* Cf. Matthew 5: 3.

159, 18 *Leipzig Gewandhaus]* One of the most important concert halls in Germany.

159, 20 *long."]* The quotation is from Strauss, *Der alte und der neue Glaube*; page reference unknown.

27 [9] Cf. section 4 of "Strauss," p. 28.

27 [10] Cf. 15 [9] in Vol. 12 of this edition.

160, 1 *Jahn]* Source not ascertained.

160, 1 *"Ode to Joy"]* "An die Freude," a poem by Friedrich von Schiller, set to music by Beethoven for the final movement of his Ninth Symphony.

27 [11] Cf. 15 [8] in Vol. 12 of this edition.

160, 2–3 *Aristotle … men.]* See Aristotle, *Politics*, 1335b, 26–1336a, 2.

27 [12] Cf. 15 [6] in Vol. 12 of this edition.

160, 8 *minds."]* Lichtenberg, *Vermischte Schriften* (Göttingen, 1867), 1: 77. This edition was part of Nietzsche's personal library. Georg Christoph Lichtenberg (1742–99), a German physicist, aphorist, and satirist, was one of Nietzsche's favorite authors and one inspiration for Nietzsche's aphoristic style.

27 [13] Cf. section 3 of "Strauss," p. 19.

27 [14]

160, 16–17 *The stupidity … famous.]* Nietzsche is alluding to the controversy that surrounded Strauss after the publication of his *Das Leben Jesu* (Life of Jesus) in 1835–36, a controversy that made Strauss and his works extremely visible.

27 [15]

160, 19 *Klopstock]* Friedrich Gottlieb Klopstock (1724–1803), a German neoclassical poet, greatly influenced Goethe. His major work, *Der Messias* (The messiah) was inspired by reading John Milton's *Paradise Lost*. Klopstock also wrote many plays that contained Teutonic-mythological themes.

27 [20] Outline for "Strauss." Cf. 27 [7, 22].

27 [21]

162, 10 *work.*] Lichtenberg, *Vermischte Schriften* (Göttingen, 1867), 1: 259.

162, 18 *people.*] Lichtenberg, *Vermischte Schriften*, 1: 261–2.

162, 21 *painted.*] Lichtenberg, *Vermischte Schriften*, 1: 264–5.

162, 21–23 *Strauss … Lessing's.]* Cf. section 10 of "Strauss," p. 61.

27 [24]

163, 15 *war]* The Franco-Prussian War (1870–71).

163, 15–19 *The war … praise.]* Cf. section 1 of "Strauss," p. 5, and also 26 [16].

27 [25]

163, 25 *manner.*] Lichtenberg, *Vermischte Schriften*, 1: 284.

163, 30 *condescended.*] Lichtenberg, *Vermischte Schriften*, 1: 299.

163, 32 *speech.*] Lichtenberg, *Vermischte Schriften*, 1: 306. See section 10 of "Strauss," p. 63.

164, 3 *fashionable.*] Lichtenberg, *Vermischte Schriften*, 1: 309.

164, 6 *idea.*] Lichtenberg, *Vermischte Schriften*, 1: 310.

27 [27]

164, 12 *stupidity.*] Schopenhauer, "Über Schriftstellerei und Stil" (On authorship and style), § 283 in his *Parerga und Paralipomena*.

27 [29] Cf. 27 [38], and 15 [10] in Vol. 12 of this edition, as well as section 12 of "Strauss," p. 70.

164, 25 *factor … farceur]* "maker" … "buffoon."

27 [30] Cf. section 12 of "Strauss," p. 70.

165, 17–18 *sub specie aeternitatis … decennii vel biennii]* "from an eternal perspective" … "[from a perspective] of ten, or perhaps only two years."

165, 19 *Büchner]* See note to 30 [20]. The reference is to Ludwig B. Büchner (1824–99), a German physician and materialist philosopher.

27 [31]

165, 20 *Unusquisque mavult credere quam judicare.]* "Each of us is more willing to trust another than to judge for himself." Seneca, *De vita beata* (On the blessed life), *Dialogues* 7.1.4.7. Quoted by Schopenhauer in "Über Schriftstellerei und Stil" (On authorship and style), §266 of his *Parerga und Paralipomena*, 2: 533.

27 [32] Cf. section 9 of "Strauss," pp. 52–53.

165, 29 *totum ponere]* "to construct a whole."

166, 15 *everything … rational]* An allusion to Hegel's philosophy, which considered everything real to be principally rational. Cf. section 2 of "Strauss," p. 15.

166, 18 *Nathan … Hermann and Dorothea]* Classical dramas by Gotthold Ephraim Lessing and Goethe, respectively.

166, 19 *bliss!"]* Strauss, *Der alte und der neue Glaube*, p. 294. Cf. section 4 of "Strauss," p. 24.

27 [33]

166, 21–22 *a simple garden house]* An allusion to the unassuming garden house in which Goethe lived in Weimar with his wife Christiane, who was from the lower classes.

27 [34]

166, 27 *cosmodicy]* See note to 21 [15].

27 [35] Cf. 15 [11] in Vol. 12 of this edition.

167, 4 *move … misplace]* Nietzsche uses the same verb here, *versetzen*, which means "to move" or "to misplace."

27 [37] Cf. 27 [77].

167, 12–13 *extra nos … praeter nos]* "outside of us" … "beyond us."

167, 14–15 *representations]* *Vorstellungen.* See note to 19 [78].

27 [38] Cf. 27 [29], and 15 [10] in Vol. 12 of this edition.

168, 1–2 *due … language]* An allusion to the Jewish descent of the German novelist, Berthold Auerbach (1812–82).

27 [39] Cf. section 10 of "Strauss," pp. 61–62.

168, 8 *creation."*] Quoted from the afterword Strauss appended to the second edition of *Der alte und der neue Glaube* (Bonn, 1873), "Ein Nachwort als Vorwort zu den neuen Ausgaben meiner Schrift *Der alte und der neue Glaube*" (An afterword as foreword to the new edition of my book *The Old and the New Faith*), p. 12.

168, 9 *writer."*] Strauss, "Ein Nachwort als Vorwort zu den neuen Ausgaben meiner Schrift *Der alte und der neue Glaube*," p. 12.

168, 12 *sublime"*] Strauss, *Der alte und der neue Glaube*, p. 359. Cf. section 5 of "Strauss," p. 30.

168, 14 *Merck*] Johann Heinrich Merck (1741–91), German scholar and critic. The quotation is taken from Strauss's "Afterword" to *Der alte und der Neue Glaube*. Cf. "Strauss," p. 62.

168, 15 *Afterword, p. 10*] Strauss, "Ein Nachwort als Vorwort zu den neuen Ausgaben meiner Schrift *Der alte und der neue Glaube*," p. 10.

27 [40]

168, 18–19 *kingdom of Prussia … kingdom of God*] *das Reich … das Reich Gottes*. The word "Reich" alludes to the founding of the German Empire under Bismarck in 1871. It must be rendered as "kingdom" here in order to retain the play on the Biblical wording.

27 [41]

168, 21 *Riehlian House Music*] Wilhelm Heinrich von Riehl published his two-volume *Hausmusik* (House music) in 1860. The term "house music" was coined in contradistinction to "salon music" and was intended to communicate that Riehl's music was the bourgeois counterpart—that is, intended for the bourgeois household—to the salon music of aristocratic society. In "Strauss," Nietzsche frequently uses the comparison with Riehl to denigrate Strauss.

27 [42] Cf. section 3 of "Strauss," p. 19. The quotation is from *Der alte und der neue Glaube*.

27 [43] Cf. section 6 of "Strauss," pp. 33–34.

27 [44] Page references are to *Der alte und der neue Glaube*.

169, 15–17 *ground" … history."*] Quotations from *Der alte und der neue Glaube*; page references not ascertained.

27 [45] Page references are to *Der alte und der neue Glaube*.

169, 21 *abysses."]* Page reference to *Der alte und der neue Glaube* not ascertained. Cf. section 10 of "Strauss," p. 60.

27 [47]

170, 1 *totum ponere]* "to construct a whole."

27 [49]

170, 13 *scantily clad]* Cf. section 10 of "Strauss," p. 60.

27 [50] Cf. section 6 of "Strauss," p. 34.

27 [51] Cf. 15 [12] in volume 12 of this edition.

171, 3–5 *Empedocles … die.]* See Diogenes Laertius, *Lives of the Eminent Philosophers*, 8.63.

27 [52] Draft for "Strauss."

27 [53] Outline for "Strauss."

172, 1 *sub specie biennii]* "from the perspective of two years"; Nietzsche is ironically playing on the standard phrase *sub specie aeternitatis*, "from the perspective of eternity." Cf. 27 [30].

172, 3 *totum ponere]* "to construct a whole."

27 [55] Cf. section 2 of "Strauss," p. 14.

172, 22 *Otto Jahn and Mozart]* Otto Jahn, one of Nietzsche's professors at the University of Bonn, was a devotee of Mozart's music and published a four-volume Mozart biography in 1856. Jahn's colleague and adversary, Friedrich Ritschl, whom Nietzsche followed from Bonn to the University of Leipzig and who became Nietzsche's primary mentor, was an adherent of Wagner's music, and it was Ritschl's wife who first introduced Nietzsche and Wagner. Nietzsche saw the differences in musical taste as symptomatic of the differences that led to the so-called "philological controversy" that erupted between Jahn and Ritschl during Nietzsche's first year of university studies in Bonn.

172, 22–23 *Jahn … Strauss … Gervinus]* Nietzsche takes the relationships of these three critics to the classical models they criticize (Mozart, Beethoven, and Shakespeare, respectively) as typical of the attitudes of the "cultural philistines."

27 [56]

173, 1 *ἄμουσος] amousos*, "crude," "uncultivated."

27 [57] *Pd* for the final title of "Strauss."

27 [58]

173, 17 *classes"]* The quotation is apparently from Strauss. The source has not been ascertained.

27 [59] Outline for "Strauss."

27 [60] Outline for "Strauss."

27 [61] Outline for "Strauss."

27 [62] Outline for "Strauss."

27 [63] Outline for "Strauss."

27 [64] Plan for publications.

27 [66] Cf. 15 [13] in Vol. 12 of this edition, and section 1 of "Strauss," pp. 6–9.

176, 16 *Vischer's statement about Hölderlin]* The philosopher Friedrich Theodor von Vischer (1807–87) gave a speech in Lauffen, the birthplace of the poet Friedrich Hölderlin, on the occasion of the poet's one-hundredth birthday. In this speech he says of Hölderlin: "he could not bear the thought that one could be a philistine and still not be a barbarian." Nietzsche cites Vischer's speech at length, including this passage, in section 2 of "Strauss," pp. 17–18.

27 [67]

176, 23 *Heraclitus]* Fragment 83, in *Die Fragmente der Vorsokratiker*, ed. Diels and Kranz, vol. 1: "To god, even the wisest human being is an ape." Cf. 26 [2].

27 [68]

177, 1–2 *They … offensive]* Cf. section 11 of "Strauss," p. 64.

177, 14–20 *Then … from?]* Cf. section 11 of "Strauss," pp. 66–69.

27 [69] Cf. Nietzsche's letter to Richard Wagner of 24 May 1875.

177, 21 *Hölderlin]* "Gesang des Deutschen" (Song of the German), in *Friedrich Hölderlin: Poems and Fragments*, trans. Michael Hamburger (Cambridge: Cambridge University Press, 1988), p. 615.

177, 26 *Delos]* A small island of the Cyclades in the Aegean Sea. In Greek mythology, the birthplace of Artemis, the goddess of the moon, and her twin brother, Apollo, the god of poetry and prophecy, who later was identified with Helios, the god of the sun.

177, 26 *Olympia]* Site of the temple and Sacred Grove of Zeus Olympius. The Olympic Games were held here during the Festival of Zeus.

27 [70] Page references are to Strauss, *Der alte und der neue Glaube*.

27 [71]

178, 5 *Next chapter]* Section 4 of "Strauss," which Nietzsche outlines here.

27 [72] Cf. 15 [14] in Vol. 12 of this edition, and also "Der Wanderer und sein Schatten" (The wanderer and his shadow), 199, in the second volume of *Human, All Too Human*.

27 [73] Outline for "Strauss"; page references are to *Der alte und der neue Glaube*.

27 [75] Final title of the first essay in *Unfashionable Observations*.

27 [77] Cf. 27 [37].

179, 9 *extra nos]* "outside of us."

27 [78] Discarded preface to "Strauss"; cf. Nietzsche's draft letter to Cosima Wagner from April 1873, *Briefwechsel: Kritische Gesamtausgabe*, ed. Giorgio Colli and Mazzino Montinari (Berlin: 1975–), pt. 2, 3: 143–44.

179, 13–14 *book … year]* Strauss's *Der alte und der neue Glaube* was so popular that it went through six printings in the first year.

179, 24–25 *Goethe … ignite]* The quotation is from Goethe's "Maximen und Reflexionen über Literatur und Kunst" (Maxims and reflections on literature and art); see the "Sophien-Ausgabe" of *Goethes Werke* (Weimar: H. Böhlau, 1887–1919), pt. 1, vol. 42, pt. 2, p. 121.

27 [79] Plan for publications.

27 [80] Apparently conceived for the final chapter of "Strauss," the idea expressed here was not employed until the second essay in *Unfashionable Observations*; cf. sections 5 and 10 of "History," pp. 115 and 158.

27 [81] First notes for "History."

[28 = Mp XIII 1]

28 [1] Cf. section 8 of "Strauss," pp. 46–48.

181, 19 *otium … otium sine dignitate]* "idleness" … "idleness without dignity."

28 [2] Like many of the writings in notebook 19, this entry, as well as 28 [4, 5, 6], is devoted to Nietzsche's planned treatise on the philosopher or the pre-Platonic Greek philosophers. See note to 19 [1].

183, 32–33 *a meager or a very considerable age*] Nietzsche's language is ambiguous. The phrase *eine kleine oder eine sehr große Zeit* can be interpreted either in terms of quality, "an unimportant or a very significant age," or in terms of quantity, "a short or a very long period of time." The rendering given here attempts to preserve this ambiguity.

184, 5 *positivis*] "positive qualities."

28 [6] Cf. 35 [11].

186, 1–2 *Ridiculous … university.*] Cf. 29 [208].

186, 9 *war*] The Franco-Prussian War (1870–71).

[29 = U II 2]

29 [1] On the theme of "truth" cf. 29 [2, 3, 4, 8, 10–21]. Titles and outlines: 29 [23, 26].

188, 8 *Kant's speech addressed to duty*] Nietzsche's allusion is to Kant's essay "Über ein vermeintliches Recht aus Menschenliebe zu lügen" (On a putative right to lie in the interest of human love). In this essay Kant rejects the thesis, proposed by Benjamin Constant, that there are certain situations in which lies are justified if they effect human good. Kant insists on the absolute duty of human beings to tell the truth, claiming that any infraction against this duty undermines the notion of truth itself.

29 [6]

189, 24 *impossible.*"] The quotation from Benjamin Constant is most likely drawn from Kant's essay "Über ein vermeintliches Recht aus Menschenliebe zu lügen" (On a putative right to lie in the interest of human love). The passage is taken from Constant's *Des reactions politiques* (On political reactions) and is in response to Kant's *Metaphysik der Sitten* (Metaphysics of morality). See note to 29 [1]. Cf. 29 [179].

189, 27 *truth.*"] Nietzsche is quoting from Goethe's translation of Denis Diderot's *Rameau's Nephew*; see Goethe, *Werke in vierzig Bänden* (Stuttgart, 1856–57), 29: 261. This collection was part of Nietzsche's personal library.

29 [8]

190, 29 *fiat veritas, pereat mundus*] "Let there be truth, and let the world perish."

190, 30 *fiat mendacium! pereat mundus]* "Let there be lies, and let the world perish."

191, 35 *credo quia absurdum est]* "I believe it because it is absurd."

192, 5 εὐδαιμονία*]* eudaimonia, "happiness."

192, 36 *on ... earth"]* Cf. 29 [181].

29 [9]

193, 1 *Penzel]* Abraham Jakob Penzel (1749–1819), adventurer and scholar.

193, 4 *soldier."]* The source of the quotation is unknown.

193, 5–6 *passage ... world.]* Cf. section 3 of "History," p. 107. The source of the Luther quotation could not be ascertained.

29 [10] Cf. 29 [13] and section 6 of "Schopenhauer," pp. 224–30.

193, 23 *republic ... scholars.]* Cf. 19 [99].

193, 24 *ochlocracy]* "mob rule."

29 [13]. Cf. 29 [10] and section 6 of "Schopenhauer," pp. 225–29.

194, 9 *adiaphoris]* "matters that are irrelevant or indifferent to faith."

196, 29–30 *Ingenii largitor venter.]* "The stomach is the dispenser of genius."

196, 30 *stomach."]* A quotation from Goethe's translation of Diderot's *Rameau's Nephew. Borborgymous:* "intestinal rumblings caused by gas."

29 [15] Cf. section 6 of "Schopenhauer," p. 225.

29 [18]

199, 13–14 *becoming ... being]* See note to 19 [67].

29 [19]

199, 15–16 *Plato ... market]* See Diogenes Laertius, *Lives of the Eminent Philosophers*, 3.19. Plato is said to have been taken prisoner and sold at a slave market in Aegina. However, he was ransomed and returned to Athens.

29 [22]

200, 7 *laissez aller]* "let it be," "leave it alone."

29 [23] Cf. 29 [26].

29 [24]

201, 9 *Zöllner]* See the forward to Johann Karl Friedrich Zöllner's *Über die Natur der Kometen: Beiträge zur Geschichte und Theorie der Erkenntnis* (On the nature of comets: contributions to the history and theory of knowledge), 2nd ed. (Leipzig, 1872). This book was part of Nietzsche's personal library. See note to 19 [94].

29 [25]

201, 16 *Schiller*] The source of this Schiller reference has not been ascertained.

29 [26] Cf. 29 [23].

29 [28]

202, 6 *conditio*] "situation," "condition."

202, 9 *Defienda … myself.*"] Cf. section 10 of "History," p. 162.

29 [29] This entry marks the transition from the theme of "truth" to that of "history." From this point onward, most of the writings in this notebook can be seen as preliminary notes for "History."

202, 22–203, 11 *If … impossible.*] Cf. section 2 of "History," p. 98.

29 [30] Cf. section 2 of "History," p. 98.

29 [31]

203, 24 *the superstition of the rationality of history*] Nietzsche is alluding to Hegel and the Hegelians, who were adherents to the view of history as a purposive and rational development.

204, 15–18 *Every … history.*] Cf. section 1 of "History," p. 90.

29 [32] Cf. section 1 of "History," p. 89.

29 [34] Cf. section 2 of "History," p. 99.

29 [35]

205, 15–17 *The antiquarians … it*] Cf. 29 [183].

29 [36] Cf. section 2 of "History," p. 96.

29 [40] Cf. section 9 of "History," pp. 153–54.

208, 1 *la femme*] "woman."

29 [41] Cf. section 9 of "History," pp. 154–55.

29 [42] Cf. section 8 of "History," p. 143.

209, 31 *sweepings*"] Heraclitus, fragment 124, in *Die Fragmente der Vorsokratitker*, ed. Diels and Kranz, vol. 1.

29 [43] The source of the Luther quotation has not been ascertained. Cf. 29 [184]

29 [44] Source not ascertained.

29 [45]

210, 13 *"un personnage haineux"*] "a malicious person."

29 [46] Cf. section 8 of "History," p. 140.

210, 24 *a disguised theology]* An allusion to Ludwig Feuerbach's famous statement that philosophy is a disguised theology.

29 [47]

211, 25 *κρᾶσις] krasis*, "intermixture," "blending."

29 [48]

211, 26–27 *the parallel … old age]* This parallel of history to the stages of human development was articulated in *Philosophie des Unbewußten* (Philosophy of the unconscious) (Berlin, 1869), by the German metaphysical philosopher Eduard von Hartmann (1842–1906). Cf. section 8 of "History," pp. 138–39. Nietzsche rails against Hartmann in the concluding sections of "History."

29 [49] Cf. section 9 of "History," p. 155.

29 [51] Beginning with this entry, Nietzsche starts to intensify his arguments against Eduard von Hartmann's *Philosophie des Unbewußten* (Philosophy of the unconscious). The 1872 edition of this treatise was part of Nietzsche's personal library; his page references, however, are to the first edition of 1869. On Hartmann in this notebook, see 29 [49, 52–55, 59, 66, 72]. Cf. "History" sections 7, 8, and 9.

212, 20 *Protestant Union]* Founded in 1863, the German Protestant Union, which emerged from the movement known as "Cultural Protestantism," sought to reform and modernize the Lutheran Church so as to reconcile it with nineteenth-century cultural and scientific developments. Its aim was to win back members who had been alienated from the church by demonstrating its relevance to modern life. It hoped thereby to turn the church once more into a popular, indeed, populist institution.

212, 25 *νοῦς] nous*, "mind," or "intellect."

212, 28 *process."]* Eduard von Hartmann, *Philosophie des Unbewußten* (Philosophy of the unconscious) (Berlin, 1869), p. 638. Further references are cited as "Hartmann" with the page number.

213, 8 *"solid mediocrity"]* Hartmann, p. 618.

213, 10 *stockbroker."]* Hartmann, p. 619.

213, 13 *future."]* Hartmann, p. 618.

213, 19 *pain."]* Hartmann, page reference not ascertained.

213, 25 *Leopardi]* Nietzsche apparently means this reference to be ironic, since Leopardi lived to be only thirty-nine.

29 [52]

213, 33 *τέλος]* telos, "end," "purpose," "final cause."

214, 17–23 *It ... humanity.]* Cf. section 9 of "History," p. 151.

214, 17 *"republic of geniuses"]* See Schopenhauer, *Der handschriftliche Nachlaß*, ed. Arthur Hübscher (Frankfurt: W. Kramer, 1966–75), 3: 188. Nietzsche returns to this idea frequently in his early writings. See section 9 of "History," p. 151, and 19 [1] and 24 [4].

214, 24–25 *Moreover ... fleas!]* Cf. section 9 of "History," p. 146.

214, 26–36 *Hartmann ... Judgment]* Cf. section 9 of "History," p. 152.

214, 33–34 *the Danaides' futile attempts to draw water]* According to Greek mythology, forty-nine of the fifty daughters of Danaus, a king of Argos, killed their husbands by order of their father and were condemned in Hades forever to attempt to draw water with sieves.

29 [53]

216, 1–2 *Hegelian ... force.]* Cf. 27 [30].

216, 2–3 *disguised theology]* See note to 29 [46].

216, 5–7 *The human being ... spirit!]* Cf. section 9 of "History," p. 146.

29 [54] Cf. section 9 of "History," p. 153.

216, 14 *animae magnae prodigus]* Literally, "prodigal of a great soul," but meaning "careless of life." The phrase is taken from Horace's *Odes*, 1.12.38.

29 [56] Cf. section 7 of "History," pp. 134–35.

217, 6 *ἦθος]* ethos, "ethos." In antiquity, "ethos" was understood in the sense of "character," the disposition, habits, etc. of an individual.

29 [57] Cf. section 7 of "History," pp. 135–37.

217, 33 *tout comprendre c'est tout pardonner]* "to understand everything is to excuse everything."

218, 3–4 *It ... labor.]* Cf. *Pd* to p. 136, lines 1–12 of "History," found on pp. 356–57 of the commentary to *Unfashionable Observations*.

218, 34–36 *First ... vulgarity!]* Cf. *Sd* to p. 137, line 21 of "History," found on p. 357 of the commentary to *Unfashionable Observations*.

29 [59] Cf. section 9 of "History," pp. 148–49.

219, 18 *ex causis efficientibus]* "by means of efficient causes."

219, 19 *ex causa finali]* "by means of a final cause."

219, 21 *age of manhood]* An unmarked quotation from Hartmann, pp. 619, 625.

219, 22 *solid mediocrity]* Hartmann, p. 618.

219, 22–23 *art … stockbrokers]* Hartmann, p. 619.

220, 6–8 *but the entire … light]* Cf. "History," p. 150.

29 [60]

220, 22 *events."]* Franz Grillparzer, "Über den Nutzen des Studiums der Geschichte" (On the utility of the study of history), *Sämmtliche Werke* (Stuttgart, 1872), 9: 40. Cf. section 6 of "History," pp. 126–27.

220, 32 *overcome."]* Grillparzer, "Über den Nutzen des Studiums der Geschichte," *Sämmtliche Werke*, 9: 45.

29 [61] Cf. section 2 of "History," p. 99. The allusion is to the conspiracy between Gaius Cassius and Marcus Brutus to assassinate Julius Caesar.

29 [62]

221, 19 *do."]* Franz Grillparzer, "Über den Nutzen des Studiums der Geschichte," *Sämmtliche Werke*, 9: 129. Cf. section 6 of "History," p. 126.

29 [64]

222, 1 *The Hungarian … professor.]* Cf. 29 [6].

222, 2–5 *History … history."]* Cf. section 8 of "History," p. 143. The quotation is pieced together from Franz Grillparzer, "Über den Nutzen des Studiums der Geschichte," *Sämmtliche Werke*, 9: 157.

222, 6 *Huart⟨e⟩]* Juan Huarte de San Juan (ca. 1529–88), Spanish physician and writer.

29 [65]

222, 26 *age."]* Grillparzer, "Über den Nutzen des Studiums der Geschichte," *Sämmtliche Werke*, 9: 159.

222, 31 *moderns."]* Grillparzer, "Über den Nutzen des Studiums der Geschichte," *Sämmtliche Werke*, 9: 187. Cf. section 4 of "History," pp. 113–14.

222, 31–32 *Who … Heine!]* Cf. Grillparzer, "Über den Nutzen des Studiums der Geschichte," *Sämmtliche Werke*, 9: 197.

29 [66] Page references are to the 1869 edition of Hartmann's *Philosophie des Unbewußten* (Philosophy of the unconscious). Cf. 29 [52].

223, 22 *victory column]* From about the mid-1800's onward, the "Germania" theme had become quite prominent in Germany in response to France's wish to make the Rhine River the border between the two countries. After the German victory over the French in 1871, victory columns sprang up all over Germany, and Nietzsche probably is alluding to this general phenomenon.

223, 29–34 *perhaps … sharp.]* Cf. section 9 of "History," p. 152.

224, 7 *the Schulze-Delitzsch model]* The German jurist and social-political theorist Hermann Schulze-Delitzsch (1808–83) supported the idea of industrial and economic cooperative associations as a counterforce to competitive capitalism. From 1849 onward he founded a number of cooperatives, among them the German Cooperative Bank in 1865.

29 [67]

224, 14–15 *Kant … himself.]* The allusion is to Kant's essay "Über ein vermeintliches Recht aus Menschenliebe zu lügen" (On a putative right to lie in the interest of human love).

29 [68]

224, 20 *meantime."]* Grillparzer, *Sämmtliche Werke*, 9: 270.

224, 24 *German."]* Grillparzer, *Sämmtliche Werke*, 8: 353. Nietzsche adopted the idea expressed in this passage in section 4 of "History," p. 111.

29 [70]

224, 28 *story."]* Polybius, *Histories*, 1.1.2.

225, 4 *fortune."]* Polybius, *Histories*, 1.1.2. Cf. section 2 of "History," p. 96.

29 [71]

225, 7 *Kölnische Zeitung]* A liberal newspaper published in Cologne and aligned after 1867 with the German National-Liberal Party.

225, 9 *Tyrtaean war trumpet]* Legend describes Tyrtaeus (seventh century B.C.) as a poor, lame Athenian schoolmaster sent to Sparta in accordance with an oracle to be a leader in the Second Messenian War. Although he was chosen intentionally in the belief that he would be ineffectual, Tyrtaeus composed poetry on military themes that inspired the Spartans and caused them to win the war.

29 [72]

225, 14–18 *Hegel … Hartmann.]* Cf. section 9 of "History," p. 148. The quotation is from Hegel's introduction to his *Vorlesungen über die Philosophie der Geschichte* (Lectures on the philosophy of history), as are the subsequent quotations here.

29 [73]

226, 17 *individuals."]* Hegel, introduction to his *Vorlesungen über die Philosophie der Geschichte.*

29 [74]

227, 4 *involved."]* Hegel, introduction to his *Vorlesungen über die Philosophie der Geschichte.*

227, 8 *Lichter's words]* The identity of the person to whom Nietzsche is referring could not be ascertained.

227, 28 *propter vitam vitae perdere causas]* "On account of life to destroy the causes of life."

29 [75]

228, 1 *imagination."]* Friedrich Schiller, *Was heißt und zu welchem Ende studiert man Universalgeschichte?* (What is and why do we study universal history?), in vol. 17 of *Schillers Werke, Nationalausgabe,* ed. Karl-Heinz Hahn (Berlin: Böhlau, 1970), p. 373. Cf. section 6 of "History," p. 127.

29 [76]

228, 7 *Goethe]* The reference is to one of Goethe's "Zahme Xenien" (Tame xenien); see the "Sophien-Ausgabe" of *Goethes Werke* (Weimar: H. Böhlau, 1887–1919), pt. 1, vol. 5/i, p. 105.

29 [77]

228, 21 *else."]* Goethe, *Gespräche mit Eckermann* (Conversations with Eckermann), 16 February 1826.

29 [78]

228, 25 *history."]* Goethe, *Gespräche mit Eckermann* (Conversations with Eckermann), 21 July 1827. Cf. section 2 of "History," p. 96.

229, 4 *on."]* Goethe, letter to Zelter dated 17 January 1831. Cf. 29 [187].

229, 6 *details."]* Goethe, letter to Lavater dated 25–30 August 1776.

29 [79]

229, 14 *be!"]* Goethe, *Gespräche mit Eckermann* (Conversations with Eckermann), 11 September 1828.

29 [80]

229, 21 *much."]* Lichtenberg, *Vermischte Schriften* (Göttingen, 1867), 1: 282.

229, 27 *worse."]* Lichtenberg, *Vermischte Schriften*, 1: 285.

229, 32 *himself."]* Goethe, *Maximen und Reflexionen* (Maxims and reflections), no. 770. Cf. 29 [186].

29 [81] Cf. section 4 of "History," p. 114.

29 [83]

230, 25 *Goethe, nature.]* See Goethe's introduction to his journal *Propyläen*, in *Sämmtliche Werke*, 40 vols. (Stuttgart, 1855–58), 40: 389. Here Goethe demands that artists imitate nature, that they study it, copy it, and produce works that are similar to the phenomena that occur in nature. Cf. 9 [85] in Vol. 10 of this edition.

230, 27–29 *in … illusion.]* The words of Hans Sachs in Richard Wagner's *Meistersinger von Nürnberg*, act 3, scene 1. Cf. section 7 of "History," p. 134.

29 [84]

231, 8 *good."]* Goethe, *Maximen und Reflexionen*, no. 694. Cf. section 7 of "History," p. 137.

231, 16 *cure."]* Goethe, from the essay "Naturphilosophie" (Philosophy of nature); see Goethe's *Sämtliche Werke: Jubiläums-Ausgabe*, ed. Eduard von der Hellen, 40 vols. (Stuttgart: Cotta, 1907), 38: 118.

29 [85] The source of the quotation is unknown.

29 [86]

231, 24 *give."]* David Hume, *Dialogues Concerning Natural Religion*, ed. Nelson Pike (Indianapolis: Bobbs-Merrill, 1970), pt. 10, p. 87. The concluding lines of verse are not from Hume, but are cited by him from John Dryden's play *Aureng-Zebe*, act 4, scene 1. Cf. 30 [2], and section 1 of "History," p. 92.

232, 23 *him."]* David Hume, *Dialogues Concerning Natural Religion*, pt. 5, p. 53.

232, 32 *sorrow."]* David Hume, *Dialogues Concerning Natural Religion*, pt. 10, p. 85.

29 [87] Notes for the initial sections of "History."

29 [88] An early draft for "History," portions of which were later incorporated, in revised form, into different sections of the published essay.

235, 11–12 *in … illusion.*] See note to 29 [83].

29 [89] Early notes for "History."

235, 31 *a disguised theology*] See note to 29 [46].

29 [90] Outline for "History."

29 [91]

236, 22–23 *they … animal.*] Cf. Franz Grillparzer, *Sämmtliche Werke* (Stuttgart, 1872), 9: 267.

236, 23 *in concreto*] "in concrete form."

29 [92]

236, 27–29 *they … laments.*] Cf. section 6 of "History," p. 128, and 29 [24]. On Zöllner, see note to 19 [94].

29 [93]

237, 1–2 *"Si … prix?"*] "If I have spoken the truth, then why my vehemence in expressing it; doesn't that diminish its worth?" The source of this quotation from Mirabeau is unknown.

29 [94]

237, 5 *Stein*] Karl Reichsfreiherr von und zum Stein (1757–1831), Prussian statesman.

237, 7 *rule."*] The source of the quotation is unknown.

29 [95]

237, 8 *fere*] "approximately."

237, 20 *girls."*] The source of the quotation is unknown. The reference is to Barthold Georg Niebuhr (1776–1831), a Prussian civil servant and historian.

29 [96] Cf. section 6 of "History," pp. 125–30.

238, 6 *the will … place.*] This thesis is consistent with the theory of art propounded by Schopenhauer in *The World as Will and Representation*.

239, 2 *intelligence."*] The source of the Swift quotation is unknown. Nietzsche adopted this statement, without identifying its author, in section 6 of "History," p. 129.

240, 2 *les historiens de M. Thiers*] "the historians who work for M. Thiers." Louis Adolphe Thiers (1797–1877) was a French historian and statesman known for his work on monumental historical projects.

29 [97] Outline for "History."

29 [98] Early draft of the opening paragraphs of section 1 of "History," pp. 87–88. Cf. 30 [2].

241, 3 *Leopardi]* Giacomo Leopardi (1798–1837), Italian poet and philosopher. Nietzsche cites Leopardi from Robert Hamerling's German translation, *Gedichte* (Hildburghausen, 1866), a book that was in his personal library.

241, 28 *imperfect] Imperfectum.* This word not only evokes the notion of imperfection, but also signifies the imperfect tense in grammar, commonly called the simple past. Thus, Nietzsche suggests by means of this pun that imperfection inheres by nature in the sense of pastness.

29 [99] For "History."

29 [100] For "History."

29 [101] Outline for "History."

242, 22–23 *Niebuhr … victorious.]* See Goethe's letter to Zelter dated 17 January 1831; quoted in 29 [78]. On Niebuhr, see note to 29 [95].

29 [102] Outline for "History."

243, 11 *Kant … lies]* The allusion is to Kant's essay "Über ein vermeintliches Recht aus Menschenliebe zu lügen" (On a putative right to lie in the interest of human love). See note to 29 [1].

29 [103]

243, 26 *daemon]* "inner voice," or "guiding spirit."

29 [105]

244, 1 *Niebuhr]* The quotations are drawn from Niebuhr's letter to Adam Moltke dated 9 December 1796. On Niebuhr, see note to 29 [95]. Count Adam Moltke (1765–1843), a close acquaintance of Niebuhr, was an author and politician.

244, 3 *Voss]* Johann Heinrich Voss (1751–1826): German poet and translator, especially of Homer (*Odyssey*, 1781, *Iliad*, 1793), but also of the major Greek dramatists and Shakespeare (with sons, Heinrich and Abraham). The irony implicit in Nietzsche's praise of Voss as a representative of German literature is that in Nietzsche's day Voss's creative work was largely forgotten and he was remembered primarily as a translator.

244, 6 *Baggesen]* Jens Baggesen (1764–1826), a leading Danish literary figure in the transitional period between Neoclassicism and Romanticism, acquainted with Klopstock, Wieland, and Schiller. A Germanophile, Baggesen was so taken with the philosophy of Kant that he took the name "Immanuel" as his own second name, in honor of the philosopher.

244, 6–7 *Almanac Schiller published this year]* Most likely Schiller's *Musen-Almanach auf das Jahr 1797* (Almanac of the muses for 1797), the so-called "Xenienalmanach" in which Schiller and Goethe published their "Xenien," their satirical attacks on contemporary writers and intellectuals.

29 [106]

244, 20 *defect."]* Hölderlin, letter to his brother dated 4 June 1799.

29 [107]

244, 26 *heavens."]* Hölderlin, letter to his brother dated 1 January 1799.

29 [108] Cf. section 2 of "History," p. 99, and 21 [22].

29 [110]

245, 10 *French."]* See Goethe's letter to Schiller dated 5 April 1797.

29 [111]

245, 16 *step."]* See Schiller's letter to Goethe dated 21 April 1797.

29 [112]

245, 19 *lacks."]* Goethe, letter to Schiller dated 7 July 1796.

245, 27 *seriously."]* Goethe, letter to Schiller dated 5 December 1796.

29 [113] Cf. section 3 of "History," p. 105.

29 [114] Cf. the opening paragraphs of section 3 of "History," pp. 102–6.

246, 8 *ancestral household effects]* See Goethe's *Faust*, part 1, line 408.

246, 18–19 *de mortuis nil nisi bene]* "one should say nothing but good things about those who are dead."

29 [115] Schematic outline for sections 2 and 3 of "History."

29 [116]

247, 7–8 *opposition … naive]* Schiller used these terms to distinguish between two fundamentally different types of poets in *Über naive und sentimentalische Dichtung* (On naive and sentimentalist poetry). For Schiller, Goethe represented the naive attitude reminiscent of the ancient Greeks, whereas Schiller identified himself with the reflective, "sentimentalist" attitude of the modern poet.

29 [117]

247, 21 *a dramatist driving on to deeds*] *zum Dran drängender Dramatiker.* The translation attempts to reproduce Nietzsche's alliteration.

247, 27–28 *Shakespeare … Englishmen.*] Cf. section 5 of "History," p. 119.

248, 11 *Prince of Homburg*] *Prince Friedrich von Homburg*, a drama by Heinrich von Kleist.

29 [118] Cf. section 4 of "History," p. 112.

29 [119]

249, 17 *Eckermann*] Goethe's *Gespräche mit Eckermann* (Conversations with Eckermann).

29 [120] Cf. Nietzsche's deliberations in 21 [3] and 25 [1] on the sculpturesque group in the dramas of Aeschylus and in Wagnerian opera.

29 [121] Cf. section 4 of "History," pp. 112–13.

250, 4 δύναμις] *dynamis*, "potential," or "power."

29 [122] Cf. section 4 of "History," pp. 112–13.

29 [123] These reflections are based on thoughts expressed by Goethe, *Gespräche mit Eckermann* (Conversations with Eckermann), 3 May 1827.

29 [124]

251, 3 *daemon*] "inner voice," or "guiding spirit."

29 [125]

251, 7 *Hyperboreans*] A legendary people that lives in a state of bliss beyond the Boreas, the north wind, in a land with a favorable climate.

251, 11 *defense."*] See Goethe's letter to Schiller dated 2 January 1804.

251, 13–14 *activity."*] See Goethe's letter to Schiller dated 19 December 1798. Cf. Nietzsche's "Foreword" to "History," p. 85.

29 [126]

251, 25 *one."*] See Schiller's letter to Goethe dated 23 July 1798.

29 [127]

251, 27 *compelled."*] See Goethe's letter to Schiller dated 21 February 1798. Cf. section 6 of "History," p. 127.

252, 6 *reason."*] See Goethe's letter to Schiller dated 31 January 1798.

29 [128]

252, 10 *others."*] See Schiller's letter to Goethe dated 2 January 1798.

29 [129]

252, 13 *totality"*] See Schiller's letter to Goethe dated 2 January 1798.

252, 16 *satisfied."*⟩] See Goethe's letter to Schiller dated 3 January 1798.

29 [130] Cf. section 5 of "History," p. 119.

252, 23 *well."*] From Goethe's essay "Shakespeare und kein Ende" (Shakespeare without end). Nietzsche cites this passage in section 5 of "History," p. 119.

252, 25 *manner."*] Goethe, "Shakespeare und kein Ende."

29 [131]

253, 8 *one."*] Goethe, "Shakespeare und kein Ende" (Shakespeare without end).

29 [133]

254, 8 *categorical imperative*] See note to 19 [113].

29 [135]

254, 24–25 *the Cologne editorialists relate to Tyrtaeus.*] See note to 29 [71].

29 [136]

255, 1 *Erwin von Steinach*] The allusion is to Goethe's essay "Von deutscher Baukunst" (On German architecture), written in Strasbourg in 1772 and dedicated to the builder of the Strasbourg cathedral, Erwin von Steinach (?–1318). In this essay, Goethe celebrates the Strasbourg cathedral as a true work of German genius. Cf. section 3 of "History," p. 103.

29 [137] Written after Nietzsche's return from Bayreuth on 5 November 1873.

255, 8 *conditio*] "prerequisite," "condition."

29 [139]

256, 7–8 *Statistics … supernumeraries*] Nietzsche plays on the words *Statistik* (statistics) and *Statisten* (supernumeraries in theater) to underscore this relationship between statistics and the masses. Cf. section 9 of "History," p. 154.

29 [141] Outline for "History."

29 [142]

257, 4 *arts."*] The source of the quotation from Jean Paul is unknown. Cf. 29 [186].

257, 6 *time,]* The source of the quotation from Gibbon is unknown. Cf. section 10 of "History," p. 159, and 29 [186].

29 [146] Outline for "History."

29 [147] Outline for "History."

29 [149]

258, 20 *Statistics … animal.]* Cf. section 9 of "History," p. 154.

29 [150]

258, 21 *von der Hagen, Minnesinger]* The reference is to vol. 2, page 2 ff. of Friedrich Heinrich von der Hagen's *Minnesinger: Deutsche Liederdichter des 12. 13. und 14. Jahrhunderts* (Minnesinger: German song poets of the twelfth, thirteenth, and fourteenth centuries), 5 vols. (Leipzig, 1838–61). Nietzsche apparently consulted this volume to determine the approximate date of the Minnesinger competition at the Wartburg, the event Richard Wagner dramatized in *Tannhäuser*.

258, 23–24 *Ludus … N⟨ovissimus⟩]* The reference is to an Antichrist drama by Ludus Paschalis, *De adventu et interitu Antichristi* (On the coming and the demise of the antichrist), contained in the six-volume collection *Thesaurus anecdotorum novissimus* (New collection of anecdotes) edited by Bernhard Pez and published from 1721 to 1729.

29 [151] Notes for "History."

29 [152] Notes for "History."

29 [153] Outline for "History."

29 [154] Notes for "History."

29 [155] Notes for "History."

29 [156] Notes for "History."

29 [157] Outline for "History."

29 [158] Notes for "History."

261, 4 *advocatus diaboli]* "devil's advocate."

29 [160] Outline for "History."

29 [162] Draft for the conclusion of "History," later discarded.

262, 9 *Schiller—Correctional facilities.]* See 29 [126].

29 [164] Outline of planned *Unfashionable Observations*.

29 [166]

263, 16 *Görres … 206.]* Joseph von Görres's *Europa und die Revolution* first appeared in 1821. Görres (1776–1848) was a writer and

Catholic political journalist. The edition Nietzsche is citing has not been ascertained.

263, 18 *Licht⟨enberg⟩ I, 206.]* Lichtenberg, *Vermischte Schriften* (Göttingen, 1867), 1: 206. This edition was part of Nietzsche's personal library.

29 [167]

263, 26 *Choephori]* The second play in Aeschylus's *Oresteia*, usually translated into English as *The Libation Bearers*.

263, 27 *Erga]* Poem by Hesiod, commonly called *Opera et Dies* (Works and days).

29 [172] Cf. section 1 of "History."

29 [174]

267, 6 *Critias]* A relative of Plato's, leader of the thirty tyrants in Athens.

267, 12 *Dion]* Plato reports in his "Seventh Letter," written in response to the murder of Dion, that the latter had encouraged him to journey to see Dionysius so that the latter could be introduced to Plato's philosophy.

29 [175]

267, 23 *Eleatics]* See note to 19 [134].

29 [176]

267, 28 *greatness,"]* Lichtenberg, *Vermischte Schriften* (Göttingen, 1867), 2: 191.

29 [177]

268, 4–5 *idleness."]* Nietzsche quotes Bolingbroke in the original English.

29 [178]

268, 9 *it."]* The source of this quotation from Aristotle could not be ascertained.

29 [179]

268, 20–21 *impossible."]* On the probable source of the quotation from Constant, see the note to 29 [6].

29 [180]

268, 25 *world."]* Cf. 29 [9] and section 3 of "History," p. 107. The source of the Luther quotation could not be ascertained.

29 [181] Cf. the final line of 29 [8].

29 [182]

269, 3–4 *Defienda … myself."*] Cf. 29 [28] and section 10 of "History," p. 162.

29 [183] Cf. 29 [35].

29 [184]

269, 10 *deal."*] The source of the Luther quotation is unknown. Cf. 29 [43].

29 [185]

269, 15 *(see above).*] Nietzsche's reference leads back to 29 [76], where these thoughts are followed through in more detail.

29 [186]

269, 16–17 *Goethe … handwork*] Goethe, *Maximen und Reflexionen* (Maxims and reflections), no. 770. Cf. 29 [80].

269, 18–19 *(s⟨ee⟩ a⟨bove⟩)*] Nietzsche's reference leads back to 29 [113]. Cf. section 3 of "History," p. 105.

269, 20 *The art … arts.*] A quotation from Jean Paul, source unknown. Cf. 29 [142].

269, 21 *time."*] A quotation from Gibbon, source unknown. Cf. 29 [142] and section 10 of "History," p. 159.

29 [187]

269, 23 *itself."*] Goethe, letter to Zelter dated 17 January 1831. Cf. 29 [78].

269, 25 *Schiller … above).*] See Goethe's remarks in *Gespräche mit Eckermann* (Conversations with Eckermann), 11 September 1828, quoted above in 29 [79].

29 [188]

270, 6 *Goethe, nature.*] See note to 29 [83].

29 [189]

270, 12 *age."*] The source of the Niebuhr quotation is unknown.

29 [190]

270, 15 *loving."*] The source of the quotation is unknown.

29 [191] Cf. section 10 of "History," pp. 166–67.

29 [192] Cf. section 10 of "History," pp. 166–67.

270, 23–24 γνῶθι σαυτόν] *gnothi sauton*, "know thyself," the inscription on the temple of Apollo at Delphi.

29 [194] Cf. section 10 of "History," p. 163.

29 [195] Cf. section 10 of "History," pp. 164–66.

29 [196] Cf. the deleted passage to p. 167, line 28 in section 10 of

"History," found on p. 363 of the commentary to *Unfashionable Observations*.

271, 24–25 *"Get ... Hamlet]* Shakespeare, *Hamlet*, act 3, scene 1, line 121.

272, 1 *"On the Scholar"]* One of the many *Unfashionable Observations* that Nietzsche planned but never finished.

29 [197] Cf. 30 [15], 35 [5]. From this entry to 29 [230], the theme of the "philosopher" once again becomes Nietzsche's primary focus.

272, 23 *vid.]* "see."

272, 23 *Bagehot]* The English economist and writer Walter Bagehot (1826–77) defended an empirical approach to science based on rigorous observation.

29 [198] Cf. 30 [15], 35 [5].

29 [199]

272, 29 *Trendelenburg]* Friedrich Adolf Trendelenburg (1802–72), a German philologist, educator, prolific writer, and philosopher, was especially critical of Kant, Hegel, and their followers, for example Kuno Fischer. Trendelenburg tended to reduce ethics to the intersection of politics, history, law, and the state.

29 [202]

273, 5 *alive."]* Hölderlin, "Socrates und Alcebiades" (Socrates and Alcebiades), in *Friedrich Hölderlin: Poems and Fragments*, trans. Michael Hamburger (Cambridge: Cambridge University Press, 1988), p. 67.

273, 14 *infant."]* Hölderlin, "Der Rhein" (The Rhien), in *Hölderlin: Poems and Fragments*, p. 411.

29 [203] Cf. 31 [8].

29 [204] Cf. section 2 of "Schopenhauer," pp. 175–76.

274, 18 *pars]* "part."

274, 22 *lacking Schopenhauer).]* The German poet and dramatist Heinrich von Kleist (1777–1804) was devastated after reading Kant's *Critique of Pure Reason* because he believed Kant had demonstrated the unknowability of absolute truth. In "Schopenhauer," pp. 188–89, Nietzsche describes Schopenhauer as "the guide ... who guides us out of the cave of skeptical disgruntlement or of critical renunciation up to the heights of tragic contemplation."

29 [205] Cf. 29 [213], 34 [37].

29 [206] Cf. section 4 of "Schopenhauer," pp. 199–200.

275, 15 ἀδιάφορα] *adiaphora*, "matters of indifference or irrelevance to questions of faith."

29 [208] Cf. 28 [6].

29 [209] Cf. section 4 of "Schopenhauer," pp. 198–99, and 29 [214].

29 [213] Cf. 29 [205], 34 [37].

277, 4 *"Physician, heal thyself!"]* See Luke 4 : 23.

29 [214] Cf. section 4 of "Schopenhauer," pp. 198–99, and 29 [209, 228].

29 [215]

277, 17 *old men's summer]* *Altmännersommer*. Nietzsche is playing on the phrase *Altweibersommer*, literally "old women's summer," but meaning "Indian summer."

29 [218] Cf. section 7 of "Schopenhauer," pp. 234–36, and 19 [223].

29 [222] Cf. section 4 of "Schopenhauer," p. 198.

29 [223] Cf. section 7 of "Schopenhauer," pp. 234–35, and 29 [218].

281, 24 *continue to procreate]* See note to 19 [10].

29 [225] Cf. section 4 of "Schopenhauer," p. 196.

29 [226] Cf. 26 [20].

29 [227] Cf. 31 [5].

29 [228] Cf. 29 [214].

29 [230]

284, 21 *Kleist]* Nietzsche describes Kleist's so-called "Kant crisis" at some length in section 3 of "Schopenhauer," p. 188. Cf. 29 [204].

[30 = U II 3]

30 [1] Title of the notebook.

30 [2] First continuous version of section 1 of "History," pp. 87–88 and 93–95.

286, 4–287, 29 *The herd … divine.]* Cf. 29 [98].

286, 14–20 *Oh … boredom!]* Giacomo Leopardi, "The Night Song of the Shepherd in Asia."

287, 19 *imperfect]* See note to 29 [98].

287, 30–298, 3 *But … degeneration.]* Cf. 29 [88].

288, 3–4 *sui generis … sui juris]* "of its own kind," or "unique" … "of its own law," or "autonomous."

288, 12–17 *Just … give."]* Cf. 29 [86]. The quotation is taken from David Hume, *Dialogues Concerning Natural Religion*, pt. 10, p. 87. See note to 29 [86].

289, 21–31 *Such … stagnation.]* Cf. 29 [88].

289, 36 *Sankhya philosophy]* One of the six major systems of Hindu philosophy, it systematically enumerates twenty-five principles, consisting of twenty-four material principles and one, wholly independent, spiritual or nonmaterial principle.

30 [3]

291, 21–22 *Winckelmann says]* The source for the reference to Winckelmann could not be ascertained.

30 [5] Cf. 6 [4] in Vol. 12 of this edition.

30 [6]

292, 13–17 *Preference … way.]* Cf. 31 [3].

30 [7] Cf. 29 [204] and section 1 of "Schopenhauer," pp. 175–76.

293, 30 *refugium]* "refuge."

30 [8]

294, 27 *detrimental to the community]* Nietzsche coins the phrase *gemeinschädlich* in analogy to the common adjective *gemeinnützlich*, "beneficial to the community" or "altruistic."

30 [9] Cf. section 2 of "Schopenhauer," p. 176.

30 [15] Cf. 29 [197, 198, 230], 35 [5].

297, 26 *Kleist]* See note to 29 [230].

298, 20 *physis]* "nature."

30 [16] Cf. 30 [18] and 30 [20], as well as the notes to those entries.

298, 21 *Ulrici]* Hermann Ulrici (1806–84), German professor of philosophy.

298, 26 *Carrière]* Moritz Carrière (1817–95), German philosophy professor in Munich.

298, 29 *thought merchants]* *Denkwirthe*. Nietzsche coins this derogatory term for philosophers who, instead of creating new knowledge or arriving at original insights, merely pass on what already is known. He uses this phrase in section 8 of "Schopenhauer," pp. 249 and 250, where he attacks academic philosophers.

30 [17] Addendum to 30 [15].

299, 1 *Kleist]* See note to 29 [230].

299, 5–6 *Plato, "Seventh Letter"]* Plato's "Seventh Letter" is addressed to the followers of Dion after the latter's murder. In the opening section of this letter, Plato admonishes Dion's followers to carry on in his spirit and transform his words into deeds.

30 [18] Addendum to 30 [15].

299, 10–11 *The five thinkers of the Augsburger Allgemeine.*] The newspaper the *Augsburger Allgemeine Zeitung* published an article praising Moritz Carrière, Immanuel Herbert von Fichte, Jakob Frohschammer, Johann Nepomuk Huber, and Hermann Ulrici as the avante-garde of German philosophy. On Nietzsche's response to this, see 30 [20].

299, 16 *The first night of Diogenes.*] According to Plutarch (*Moralia*, 77–78), Diogenes of Sinope was converted to a simple, philosophical manner of life during an all-night celebration in Athens. Upon seeing a mouse eat the crumbs of his own meal, Diogenes abandoned his resentment about not being part of the celebration and began his project of simplifying his life to the greatest possible extent.

299, 17 *apices*] "summits," or "highest honors."

299, 26 *Rameau's Nephew*] Diderot's *Rameau's Nephew*, which Nietzsche read in Goethe's German translation. Cf. 29 [6].

30 [19]

300, 1–2 *commerce in thought*] *Denkwirtschaft*. See note to 30 [16].

30 [20] Cf. the *Sd* to section 8 of "Schopenhauer," p. 247, line 29, found on p. 371 of the commentary to *Unfashionable Observations*.

300, 3 *"nation of thinkers"*] A common saying refers to the Germans as "the nation of poets and thinkers" (*das Land der Dichter und Denker*).

300, 4 *commerce in thought*] *Denkwirtschaft*. See note to 30 [16].

300, 6–7 *an exceptionally public forum*] The *Augsburger Allgemeine Zeitung*; see note to 30 [18].

300, 9 *Frohschammer, Huber*] Jakob Frohschammer (1821–93) and Johann Nepomuk Huber (1830–78) were both German theologians and philosophers. See 30 [16] for Ulrici and Carrière.

300, 14 *none."*] The source of the quotation from Ludwig Büchner—if it is not an invention of Nietzsche's—is unknown.

300, 14–15 *fanatical friend of the material*] Ludwig Büchner (1824–99) was one of the most avid defenders of modern philosophical materialism in Germany.

300, 29 *thought merchants]* *Denkwirthe*. See note to 30 [16].

300, 32–33 *"Reich" … spirit.]* A pun on the word *Reich*, which designates the German "Empire" but also the "kingdom" of God, and it is to this Biblical meaning that Nietzsche is alluding here. The German word *Geist*, "spirit," also means "intellect," so that Nietzsche is simultaneously denying the intelligence of these German "philosophers."

30 [23] Cf. 37 [11].

30 [24]

301, 14–15 *Minna von Barnhelm]* Dramatic comedy by the German Enlightenment author Gotthold Ephraim Lessing (1729–81).

301, 21 *Schleiermacher]* Nietzsche's remark is meant to underscore the fact that there is no room for moral philosophy in the work of Schleiermacher, since all ethical questions are resolved (or dissolved) into religious ones.

30 [25]

301, 24 *newspaperish]* Nietzsche's neologism, *zeitungsgemäss*, is derived from the noun *Zeitung* ("newspaper") and the adjective *zeitgemäss* ("timely" or "fashionable"). The implication is that whatever in his time is fashionable or "timely" is merely fit for the daily news, that is, sensational but ephemeral. Nietzsche first employed this term in section 8 of "Strauss," p. 48.

30 [30]

302, 26 *"philosophy"]* Etymologically the word "philosophy" derives from the Greek and means "love of wisdom."

30 [31] Cf. section 2 of "Schopenhauer," p. 181.

303, 21 *Smiles).]* Samuel Smiles (1812–1904), English writer and physician.

30 [33]

303, 30 *adiaphora]* "matters of indifference or irrelevance to questions of faith."

30 [34]

304, 1 *Gracián]* Balthasar Gracián (1601–58), Spanish philosopher and writer.

30 [38]

305, 7 *{Social} Relations.]* Nietzsche's word, *Verkehr*, is somewhat cryptic and could refer either to economic relations ("commerce") or social relations ("social intercourse"). Since in other outlines of the *Unfashionable Observations* he often included an essay on social matters (see, for example, 29 [164]), I have interpolated the adjective "social" here.

[31 = Mp XIII 5]

31 [2]

306, 10 *Pericles]* See Thucydides, 2, 38.

306, 13–14 *Schiller ... edification.]* This is the central argument in Schiller's treatise *Über die ästhetische Erziehung des Menschen* (On the aesthetic education of humankind).

31 [3] Cf. 30 [6].

307, 25 *Marwitz letter]* Friedrich August Ludwig Marwitz (1777–1837) was a Prussian general and politician. The letter to which Nietzsche refers has not been ascertained.

31 [4]

308, 25 *impotentia]* "impotence," "weakness."

31 [5] Cf. 29 [227].

31 [6]

309, 15–16 πάντων μέτρον ἄνθρωπος] *panton metron anthropos,* "the human being is the measure of all things."

309, 22–25 *When ... us.]* Suetonius Tranquillus, "Caesar Augustus," *The Lives of the Twelve Caesars,* XCIV.

31 [7]

309, 27 *Platonopolis]* The city envisioned by Plato in his *Republic.*

31 [8] Cf. 29 [203] and section 4 of "Schopenhauer," pp. 199–200.

31 [10]

311, 3 *the first night of Diogenes]* See note to 30 [18].

31 [11] Cf. 30 [23].

311, 17 *apices]* "summits."

[32 = U II 5a]

32 [3]

313, 17 *Erga]* Poem by Hesiod, commonly called *Opera et Dies* (Works and days).

313, 19 *Choephori*] The second play in Aeschylus's *Oresteia*, usually translated into English as *The Libation Bearers*.

313, 19 *Oedipus rex*] *Oedipus the King*, drama by Sophocles.

313, 20 *de corona*] *On the Crown*, oration by Demosthenes.

313, 21 *Phaedo*] Philosophical dialogue by Plato.

32 [4]

313, 31 *One-year Volunteer*] Nietzsche enlisted as a one-year volunteer in an artillery brigade and served from October 1867 to October 1868. His experiences in the military, which were quite positive, probably were intended to serve as the basis for the planned essay that in other outlines for *Unfashionable Observations* (see, for example, 19 [330]) is called "Soldier Culture." In general, Nietzsche was opposed to the Prussian practice of allowing those who pursued advanced schooling or training to serve a reduced, one-year military term instead of the usual two-year term. See Nietzsche's letter to Carl von Gersdorff dated 18 January 1874.

32 [5] Probably plans for university lecture courses. The list for each year consists of one book of Thucydides' *Histories*, a drama, a philosophical treatise, and an oration.

314, 10 *Persians*] A drama by Aeschylus.

314, 10 *Gorgias*] Philosophical treatise by Plato.

314, 11 *Pro corona*] Nietzsche probably intended to write *De corona*, *On the Crown*, an oration by Demosthenes.

314, 12 *Trachinian Women*] Drama by Sophocles.

314, 14 *Antigone*] Drama by Sophocles.

314, 16 *Oed{ipus at} Col{onus}*] Drama by Sophocles.

314, 18 *Frogs*] Drama by Aristophanes.

314, 18 *Leges*] *Laws*, philosophical dialogue by Plato.

314, 19 *Birds*] Drama by Aristophanes.

32 [7]

314, 27 διαδοχαί] *diadochai*, "successions," or "successors." See note to 19 [59].

32 [8] *Pd* for 33 [1]. Cf. section 7 of "Wagner," p. 292. From here to 32 [61], the entries in this notebook constitute preliminary notes for "Wagner."

32 [9] *Pd* for 33 [2].

32 [10] *Pd* for 33 [3, 4, 5]. Cf. 32 [49].

32 [11] *Pd* for 33 [6, 7].

32 [12] *Pd* for 33 [7].

32 [13] *Pd* for 33 [8, 9, 10].

32 [15] *Pd* for 33 [11, 12, 13, 14, 15, 16].

318, 20–21 *Sachs-Wotan … Tannhäuser]* Characters in Wagner's operas *Die Meistersinger*, *The Ring of the Nibelungen*, and *Tannhäuser*.

32 [17]

319, 1 *Beckmesser]* A character in Wagner's *Meistersinger*.

32 [18] Drafted in January 1874; cf. Nietzsche's letter to Malwida von Meysenbug dated 11 February 1874.

32 [22]

320, 7 *camera]* "chamber."

320, 11 *"Imperial March"]* The march Wagner composed in 1871 to celebrate the Prussian victory over the French.

32 [27]

321, 15 *orchestics]* Nietzsche is thinking of the original Greek meaning of this word, "to dance," and its association with the chorus in ancient Greek tragedy.

321, 23 *Hans Sachs]* Like Beckmesser, a character in Wagner's *Meistersinger*.

32 [39]

324, 15 *K⟨ing⟩ o⟨f⟩ B⟨avaria⟩]* King Ludwig II of Bavaria, who was an inspired devotee of Wagner's music.

324, 19 *the revolution]* The Revolution of 1848, in which Wagner sided with the cause of the revolutionaries.

32 [45]

327, 8 *"Opera and Drama"]* One of Wagner's early theoretical works.

32 [49] Cf. 32 [10], 33 [3].

327, 22 *27, 507]* The reference is to Goethe, *Aus meinem Leben: Fragmentarisches* (From my life: Fragments), *Sämmtliche Werke*, 40 vols. (Stuttgart, 1856–57), 27: 507. This collection was part of Nietzsche's personal library. Cf. 32 [3].

32 [50]

327, 24 *"nude figure music"]* *Actfigurenmusik*; Nietzsche is apparently thinking of a form of music that would invoke the nude poses (*Act*) of sculpture and painting. Cf. in this regard his reflections on the sculpturesque aspect of Aeschylus's dramas in 21 [2, 3] and especially 25 [1].

32 [52]

329, 24–25 *"Coriolan Overture"*] Beethoven's overture to *Coriolan*, by the Austrian poet and dramatist Heinrich Josef von Collin (1771–1811).

330, 10 *sculpturesque*] See note to 21 [2].

32 [61]

333, 8 *mass*] Nietzsche is thinking of the collective conditions of artistic reception inherent in the large theatrical audience, as opposed to the individual, contemplative conditions of reception for other art forms.

333, 11 *theatrocracy*] Nietzsche's neologism refers to the institutional powers that held sway in the world of theater and that resisted Wagner's innovations.

333, 14 *tyrannis*] "reign of tyranny."

32 [62]

333, 27 *one-year flies*] *Einjahrsfliegen*. A reference to the Prussian practice, extended to all of the German Empire under Bismarck, of allowing those who pursued advanced schooling or training to serve a reduced, one-year military term instead of the usual two-year term. Nietzsche served as a one-year volunteer from October 1867 to October 1868. See note to 32 [4].

334, 1 *The Greeks made Sophocles into a general*] In 440 B.C., in recognition of the political wisdom displayed in his drama *Antigone*, Sophocles was appointed by the Athenians to be one of the ten *strategi*, or generals, in the war against the aristocratic faction of Samos.

32 [67]

335, 24–25 *They … crushed.*] The idea that existence is hostile to the individual is a principal tenet of Schopenhauerian pessimism. Nietzsche's view of tragedy, as the reintegration of the individual into the circle of life, reflects this pessimistic principle.

336, 9–10 *ultramontanists*] A movement within Catholicism that defended the primacy of the Pope. In the nineteenth century, the ultramontanists were responsible for a split within German

Catholicism and "ultramontanism" became a catchphrase for conservative resistance to the Enlightenment, liberalism, and Protestantism.

336, 11 *sensu proprio]* "in the strict sense."

32 [71] Cf. 32 [80].

337, 27 *philalethes]* "lovers of truth." Cf. 34 [36].

32 [72]

338, 11 *J⟨acob⟩ B⟨urckhardt⟩]* Burckhardt (1818–97) was an esteemed art historian and one of Nietzsche's most distinguished colleagues at the University of Basel. They were close acquaintances during Nietzsche's Basel years and shared a mutual intellectual respect.

32 [75]

338, 26 *University philosophy]* Schopenhauer wrote a treatise on the woes of university philosophy, "Über die Universitäts-Philosophie," in vol. 1 of his *Parerga und Paralipomena.* Nietzsche returned to this subject in section 8 of "Schopenhauer," for which this represents a preliminary outline.

32 [76] Notes for section 8 of "Schopenhauer" on the problems of university philosophy.

32 [77] Notes for section 4 of "Schopenhauer," pp. 201–7. Cf. 34 [4].

32 [80] Cf. 32 [71]. Preliminary notes for section 6 of "Schopenhauer," pp. 215–24, which deals with the question of culture.

32 [82] Cf. 34 [9].

32 [83] Preliminary notes for sec. 6 of "Schopenhauer," pp. 215–24.

342, 30 *Dubois-Reymond]* The German philosopher Emil Dubois-Reymond (1818–96) argued for the founding of a German language academy following the French model. Nietzsche remarks critically on this proposal in section 6 of "Schopenhauer," p. 221.

[33 = Mp XIII 4, 1–5]

33 [1] *Pd:* 32 [8]. Cf. section 7 of "Wagner," p. 292.

33 [2] *Pd:* 32 [9].

344, 4 *Schröder-Devrient]* Wilhelmine Schröder-Devrient (1804–60), a German singer.

33 [3] *Pd*: 32 [10]. Cf. section 8 of "Wagner," p. 297.

344, 22 *insane."]* Goethe, *Aus meinem Leben: Fragmentarisches* (From my life: Fragments), *Sämmtliche Werke in vierzig Bänden* (Stuttgart, 1856–57), 27: 507. This collection was part of Nietzsche's personal library. Cf. 32 [49].

33 [4] *Pd*: 32 [10].

33 [5] *Pd*: 32 [10].

33 [6] *Pd*: 32 [11].

33 [7] *Pd*: 32 [11, 12].

33 [8] *Pd*: 32 [13].

33 [9] *Pd*: 32 [13].

33 [10] *Pd*: 32 [13].

33 [11] *Pd*: 32 [15].

33 [12] *Pd*: 32 [15].

33 [13] *Pd*: 32 [15].

33 [14] *Pd*: 32 [15].

33 [15] *Pd*: 32 [15].

33 [16] *Pd*: 32 [15].

347, 25 *the revolution]* The Revolution of 1848, in which Wagner sided with the cause of the revolutionaries.

[34 = U II 6]

34 [1] First title for "Schopenhauer." The entire notebook contains preliminary notes for this essay.

34 [4] Notes for section 4 of "Schopenhauer," pp. 203–7. Cf. 32 [77].

34 [8] Cf. sections 3 and 4 of "Schopenhauer," pp. 194–95; 195–96.

34 [9] Cf. 32 [82].

34 [10] Outline for section 4 of "Schopenhauer."

350, 7 *See left.]* Nietzsche's note directs him to the opposite page of the notebook; the reference is presumably to either 34 [5] or 34 [6].

34 [11]

350, 13 *p. 392, Parerga II]* The reference is to §177 entitled "Über das Christenthum" (On Christianity) in vol. 2 of Schopenhauer's *Parerga und Paralipomena*, *Sämmtliche Werke*, ed. Julius Frauenstädt (Leipzig, 1873–74), p. 392.

34 [12]

350, 14 *esse]* "being," or "essence."

34 [14] Cf. section 5 of "Schopenhauer," p. 211.

34 [15] Cf. section 6 of "Schopenhauer," pp. 218–24.

34 [16] Cf. section 6 of "Schopenhauer," p. 231.

34 [21] Cf. section 5 of "Schopenhauer," p. 212.

34 [22] Cf. section 6 of "Schopenhauer," pp. 220–21.

34 [23] Cf. section 6 of "Schopenhauer," p. 223.

34 [24] Cf. 35 [14].

354, 13–16 *Every ... sociability.]* Cf. section 5 of "Schopenhauer,"
    p. 211.

34 [29] *Pd* for section 6 of "Schopenhauer," pp. 220–21.

34 [31] Cf. section 4 of "Schopenhauer," pp. 203–7.

34 [36] Outline for "Schopenhauer."

358, 10–11 *chapter on his dangers]* Section 3 of "Schopenhauer."

358, 23 *philalethes]* "lovers of truth." Cf. 32 [71].

34 [37] Cf. 29 [205, 213], and section 6 of "Schopenhauer," pp. 221–
    22.

359, 9 *war with the French]* The Franco-Prussian War (1870–71).

359, 17–19 *Renan ... Hausrath]* The French historian and philoso-
    pher Ernest Renan (1823–92) wrote a biography of Jesus, as did
    David Strauss. See note to 27 [1]. The German theologian Adolf
    Hausrath (1837–1909), one of the cofounders of the Protestant
    Union, was one of Strauss's supporters and published a book
    entitled *D. F. Strauss und die Theologie seiner Zeit* (D. F. Strauss and
    the theology of his age) between 1876 and 1878.

34 [42] Cf. section 5 of "Schopenhauer," pp. 209–10.

34 [45]

361, 24 *Odysseus ... shades]* See Homer, *The Odyssey*, 11.23–50, where
    Odysseus sacrifices a black sheep to the gods to ensure his safe
    return to Ithaca before descending to the underworld.

361, 26 *Philosophia academica delenda est]* "Academic philosophy is
    to be eradicated."

34 [46]

361, 27 *Ils se croient profonds et ne sont que creux.]* "They take them-
    selves to be profound but are merely hollow." The source of
    this statement is unknown. Cf. *Sd* to section 8 of "Schopen-

hauer," p. 247, line 29 to p. 248, line 25, found on p. 372 of the
commentary to *Unfashionable Observations*.

34 [47] Outline for "Schopenhauer."

362, 7 *La Trappe]* A Cistercian monastery in Normandy, founded
in 1140. Nietzsche recounts Schopenhauer's reaction to a portrait of Armand-Jean Le Rancé (1626–1700), who as abbot re-
formed this monastery in 1664, in section 3 of "Schopenhauer,"
p. 191. This episode from Schopenhauer's life is related by Wilhelm Gwinner in his *Arthur Schopenhauer aus persönlichem Umgange
dargestellt* (Arthur Schopenhauer, portrayed on the basis of personal acquaintance) (Leipzig, 1862), 108.

[35 = Mp XIII 3]

35 [4] The quotation from Aristippus can be found in Diogenes
Laertius, *Lives of the Eminent Philosophers*, 2.68. For the quotation from Ariston see Plutarch's *Moralia*, 426.

35 [5] Cf. 29 [197, 198], 30 [15].

35 [6]

364, 7 *them."]* Goethe, distich no. 43 from the collection "Vier
Jahreszeiten" (Four seasons). Originally published in Schiller's
Musen-Almanach auf das Jahr 1797 (Almanac of the muses for 1797)
under the title "Guter Rat" (Good advice).

35 [8]

364, 26 *death."]* Giacomo Leopardi, "Il pensiero dominante"
(The dominant thought). Nietzsche again cites Leopardi from
Robert Hamerling's German translation, *Gedichte* (Hildburg-
hausen, 1866), which was in his personal library.

35 [9] Cf. section 5 of "Schopenhauer," p. 208.

35 [10] Cf. section 5 of "Schopenhauer," p. 208.

35 [11] Cf. 28 [6].

365, 9–10 *"behold … human being!"]* An allusion to "Ecce homo,"
the words of Pontius Pilate in reference to Jesus, John 19 : 5.

365, 18 *e contrario]* "on the contrary."

35 [12]

366, 28 *is not of this world]* An allusion to Jesus's remark to Pilate,
"My kingdom is not of this world," John 18 : 36.

366, 32 *Aristotle's claim]* The claim, made in the *Poetics*, that art
imitates nature.

367, 3–6 *It … use."*] Cf. section 5 of "Schopenhauer," pp. 213–14. The statement by Goethe is taken from his letter to Charlotte von Stein dated 3 March 1785.

367, 5 *causa finalis*] "final purpose," "ultimate aim."

367, 27–35 *By means … shackling.*] Cf. section 6 of "Schopenhauer," p. 220.

368, 10–19 *Thus … conflagration.*] Cf. section 6 of "Schopenhauer," p. 220.

368, 23–31 *And … obscenities.*] Cf. section 6 of "Schopenhauer," pp. 220–21.

368, 31–369, 4 *And it is … nose.*] Cf. 34 [29] and section 6 of "Schopenhauer," p. 221.

369, 5–370, 24 *The Germans … idols. —*] *Pd* for section 6 of "Schopenhauer," p. 221, line 14 to p. 222, line 29.

369, 6 *war with France*] The Franco-Prussian War (1870–71).

369, 18 *Dubois-Reymond*] See note to 32 [83].

369, 21–26 *and we can … both!*] Cf. the *Pd* to section 6 of "Schopenhauer," p. 221, line 33, found on p. 369 of the commentary to *Unfashionable Observations*.

370, 22 *fire.'*] Richard Wagner, "Über das Dirigieren" (On conducting), *Gesammelte Schriften und Dichtungen* (Leipzig, 1871–73), 8: 387.

371, 6–21 *that haste … enjoying.*] *Pd* for section 6 of "Schopenhauer," p. 222, line 32 to p. 223, line 12.

371, 31–372, 20 *When I … pseudophilosophies*] *Pd* for section 6 of "Schopenhauer," p. 223, lines 13–36.

35 [13] The source of the statement attributed to Schopenhauer is unknown.

35 [14]

373, 5–375, 13 *Human beings … sociability.*] *Pd* to section 5 of "Schopenhauer," p. 209, line 5 to p. 211, line 16.

375, 9–25 *every moment … property*] Cf. 34 [24].

[36 = U II 7b]

36 [1] List of planned philological works.

36 [2] Plans for the publication of further *Unfashionable Observations*.

36 [3] See Curt Paul Janz, "Friedrich Nietzsches akademische Lehrtätigkeit in Basel 1869–1879," *Nietzsche-Studien* 3 (1974): 192–203.

[37 = U II 7c]

37 [1] The entries here are stylistic études that concentrate on words that begin in German with the prefix "ab." Instead of translating them, I have left them in the original German. Nietzsche's explanatory comments, if included, have been translated. It is possible that these stylistic exercises are notes for the planned essay on the topic "Reading and Writing." Cf. 26 [20], 29 [226]. These exercises in style and vocabulary may also have been a response to Nietzsche's self-doubts about his own writing style, initiated by Cosima Wagner's critical response to "Utility and Liability" in April 1874. In this regard, see the "Translator's Afterword" to *Unfashionable Observations*, pp. 403–4.

377, 1 *degenerare]* "degenerate."

377, 2 *depascere]* "depasture."

378, 20 *ablatio ciborum]* "deprivation of food."

37 [2] Stylistic exercises centered around words beginning with "e." See note to 37 [1].

37 [3]

380, 18 *artem tegere]* "concealing the craft."

37 [4]

381, 7 *unfortunate idea of an academy]* See note to 32 [83].

381, 21 *Keller]* Gottfried Keller (1819–90), Swiss realist writer. For Berthold Auerbach, see note to 19 [259].

381, 32 κοινή *] koine*, "standardized language." In classical studies, *koine* refers to the common, pan-Hellenic language, based on Attic dialect, that emerged in the fourth to third centuries B.C.

37 [5]

382, 13 *Five-year Pythagorean prohibition on reading.]* In his *Lives of the Eminent Philosophers* (7.10), Diogenes Laertius claims that the students of Pythagoras were required to listen in total silence to their master for five years before taking their examination. Nietzsche is transferring this Pythagorean prohibition to reading. Cf. section 1 of "Wagner," p. 262.

[38 = Mp XII 5]

38 [1] Nothing is known about Nietzsche's sketches on Prometheus. As early as 1859 Nietzsche had planned a joint treatise on Prometheus with his friend Wilhelm Pinder (1844–1928), but it

is unclear whether there is any relationship between this early plan and the entries in this notebook.

387, 5–6 *He ... son.]* According to one of the legends about Prometheus, he was a seer who knew that if Zeus were to have a son with Thetis, this son would dethrone him. Prometheus repeatedly refused to reveal this knowledge to Zeus or his emissaries.

387, 9 *in summa]* "in sum."

38 [3]

388, 24–25 *Prometheus ... Mecone!]* When the gods and human beings were disputing with one another at Mecone, Prometheus attempted to deceive Zeus by cutting up a bull and dividing it into two parts: the best parts he wrapped in the skin, but placed the stomach, the worst part, on top; the second pile consisted of the bones covered with fat. Zeus chose the latter.

Translator's Afterword

Richard T. Gray

Nietzsche recorded the unpublished writings translated in this volume during the two and one-half years from the summer of 1872 to the end of 1874. The major works published in this period were the first three *Unfashionable Observations*, "David Strauss the Confessor and the Writer," "On the Utility and Liability of History for Life," and "Schopenhauer as Educator." Notebooks 26 to 35, in particular, contain many notes and preliminary drafts for these texts. However, the content of the notebooks in general extends far beyond the themes of these published essays, embracing many of Nietzsche's ideas for further, but never completed, *Unfashionable Observations*, as well as diverse topics related to the courses he was teaching in the field of classical philology at the University of Basel. Scattered among the unpublished writings from this period we find notes for treatises on "The Afflictions of Philosophy," "On Truth and Lie in an Extra-Moral Sense," "On Decorative Culture," "Reading and Writing," "One-Year Volunteers," "We Philologists," and "Richard Wagner in Bayreuth," all of which were conceived as *Unfashionable Observations*. "Richard Wagner in Bayreuth" is the only planned essay in this group that was actually realized; however, this was not until 1876. Only Nietzsche's initial notes for the Wagner essay are found among the notebooks translated here.[1] Beyond notes and plans for *Un-*

---

1. Notebooks 32 and 33 are devoted primarily to Nietzsche's reflections on Wagner. However, since the major work on "Richard Wagner in Bayreuth"

fashionable Observations, these notebooks encompass numerous sketches related to Nietzsche's major philological project from this period, a book on the "pre-Platonic Greek philosophers," Nietzsche's preferred designation for what are commonly termed the pre-Socratic philosophers. The closest Nietzsche came to bringing this material on the earlier Greek philosophers into publishable form is the incomplete manuscript "Philosophy in the Tragic Age of the Greeks."[2] The Basel lecture course on "The Pre-Platonic Philosophers," which Nietzsche gave in the winter semester of 1869–70, the summer semester of 1872, the winter semester of 1875–76, and again in the summer semester of 1876, is closely tied to this project.[3] In the unpublished writings, this material is designated with various titles, ranging from the dry and matter-of-fact "The Philosopher of the Tragic Age" (19 [13]) to more provocative and more broadly conceived titles such as "The Last Philosopher" (19 [36, 318]), "Wisdom and Science" (19 [85]), "The Philosopher: Observations on the Struggle Between Art and Knowledge" (19 [98]), "The Philosopher as Physician of Culture" (23 [15]), and "The Justification of Philosophy by the Greeks" (19 [316]).

   Nietzsche scholarship has tended to refer collectively to the material connected with this work on the pre-Platonic philosophers as Nietzsche's "philosophers book,"[4] and this generic

---

was accomplished between fall 1875 and summer 1876, the bulk of the unpublished writings related to this text can be found in Vol. 12 of this edition, *Unpublished Writings from the Period of* Human, All Too Human. On the genesis of "Richard Wagner in Bayreuth," see the "Translator's Afterword" to *Unfashionable Observations*, 405–6.

   2. Because this text is closely related to Nietzsche's work on *The Birth of Tragedy*, it is published in Vol. 1 of the present edition.

   3. Nietzsche's notes for his lecture course "Die vorplatonischen Philosophen" (The pre-Platonic philosophers) can be found in Colli and Montinari's *Kritische Gesamtausgabe*, part 2, vol. 4, edited by Fritz Bronmann and Mario Carpitella (Berlin: De Gruyter, 1995), 206–362.

   4. The so-called Musarion-Ausgabe of Nietzsche's collected works collated the fragments related to Nietzsche's "philosophers book" under the title

designation most aptly captures the breadth and diversity of the material Nietzsche included in this project. Indeed, the ideas that emerge around Nietzsche's deliberations on these early Greek thinkers are absolutely central to his thought from this period and contribute in significant ways to the development of the major themes he addresses: the role of the philosopher vis-à-vis his age and the surrounding culture; the relationships linking philosophy, art, and culture; the metaphorical nature of language and its relationship to knowledge; the unmasking of the drive for absolute "truth" as a palliative against the horror of existence; and last but not least, Nietzsche's "unfashionable" attack on modern science and modern culture, especially on the Germany of the Bismarck Reich. Moreover, Nietzsche's ideas for this "philosophers book" ultimately are what give these notebooks their coherence, since these thoughts run like a connective thread throughout the notes of this period. Notebook 19, from the summer of 1872 to early 1873, is almost entirely composed of sketches related to the "philosophers book"; in subsequent notebooks, these thoughts are displaced temporarily by notes for other projects, only to resurface once again, like the primary theme of a musical composition. Indeed, Nietzsche's thought from 1872 through 1874 is so dominated by his reflections for this work on the philosopher that one could just as easily justify calling the current volume "Unpublished Writings from the Period of 'The Philosophers Book'" as "Unpublished Writings from the Period of *Unfashionable Observations*." As we will see, the notebooks from the summer of 1872 to the end of 1874, especially the notes for the "philosophers book," represent important transitional documents in Nietzsche's intellectual de-

---

"Vorarbeiten zu einer Schrift über den Philosophen" (Preliminary sketches for a work on the philosopher); see Nietzsche's *Gesammelte Werke* (Munich: Musarion, 1922), 6: 3–120. The reception of this reconstructed text, which was translated into French, had a decisive influence on the post-structuralist interpretation of Nietzsche.

velopment, marking, among other things, the shift from philological to philosophical studies and the turn to unabashed cultural criticism.

The year 1872 is a crucial one in Nietzsche's biography. It was punctuated by three major crises: the unsettling of his professional self-conception as a classical philologist; the shattering of his ambitions to compete with Richard Wagner on the latter's own turf, in the area of musical composition; and the move of the Wagners from Tribschen, with its proximity to Basel, to Bayreuth, and the progressive alienation between the Wagners and Nietzsche from 1872 through 1875. These three events contributed in significant ways to the redirection of Nietzsche's intellectual activities at this time, his turn away from the philosophically tinged philology of *The Birth of Tragedy* and "Philosophy in the Tragic Age of the Greeks" to the vociferous cultural criticism characteristic of *Unfashionable Observations*, on the one hand, and the critical philosophy of *Human, All Too Human*, on the other.

When Nietzsche wrote in his preliminary notes for "Richard Wagner in Bayreuth" that in his youth Wagner is "a many-sided dilettante who seems destined to come to nothing" (32 [18]),[5] he also could have been thinking of himself; for this observation applies, *mutatis mutandis*, to Nietzsche, as well. Classical philology, philosophy, musical composition, poetry: these are only his most widely recognized pursuits. It is little known, however, that during his first year of university studies in Bonn, Nietzsche also enrolled as a student of theology, or that following the completion of his studies in Leipzig and prior to his appointment as professor at the University of Basel, he considered reentering the university to study chemistry.[6] While all this certainly speaks for Nietzsche's manifold interests and tal-

---

5. Nietzsche expands on this observation in the published text of "Richard Wagner in Bayreuth"; see *Unfashionable Observations*, 263.

6. See Nietzsche's letter to Erwin Rohde dated 16 January 1869.

ents, it also points to the danger that he might dissipate his energies, especially given his ever weakening constitution and his threatened health. Moreover, following the assumption of his professorship in 1869, his professional responsibilities demanded major investments of time, and this made it all the more important for him to be able to lend focus to his intellectual activities. Indeed, Nietzsche's well-known animosities toward his teaching duties stemmed in part from his recognition that they sapped away precious time he could invest in his other pursuits. He certainly was thinking of his responsibilities as professor when he claimed in note 29 [231]: "I never would let a professional position rob me of more than a quarter of my energy." Whether it really was possible for Nietzsche to adhere to this assertion is doubtful.

The Wagners' move from Tribschen to Bayreuth in April 1872 constituted the necessary external condition for Nietzsche's gradual but decisive alienation from Richard Wagner and his Bayreuth project in the years that followed. The closeness Nietzsche experienced to the Wagners from April 1869 to April 1872, when he was a welcome and regular, even unannounced, guest in their house and actively participated in their intellectual exchanges and their plans for the future, never could be recaptured after the Wagners moved to Bayreuth. As early as December 1872 there were signs that the geographical distance from Bayreuth already was giving rise to emotional and intellectual distance from Wagner: although he was invited to spend the first Bayreuth Christmas with the Wagners, adhering to a tradition established in Tribschen, Nietzsche bypassed Bayreuth and celebrated the holiday with his mother and sister in Naumburg instead. As a substitute for his own presence, he sent Cosima Wagner the "Five Prefaces to Five Unwritten Books," intended as a belated Christmas present. But far from assuaging the Wagners' peevishness at their friend's rejection of their invitation, this present merely intensified it: in her diaries, Cosima complained of the "awkward gruffness" that surfaced in these pieces, a quality the Wagners perhaps were now inclined to see in Nietzsche's character in general.[7]

Nietzsche's growing alienation from Wagner's Bayreuth project made itself evident in the lack of enthusiasm he evinced when given the task in October 1873 of writing an "Admonition to the German Nation" to rally financial support for construction of the Bayreuth festival theater, which was falling precariously behind schedule due to lack of funds. To his friend Erwin Rohde Nietzsche confessed the displeasure with which he faced this task, and he even went so far as to try to enlist Rohde's assistance in writing this public appeal.[8] Despite his reluctance, Nietzsche finally composed his "Admonition to the Germans" on October 22 and submitted it to the delegates at the meeting of the patrons of Wagner's Bayreuth project at the end of the month. But the delegates rejected Nietzsche's manuscript, and he, in turn—perhaps out of spite—refused to revise it, recommending instead that the task be given to someone else. This event is significant, for it testifies to Nietzsche's ambivalence toward Wagner and Bayreuth at this early date and signals Nietzsche's retreat from his commitment, already evident in *The Birth of Tragedy*, to devote his writings to the glorification of Wagner, his music, and the cultural renewal they represented for the young Nietzsche. It is perhaps no coincidence that Nietzsche's first notes for "Richard Wagner in Bayreuth" were written shortly after this experience, in the early months of 1874. These writings, found in notebooks 32 and 33 of the present volume, already contain many of the germinal ideas later elaborated in the fourth essay in *Unfashionable Observations*, "Richard Wagner in Bayreuth"; however, the tone in which Nietzsche presents them is decidedly more skeptical and critical than in the published essay, in which Nietzsche takes pains

---

7. For a detailed description of the events surrounding Nietzsche's refusal to travel to Bayreuth in December 1872, see Curt Paul Janz, *Friedrich Nietzsche: Biographie*, 3 vols. (Munich: Hanser, 1978–79), 1: 495–98.

8. See Nietzsche's letter to Erwin Rohde dated 18 October 1873.

to demonstrate the dialectical process by which Wagner's deficits work to his advantage. This subtle strategy is not yet in evidence in the early writings on Wagner from these notebooks.

Nietzsche always displayed a peculiar fervor for music, and he wrote his own musical compositions beginning with his early youth. In 1872, Nietzsche for all practical purposes abandoned this pursuit; and although it must have been extremely difficult for him to deny himself this pleasure, the cause of this turn from musical composition was in important respects self-imposed. In spring 1872, Nietzsche wrote a piano piece for four hands, inspired by Robert Schumann's "Manfred Overture"—itself inspired by Byron's drama *Manfred*—to which he gave the title "Manfred Meditation." At about this same time, Nietzsche began to cultivate the friendship of Hans von Bülow, one of Wagner's students, the previous husband of Cosima Wagner, and a well-known pianist and composer in his own right. In July 1872, Nietzsche included a copy of the music to his "Manfred Meditation" in a letter to von Bülow, with the veiled request that the experienced musician pass judgment on its merits. The language in which Nietzsche couched this request is significant: "If you should find," he writes, "that your patient [i.e., Nietzsche himself] writes terrible music, then you are knowledgeable in the secret of the Pythagorean art of curing him by means of 'good' music. But with this you would win him back for philology."[9]

Especially curious is Nietzsche's suggestion that his pursuits in the area of musical composition somehow detract from or substitute for his philological studies; and it almost seems as if he was asking von Bülow either to rescue him from philology by recognizing his talent as a composer, or, following Nietzsche's own words, win Nietzsche back for philology by convincing him that he has no calling as a composer. At any rate, the latter is what von Bülow in fact did: in his response, he mercilessly disparaged Nietzsche's "Manfred Meditation,"

---

9. See Nietzsche's letter to Hans von Bülow dated 20 July 1872.

calling it "the most extreme example of fantastic extravagance, the most unpleasant and antimusical notes on music paper that I have seen in quite some time."[10] As is to be expected, Nietzsche was devastated by this unusually vicious—if frank and honest—critique. Yet perhaps this episode had precisely the effect Nietzsche secretly desired, for von Bülow's critique cured him almost completely of his musical ambitions. To be sure, in the end, this was not enough to "win him back" for classical philology; but after this experience, Nietzsche composed only one further musical work, his "Hymn to Friendship," which dates from 1873–74.

The final crisis of the spring and summer of 1872, and perhaps the most decisive one for Nietzsche's further development, was initiated by the vehement rejection of his *Birth of Tragedy* in philological circles. In this first philological book, Nietzsche had attempted to practice a kind of engaged scholarship by arguing the parallel between the structure of ancient Greek tragedy and Wagner's operatic "total work of art," and it probably was inevitable that his fellow philologists would find his scholarly practice at best questionable, and at worst reprehensible. It was inherent in Nietzsche's own genius, in the audacity of his ideas and the forceful, exuberant, confident—sometimes even arrogant—manner in which he presented them, that he was fated to be "unfashionable," at odds with all the common trends and accepted practices, in his philological writings, as well. The only exceptions to this are some of the essays he wrote under the influence of his teacher Friedrich Ritschl, which conform to the demands and expectations of the historical scholarship that was part and parcel of studies in classical philology during Nietzsche's day. By the same token, however, Nietzsche believed that his own "unfashionableness," his ability to take a critical stance on the cultural and intellectual fashions of Bismarckian Germany, was fundamentally predicated on his training as a classical philologist. In the

---

10. See Hans von Bülow's letter to Nietzsche dated 24 July 1872.

"Foreword" to "On the Utility and Liability of History for Life," for example, he asserted "that it is only to the extent that I am a student of more ancient times—above all, of ancient Greece" that he could be so "unfashionable" as to have doubts about the utility of historical studies.[11] To be sure, Nietzsche had doubts about his suitability as a classics scholar long before the rejection of *Birth of Tragedy*, and his letters from his student days are filled with attacks on the boring, stuffy, and narrow-minded way even great philologists like his teacher Ritschl pursued their research. But despite this, he seemed to hold onto the hope that, with the support of his friend and fellow philologist Erwin Rohde, he somehow could usher in a new scholarly manner in classical studies.

In his career as a philologist Nietzsche paid dearly for his compulsion to resist the research standards dictated by the community of scholars. In January 1872, *The Birth of Tragedy from the Spirit of Music* appeared with the same publishing house that published Wagner's works, E. W. Fritsch in Leipzig. This fact alone might have sufficed to call the philological rigor of Nietzsche's treatise into question. It certainly contributed to the impression that Nietzsche's philological arguments were mere scholarly facades for the defense of Wagner's "Kunstwerk der Zukunft," his "artwork of the future."[12] The young philologist Ulrich von Wilamowitz-Moellendorff, who was four years Nietzsche's junior and had attended the same high school as his senior colleague, ironically alluded to the Wagner-Nietzsche connection in his vituperative polemic against Nietzsche and

11. Nietzsche, *Unfashionable Observations*, 86.

12. Wagner's programmatic treatise "Das Kunstwerk der Zukunft," in which he laid out his theory of combining music, poetry, and theater in a "Gesamtkunstwerk," a total work of art, appeared in 1849 and gave rise to the association of Wagner with the term "Zukunftsmusik," "future music." This German term came to be derogatorily associated with the notion of utopian, impractical ideals or pipe dreams, a meaning it still carries in contemporary German usage. Wagner defended his conception of the artwork of the future in a later essay that bore the title "Zukunftsmusik" (Future music).

his book, "Zukunftsphilologie! Eine Erwiderung auf Friedrich Nietzsches *Geburt der Tragödie*" (Future philology! A response to Friedrich Nietzsche's *Birth of Tragedy*). Wilamowitz-
Moellendorff's review presented a scathing critique that left
no aspect of Nietzsche's book untouched, and it culminated
in the demand that Nietzsche vacate his professorial chair,
since he clearly was not suited for training the philologists of
the future. In the wake of this highly visible scholarly attack,
Nietzsche and his work became a philological scandal to such
an extent that, as Nietzsche reports, Hermann Usener, a professor of philology in Bonn, declared Nietzsche "finished as a
scholar." [13] His friend Wagner, who published a public letter in
the *Norddeutsche Allgemeine Zeitung* defending Nietzsche against
Wilamowitz-Moellendorff's polemic, probably just made matters worse, since his plea on Nietzsche's behalf merely con-
firmed for many the belief that the author of *The Birth of Tragedy*
was one of Wagner's literary lackeys.

Nietzsche's response to this controversy runs counter to the
commonly held belief that he did not place much stock in
his position as a philologist and a scholar. He first enlisted
the services of his close friend and fellow classical philologist Erwin Rohde to write an explicitly scholarly rebuttal of
Wilamowitz-Moellendorff's treatise. Furthermore, in his correspondence of this period, Nietzsche constantly bemoaned
the loss of his scholarly reputation and its consequences, above
all that fact that in winter semester of 1872–73 not a single
student of philology enrolled in his university courses. [14] Of
course, Rohde was the second-to-last person — after Wagner —
who could launch an adequate defense of Nietzsche, since he
already had published a review in support of *Birth of Tragedy*
before the appearance of Wilamowitz-Moellendorff's attack,
and it was widely known that he and Nietzsche were close
friends and confidantes. Nietzsche's other strategy was to win

---

13. See Nietzsche's letter to Erwin Rohde dated 25 October 1872.
14. See Nietzsche's letter to Richard Wagner from mid-November 1872.

the support of Friedrich Ritschl. However, this strategy like-wise failed,[15] and it was only after being rejected by Ritschl, his own academic mentor and the person responsible for his appointment as professor in Basel, that Nietzsche admitted he had "fallen from grace" and been excluded from the "guild" of philologists.[16]

But even then, Nietzsche did not give up the fight to gain recognition and acceptance as a philologist. In July, he finished the second installment of a purely philological essay on the competition between Homer and Hesiod, the first part of which had appeared in the *Rheinishes Museum*, a journal under Ritschl's editorship, and in early August, he sent the completed manuscript to his mentor. In the cover letter to Ritschl, Nietzsche defended himself and Rohde against Ritschl's criticism, voiced in a letter to Nietzsche,[17] that they were engaged in a "struggle against philology" or were mounting an attack against "history."[18] It is not surprising, of course, that Ritschl would express this fear, since he consciously pursued a type of philology that had a strict historical orientation and hence could not help but feel threatened by the superhistorical, highly speculative arguments Nietzsche made in *The Birth of Tragedy*. What is surprising, however, is that the same Nietzsche who a year and a half later, in February 1874, would publish a virulent attack on historical scholarship in his second *Unfashionable Observation*, could so innocently claim in his response to Ritschl that he had no intention of discrediting "history" as such. Indeed, it is certainly possible that the venom of Nietzsche's later vendetta against history derives from his animosity toward his fellow classical philologists and the discipline that refused to recognize his own work as legitimate scholarship. At any rate,

---

15. See Nietzsche's letter to Ritschl dated 26 June 1872 and Ritschl's response from 2 July of that year.

16. See Nietzsche's letter to Erwin Rohde dated 7 July 1872.

17. See Friedrich Ritschl's letter to Nietzsche dated 2 July 1872.

18. See Nietzsche's letter to Friedrich Ritschl dated 12 August 1872.

in the cover letter to Ritschl, Nietzsche made it clear that he sought his own rehabilitation as a philologist and a scholar: "I am trying to save my skin as a philologist, people are refusing to acknowledge *me* as a *philologist*," he wrote, as if his qualifications for philological scholarship scarcely could be put in doubt. But Nietzsche's self-defense remained fruitless: the final break with Ritschl came a year later, in December 1873, and Nietzsche was condemned to remain a scholarly outsider in his discipline.

Nietzsche's resentment for this ostracization by his fellow philologists expressed itself at this time in his identification with other scholarly outsiders, especially with Schopenhauer, whose lack of recognition Nietzsche would lament in "Schopenhauer as Educator," but also with the physicist Johann Karl Friedrich Zöllner. In the preface to his book *Über die Natur der Kometen: Beiträge zur Geschichte und Theorie der Erkenntnis* (On the nature of comets: Contributions to the history and theory of knowledge), Zöllner criticized his fellow scientists and scholars for their shoddy and lax research methods. This critique, not surprisingly, aroused the vehement disapproval of Zöllner's colleagues, who lost no opportunity to launch a counter-offensive against Zöllner. Nietzsche owned a copy of *Über die Natur der Kometen* and he frequently lauded this book and its author. As is clear from his repeated remarks on Zöllner in his notebooks, he identified not only with the critical stance Zöllner assumed with regard to the sciences, but also with the physicist's banishment from the hallowed halls of "accepted" scholarship.[19]

It was against the backdrop of this controversy surrounding *The Birth of Tragedy* that Nietzsche's reflections for his "philosophers book" emerged. In fact, Nietzsche conceived this work on the pre-Platonic philosophers as a companion piece to *The Birth of Tragedy*, and his intention was to defend his arguments

---

19. On Nietzsche's response to Zöllner, see entries 19 [94, 259] and 29 [24, 92, 200] in the present volume.

about the relationship between Greek tragedy and the world view of the preclassical Greeks by demonstrating that one could arrive at the same conclusions by examining the "tragic" philosophy of these earlier thinkers. Just as Wagner functioned in *The Birth of Tragedy* as a touchstone to relate the nature of tragedy to contemporary cultural developments, Schopenhauer was the lodestar that guided Nietzsche's deliberations on the pre-Platonic philosophers and connected these ideas with Nietzsche's reflections on the cultural situation in contemporary Germany. This is demonstrated both by the presence of Schopenhauer throughout the notes for this project, as well as by the citations from Schopenhauer's magnum opus, *The World as Will and Representation*, in support of his arguments in the incomplete manuscript "Philosophy in the Tragic Age of the Greeks." Indeed, many of the general observations Nietzsche first made about the pre-Platonic philosophers in the context of his "philosophers book" eventually appeared in more generalized form in "Schopenhauer as Educator."

Nietzsche's planned book on the pre-Platonic philosophers is perhaps the most representative work of his early Basel years in one crucial respect: its willful and pervasive imbrication of philological and philosophical questions. Even before assuming his professorship in Basel, Nietzsche remarked that, when viewed from the perspective of the history of culture, philologists were simply "factory workers" in the service of "some great philosophical demigod," and he named Schopenhauer as the greatest philosophical demigod of the past millennium.[20] And Nietzsche announced in no uncertain terms to the audience attending his inaugural lecture in Basel on "Homer and Classical Philology" that philosophy, not philology, was his ultimate aim: "philosophia facta est quae philologia fuit" (what was philology has been made into philosophy), he boldly asserted at the conclusion of this lecture that marked the inception of his career as a professor of classi-

---

20. See Nietzsche's letter to Paul Deussen from September 1868.

cal philology. This maxim would prove true for Nietzsche's teaching, as well, where his lecture course on the pre-Platonic philosophers became one of his favorite and most frequently offered subjects.

However, while the unpublished writings from 1872 to 1874 corroborate the assertion that for Nietzsche philology always was philosophy, they also demonstrate the opposite: namely, that in this period, at least, philosophy always was tied to philological concerns. This is possibly the most significant general recognition that one can derive from the study of these notebooks: that Nietzsche's early philosophical positions were married to, and developed to a large extent in conjunction with, his thoughts about the ancient Greeks. In the final analysis, therefore, it is immaterial whether one interprets Nietzsche's philosophy as an outgrowth of his philological studies or whether one reads his philological interpretations as projections of his own philosophical and cultural standpoints.[21] Thus, these notebooks throw into question the common notion that Nietzsche was foremost a philosopher and only a philologist in spite of himself. Indeed, the unpublished writings from this period demonstrate precisely how closely Nietzsche's philological positions were interwoven with his fundamental philosophical attitudes.[22]

In the notebooks from the summer 1872 to the end of 1874 it is possible to trace how some of Nietzsche's central philo-

---

21. On the debate regarding Nietzsche's interpretation of the pre-Socratic philosophers see Tilman Borsche, "Nietzsches Erfindung der Vorsokratiker," in *Nietzsche und die philosophische Tradition*, ed. Josef Simon, 2 vols. (Würzburg: Königshausen & Neumann, 1985), 1: 62–87; David R. Lachterman, "Die ewige Wiederkehr des Griechen: Nietzsche and the Homeric Question," in *Nietzsche und die antike Philosophie*, ed. Daniel W. Conway and Rudolf Rehn (Trier: Wissenschaftlicher Verlag Trier, 1992), 13–35; Rudolf Rehn, "Nietzsches Modell der Vorsokratiker," in *Nietzsche und die antike Philosophie*, 37–45.

22. See Herbert Cancik, *Nietzsches Antike: Vorlesung* (Stuttgart: Metzler, 1995), 2–4. Cancik defends the thesis that Nietzsche the philologist is omnipresent in all of Nietzsche's philosophy.

sophical doctrines were first expressed in the context of his philological studies, in particular in the writings devoted to his "philosophers book" and in his investigation of the pre-Platonic Greek philosophers.

The predominant theme of Nietzsche's "philosophers book" is the relationship between the philosopher and culture, in particular the role the former plays in generating a common, unified culture for any people or nation. In his deliberations on the pre-Platonic philosophers, Nietzsche delineates the distinction between true "culture" as a uniform, form-giving set of shared values, and false "cultivation," the superficial, ephemeral values that define and shape everyday life. For the Nietzsche of the period of *Unfashionable Observations*, culture is a deep structure concerned with the eternal issues of humankind, with life, existence, death; as such, it dwarfs and minimizes all the transitory questions of politics, economic and social status, even science and scholarship. Thus, Nietzsche's interpretation of the pre-Platonic philosophers and their relationship to these more banal concerns already prefigures the concept of "unfashionableness" that is so central to his thought at this time. In entry 19 [9], one of the earliest from this period, he writes, for example: "Those Greek philosophers *overcame the spirit of the age* in order to be able to gain a sense for the spirit of the Hellenic: they express the need for solutions to eternal questions." This Hellenic spirit is that deep structure, that commitment to imperishable existential problems, that defines a true culture, but such an overriding culture can be attained only by overcoming the spirit of the age, the "fashionable" proclivities and transitory aspects of the life of the individual. In their attack on the "spirit of the age," the earlier Greek philosophers already model the hostile stance toward "cultivation," the false culture of the transitory, that Nietzsche himself assumed in the cultural critique of the *Unfashionable Observations*. Prerequisite for such a unitary culture, Nietzsche argues in entry 19 [42], is an "enormous power of appropriation," the ability to transform all one's experiences into "life," instead of merely turning everything into dead knowledge. For Nietzsche, the early Greeks provide the prototype for this power to assimilate everything for the benefit of life. It is but a small step from this reflection on the appropriative power of the Greeks to Nietzsche's arguments in the second of the *Unfashionable Observations* that a civilization concerned predominantly with historical knowledge becomes unfit for life. In this essay, echoing the language of entry 19 [42], he argues that the "most powerful" historical sensibility would be one that could "assimilate or forcibly appropriate" the past, "transforming it, as it were, into its own blood."[23]

Closely connected with this ability to appropriate is a second capacity that is central to Nietzsche's conception of culture at this time: the power to concentrate and lend focus, to refer all experience to the profound and shared world view that forms the nucleus of any true culture. One of the recurrent themes in these notebooks is the insistence that this task of giving focus and concentrating a people's drives falls to the philosopher and that he therefore plays the all-important role of paving the way for culture. "*The supreme dignity of the philosopher*," Nietzsche claims in entry 19 [27], "*is revealed when he gives focus to the limitless drive for knowledge, controls it by giving it unity.*" As he goes on to maintain in the same entry, it is once again the pre-Platonic Greek philosophers who exemplify this ability to control and focus the drives of the people and thereby to make them culturally productive. The stress Nietzsche places on the unitary, organic nature of the culture represented by the early Greeks ultimately would be brought to bear on Nietzsche's attack on his fellow Germans and their lack of style and culture. In section 1 of "David Strauss the Confessor and the Writer," the first of the *Unfashionable Observations*, Nietzsche defines culture as "a unity of artistic style that manifests itself throughout all the vital self-expressions of a people," and he calls the Germans barbarians because they lack any such unitary style.[24] No

---

23. "On the Utility and Liability of History for Life," 90.
24. "David Strauss the Confessor and the Writer," 9.

doubt the reason why at this time Nietzsche attached so many hopes to Richard Wagner's music and the project of the Bayreuth festival theater was because he envisioned Wagner's art as the embodiment of a specifically German cultural style.

In the unpublished writings, this opposition between an intrinsic, organic artistic style and an extrinsic, purely formalistic one often is presented in terms of the opposition between Greek and Roman culture. This was the intended theme of the essay for *Unfashionable Observations* Nietzsche planned, but never completed, under the title "On Decorative Culture," with which he also frequently associated the name of Cicero.[25] These reflections revolve around the dichotomy between nature and convention, between an essentially innate culture whose coherence emerges from its own vital substance and a purely conventional culture that is given structure by nonessential formal qualities imposed upon it from without. Nietzsche apparently planned first to expose this dichotomy by contrasting Greek and Roman cultures, and then to apply this model to a juxtaposition of the cultures of Germany and France.

Another one of Nietzsche's predominant concepts from this period first arises in the context of his arguments about the early Greek philosophers. This is the notion of control, of *Bändigung*, especially control of the drive for knowledge. It is difficult to render in English all the nuances of the German word *Bändigung*. Derived from the verb *bändigen*, it implies control in the sense of restraint, of reining in and giving direction to an otherwise unfettered drive. Thus, the verb *bändigen* is employed in the domain of animal husbandry in the sense of "to tame," and this signification is relevant for Nietzsche's use of the term. In entry 19 [27] quoted above, Nietzsche already utilizes this concept in the context of the earlier Greek philosophers. Immediately following the cited passage, he remarks: "This is how the earlier Greek philosophers are to be understood, they control the drive for knowledge. How did it come

25. See, for example, 19 [266, 290, 291], 24 [11, 12], 29 [117], 32 [2, 14].

about that after Socrates it gradually slipped from their grasp?"
The historical development Nietzsche outlines in this entry
closely parallels the one he constructed in *The Birth of Tragedy*:
Socrates is viewed as the hinge point between the tragic culture of the early Greeks and the age of scientific knowledge,
of "truth." What distinguishes these two historical epochs in
Nietzsche's understanding is precisely the role of the philosopher: that is why the pre-Platonic philosophers become the
avatars of mythic, tragic culture and Socrates the emblem for
the world of science and absolute knowledge. According to
Nietzsche, these earlier thinkers still possessed the ability to
control, restrain, and tame the uninhibited drive for knowledge; and this controlling force constituted the precondition
for the emergence of culture. Socrates introduced the unrestrained drive for truth, and hence he marks the end of true
"culture" in Nietzsche's sense and the beginning of "science,"
the will to unqualified, infallible truth.

Through his analysis of the early Greeks, the young Nietzsche diagnoses a series of antidotes to unimpeachable truth and
the indubitability of scientific knowledge. Control, imagination, intuition: these are the traits he opposes to the uninhibited
knowledge, logic, and abstraction of scientific thought. All of
the terms of this opposition can be subsumed under the dichotomy between "illusion," on the one hand, and "truth," on
the other. Nietzsche's valorization of illusion and semblance,
which he associates with the tragic culture of the early Greeks,
over objective truth and veracity will remain one of the distinguishing traits of his philosophy. In these early notebooks,
illusion is identified not only with art, but with philosophy,
as well. Indeed, here, for each of those philosophers Nietzsche values—whether the pre-Socratic Greeks, Schopenhauer,
or even Kant—it is the artistic element of their philosophy that
establishes their worth. Nietzsche expresses this relationship
most clearly in entry 19 [45].

> How does the philosophical genius relate to art? Little can be
> learned from his immediate conduct. We have to ask: Is there

anything in his philosophy that is art? Work of art? What *remains* when his system, as science, has been destroyed? But it must be precisely this remaining element that *controls* the drive for knowledge, that is hence the artistic element. Why is such control necessary? For, when considered scientifically, his system is an illusion, an untruth that deceives the drive for knowledge and affords only temporary satisfaction. In this control, the value of philosophy does not lie in the sphere of knowledge, but in the sphere of life: the *will to existence uses philosophy* for the purpose of a higher form of existence.

"Art," "illusion," "untruth" are the names of those controlling forces that rein in the drive to truth and knowledge. Only when philosophy makes use of these controlling powers does it serve a higher purpose than the drive for knowledge. Only then does it serve the will to existence, to *life*.

With this we see how fluid the transition is from Nietzsche's arguments about the value of the philosopher in his "philosophers book" to his attack on history in the second of the *Unfashionable Observations*. Indeed, in the early writings from notebook 29, which represent preliminary notes for "On the Utility and Liability of History," the notion of control and the significance of illusion figure prominently.[26] Thus, in entry 29 [52], in which Nietzsche reacts to Eduard von Hartmann's *Philosophie des Unbewußten* (Philosophy of the unconscious), he openly asserts "*that consciousness is promoted* and developed *only by ever loftier illusions*." The ultimate standard by which the early Nietzsche measures value, including the value of truth and knowledge, is the standard of life, of existence, and what existence above all requires, according to Nietzsche, is illusion, art, and imaginative philosophy, for only these can function as palliatives against the horror of existence and thereby make life sufferable.

---

26. See, for example, 29 [51], in which Nietzsche calls for the control of the historical sensibility so rampant in his age and attacks Eduard von Hartmann for his merciless destruction of illusion.

In an important sense, then, Nietzsche's assault on the historical disciplines in "On the Utility and Liability of History for Life" stands in for this greater struggle against the unlimited drive for knowledge in all its manifestations. What distinguishes Nietzsche's strategy in this essay is his decision to lay out the dangers of absolute knowledge on the example of precisely that scholarly discipline his age held in highest esteem: historical study. This will to associate the major cultural ailments Nietzsche diagnosed in the Germany of his day with precisely those institutions his contemporaries most venerated—historical scholarship, the exact sciences, cultivation, the state, the university, to name just a few—is the defining reflex of his "unfashionableness." And the ancient Greeks always are the standard with which contemporary Germany is compared and found lacking. To be sure, Nietzsche's interpretation of the Greeks is just as "unfashionable," radical, and contrary as his interpretation of contemporary cultural and political phenomena, for he opposes to the common, classical German understanding that stressed the simplicity, grandeur, optimism, and rationality of Greek civilization the darker vision of a people who had recognized existence in all its brutality and who consequently turned to illusion, religion, and myth as ways to assuage the anxiety concomitant with this existential knowledge. There was little prospect that Nietzsche's fellow philologists would embrace this revolutionary reinterpretation and revaluation of ancient Greek culture.[27]

---

27. On the revolutionary aspects of Nietzsche's reinterpretation of the Greeks, see Tilman Borsche, "Nietzsches Erfindung der Vorsokratiker," *Nietzsche und die philosophische Tradition*, 81–84, and Hubert Cancik, *Nietzsches Antike*, 35–36. The philosopher Martin Heidegger, of course, was profoundly influenced by Nietzsche's interpretation of the pre-Socratics. Heidegger even suggests that the philologist Hermann Diels, who published a critical edition of the texts of the pre-Socratic philosophers in 1903, the same year that Nietzsche's treatise on the pre-Socratics became known, was influenced by Nietzsche's interpretation of these thinkers. See Martin Heidegger, *Holzwege* (Frankfurt: Klostermann, 1950), 317.

Three major concepts that will remain fundamental to his later philosophy already inform Nietzsche's "unfashionable" reassessment of the pre-Platonic philosophers: these are the notions of imagination, intuition, and the game or contest. The first two concepts, as we have seen, are closely tied to Nietzsche's belief in the value of illusion, the beneficial effect of semblance for human life. Nietzsche refuses to reduce philosophical thought to logic and mathematics; on the contrary, philosophy and art are closely related activities because both rely on speculative thought, the imaginative leap. In entry 19 [75] Nietzsche thus contrasts philosophical thinking with scientific thought, or "reason," defining the former as "flight of imagination, that is, a leaping from possibility to possibility, with these possibilities for the moment being taken as certainties." Instead of being held back by the test of validity or truthfulness, philosophical thought tests possibilities through flights of fancy. As Nietzsche goes on to argue in the next entry, 19 [76], this "*unprovable* philosophizing" has a greater worth than all the proven postulates of scientific knowledge precisely because philosophical thought manifests an "*aesthetic* drive." This aesthetic dimension gives "the inadequately proven philosophy of Heraclitus . . . far more artistic value than all the propositions of Aristotle."

Here we see once more the "unfashionable" side of Nietzsche's treatment of the Greeks, his approbation of the little-known pre-Socratic philosopher Heraclitus, whose work was passed down only in obscure fragments, and his deprecation of Aristotle, the "classical" Greek thinker who often is viewed as the paragon of the ancient philosopher. These reflections on the significance of imaginative, intuitive thought for philosophical reflection culminate in the arguments Nietzsche formulated in the fragmentary essay "On Truth and Lie in an Extra-Moral Sense," which was conceived as another of the *Unfashionable Observations*. Nietzsche's celebration in this unfinished treatise of the intuitive human being over the rational one is symptomatic of his interpretation of the earlier Greek philosophers.

The notion of competition, play, or rivalry also was central to Nietzsche's understanding of the pre-Platonic Greek philosophers. Nietzsche cast the philosophical reflections in his last philological essay on the competition between Homer and Hesiod into a more general philosophical form in "Homer's Competition," the fifth of the "Five Prefaces for Five Unwritten Books" that he presented to Cosima Wagner for Christmas 1872.[28] Nietzsche understood the competition between two geniuses of equal caliber as the necessary precondition for their respective creative developments. At the same time, this counterbalance between two competing geniuses assures that neither will be able to assume a position of absolute mastery and tyranny. Nietzsche believed that the productive tension that arose from this competitive situation gave rise to the tremendous creativity of Hellenic culture, as he elucidates in the example of Homer and Hesiod. Moreover, Nietzsche's transposition of this agonal pattern onto his interpretation of the pre-Platonic philosophers produces another controversial, "unfashionable" philological theory: it allows Nietzsche to question the widely accepted notion of the *diadochai*, of a developmental succession from one philosopher and philosophical school to another, replacing it with this more dialectical theory of mutual contestation.[29] As Nietzsche makes clear in 26 [8], a preliminary note for "Philosophy in the Tragic Age of the Greeks," his intention was to adopt for his own portrayal of these philosophers the manner in which, according to his interpretation, they actually had related to one another: "the task," he contends, should be "to tell about [these philoso-

---

28. "Homer's Competition" and the other four short essays that comprise the "Five Prefaces to Five Unwritten Books" are published in Vol. 1 of this edition.

29. For Nietzsche's reflections on the *diadochai*, see, for example, entries 19 [59, 169], and 32 [7].

phers] in the same way as they told about their predecessors and about their points of contact; that is, the *struggle* among them." Thus, the prototype for Nietzsche's agonal theory of culture and cultural productivity already is present during these early years in his understanding of the competitive element in ancient Hellenic culture. Nietzsche's biographer Werner Ross has even speculated, with some justification, that Nietzsche may have conceived his relationship with Wagner at this time along the lines of just such a productive competition between two geniuses.[30]

One final concept that is decisive for Nietzsche's thought of this period must be touched upon here: the notion of *Übertragung*, a term that defies simple rendering into English because of its extensive semantic scope. On the most literal level, the verb *übertragen* means "to carry over," and the noun *Übertragung*, which is derived from this verb, commonly signifies "transference." But *Übertragung* also can imply a transference in the stronger, more subjective sense of "projection," as when one projects a meaning or an interpretation onto a certain set of data. Moreover, in the sphere of rhetoric, *Übertragung* is the common German word for "metaphor," which itself derives from a Greek verb meaning "to carry over" or "to transfer." Finally, this word also can carry the signification of "translation." All four of these meanings, "transference," "projection," "metaphor," and "translation," are germane to Nietzsche's understanding and use of this word, and as a result it proved impossible to translate it consistently throughout these notebooks.[31] The concept of *Übertragung*, understood broadly

---

30. Werner Ross, *Der ängstliche Adler: Friedrich Nietzsches Leben* (Stuttgart: Deutsche Verlags-Anstalt, 1980), 347.

31. Because of the significance of the concept of *Übertragung* in Nietzsche's thought of this period, I have made a point of documenting in my annotations the occurrence of this term, along with my rendering in individual instances. By referring to these notes, the reader can trace Nietzsche's use of this concept in various contexts.

as a kind of creative transference of an idea from one context to another, as a principally nonlogical leap connecting one thought with another, is fundamental to the theories of knowledge and language Nietzsche developed between the years 1872 and 1875.

Like many of Nietzsche's principal ideas from this early period, the notion of *Übertragung* also is fundamentally connected to one of his primary theses about the early Greek philosophers: the anthropomorphic character of their thought. Thus, he argues that the pre-Platonic philosophers practiced a kind of ideation that, akin to Greek mythological thought, projects the human being onto all of nature. As is typical of Nietzsche's thought patterns at this time, he then extrapolates this quality from the pre-Platonic philosophers and generalizes it as a characteristic of the philosopher per se. In entry 19 [237], for example, he apodictically asserts: "The philosopher does not seek truth, but rather the metamorphosis of the world into human beings: he struggles to understand the world by means of self-consciousness. He struggles for an *assimilation*; he is satisfied when he has explained something anthropomorphically." The language of this entry reveals the close connection between anthropomorphic projection and the creative power of assimilation, its relationship to the creative process and the intuitive leap so central to Nietzsche's understanding of culture and the philosopher's role in the development of culture. Assimilation, metamorphosis, anthropological projection, transference, metaphor: these are the epistemological processes the early Nietzsche prized, not logical relations, deductive thinking, causality, ratiocination.

In the notes for the planned essay "On Truth and Lie in an Extra-Moral Sense," which Nietzsche dictated to his friend Carl von Gersdorff in summer 1873, Nietzsche's reflections on the fundamentally illogical process by which concepts and words come into being receive their definitive formulation. Here the concept of *Übertragung* in its various meanings is the key to Nietzsche's reflections. As Andrea Orsucci recently has shown, it is likely that Nietzsche's use of this term owes much to Gustav Gerber's *Die Sprache der Kunst* (The language of art), a book Nietzsche borrowed from the Basel university library in September 1872.[32] What Gerber's and Nietzsche's theories have in common, at any rate, is a stress on the fundamental metaphoricity of language. In the writings from the notebooks of this period it is possible to trace the development of Nietzsche's epistemological thinking out of his anthropomorphic assumptions about the ancient Greeks, through theories about the ineluctably sensual nature of all knowledge, to reflections about the rhetoricity of language and consciousness.

Entries 19 [216] and 19 [217] provide an instructive example of how thoughts first formulated in the context of Nietzsche's "philosophers book" are immediately expanded into a more general theory of knowledge. The first of these entries is concerned with the shift from the intuitive, "illogical" philosophizing of the pre-Socratics, the emergence of what Nietzsche calls the "pathos of truth," and the identification of philosophy and logical thought with Socrates. Significant here is Nietzsche's premise that the philosophical mode of the pre-Socratics is identical with the process by which language emerges: "We observe how *philosophy* is at first carried on in the same manner in which *language emerged*, that is, illogically." Of course, illogicality does not carry negative connotations for Nietzsche; on the contrary, it marks that creative, aesthetic process to which he attributes the ultimate value of any philosophy, of any mode of thought. Meta-phor, trans-ference, *Über-tragung*—the illogical leap from one domain to another—thereby becomes the principal operation of human language and thought, not rational structures and deductive processes.

---

32. Andrea Orsucci, "Unbewußte Schlüsse, Anticipationen, Übertragungen: Über Nietzsches Verhältnis zu Karl Friedrich Zöllner und Gustav Gerber," *'Centauren-Geburten': Wissenschaft, Kunst und Philosophie beim jungen Nietzsche*, ed. Tilman Borsche, Federico Gerratana, and Aldo Venturelli (Berlin: Walter de Gruyter, 1994), 193–207, esp. 202–4.

In 19 [217], Nietzsche succinctly formulates this radical epistemological insight: "Our sensory perceptions are based on tropes, not on unconscious inferences. Identifying similar thing with similar thing—discovering some similarity or other in one thing and another thing is the primordial procedure. *Memory* thrives on this activity and constantly practices it. *Misapprehension* is the primordial phenomenon.—This presupposes the *perception of structures*." Once again, in typical Nietzschean fashion, "misapprehension" is revalued, lent a positive connotation, for it serves as the necessary precondition for all conceptualization. Only when we segregate primary from secondary features, ignore the latter, and group things according to the former do we arrive at general concepts or words. But, as Nietzsche insists in 19 [67], this capacity to segregate and compare is essentially a creative reflex. "There exists within us a power that allows us to perceive the *major* features of a mirror image with greater intensity," he notes, "and another power that stresses similarity in rhythm despite actual imprecision. This must be an *artistic* power. For it *creates*. Its primary operations are *omitting, overlooking,* and *failing to hear*."

As Arthur Danto has argued, this epistemological insight is one of Nietzsche's major achievements from the years between 1872 and 1874, an insight that remains central to his later philosophy.[33] Indeed, since the ground-breaking study by Karl Schlechta and Anni Anders in the early 1960's, which argued the connection between the reflections in Nietzsche's unpublished notebooks from the early 1870's and his later philosophical positions, scholars frequently have cited the importance of these notebooks for our understanding of Nietzsche's intellectual development.[34] One of the peculiar paradoxes of the

---

33. Arthur Danto, *Nietzsche as Philosopher* (New York: Macmillan, 1965), 38.

34. Karl Schlechta and Anni Anders, *Friedrich Nietzsche: Von den verborgenen Anfängen seines Philosophierens* (Stuttgart: Frommann, 1962), esp. 7–8. See also David Breazeale's introduction to *Philosophy and Truth: Selections from Nietzsche's Notebooks of the Early 1870s* (Atlantic Highlands, N.J.: Humanities Press,

period of *Unfashionable Observations* is that the importance scholars have attributed to the unpublished notebooks from these years stands in inverse proportion to the relatively little significance attached to the published works, with the exception of "On the Utility and Liability of History for Life." This indicates that the significance of the *Unfashionable Observations* perhaps has been perennially underestimated, for, as I have attempted to demonstrate here, the ideas that emerge in the unpublished writings, although they appear in transmogrified form, in many ways shape and focus the cultural critiques voiced in the *Unfashionable Observations*, especially in the first three pieces.

A remark Nietzsche made to Erwin Rohde in the summer of 1872 sheds light on this relationship between the unpublished and published works of this period. "At the moment I am swamped by plans that occur to me in rather helter-skelter fashion: and yet I sense that I am always following *one single* course—there is no confusion."[35] As I have indicated, it is the plan for his "philosophers book" that gives structure to the diversity of Nietzsche's thought in this period. If, as Nietzsche claimed in 29 [211], "*every* philosophy must be able to do what I demand, concentrate the human being," then his own thought was becoming philosophical in the sense that it was undergoing precisely such a process of concentration in the years from 1872 to 1874.

The "philosophers book"—a work conceived initially as a contribution to classical philology—provided Nietzsche with the necessary framework to formulate and organize his philosophical thought. However, the primary problem of this period was the struggle to find the proper form in which to express these philosophical positions. The negative reception of *The Birth of Tragedy* and the professional repercussions that fol-

---

1979), xiii–xlix, and Rüdiger Schmidt, *"Ein Text ohne Ende für den Denkenden":* *Zum Verhältnis von Philosophie und Kulturkritik im frühen Werk Friedrich Nietzsches* (Königstein: Forum Academicum, 1982).

35. See Nietzsche's letter to Erwin Rohde dated 26 August 1872.

lowed must have made it evident to Nietzsche that the strategy of engaged scholarship, classical philology as a kind of cultural criticism, was doomed to failure in the Germany of the 1870's. Indeed, it would not be until almost exactly one hundred years later that an engaged scholarship of the sort Nietzsche attempted to practice finally would be able to establish itself in the philological disciplines—although it is once again under attack today. At any rate, Nietzsche's insights into the problematics of such applied scholarship probably were a significant contributing factor in his failure to complete his "philosophers book."

Philological scholarship was an inadequate vehicle for Nietzsche's cultural critiques for at least two reasons. First, the audience for such scholarship was much too limited, and the philologists themselves were not inclined to accept Nietzsche's "unfashionable" reorientation of their discipline. But more important, perhaps, was that Nietzsche's cultural critique was directed primarily at scholars, at Germany's intellectual elite, whom he never tired of attacking for being neither intellectual nor elite enough. For this reason alone his ideas required dissemination among a broader popular-intellectual public, and this is precisely the audience he sought to reach in the *Unfashionable Observations*. It is difficult to overestimate the importance of the first of these essays, "David Strauss the Confessor and the Writer," given this need to find resonance in a wider intellectual community. Strauss's book, after all, had struck a nerve among Germany's intellectuals, as demonstrated by its popularity, and Nietzsche's attack was calculated to catapult him into the public limelight and help him win a more diverse audience. The transition from the engaged philological scholarship of *The Birth of Tragedy* or "Philosophy in the Tragic Age of the Greeks" to the popular essay form of the *Unfashionable Observations* thus represents a shift in the vehicle by which Nietzsche presented his ideas, not a radical change in those ideas themselves. This clearly is evidenced by the manner in which the chief concepts from the unpublished writings are reformulated and recontextualized in the *Unfashionable Observations*, as they are, in fact, throughout the unpublished notebooks themselves. This practice of resituating kernel thoughts in varied conceptual contexts prefigures the perspectivism that later would become the defining trait of Nietzsche's intellectual productivity and creativity.

More important, perhaps, is that the relationship between the published and unpublished work of the early 1870's brings to light just how natural the more fragmentary, occasional form of the notebooks was for Nietzsche's manner of thought. Indeed, when viewed against the backdrop of the unpublished writings, the essays of the *Unfashionable Observations* appear to be artificial, almost accidental constructs, texts that seem to have been arbitrarily cut out of the overall fabric of Nietzsche's thought from this period.[36]

But if the *Unfashionable Observations* represented an improvement over philological scholarship as a vehicle for Nietzsche's ideas, the pretense to sustained argumentation inherent in the essayistic form still imposed too many logical and structural constraints. Already at this early stage of his philosophizing, the fragmentary form of the unpublished notebooks represents the ideal medium for Nietzsche's reflections. In this sense, the development of Nietzsche's characteristic aphoristic style in *Human, All Too Human* can be seen as a natural outgrowth of this search for the proper textual vehicle in the early 1870's and Nietzsche's recognition that, like Georg Christoph Lichtenberg, whose aphoristic scratch books provided Nietzsche with an important stylistic model, his own thought was ideally suited to a form that more closely approximated the freedom and dynamic intermingling of ideas present in his notebooks.

The close interrelationship between the unpublished and published works from this period points to one of the major challenges the translator faces when rendering Nietzsche's

---

36. Curt Paul Janz argues a similar point for the entirety of Nietzsche's thought and works; see his *Friedrich Nietzsche: Biographie*, 1: 558.

notebooks: the need to reflect the consistency of Nietzsche's
ideas and terminology as they move from unpublished to published form, and yet simultaneously to capture the subtle modi-
fications they sometimes undergo. This problem is especially
severe in the case of entries that represent initial expositions
or preliminary drafts for passages from the *Unfashionable Observations*. One of my aims as translator has been to mirror as
faithfully as possible even the most minor variations between
the German of the unpublished writings and the language of
the corresponding published text. This holds not only for matters of semantics, that is, for the choice of words and phrases,
but also for syntactical constructions and punctuation. In addition, in the notes I have provided a more complete inventory
of correspondences between unpublished and published writings of this period than is currently available in the yet incomplete commentary to Colli and Montinari's German edition.[37]
Thus, my English translations provide a detailed map of the
textual relationships between unpublished and published texts,
and hence they can serve as a preliminary guide for philological examinations of Nietzsche's writings from 1872 to 1874.
Of course, translations always can serve only as waysigns, and

---

37. The annotations for the unpublished writings of this period, published
in volume 14 of the *Kritische Studienausgabe*, are deficient in many respects, and
they represent at best a skeleton of what we might expect from the annotations for the definitive critical edition, which is yet to appear. Consequently,
I have found it necessary to supplement the notes made available in the *Kritische Studienausgabe*. This is especially true for many of the texts and authors
Nietzsche quotes in the fragments, as well as for his many references and
allusions to Greek authors and their doctrines. I would like to recognize here
the outstanding work of my research assistant, Stephanie Dawson, who accomplished much of the preliminary work for these supplementary notes. I
would also like to thank my colleagues in the Classics Department of the University of Washington, especially Stephen Hinds, Mary Blundell, and James
Clauss, for their assistance in tracking down some of Nietzsche's references
to classical authors and for editorial assistance with the notes to Greek and
Latin passages.

truly text-critical philology will need to return to the original German texts.

In entry 37 [4] of these notebooks, Nietzsche expresses the following recommendation for the translator: "Never shy away from being clearer than the author." While this is a maxim the translator is well advised to follow in the instance of published texts, in the case of an author's literary estate, especially when it takes the form of often hastily recorded entries in notebooks, the pertinence of this principle becomes much more problematic. For one thing, to give Nietzsche's unpublished writings the clarity and polish of his published works would give a false impression about the actual nature of these notebooks, which still display the spontaneous, impromptu character of notes recorded for later use but not subjected to rigorous critical scrutiny. I have attempted to preserve this quality of Nietzsche's notebooks in my translation. On the other hand, in cases of ambiguity or even apparent contradiction, it often is possible to discern from the nuances of the German original, or based on a comparison with another fragment that treats a similar idea, the direction and probable meaning of Nietzsche's thought. In such cases I have not hesitated to try to be "clearer" than Nietzsche himself. Moreover, there are instances in which Nietzsche's wording is clumsy, at best, and decidedly equivocal, at worst. Whenever these equivocations could not be resolved, or when they seemed deliberate, I have attempted to reflect their ambiguity in my English rendering. Where this proved impossible, or where it could be accomplished only by deviating flagrantly from Nietzsche's German text, I have supplied an annotation. Characteristic of the fragmentary form of these notebooks is the often truncated or faulty syntax: I have sought to retain this element in my translation. However, whenever it seemed to me that clarity demanded interpolations on the part of the translator, I have marked these by inserting them in braces.

If the most difficult task confronting the translator of Nietzsche's stylistically honed published works is the adequate rendering of his semantic nuances, his rhetorical flourishes, and his penchant for puns and plays on words, the translator of the unpublished notebooks must solve problems of a completely different sort. Especially given the brevity of some of these notes and the consequent lack of an extended hermeneutical context, it often is difficult to identify the precise semantic import of a word or statement. In such instances the translator must rely on his or her familiarity with the author and make educated guesses about the precise meaning of the fragment in question. Although they never can be wholly adequate, I hope that my hermeneutical reconstructions will at least prove to be accurate. Above all, I hope that I have succeeded in retaining the sketchbook quality of Nietzsche's thought in these notebooks, without, however, sacrificing the philosophical and intellectual rigor they often evince.

Index

In this index an "f" after a number indicates a separate reference on the next page, and an "ff" indicates separate references on the next two pages. A continuous discussion over two or more pages is indicated by a span of page numbers, e.g., "pp. 57–58." *Passim* is used for a cluster of references in close but not consecutive sequence.

losophy, 28, 145–46, 199, 483, 486; and pleasure, 198–99; and religion, 192; and scholarship, 193f, 196–97, 200f; Schopenhauer on, 348–49, 358, 366; and science, 341, 489; and sense perception, 71; and skepticism, 191–92; and society, 55; and strength, 18, 37; and suffering, 336, 340f; and tautology, 80; and tragedy, 37; unknowability of, 117, 199; and untruth, 16ff, 189, 193, 197, 356, 481

Überweg, Friedrich, 144, 418–19
Ulrici, Hermann, 298, 300, 449f
Ultramontanism, 336, 455–56
Unconscious, 12, 37, 48, 51, 68, 219, 223, 235, 265, 374, 399
Unity, 27, 30, 34, 46f, 74, 92, 382; and culture, 17f, 21, 69, 98, 121, 175f, 211, 316, 478; and history, 211; and language, 383, 385; and love, 128–29; and metaphor, 98, 386; of opposites, 124; and religion, 27, 264; of style, 175f; and Wagner's practice, 316, 321; and will, 105
Universality, 39, 45, 205f
Universities, 171f, 182f, 186, 276, 338, 351, 362, 404, 482
Unknowability, 119, 199
Usener, Hermann, 472
Utilitarianism, 256
Utility, 26, 54, 76, 205f, 272, 286, 290–91

Vegetarianism, 308, 311
Vischer, Friedrich Theodor von, 176, 428
Vision, 64–65, 399, 416

Vitalism, 406
Vivisection, 202, 204
Voltaire, 157, 162, 170, 422
Voss, Johann Heinrich, 244, 440

Wagner, Cosima, 461, 467–68, 469, 484
Wagner, Richard, 10, 81ff, 88f, 91, 108, 139, 255, 306, 313f, 315–33, 335, 343–47, 351, 370, 406ff, 413, 420, 427, 444; music of, 83, 85, 87, 315–33, 343–47, 406f, 454, 468, 470f, 479; and relations with Nietzsche, 427, 466–69, 471–72, 475, 479, 485
War, 26, 38, 72, 84, 94, 152, 154, 163, 182, 254, 305, 333–34, 354, 359, 369, 388, 404
Weakness, 224, 234ff, 289f, 293–95, 297, 307f, 360f
Wealth, 371–72
Weisse, Christian Hermann, 89, 409
Wieland, Christoph Martin, 440
Wilamowitz-Moellendorff, Ulrich von, 471–72
Will: and art, 18; and asceticism, 105; and causality, 64; freedom of, 38, 53; Hellenic, 17; imperishability of, 5, 394; and morality, 19; omnipotence of, 19; and philosophy, 18; Schopenhauer on, 44, 326, 350, 365, 394, 400; and sensation, 51; and unity, 105
Winckelmann, Johann Joachim, 88, 291, 408f
Wisdom, 279, 282, 290, 298, 301, 302–3, 363, 389
Working class, 277
World history, 225–26, 227

The Complete Works of Friedrich Nietzsche

Library of Congress
Cataloging-in-Publication Data

Nietzsche, Friedrich Wilhelm, 1844–1900.
[Selections. English. 1999]
Unpublished writings from the period of
Unfashionable observations, / Friedrich Nietzsche ;
translated, with an afterword, by Richard T. Gray.
p.   cm. — (The complete works of Friedrich
Nietzsche ; v. 11)
Includes bibliographical references and index.
ISBN 0-8047-2884-4 (cloth : alk. paper) ;
ISBN 0-8047-3648-0 (pbk. : alk. paper)
1. Philosophy.   I. Gray, Richard T.   II. Title.
III. Series: Nietzsche, Friedrich Wilhelm, 1844–1900.
Works. English. 1995 ; v. 11.
B3312.E5G78   1999   193—dc21   98-37649   Rev.

⊗ This book is printed on acid-free paper. It was typeset
in Monotype Garamond by Tseng Information Systems, Inc.
Designed by Copenhaver Cumpston

Original printing 1999
Last figure below indicates year of this printing
08 07 06 05 04 03 02 01 00 99